Thinking in the World

Series Page

Thinking in the World combines the work of key thinkers to pioneer a new approach to the study of thought. Responding to a pressing need in both academic and wider public contexts to account for thinking as it is experienced in everyday settings, the Reader and Book Series explore our thinking relationship to everything from illness to built environments, to ecologies, to other forms of life and technology.

Bringing together phenomenology with recent trends in cognitive science and the arts, this unique, field-defining collection illuminates thinking as a practical activity. It interweaves a series of distinctive essays and commentaries into a compelling whole, constituting a new framework and set of resources for analysing thinking in real-world situations. Rather than simply thinking *about* the world, the authors examine the ways in which we think *in and with* the world in its physical, material and social dimensions. A philosophy of thinking in action, it provides a multifaceted but sustained account of neurobiological experience and its inexorable connection to the world.

Thinking in the World

A Reader

EDITED BY
JILL BENNETT AND MARY ZOURNAZI

BLOOMSBURY ACADEMIC
LONDON • NEW YORK • OXFORD • NEW DELHI • SYDNEY

BLOOMSBURY ACADEMIC
Bloomsbury Publishing Plc
50 Bedford Square, London, WC1B 3DP, UK
1385 Broadway, New York, NY 10018, USA

BLOOMSBURY, BLOOMSBURY ACADEMIC and the Diana logo are trademarks of Bloomsbury Publishing Plc

First published in Great Britain 2020

Cover design by Peter Somogyi

A catalogue record for this book is available from the British Library.

A catalog record for this book is available from the Library of Congress.

ISBN: HB: 978-1-3500-6921-3
PB: 978-1-3500-6922-0
ePDF: 978-1-3500-6920-6
eBook: 978-1-3500-6924-4

Series: Thinking in the World

Typeset by Deanta Global Publishing Services, Chennai, India

We dedicate this book to Michel Serres – a truly original thinker who continues to inspire us and our thinking in the world.

Contents

Illustrations

Contributors

Mieke Bal is a cultural theorist, critic, video artist and occasional curator. She works on gender, migratory culture, psychoanalysis and the critique of capitalism. Her thirty-eight books include a trilogy on political art: *Endless Andness* (on abstraction), *Thinking in Film* (on video installation), both 2013, and *Of What One Cannot Speak* (on sculpture, 2010). Her work comes together in *A Mieke Bal Reader* (2006). In 2016 appeared *In Medias Res: Inside Nalini Malani's Shadow Plays* (Hatje Cantz), and in Spanish, *Tiempos trastornados,* on the politics of visuality (AKAL 2016). Her video project with Michelle Williams Gamaker, *Madame B*, is widely exhibited, in 2017 in Museum Aboa Vetus & Ars Nova in Turku, and combined with paintings by Munch in the Munch Museum in Oslo. Her most recent film is *Reasonable Doubt* on René Descartes and Queen Kristina (2016). <www.miekebal.org> [accessed 01 August 2017].

Jill Bennett is Professor of Experimental Arts and founding Director of NIEA, and formerly Associate Dean Research, UNSW Art & Design (2006–16). A writer and curator, she has published widely on visual culture, new media and transdisciplinary aesthetics. Her research is particularly focused on aesthetics (broadly understood as the analysis of sensori-affective perception and interaction) and its 'practical' deployment both in art/exhibitions and in social and scientific areas beyond traditional art practice. In 2014 Jill curated *Amnesia Lab* at UNSW – an exhibition and 'live lab' bringing together artists and cognitive neuropsychologists researching memory loss. With Volker Kuchelmeister, she has led the development of the 3D immersive *Amnesia Atlas,* a media installation designed to investigate processes of memory retrieval. Jill's recent books include *Practical Aesthetics: Events, Affects and Art After 9/11* (IB Tauris, Radical Art: Radical Aesthetics, 2012), for which she received the Sterling and Francine Clark Fellowship (Clark Institute, Massachusetts) in 2009 and an ARC Discovery Grant; and *Curating Sydney* (UNSW Press, 2014; with Saskia Beudel), the outcome of an ARC Linkage Grant. Her previous books include *Empathic Vision* (Stanford UP, 2005), a study of art and trauma, and several monographs on new media art.

Havi Carel is Professor of Philosophy at the University of Bristol, where she also teaches medical students. She is currently a Wellcome Trust Senior Investigator, leading a five-year project, the Life of Breath (www.lifeofbreath.org). Her third monograph, entitled *Phenomenology of Illness*, was published by Oxford University Press in 2016. Havi was voted by students as a 'Best of Bristol' lecturer in 2016. Havi is the author of *Illness* (2008, 2013), shortlisted for the Wellcome Trust Book Prize, and of *Life and Death in Freud and Heidegger* (2006). She is the co-editor of *Health, Illness and Disease* (2012) and of *What Philosophy Is* (2004). She uses film in teaching and has co-edited a volume entitled *New Takes in Film-Philosophy* (2010). She also co-edited a special issue of *Philosophy* on 'Human Experience and Nature' (2013). She previously published on the embodied experience of illness, epistemic injustice, well-being within illness and the experience of respiratory illness in the *Lancet, BMJ, Journal of Medicine and Philosophy, Journal of Medical Ethics, Journal of Applied Philosophy, Theoretical Medicine and Bioethics, Medicine, Healthcare and Philosophy*, and in edited collections. In 2009–11 Havi led an AHRC-funded project on the concepts of health, illness and disease. In 2011–12 she was awarded a Leverhulme Fellowship for a project entitled 'The Lived Experience of Illness'. In 2012–13 she held a British Academy Mid-Career Fellowship.

Edward S. Casey is Distinguished Professor of Philosophy at SUNY, Stony Brook, and former president of the America Philosophical Association, Eastern Division. He is the author of ten books, including four volumes on place. His most recent publications are *The World at a Glance* and *The World on Edge*.

Wayne Christensen's research interests include the evolution of cognition, skill, agency, and the development of mindreading. He completed his PhD in philosophy of biology and in philosophy of cognitive science at the University of Newcastle (Australia), and he has been a lecturer and researcher at the ANU, the Konrad Lorenz Institute for Evolution and Biology, The University of Adelaide and Macquarie University. He is currently a research fellow at the University of Warwick and is engaged in projects on skilled action and the sense of commitment.

Lynn Froggett has a cross-disciplinary academic formation in the Humanities and Social Sciences, and is Professor and Director of Psychosocial Research at the University of Central Lancashire. She holds visiting professorships at the Universities of Stavanger, in Norway and Roskilde, in Denmark, and an ongoing research collaboration with UNSW Art & Design, Sydney. With a background in social policy, welfare and innovation and public mental health, a key focus of her current work is in the socially engaged arts. She has led a succession of empirical projects in clinical, cultural and community settings as diverse as youth justice, museums, hospitals, new model arts institutions, primary care, regeneration contexts, schools and festivals. Her recent projects have been particularly concerned with cultural citizenship and regeneration, including the role of digital media and both durational and permanently sited public art in civic discourse. The theoretical and conceptual development from this body of work is cumulative and rests on the development of in-depth, hermeneutic, ethnographic, narrative and visual methodologies. Recent themes have been the relationship between symbolization and personal or community transformation, the role of illusion and delusion in social change processes, and the use of the aesthetic faculty in apprehending complex social phenomena.

Andrew Geeves is a qualitative researcher from Sydney who is interested in psychoanalysis, the experience of expert performance and the emotions involved in this experience, especially for musicians. He was awarded his PhD in psychology from Macquarie University, Sydney, in 2012 and examined the experience of music performance for the professional musician for his dissertation. He has worked as a lecturer, tutor, research assistant and music performance coach. He currently works as a psychologist in private practice.

Petra Gemeinboeck is Senior Lecturer in Interactive Media Arts at UNSW Art & Design, Sydney, and formerly Deputy Director of the NIEA Creative Robotics Lab, and Director of UNSW Art & Design Postgraduate Research. An artist and researcher, Petra's creative practice crosses robotics, performance and feminist theory, exploring our entanglements with machines, and making tangible the vulnerabilities and politics involved. Her earlier works developed new aesthetic experiences through interactive installation and virtual reality. She currently leads an ARC Discovery Project, which investigates the potential of movement, and dance in particular, for reimagining how machines look, learn and affect us. Petra publishes widely on non-human agency, machine creativity and issues of embodiment, and has co-edited a special *Fibreculture* issue on creative robotics. Her artworks have been exhibited internationally, including at the Ars Electronica Festival; International Triennial of New Media Art at NAMOC, Beijing; Centre des Arts Enghien, Paris; Foundation for Art and Creative Technology (FACT), Liverpool; Gallery of Modern Art, Brisbane; ICC, Tokyo; and MCA, Chicago.

Katherine Gibson is a Professorial Research Fellow in the Institute for Culture and Society at the Western Sydney University. She is an economic geographer with an international reputation for innovative research on economic transformation and over thirty years' experience of working with communities to build resilient economies. As J. K. Gibson-Graham, the collective authorial presence she shares with the late Julie Graham (Professor of Geography, University of Massachusetts, Amherst), her books include *The End of Capitalism (As We Knew It): A Feminist Critique of Political Economy* (Blackwell, 1996) and *A Postcapitalist Politics* (University of Minnesota Press, 2006). Her most recent books are *Take Back the Economy: An Ethical Guide for Transforming Our Communities,* co-authored with Jenny Cameron and Stephen Healy (University of Minnesota Press, 2013); *Making Other Worlds Possible: Performing Diverse Economies,* co-edited with Gerda Roelvink and Kevin St Martin (University of Minnesota Press, 2015); and *Manifesto For Living in the Anthropocene*, co-edited with Deborah Bird Rose and Ruth Fincher (Punctum Press, 2015).

Michael Hardt is an author, most recently of *Assembly* (with Antonio Negri). He teaches at Duke University and serves as editor of *The South Atlantic Quarterly.*

Tim Ingold is Chair of Social Anthropology at the University of Aberdeen. He has carried out fieldwork among Saami and Finnish people in Lapland, and has written on environment, technology and social organization in the circumpolar North, on animals in human society, and on human ecology and evolutionary theory. His more recent work explores environmental perception and skilled practice. Ingold's current interests lie on the interface between anthropology, archaeology, art and architecture. His recent books include *The Perception of the Environment* (2000), *Lines* (2007), *Being Alive* (2011), *Making* (2013) and *The Life of Lines* (2015).

Alphonso Lingis is Professor Emeritus of Philosophy at the Pennsylvania State University. He has published *Excesses: Eros and Culture* (1984), *Libido: The French Existential Theories* (1985). *Phenomenological Explanations* (1986), *Deathbound Subjectivity* (1989), *The Community of Those Who Have Nothing in Common* (1994), *Abuses* (1994), *Foreign Bodies* (1994), *Sensation: Intelligibility in Sensibility* (1995), *The Imperative* (1998), *Dangerous Emotions* (1999), *Trust* (2003), *Body Modifications: Evolutions and Atavisms in Culture* (2005), *The First Person Singular* (2007), *Contact* (2010) and *Violence and Splendor* (2011).

Lambros Malafouris, PhD (Cambridge, Darwin College), is Johnson Research and Teaching Fellow in Creativity, Cognition and Material Culture at Keble College, and the Institute of Archaeology, University of Oxford. He was

Balzan Research Fellow in Cognitive Archaeology at the McDonald Institute, University of Cambridge between 2005 and 2008. His research interests lie broadly in the archaeology of mind and the philosophy of material culture. His publications include *How Things Shape the Mind: A Theory of Material Engagement* (MIT Press, 2013), *The Cognitive Life of Things: Recasting the Boundaries of the Mind* (with Colin Renfrew, 2010), *Material Agency: Towards a Non-anthropocentric Approach* (with Carl Knappett, 2008) and *The Sapient Mind: Archaeology Meets Neuroscience* (with Colin Renfrew and Chris Frith, 2008).

Jeff Malpas is Distinguished Professor at the University of Tasmania, Hobart, and Adjunct Professor in Architecture at RMIT University, Melbourne. Growing up in New Zealand, but working most of his academic life in Australia, he is the author or editor of twenty or more books with some of the world's leading academic presses, and has published numerous scholarly articles on topics in philosophy, art, architecture and geography. His work is grounded in post-Kantian thought, especially the hermeneutical and phenomenological traditions, as well as in analytic philosophy of language and mind, and draws on the thinking of a diverse range of thinkers including, most notably, Albert Camus, Donald Davidson, Martin Heidegger and Hans-Georg Gadamer.

Doris McIlwain was Associate Professor of Psychology at Macquarie University, Sydney. Her teaching and research addressed personality, psychoanalysis and emotion, with particular interests in affiliation to new religious movements, narcissism and Machiavellianism, and skilled movement. She sought to integrate qualitative and psychometric methods, treating psychology as a portable science in a range of real-world settings. Doris McIlwain died in 2015.

Hélène Mialet is currently a faculty member in the Department of STS at York. She is the author of *L'Entreprise Créatrice* (Hermès, 2008), *Hawking Incorporated* (Chicago: University of Chicago Press, 2012) and *A la Recherche de Stephen Hawking* (Odile Jacob, 2014). Presently, she is working on a book-length manuscript entitled *Rethinking the Actor of Invention*, which is a theoretical reflection on the history and sociology of ideas about the knowing subject, and formulating a new project on type-1 diabetes and its management, which engages with notions of the self, personhood, and control. More specifically, this book tentatively entitled *Tracking the Trackers: An Ethnographic Study of Sensibility in Translation* focuses on issues having to do with lay and expert knowledge in the management of chronic disease; with the use of prosthetics, computer-driven monitoring devices, algorithms and extended medical networks involving assemblages of caregivers, patients, animals and machines; and on questions of management and control, and their relationship to experience, sensation and expertise.

Ethan Miller is Lecturer in Politics, Anthropology and Environmental Studies at Bates College in Lewiston, Maine, and is a member of the Community Economies Collective. His current work focuses on challenging problematic distinctions between 'economy', 'society' and 'environment' in regional development processes, and on developing cross-cutting and integrative conceptual tools to strengthen transformative, post-capitalist organizing efforts. Ethan has also been engaged for the past fifteen years with an array of projects focused on cooperative and ecological livelihood, including the Data Commons Cooperative, Grassroots Economic Organizing (GEO), the JED Collective cooperative homestead, and Land in Common community land trust.

Alberto Pérez-Gómez was born in Mexico City in 1949, where he studied and practiced architecture. In 1983 he became Director of Carleton University's School of Architecture. Since January 1987, he has occupied the Bronfman Chair of Architectural History at McGill University, where he founded the History and Theory post-professional (Master's and Doctoral) programmes. His research takes as its core the phenomenological and embodied experience of architecture, and investigates its performative and narrative aspects. He has lectured extensively around the world, and is the author of numerous articles published in major periodicals and of books. His book *Architecture and the Crisis of Modern Science* (MIT Press, 1983) won the Hitchcock Award in 1984. His later books include *Polyphilo or The Dark Forest Revisited* (1992), *Architectural Representation and the Perspective Hinge* (co-authored with Louise Pelletier, 1997), *Built upon Love: Architectural Longing after Ethics and Aesthetics* (2006) and most recently *Attunement: Architectural Meaning after the Crisis of Modern Science* (2016).

Ralph James Savarese is the author of *Reasonable People: A Memoir of Autism and Adoption* and the co-editor of a special issue of *Disability Studies Quarterly*, 'Autism and the Concept of Neurodiversity', the first collection of its kind. He has published some twenty-five articles on autism. His new book, under contract at Duke University Press, is titled *See It Feelingly: Classic Novels, Autistic Readers, and the Schooling of a No-good English Professor.*

Michel Serres was a member of the Académie Française. He has written numerous essays and books on philosophy and the history of science, including *The Five Senses* (Bloomsbury), *Genesis* (Grasset/University of Michigan) and *Biogée* (Le Pommier/Univocal Press).

John Sutton is Professor of Cognitive Science at Macquarie University in Sydney, where he was previously Head of the Department of Philosophy.

His current research addresses embodied and distributed cognition, autobiographical and collaborative memory, and the cognitive humanities

Mary Zournazi is an Australian author, philosopher and film-maker. She is Associate Professor in the School of Social Sciences at the University of New South Wales, Sydney. Her most recent film is *Dogs of Democracy* (2017) and forthcoming is *Rembetika Blues* (2020). She is the author of several books including *Hope – New Philosophies for Change* and *Inventing Peace* with the Oscar-nominated German film-maker Wim Wenders.

Acknowledgements

Thanks to Peter Cowley and Margaret Sankey for the written translation of Michel Serres (Chapter 1) and to Waddick Doyle for interpreting the conversation with Michel Serres in Paris.

A revised version of the paper by John Sutton, Doris McIlwain, Wayne Christensen and Andrew Geeves (Chapter 5, 'Embodying thought in skilful action') was previously published as 'Applying Intelligence to the Reflexes: Embodied Skills and Habits between Dreyfus and Descartes', in the *Journal of the British Society for Phenomenology* 42 (1), 2011, 78–103. Earlier versions of parts of this material were presented at seminars at Monash University, Macquarie University and Lewis and Clark College; to the annual conference of the Australasian Association of Philosophy; and to the Skill Acquisition Research Group at the Australian Institute of Sport.

Lambros Malafouris' work (Chapter 6, 'What does the stick do for the blind?') was assisted by the John Templeton Foundation Grant, *Self-Bound: The Making of Human Consciousness* (ID 60652).

Tim Ingold's work (Chapter 10, 'Thinking through the cello') was assisted by the European Research Council Advanced Grant, *Knowing From the Inside: Anthropology, Art, Architecture and Design* (323677-KFI, 2013–18).

Jill Bennett and Lynne Froggett's work (Chapter 11, 'Aesthetic intelligence') was assisted by an Australian Research Council (ARC) Linkage Grant, *Third Space*.

Havi Carel's paper (Chapter 13, 'The philosophical role of illness') was first published as 'The Philosophical Role of Illness' in *Metaphilosophy*, 45(1): 20–40, 2014. We are grateful to Wiley Publishers for their permission to reprint it here. This paper was written during a period of research leave funded by the Leverhulme Trust and revised during a period of leave funded by the British Academy.

Thanks to Ally Bisshop for her assistance with the manuscript. Work on this book has been supported by UNSW Sydney.

Introduction: Thinking in the world

Jill Bennett and Mary Zournazi

I

The expansive concept of 'thinking in the world' is a radically different proposition to the contemplative endeavour of 'thinking *about* the world'. *Thinking in* evokes an embedded, engaged activity – a praxis and process, rather than simply a reflection. As such, this study of thinking is not the exclusive province of philosophy and cognitive science. Both philosophy of mind and cognitive science have, in recent times, evolved understandings of thinking as embodied and situated. But such a shift itself implies the necessity of a transdisciplinary turn; *situated* thinking is imbricated with material environments (the term is often associated with science and technology studies) and *embodied* thinking has physical, affective, sensory and aesthetic dimensions (and hence has resonance across arts and humanities, as well as psychology). To study thinking in the world is to study experience, and its corollary, engagement. Thinking – as theories of extended cognition argue – does not merely take place in the brain but in the circuits that link cognitive processes to real-world settings, to technology, to place and to other people. These relationships are shaped through interpersonal and social connections, by machines and other resources; they enfold the world, are shaped by the world, and are the means of imagining and making the world.

This Reader aims to open out questions of how to consider thinking *in* and *with* our environments. It examines the ways in which thinking is activated and enacted in the world, and draws upon fields of practice where thinking is understood in dynamic relation to the development of technologies, the built environment, creativity and politics. In so doing, it draws on authors who combine different phenomenological, philosophies of mind and cognitive science perspectives, without privileging any one approach, but working towards an expanded philosophy of thinking.

The French philosopher Michel Serres, who works across the sciences, arts and humanities, provides a useful touchstone for this study of thinking. Serres reflects on the transdisciplinarity of research and a 'practise of science' that he ascribes to Leibniz, and which he sees as a productive mode or method that can embrace different fields of knowledge:

> Let us eliminate distance, enter into the effective workings of science. Let its discourse speak. An attentive listener will easily hear its implicit philosophy. Is this really a method? Yes. A method is acceptable, not only when the organon which promotes or justifies it is rigorous, or when it stands on its own as a systematic or normative monument – hence the derisory efficiency of most traditionally taught 'methods' (by efficiency we mean the ratio between results and the power of the constructed device) – but when it is fecund, here and now. A method is preferable by virtue of what it does, not by what it thinks. At stake here is not to speak of, around, about, on (meaning 'above') science, but simply to speak science, one science, this part, that theorem.[1]

For Serres, the world itself thinks, in ways in which we have yet to understand: all animate (human and non-human species) and inanimate objects (rocks, minerals, and so on) in this world share a form of *information* exchange; it is this 'communication' that we share in common, and which can bring together new and intimate ways of understanding the world. In many of his books, including *Eyes* and in his contribution to this volume, he suggests how the empirical world may be understood as processes of exchange in which human perception is not dominant.[2] Rather than merely being the object of perception, the world itself perceives, engages and activates thinking; humans are a *small* part of this process of engagement. His approach, in the broadest terms, resonates with accounts of perception and cognition as an extended or enactive process, coupling the organism and its environment (cf. Evan Thompson, Francisco J. Varela and Aloe Noë).[3]

Thinking as a form of engagement opens out a dialogue with the world, and this process, Serres suggests, enables humans to move from being *parasites* of the world to working in *symbiosis* with it. Such a radical shift may occur across the spectrum of knowledge practices: economic, social and environmental. But with our human-centred vision, there have been fundamental misadventures in our thinking, and because of this, the world has become the 'silent' partner in histories of human ignorance and waste. It is by opening a global conversation that can include other forms of thinking and knowing that we can extend the world as we know it. This involves challenging any one world view so as to promote dialogue that actively engages *listening* to the world: where thinking is grounded in encounters with the world, and those worlds that we have yet to experience.

This insistence on attentiveness to the world is present in other phenomenological works. The French philosopher Gaston Bachelard similarly recovers a mode of 'worldly' vitality: because it is thinking as the engagement and inhabitation in the world that connects us, and shapes our feelings and perceptions. In an interview conducted in 1961, Bachelard spoke about living the life of a gardener; this life is grounded in the flows and changes of a material world.[4] He reflects on the first time he saw trees blossoming in the country, and notes how capitalist functions cannot control the advent of blossom. For Bachelard, each moment has an imaginative potential to create and transform how we engage with and understand our surroundings.

This type of sensibility shapes our encounters in the world, and necessitates thinking with the 'intelligence' of other species and plants as Alphonso Lingis has addressed (across his writings, and in this volume).[5] Attunement with place thus implies a worldly consciousness and awareness of processes of transformation – an ecological sensibility. Such an approach to thinking in place is most thoroughly developed in the phenomenological writings of Ed Casey (both Casey and Jeff Malpas extend these lines of thinking and engagement across their works, and in this collection).

Thinking as worldly and affective invokes a sensory engagement with the environment, and enables what might be considered as atmospheric attunement: embodied thinking in relation to environment and place. As Alberto Pérez-Gómez argues in this collection, human consciousness is shaped through and with relations to the physical environment. In this way, he follows authors such as Juhani Pallaasma working across phenomenology and neuroscience[6] in exploring architecture's attunement to embodied experience, and hence, how attention to the environment can enhance forms of consciousness that are predicated on well-being and health, not simply on utility and function.

In a similar vein, modes of thinking that are embodied in skilled actions – playing instruments, dance or sporting activities – might also be considered as atmospheric and ecological. Philosopher Maurice Merleau-Ponty's seminal works on perception provide various authors in this collection with ways to envisage and expand where we can locate thinking, materiality and action.[7] But as Lambros Malafouris – following the philosopher Andy Clark – asks, 'How do we put brain, body and the world back together again?'[8] How does the study of material culture broaden the conception of 'mind'? To respond to this challenge, we need to engage a much wider range of practices than is traditionally encompassed within philosophy or the study of thought.

The stakes of such a process-based or 'extended cognition' paradigm are perhaps most evident when we consider the exclusions of narrower, normalized models of cognition and thinking. How, for example, do minds operate when they are embodied in ways that couple with assistive technologies (viz., Hélène Mialet's study of Stephen Hawking)? This question – foreshadowed by Merleau-Ponty's famous discussion of the blind man's stick as a scaffold for cognition and experience – has become emblematic in an age of artificial intelligence, and as human-machine couplings become more visible. And it is no coincidence that it has been feminist-inspired authors who have pioneered the study of machinic bodies: Donna Haraway's writing on cyborg culture;[9] Lucy Suchman's human-machine reconfigurations,[10] which begin with the photocopier – and in this volume Mialet; and robotics artist Petra Gemeinboeck. Similarly, Suchman asks us to consider the problem of 'situational awareness' – how new forms of perception and non-human devices implicate us.[11]

Feminism, in common with disability theory, debunks the humanist myth of natural ability. Eli Clare rightly insists that the term *enabled* is more suitable than able-bodied, the latter effacing the degree to which the dominant neurotypical, non-disabled normalized body is implicitly assisted by *all* social systems, workplace and learning practices, and architectural and design solutions.[12] A radical and necessary step is to understand how all bodies and minds – whether labelled able or disabled – are interdependent and assisted.

As John Sutton and colleagues' work shows, the mind has never been a self-contained proposition, independent of its corporeal, social and environmental scaffolding. Thinking is thus a process and product of embodied conditions. Illness or neurodivergence (see Havi Carel and Ralph Savarese's chapters) may be material to thought. It is not a question of whether illness and/or neurodivergence impair or enhance thinking (they may in specific instances do either or neither). It is rather that they challenge the very assumption of neuronormativity: the belief that thinking is ever NOT inflected by our diverse and specific embodied experiences. This de-centring is at the heart of the *Thinking in the World* project.

Neurodiversity represents a revolutionary shift in thinking (extended in this volume by Ralph Savarese). Coined by the Australian activist Judy Singer,[13] and now taken up by a global movement, the concept of neurodiversity asserts the principle that natural and normal variations in the human genome and acquired characteristics (like brain lesions) produce diversity: a spectrum of subtle differentiation that cannot be reduced to a binary distinguishing abnormality or 'disorder' by virtue of deviation from a norm. Neurodivergent or autistic modes of thinking require exploration and representation; because they arise from specific sensory-perceptual conditions, they in turn give rise to new aesthetics, new forms of engagement.

In this regard, we understand the politics of neurodiversity, and more generally, of difference, to be bound up with the diversification of thinking modalities. To explore the political implications and potential of neurodiverse thinking must entail an openness to aesthetic experimentation, which in turn must be open to co-option and transformation. Aesthetics in this sense is not a discipline but a means.

* * *

This volume pursues the questions of the materiality of experience, and experience itself as a process, in turn informing intervention and social action. This involves an embodied form of action, based at the very heart of social movements and collectives, that Michael Hardt has explored in various ways in the radicalization of political thinking (along with Antonio Negri).[14] This thinking involves our affective lives and labour and our sense of common resources, habitats and ecology. It involves systems of thinking and connection that embed and expand social relations, and that recognize the inherent exchange within the worlds in which we live – which are explored in different ways in this volume (see Hardt and Zournazi, and Gibson and Miller's chapters). It is this reactivation of materiality, ecology and the world that shapes new processes of thinking and sociality: re-envisaging the actions and relationships that produce, engage and extend our worlds in social and political terms.

Cutting across all these approaches to thinking are the textures of feeling, sensory and affective experience, and attunement to the world. Thinking – if it is located in a sensing, affective body, in place, or in action – calls for diverse methodological approaches to its study. In this Reader, we consider the practice of thinking as an empirical venture – an experience – that shapes meaning and knowledge production.

II

This Reader encompasses different styles and modes of thinking through written essays as well as dialogue: conversational essays to emphasize the way thinking is generated in the world. This is a *thinking in action*: different authors thinking together to share and extend the accounts and ways of perceiving and addressing the world. The Reader is divided into different parts to navigate the various approaches and responses to the *Thinking in the World* project. Each chapter engages with the challenge of thinking *in and with* the world to provide a lens through which to reconsider how we might approach critical junctures of meaning and action today.

Part I, *Thinking worlds,* establishes a call to action: a radicalization of perception that arises from the question, 'How does the world itself think?' Drawing on her work on dialogic modes of creativity and reflection,[15] Mary Zournazi engages with philosopher Michel Serres to examine the questions of worldly thinking and the implications of thinking for perception in their chapter, 'Revolutions in Thinking'. This investigation involves old and new questions in science, what information and exchange mean today, and how we might listen to and learn from the world. This promotes a re-orientation of thinking to move beyond a human-centred vision to multi-vocal perceptions of the world: a respect for and engagement with animate and inanimate objects in this world – whether they be human, animal, plant or mineral. It also provides a framework of rethinking the limitations within Western forms of knowledge, and the possibilities of engaging with other ways of thinking and knowing the world. This radicalization of perception provides an ecological framework: a philosophy for the future and a philosophy for the world.

In 'The thinking that is in the world', Alphonso Lingis argues that the mind and thinking are part of a response to the world, a mode of dwelling within it (borrowing from Heidegger's notion of dwelling) – 'thinking is dwelling with things, in the world'. In this chapter, Lingis brings to light how we think, by means of the intelligence of other species and plants; thinking then opens out forms of consciousness beyond our own. This provides insights into how we might consider our relations to the world, which might also inform a different social consciousness that emerges through the respect for other ways of navigating and responding it.

Part II, *Senses of place,* brings together the relationship of thinking, feeling and place, and the ways that our sense of place provides the means for articulating experience, intelligence and perceptual worlds. The conversation between Ed Casey and Jeff Malpas, 'A phenomenology of thinking in place', sheds light on how the *feeling* of place is – implicitly and effectively – the *thinking* of it. They are concerned with rethinking a sense of place and notions of memory. By exploring various philosophers such as Robin George (R. G.) Collingwood, Gaston Bachelard and Martin Heidegger, and authors such as Albert Camus, they discuss how thinking evokes the layering of memory, feeling and the experience of place.

In his chapter, 'Attunement as architectural meaning', Alberto Pérez-Gómez argues how architecture is central to our foundational sense of being and of knowing the world. His notion of attunement and the related concept of atmosphere involve a reconsideration of how architectural forms influence and shape human consciousness. For Pérez-Gómez, through a sense of embodied cognition and place, the way in which we structure our cities and worlds becomes part of the process of thinking in and through them. He argues for the essential connection between embodied experience and built environments in shaping our knowledge and well-being – both historically and into the future.

In Part III, *Extended minds and bodies*, body, culture and mind are envisaged as part of a rich ecology of actions and relations that shape thinking in the everyday; the materiality of experience becomes the basis for the examination of our habits, cultural artefacts and actions. In John Sutton and colleagues' chapter, 'Embodying thought in skilful action', the authors argue how mindful action and its attunement to and with body and world generate thinking that is grounded in the very act of movement itself. They rethink accounts of memory and the body, which unsettles – both historically and conceptually – the very idea of reducing complex embodied action to mere reflex, and by rethinking these categories, they enrich both traditionalist and phenomenological accounts of body and habit. For example, in complex settings such as in sport, dance or music, actions or movements incorporate technological, material, cultural, affective and collaborative resources into what are best understood as dynamic 'cognitive ecologies'. As such, they argue for a thinking that is grounded in the embodied and skilful actions of practitioners, and by doing this they recast the problem of cognition and thinking as not separate from the movement and kinaesthesia of the body.

In his chapter, 'What does the stick do for the blind?', Lambros Malafouris builds on the emerging field of 'neuroarchaeology' and anthropological approaches to mind and culture. Malafouris returns to the classic case (invoked by Merleau-Ponty) of the 'blind man's stick' as an extension of the mind, to examine how such a prosthetic device may be intrinsic to the way in which humans learn to identify, attend to and transform their world. Malafouris suggests how the world and the co-evolving of forms and technologies are part of the ways in which our minds extend, and how thinking is dynamically modelled in and through behaviours that are often mediated by material objects; a complex relation between brain, body and world. His 'material engagement theory' traces this materiality of thought as a creative process embedded and emergent in lived histories, thus demanding a reappraisal of assumptions about cognitive evolution.

Part IV, *Technologies,* examines the thinking that emerges in and with human and non-human relations. In her chapter, 'The distributed-centred subject', Hélène Mialet looks at human and non-human relations in the constitution of the self. Through her case study of Stephen Hawking, she argues how technologies are part of the formation of the self: instruments, devices and machines (*and* humans) are part of knowledge production. She posits that thinking involves non-humans, and that the creation and distribution of ways of knowing may also involve different forms of agency. The frontier between machines and humans are blurred, and in this reconstitution of the subject, the perceptual and habitual pathways of what makes us human are challenged.

In Petra Gemeinboeck's chapter, 'Dancing with the non-human', she explores our relations with artificial intelligence. Gemeinboeck looks at the implications of this through her project, *Machine Movement Labs*, demonstrating the ways in which learning to think with and through different bodies – human and non-human – provides a way of establishing mutually relational thoughts. She posits thinking as a kind of mutual reconfiguring *with* the world; embodied and entangled thinking that is always situated, relational and materially anchored.

Part V, *Creativity,* considers how thinking is established through the movement and relational aspects of aesthetic sensibilities and experience. By considering thinking as atmospheric and collective, we open out our notions of feeling, memory and relations to and with the world. Mieke Bal's chapter, 'Thinking in film', investigates thought as movement, and the trajectories of affect and perception that are established through the practice of art. Reflecting on her inspirations and her film projects *Madame B* and *Reasonable Doubt – Scene from Two Lives*, Bal argues how thinking never happens alone but is always a social process. She evokes how the movement of thinking is akin to the movement of images: enduring while also continually transforming, and sustained through collective and social practices

In his chapter, 'Thinking with the cello', Tim Ingold asks us to reconsider the nature of thought, and argues for the necessity of thinking about mind, body and self as a fusion with and through the world. Where silence is usually considered as containing no movement or sound, Ingold draws on his own experiences of playing the cello to argue how silence – and by extension, thought – is alive with sound and feeling. Through a carefully woven argument, Ingold shows how sound is neither a physical impulse nor a mental sensation, but a phenomenon of atmosphere brought about by the blending of the cosmic and the affective. He suggests that, like light, sound is generated by a fission/fusion reaction that unites us with the cosmos even as it divides us against ourselves. As such, *thinking-in-doing* is not cognitive but atmospheric in its spaciousness and embodied experience.

Jill Bennett and Lynn Froggett's chapter, 'Aesthetic intelligence', reflects on how aesthetic sensibility relates to our everyday experience and intersubjective relations. Drawing on their collaborative work – blending Bennett's concept of practical aesthetics and Froggett's psychosocial methodology – they consider the importance of the concept of aesthetic intelligence and the implications of this embodied experience for understanding, which is attentive to the sensory-affective dimensions of engagements with the world.

Part VI, *Spectrums of experience*, examines thinking in terms of a neurodiverse spectrum (recognizing that variations in the human genome create varieties of thinking experience) and also the variations in human health, which do not simply divide the well from the unwell but constitute embodied experiences that gives rise to forms of thinking.

Ralph Savarese's chapter, 'Reading Leslie Marmon Silko's *Ceremony* with autist Jamie Burke', enacts what he calls 'neurocosmopolitanism' – an ethical principle derived from the scientifically grounded, activist vision of neurodiversity. Modelling a form of cognitive hospitality that decentres the neurotypical brain and rejects a deficit account of autism, Savarese's reading with Burke is an imaginative interaction of neurodiverse perceptions, showing instead how autistic worlds inspire different modes of embodied thinking.

In her chapter, 'The philosophical world of illness', Havi Carel asserts thinking as part of the embodied experience of difference – illness as a bodily modality or process that enables the reawakening of notions of selfhood. Her chapter opens out the question of what makes us human, and how human relationships and ethics would be incomplete if they did not take into account the full spectrum of human life and experience, spanning sickness and health, childhood, adulthood and old age. Carel shows how illness can undermine taken-for-granted expectations, destroying the assumptions that underpin values attached to longevity, capability and autonomy. She argues for the importance of embodied difference in our real-world experience.

Part VII, *Economies, ecologies, politics*, considers *thinking together* as a mode of political engagement and material action. This resonates with the idea of embodied and situated knowledges explored in previous chapters, but this *thinking together* concerns what thinking might mean through the political process itself, and as such, understanding the different social contexts and conditions for political thought. In their chapter, 'Thinking love and politics in the world', Michael Hardt and Mary Zournazi explore how *thinking with politics* might evolve, and how love as the co-substantiation of thought in the political sphere might enable different relations, negotiations and exchanges to emerge across and between different systems of political thought and action.

In their chapter, 'Thinking with interdependence', Katherine Gibson and Ethan Miller consider the need to move beyond theorizing notions of economy and environment, to thinking towards ecological livelihood. They argue for the importance of *thinking with* the challenges of climate change and the suffering of fellow humans, and they ask how the work of social theorists and action researchers might open out new pathways of thought. They seek to engage with the world in which the materiality of thinking is the process of learning with and through our common resources; and to learn from those that have already been part of this collective experience. In so doing, they offer new paradigms for thinking relationships of social change and ecological life.

* * *

What we hope to offer in this Reader is a sense of how thinking evolves in real-world situations. In so doing, we seek to inspire further engagement with a sociality of experience that is neurodiverse, differently embodied, human and non-human in scope. This is a broad-ranging philosophy of *thinking in action* – an emergent and multifaceted account of embodied experience and its inexorable connection to the world. We invite others to participate in this *Thinking in the World* project, and its possibilities towards a philosophy for the future.

Notes

1 Michel Serres, 'Transdisciplinarity as Relative Exteriority', in Special issue on 'Transdisciplinary Problematics', eds Peter Osborne, Stella Sandford and Eric Alliez, Theory, Culture & Society 32.5–6 (2015), p. 43.

2 Michel Serres, *Eyes,* trans. Anne-Marie Feenberg-Dibon (London: Bloomsbury, 2015) is published as part of the 'Thinking in the World' Series. Other texts relevant here include Serres' *The Natural Contract*, trans. Elizabeth MacArthur and William Paulson (Ann Arbor: University of Michigan Press, 1995), and *Biogea*, trans. Randolph Burks (Minneapolis: Univocal Publishing, 2012).

3 See Francisco J. Varela, Evan Thompson and Eleanor Rosch, *The Embodied Mind: Cognitive Science and Human Experience* (Cambridge, MA: MIT Press, 1991). See also Alva Noë, *Action in Perception* (Cambridge, MA: The MIT Press, 2004), and Humberto Maturana and Francisco Varela's texts: *Autopoiesis and Cognition: The Realisation of the Living* (Boston: D. Reidel Publishing, 1980) and *The Tree of Knowledge: The Biological Roots of Human Understanding* (Boston: New Science Library, 1987).

4 See Gaston Bachelard's interview on 'Cinq Colonnes à la Une', NA.fr archival website, https://www.youtube.com/watch?v=qu70lxwFoTA (accessed 25 July 2018). See also his texts: *The Poetics of Reverie*, trans. D. Russell (Boston: Beacon Press, 1971); *On Poetic Imagination and Reverie*, trans. C. Gaudin (Dallas: Spring Publications, 1987); *The Poetics of Space*, trans. M. Jolas (Boston: Beacon Press, 1994); *The Dialectic of Duration*, trans. M. McAllester Jones (Manchester: Clinamen Press, 2000); *Earth and Reveries of Will: An Essay on the Imagination of Matter*, trans. Kenneth Haltman (Dallas: Dallas Institute Publications, 2002).

5 In addition to his contribution to this Reader, see, for example, Lingis' *Violence and Splendour* (Evanston, IL: Northwestern University Press, 2011).

6 See, for example, Juhani Pallasmaa, *The Eyes of the Skin* (Chichester: Wiley-Academy; Hoboken, NJ: John Wiley & Sons, 2005).

7 See Maurice Merleau-Ponty, *The Primacy of Perception*, ed. James M. Edie (Evanston, IL: Northwestern University Press, 1964) and *The Phenomenology of Perception*, trans. Donald A. Landes (New York and London: Routledge, 2012).

8 As well as in his contribution to this Reader, Lambros Malafouris make a similar argument in *How Things Shape the Mind: A Theory of Material*

Engagement (Cambridge, MA: MIT Press, 2016). See also Andy Clark, *Being There: Putting Brain, Body and World Together Again* (Cambridge, MA: MIT Press, 1997).

9 Donna Haraway, *Simians, Cyborgs and Women: The Reinvention of Nature* (London: Free Association Books, 1991).

10 See, for example, Lucy Suchman, *Plans and Situated Actions: The Problem of Human-Machine Communication* (Cambridge, MA: Cambridge University Press, 1987).

11 See, for example, Suchman's 'Situational Awareness and Adherence to the Principle of Distinction as a Necessary Condition for Lawful Autonomy', in *Lethal Autonomous Weapons Systems: Technology, Definition, Ethics, Law & Security*, ed. Robin Geiß (Berlin: German Federal Foreign Office, 2017), pp. 273–83.

12 This is expressed across Eli Clare's work, including texts such as *Brilliant Imperfection: Grappling with Cure* (Durham, NC: Duke University Press, 2017), and *Exile and Pride: Disability, Queerness, and Liberation* (Cambridge, MA: South End Press, 1999).

13 See, for example, Judy Singer, *NeuroDiversity: The Birth of an Idea* (Kindle e-Book, 2016).

14 See, for example, Michael Hardt and Antonio Negri, *Multitude* (New York: Penguin Books, 2004).

15 See Mary Zournazi, *Hope – New Philosophies for Change* (New York: Routledge, 2003), and Wim Wenders and Mary Zournazi, *Inventing Peace – A Dialogue on Perception* (London: I. B. Tauris, 2013).

References

Bachelard, G., *The Dialectic of Duration*, trans. M. McAllester Jones, Manchester: Clinamen Press, 2000.

Bachelard, G., *Earth and Reveries of Will: An Essay on the Imagination of Matter*, trans. Kenneth Haltman, Dallas: Dallas Institute Publications, 2002.

Bachelard, G., Interview on the television program 'Cinq Colonnes à la Une', NA.fr archival website, https://www.youtube.com/watch?v=qu70lxwFoTA (accessed 25 July 2018).

Bachelard, G., *On Poetic Imagination and Reverie*, trans. C. Gaudin, Dallas: Spring Publications, 1987.

Bachelard, G., *The Poetics of Reverie*, trans. D. Russell, Boston: Beacon Press, 1971.

Bachelard, G., *The Poetics of Space*, trans. M. Jolas Boston: Beacon Press, 1994.

Clare, E., *Brilliant Imperfection: Grappling with Cure*, NC: Duke University Press, 2017.

Clare, E., *Exile and Pride: Disability, Queerness, and Liberation*, Cambridge, MA: South End Press, 1999.

Clark, A. and D. J. Chalmers, 'The Extended Mind', *Analysis* 58:1 (1998), pp. 7–19.

Haraway, D. J., *Simians, Cyborgs and Women: The Reinvention of Nature*, London: Free Association Books, 1991.
Hardt, M. and A. Negri, *Multitude*, New York: Penguin Books, 2004.
Lingis, A., *Violence and Splendour*, Evanston, IL: Northwestern University Press, 2011.
Merleau-Ponty, M., *The Phenomenology of Perception*, trans. D. A. Landes, New York and London: Routledge, 2012.
Merleau-Ponty, M., *The Primacy of Perception*, James M. Edie (ed.), Evanston, IL: Northwestern University Press, 1964.
Malafouris, L., *How Things Shape the Mind: A Theory of Material Engagement*, Cambridge, MA: MIT Press, 2016.
Maturana, H. R. and F. J. Varela, *Autopoiesis and Cognition: The Realisation of the Living*, Boston: D. Reidel Publishing, 1980.
Maturana, H. R. and F. J. Varela, *The Tree of Knowledge: The Biological Roots of Human Understanding*, Boston: New Science Library, 1987.
Noë, A., *Action in Perception*, Cambridge, MA: The MIT Press, 2004.
Pallasmaa, J., *The Eyes of the Skin*, Chichester: Wiley-Academy; Hoboken, NJ: John Wiley & Sons, 2005.
Serres, M., *Biogea*, trans. R. Burks, Minneapolis: Univocal Publishing, 2012.
Serres, M., *Eyes*, trans. A-M. Feenberg-Dibon, London: Bloomsbury, 2015.
Serres, M., *The Natural Contract*, trans. E. MacArthur and W. Paulson, Ann Arbor: University of Michigan Press, 1995.
Serres, M., 'Transdisciplinarity as Relative Exteriority', in P. Osborne, S. Sandford and E. Alliez (eds), Special issue on 'Transdisciplinary Problematics' *Theory, Culture & Society* 32.5–6 (2015): 41–4.
Singer, J., *NeuroDiversity: The Birth of an Idea*, Kindle e-Book, 2016.
Suchman, L., *Human-Machine Reconfigurations: Plans and Situated Actions*, Cambridge, MA: Cambridge University Press, 2007.
Suchman, L., 'Situational Awareness and Adherence to the Principle of Distinction as a Necessary Condition for Lawful Autonomy', in R. Geiß (ed.), *Lethal Autonomous Weapons Systems: Technology, Definition, Ethics, Law & Security*, Berlin: German Federal Foreign Office, 2017: 273–83.
Varela, F. J., Thompson, E. and E. Rosch, *The Embodied Mind: Cognitive Science and Human Experience*, Cambridge, MA: MIT Press, 1991.
Wenders, W. and M. Zournazi, *Inventing Peace – A Dialogue on Perception*, London: I. B. Tauris, 2013.
Zournazi, M., *Hope – New Philosophies for Change*, New York: Routledge, 2003.

PART ONE

Thinking worlds

1

Revolutions in thinking

Michel Serres (MS) and Mary Zournazi (MZ)

Introductory remarks

How does the world think? This is a question that invites us to consider the nature of perception and the materiality of the world. If the world thinks – if mountains, rivers, trees and rocks perceive the world – how does this reorient philosophies of perception? It is these questions that invite us to reconsider the relations between art, philosophy and science to pose new directions in thinking. In this chapter, Michel Serres and Mary Zournazi explore the fundamental questions of what thinking in the world might mean, and how the world itself thinks. For Serres, all animate and inanimate objects in this world share a form of information exchange; it is this 'communication' that we share in common, and it is this *commonality* that calls for a radical philosophy of perception – a philosophy that ask us to move beyond a human-centred vision to multi-vocal perceptions of the world.

To rethink perception, then, is central to all of knowledge practices and relationships: economic, social and environmental. With our human-centred vision, there have been fundamental misadventures in our thinking, and because of this, Serres suggests two parallel gaps that have emerged in the world. First, there is the belief that humans have control over nature, and second, that the objects of human production such as money, economics and power relations are not seen as products of human invention.[1] The world has become the 'silent' partner in histories of human ignorance and waste.

In *The Natural Contract*, Serres give us a very precise image of this type of violence using Goya's painting, 'Men Fight with Sticks': two duellists striking blows at each other, and with each blow they sink further and further into a muddied quicksand. Serres notes that the earth will swallow up the fighters before they, and the gamblers, have had a chance to settle accounts'.[2] As a result of this battle among ourselves, we are at the borderline: we are now faced with a world that may no longer be able to support our ongoing violence and destruction to life and habitat.

Over many decades, Michel Serres's illustrious writings and philosophical inventions show the deep concern for the ecology of the world, because as he reminds us there are 'thoughtful subjects everywhere'. Together Serres and Zournazi discuss some of these subjects, and the elements for thinking *with* the world, not about the world.

Things of the world

MZ: I want to start by asking you about *how the world thinks*? In your books *Biogea* and *the Natural Contract,*[3] you talk about aspects of the world's thinking that can take place without humans ... We spoke about this previously together, and the role of 'information' but let's start with thinking.

MS: Our Western way of thinking makes a clear distinction between us humans as active subjects, and the objects of the world, which are passive. There are three ways of understanding this. Firstly, we think the world, and the world is thought by us. Secondly, we act on the world, and the world is the object of our actions. And thirdly, we have rights over the world, whereas the world has none over us. That is how we think, and this way of thinking has been very fertile, very fecund, very useful, and has led us to an unparalleled exploitation of the world – as a result of which we have made the most of the world, become rich, knowledgeable and comfortable. All well and good. However the inevitable conclusion of these three actions is that we find ourselves today facing a serious problem, namely, that we are destroying the world. And we are doing so because we consider ourselves the only active subjects, and think that we can exploit our passive world intellectually, actively and legally.

So we might say that these three ways of thinking – intellectual, practical and legal – have enabled us to make considerable progress, but we have reached an impasse. And these three points are the focus of my thinking: the intellectual, the practical and the judicial. I began with the third point, namely, that we have all possible rights over the world, whereas things in the world have none over us. Do you see? You who come from Australia, you know that there are cultures other than ours for which things in the world are not mere passive objects, are not to be exploited, are not objects, bereft of rights. You see that there are other cultures that teach us a wisdom we have forgotten. For instance, I exposed that wisdom in *The Natural Contract*, where I propose that the things of the world should become legal subjects.[4] This is unthinkable under Western law, precisely because we alone can be legal subjects.

Indeed, since I wrote *The Natural Contract*, many countries – Brazil, the US, occasionally even France – have begun to evolve, judicially speaking, and to consider that it might be possible, for example, for a state forest to defend itself against its users: the forest would, in these circumstances, be considered a legal subject and would have the right to sue its users. This was unthinkable before *The Natural Contract*, because there was no such definition of objects as legal subjects, that is having the right to take human beings to court.

That is the legal side. Naturally the practical side is even more difficult. In other words, can we consider that objects might not be merely passive? This is where the notion of information, about which we spoke last time, comes to bear on the problem. Here is more or less what I said: When we take a living being, we can define it as receiving information, emitting information, storing information and processing information. Such is the life of a living being. Once you understand these four rules concerning living beings and information, you long to use them to define life itself. You say, 'Hang on, life is precisely these four operations'. Well, not quite, because I do not know a single inert object about which one cannot also say that it receives, emits, stores and processes information. This is true of a crystal, of a gem stone, of a metallic object and so on. And it's equally true of a continent, a star, a planet or of any other object in the world. This is an odd thing to say, because we wonder: what is a human being? A human being is someone who emits, receives, stores and processes information. You realize that these four rules are shared by human beings, alone or in groups, living beings and objects – and that is a significant modern discovery.

Once we have defined these four rules of information, namely, emitting, receiving, storing and processing, we notice something surprising, which is that these four rules are true for life, for the inert and for human activity, whether individual or otherwise. At the moment, I am emitting information, receiving information from you, storing it inside myself and processing it, obviously. Any group of humans, whether a family, a village, a nation and so on, is also a cluster of beings emitting, receiving, storing and processing information. As a result, these four rules are universally true, and bring together living beings, inert objects and humans in new and intimate ways, and that is indeed a new discovery.

MZ: If we consider that this process of information is universal, how does it redefine what it means to be human? How do we understand our sense of 'collective', whether it is a family, village or nation? And how does this provide another sense of intimate relations and connexions with the world?

MS: In the past, when we thought about family relationships, we thought about how the family related to the city. And when we thought about a city in terms of its relationships, we wondered how the city might relate to the nation. However, what I am proposing shows that whether we're talking about a family, a city or a nation's relationships, they are all situated in the world. And this allows us to understand our new relationships with the world. Here is an example. For the ancient Romans, the word *familia* designated father, mother, children, ancestors, but also cattle, sheep, wheat, life and their farming tools. So family meant human relationships, relationships with living beings, and at the same time their relationship to the land they cultivated. I would like to restore this ancient sense of relationships. Today, we need to broaden our relationships so that they resemble something a bit like the Roman *familia*.

MZ: Returning to the four functions – emitting, receiving, storing and processing information – that exist in objects that we would not have thought had this capacity, what does this mean for how we understand the thought processes of objects? How do we come to understand this 'difference', and appreciate it without oppressing or pushing our own thinking onto objects? What does this revolution in thought mean?

MS: Well this is an old question, that science has been asking since the beginning. We don't impose our way of thinking on the world. Simply observing objects, or understanding what law governs them, is already a way in which human beings can listen to objects. In other words, we receive information from these objects. Do you see what I mean? Consequently we cannot say that they think, obviously, but the mere fact of observing them is a kind of respect that we can show towards objects. We do not impose our way of thinking on them – quite the contrary. We are, so to speak, passive recipients of the information they broadcast to us.

I think what I'm proposing is a veritable revolution in how we think, because for several decades now we have been concerned by the destruction of biodiversity, alarmed by climate change and global warming, and so we are paying more and more attention to animal behaviour, to the ecology of living species, to the physicality of the planet and to the changing climate.

The fact that entities other than humans are sending us information allows us to consider the world differently to how we have done in the past. In the past, we considered the world to be an array of passive objects, and now we genuinely take them to be our partners in global conservation.

MZ: I'd like to talk more about the notion of listening, and taking part in a genuine conversation – how do we listen, and what does that involve in your scheme of the cosmos?

MS: I think listening is a good metaphor. I really do believe that we receive signals from the world. Naturally we hear its background noise, or chaos if you will, but we also hear all kinds of other signals: from the Big Bang, from distant galaxies, etc. As a result, the whole science of cosmology revolves around listening to these signals, and processing them. And this is of course true of many other sciences. I believe that the world emits noise and transmits signals to us, and that listening to those signals is the very essence of science.

MZ: Now I'm interested in the signals, and that information relationship that every object in the world has – humans, inanimate objects, etc. Can you tell me a little bit more about what these signals are?

MS: Once you consider all the sciences together it becomes quite clear that optics studies signals from the visual world, acoustics studies signals from the auditory world and that all the sciences occupy a sort of region on the signal scale. There are non-visible signals, visible signals, signals which can only be heard with highly sophisticated apparatus and so on – do you see what I mean? So I think you can do something like a classification of the sciences along the scale of possible signals.

MZ: What would this scale of possible signals look like? How do we understand these signals in their own terms, and not for our benefit or exploitation?

MS: This is a question that very much piqued my interest, because entities other than human do indeed send us signals. How then do we hear them? What are these signals? Et cetera. It's quite simple – the answer is an easy one: it goes back to Galileo's explanation that the world is written in the language of mathematics. The language of mathematics encompasses all of these signals, which is how it gives us acoustics and optics, and even a discipline called signal processing. As a result, it can be said that mathematics is the language of the world. And that is a true miracle, and a true paradox, because the more abstract mathematics becomes, the more it deals with the most concrete, the most subtly concrete things in the world. This is what Einstein said, namely, that the most incomprehensible thing about the world is that it is comprehensible. Simply that. We listen to the world, and mathematics gives us to language to do so.

Mythologies

MZ: The way in which we perceive the world influences our language of it, and science has one way of looking at all of this, but there is also mythology and art. What is the interrelationship between these things so that we can really hear and respect the world as it speaks and as it thinks?

MS: That is interesting. I spoke earlier about your Australian origins, where the indigenous people, the Aborigines, have particular mythologies, just as we Europeans, we others, inhabit a land where our ancestors had their own. I've taken a particular interest in these very mythologies, which have a world view different to our own. Let me give you an example. We Western others, when we speak of the world, genuinely believe that everything in the world, be it human bodies, other living bodies or inert objects, is made from the same matter: oxygen, nitrogen, carbon and so on. But the question then becomes: how do we come to have a rock here, a snake over there, my translator right here in front of me ... all quite distinct individuals. Moreover we have a sort of dualism which tells us that all matter is the same, but that souls are different. Mme Zournazi's soul is not the same as my translator's, nor the same as an animal, etc. Well, there are mythologies where the opposite is true. And we need to bear in mind these mythologies, which are the opposite of our own. Animists, for instance, believe that the whole world shares one soul, and that physical bodies are all distinct. Quite the opposite. I believe that if we study in detail the world views entailed in these mythological strands, we can only enrich philosophy in extraordinary ways. In other words, we apprehend that our own view of the world is most certainly a choice, whereas the view that I have just described is symmetrical, different, opposite. And suddenly, as soon as I perceive an opposing world view (which I am calling a mythology), a new world opens up entirely before me – perhaps the real world. Who is to say that this new world is not more real than my own?

That is, once we have understood that there exists a mythology completely symmetrical with and the opposite of ours, we can see that for some people, or at certain historical moments ... the world was not the same for them as it is for us. It wasn't the same world, you understand. And nothing is more instructive than that. For example, in Western philosophy there are theories, for example Stoicism, concerned with the world soul. And so that philosophy was quite close to the mythologies about which you are talking, you understand. I even wrote a book expressly to show that many scientific, philosophical and artistic studies sometimes came from a mythology in the distant past, which inspired that very philosophy. It is called *Writers, Scholars and Philosophers Travel the World.*[5]

MZ: Can I ask you about the world soul, and if we think the idea of a world soul maybe exists for us now, what does that say, or how can that help us on the one hand to understand the new technologies, and on the other hand, make the world more just, a more just place for nature and for ourselves? It's a big question.

MS: I don't believe that one can literally apply an old theory like that to today's world. No, not at all, I do not believe that that is possible. But what is interesting is the idea of being inspired by another vision of the world, in order to try to understand the present-day world.

What is remarkable today is that we are living out the end of the Industrial Revolution, which was based on the world vision about which I have just been speaking to you. That is, one in which the objects in the world are inert and completely passive, and in which they are our property and we can exploit them. Consequently, we are in the last stages of this world vision, and the Industrial Revolution – that I now call 'hard' – has just come to an end, to be replaced by another world, which is, I believe, much 'softer'. That is, it is no longer the Industrial Revolution of the past, but is based on our science: for example, the life sciences, the earth sciences and the information sciences. We are at present living through a complete change in world vision. That is why we have to work on the question that you are asking. We are moving from a 'hard' age to a 'soft' age.

Revolutions in thought

MZ: Given this movement from hard age to soft age, what is the relationship between biology or life and information today?

MS: I think that today the information sciences are theoretically and practically those that lead to thinking. Today there would be no biology if there were no information science leading straight to biology. There would be almost no science at all if there were no information theory. We can no longer do without it now; it's as though it were, in a certain sense, the fundamental science. That is, the science which leads both to our techniques and thinking. Consequently, there would be no biology without that, nor astronomy, nor sociology.

Basically our main tool today is the computer. It's very simple. When I was young and entered an office where someone was looking at the sky with a telescope I said, 'he is an astronomer'. When I went into a laboratory and saw a man in a white coat with coloured stains on it I said, 'he must be a chemist'; when I went into a room where there was a man with a stick of chalk writing equations on the blackboard, I said, 'he must be a mathematician'. So I could distinguish the sciences merely by looking at people's appearance and what they were doing. Today, when I go into a room they are all at their computers – whether they are astronomers, physicists, sociologists or poets. So, the computer has become the universal tool for understanding, and consequently information theory theoretically dominates all knowledge.

That is why I say that we are moving into a new age – into which science moreover has already moved, and into which our social practices are increasingly moving – that I call the 'soft' age.

MZ: How do we understand this shift in practice, technologies from 'hard to soft'?

MS: I believe personally that the technology that we have used until now was a technology determined by, and constructed on the basis of, the Industrial Revolution, at the end of the eighteenth and beginning of the nineteenth centuries. This technology was founded on energy, that is, on petroleum, electricity, and nuclear energy, etc., and today this technology, founded on energy, is gradually coming to an end. That is, we will exhaust petroleum resources and we will find that coal resources are too polluting, etc. We are obliged to have a technological revolution.

Once, technology was founded on thermodynamics, on energy. Today I believe that technology must be founded on information; that is why I am talking about information. But also, I believe that the technologies of today should be founded on what we call in French *SVT*, the life and earth sciences. The life and earth sciences are sciences that are very aware of the protection of life, the protection of species and the protection of the earth. Consequently they are 'soft' sciences, in contrast to 'hard' technologies. And so the technological revolution must be founded on the life and earth sciences, and on the information sciences. So there is a sort of technological revolution which is in process today, and it is to be hoped that it will come about. That is how we should respond to the question of technology.

MZ: So, in a way, technology can open out a pathway for the good, so to speak ...

MS: Technology is always a means to an end, and means are good or bad according to how they are used, depending on the end to be achieved. So it is up to us to decide whether the means are good or bad, but I believe that the technology that I am proposing, the technology that is emerging, is 'softer'. It is not of question of 'good and evil', but rather of 'soft' and 'hard'. The old technology was 'hard' and the new technology is much 'softer'.

MZ: And all of your work is looking at the means of technology, and how we understand and use it. In other words, the necessity of 'information' as you conceive it, as part of this process of change ...

MS: I believe that everything that I am attempting to do is a philosophy of knowledge – a philosophy of technology which would be truly adapted to the transformations that we are experiencing. When all is said and done, the principal aim of philosophy today is to foresee the world of tomorrow, to avoid catastrophes, to avoid ecological collapse and to prepare for future generations and the future world. It is consequently necessary to prepare seriously a philosophy of knowledge, science and technology for the future world, for the future.

MZ: That's why we need to listen to the world.

MS: That's right. That is ... whether it is knowledge or technology, I call it 'soft', ... we must be open to the world, rather than considering it as merely consisting of passive objects, and ... consider these objects as existing at the same time as us. I wrote a book on parasites once, and contrasted parasitism and symbiosis.[6] In the past we were parasites, now we must become symbiotes.

Eyes

MZ: In entering this new 'soft' age, how do we come back to this central issue of listening to the world, and how the world thinks? What is the relationship?

MS: I have written a book called *Eyes*.[7] Traditionally a book about seeing consisted in speaking about all the different views that one can have of the world: a broad view, as in astronomy, or a narrow view, as for atoms and molecules, and then views such as those of the painter or poet, etc. But my book was not at all about that.

My book was rather: Does a fly see the world? Does a snake see the world? Does a whale see the world? How do they see it? How does an animal see the world? And I should like to construct a museum where the masterpieces would not be the human way of seeing the world, but each image would be the world view of the mouse, fly, spider, eagle and so forth.

So you can easily see the reversal that I can bring about, by saying that we see the world but we never think that the world sees, and that animals see. And I went even further, I said that when I go into a jewellery shop and see the precious stones, these gemstones reflect each other, as if they could see each other. Consequently my whole book consists in saying how the world sees, and not only how I see the world. That is the reversal I am bringing about.

Constructing a museum or an exhibition in which the images would be what the fly sees, the snake sees, or the bird or fish sees. It would be an extraordinary museum, which would be completely different [from traditional museums]. I remember in the centre of Australia there is a small town called

Alice Springs, and outside Alice Springs there is a museum that resembles this dream of mine. That is, one goes into the desert, and then there are little signs attached to objects, naming them, as if one had not done anything but simply name this or that object. My idea would be to create that museum, to change the point of view, to go beyond human narcissism. We are all Narcissus, we see only our world. But one doesn't allow perception in the same way as one allows speech. Allowing things to speak means allowing them to see. One allows vision in the same way as one allows speech.

MZ: Yes, in your book *Eyes* you suggest that we ourselves do the looking but we are also being looked at. What are the implications of this radical transformation of perception and 'speaking'?

MS: Our perception varies greatly depending on whether you are a teacher or a sailor, an artist or a physicist or a biologist, and so on. Be that as it may, these are all human perceptions of the world. As a result, humankind constructs a certain world. But we do not know what kind of world is constructed by frogs, snakes, eagles, doves, whales, fish and so forth, because they have very different eyes, and brains that process information very differently. It's for this reason that I believe that we will never truly know what the world is until we have an idea of the sum total of these constructions of the world by other beings. This is why I dream of the museum I mentioned earlier, in which we would not see paintings imagined by painters – humans, men, women – but in which we might see paintings as seen by frogs, snakes, eagles, flies, whales, fish, etc. And in its totality, this new museum might give us access to the real world. But we do not know that world. That is why I've written this book on animal perception

MZ: How do we make sense of these 'multiple perceptions'?

MS: We can also generalize and say that when walking in the mountains and seeing a lake, we sometimes think that the sky as seen by the lake – seen in the lake – is more beautiful than the sky itself. We have the impression that the lake reflects the colour and a vision of the sky. Consequently, there too we have a vision of the world as seen by the world, by things in the world. So there you have a generalization of my idea about animals.

MZ: In this way, this vision that you are talking about will transform how we understand both ourselves and the world. Is this how we think?

MS: Both. From the moment one is conscious of the way in which non-humans perceive the world, one realizes quite quickly that the world is not necessarily what we see. It broadens completely our view of the world. It generalizes it, if you like.

MZ: And then this changes our thought processes once more?

MS: We always believe that the world is quite close to our representation and that the world is our representation – I mean that of scholars, of Mme Zournazi, or my own, etc. – but essentially that it is ours. And the idea that the world is other than our representation, and can also be that of animals, radically broadens our way of thinking about the world. One no longer thinks in the same way.

In philosophy, it is often said that there are two fundamental theories: idealism and realism. Idealism says that the world is how we represent it. Realism says that the world is outside our representation. In this respect, I would willingly be a realist. To be sure, it is our representation, but also that of thousands of other living beings. It escapes and goes above and beyond our representation.

MZ: So different systems of 'life' can co-exist with us – and therefore, we are no longer the centre of the universe and our representations have their limits. How does this broaden our knowledge more precisely, or how does it give us more freedom to understand the world as it is?

MS: This is a bit like what we discussed before, the problem of perception. The English word 'environment' comes from the French word, which means 'environs'. It's as though you have a circle with man in the middle of that circle and nature around him. Well, no – that's just narcissism. There are other lives, other perceptions of the world; therefore it isn't true, we are not, in fact, the centre of the world. So I come full circle and say again that the world we construct, the real world, cannot be imagined until we have aggregated all possible representations of it by other living beings.

MZ: This reversal of thought is quite challenging. What are the implications for ensuring that the world survives? What are the practical tools for this transformation of perception?

MS: The general project of my books is to prepare the foundations of a philosophy which would be the philosophy of the future. Just now I said that today, we are worried about the future of the world. The philosophy which preceded us laid the groundwork for the destruction of the world, and consequently, we must invent a philosophy which prepares for a future in which the world would not be destroyed. That is why I am proposing the foundations of a philosophy of knowledge which makes a complete break with the philosophy that has contributed to this destruction. That is the change that I am proposing.

MZ: With this revolution in perception comes a voyage into darkness, a different model of how we might understand truth and knowledge.

MS: Traditional philosophers, like Plato in the myth of the cave or the Enlightenment philosophers of the eighteenth century, be they English or

European, give a kind of model of knowledge. This model is usually daylight, and in particular, the light of the sun. The criticism that I make of this model is that there is only one sun, and if it is really the model for knowledge, then there would be only one truth, and that is firstly false and secondly, dangerous.

Personally I prefer to focus on the idea of night, the shadow of night. What do I see at night? Well, I see multiplicities of stars grouped into constellations with galaxies – which, moreover, are sometimes more visible in the southern than in the northern hemisphere. These galaxies, constellations and stars are all different: different in intensity, luminosity, colour, disposition, position and grouping in the sky. Consequently, that is the real model of knowledge with disparate truths, completely different truths, grouped in addition in a somewhat random fashion. There are mathematical truths, physical truths, historical truths, mythological truths, any number of truths – or human truths. And so there are constellations and, as well, lights that are all different, and really correspond to disparity and the differentiation of knowledge, and are illuminated and visible as a sort of figure against the dark background of night. The dark background of night is obviously non-knowledge, what we don't know, our ignorance, what is not known and, perhaps tomorrow, will become a field of knowledge and allow human beings to capture light from darkness. And it is true that, over time, we see new lights emerge and, conversely, other stars disappear. This evolving and disparate aspect of night is much more interesting as a model for knowledge than the model of daylight, in which there is in fact only one truth, which is very dangerous and is called 'ideology', and as a consequence often leads to crime. So I prefer night to day as a model for knowledge.

Cosmocracies

MZ: To return to *Biogea*, you present the argument for a 'cosmocracy' of the world … in other words, how to let the world speak.

MS: Yes, in *Biogée*, I attempted something very difficult to accomplish – to let the world speak. For example, I spoke of earthquakes, volcanos, etc. What information does the world give us? I began by retelling the story of the Great Flood, with Noah first hearing the cracking sounds that the Mediterranean made before flooding the Black Sea, the hollow of the Black Sea; thus he heard the world.[8] The world had spoken. And so that gives a completely different sort of vision of the world – one in which one lets the world speak. It is not just we who have a voice, but the world also has a voice.

That is why I spoke of signals and so in *Biogée*.
I let living things speak,
I let the world speak.
That is my aim.

Afterword

I am grateful to Michel Serres for his wisdom, and for his time and patience as we moved between different languages, concepts and models for thinking in the world. When I reflect back over this conversation, and as I understand more and more the necessity of 'information' as a new concept for living and thinking today, I am awestruck by Michel's truly innovative direction for the future of philosophy, and for the future of the world.

The written translation of Michel Serres is by Peter Cowley and Margaret Sankey. Thanks to Waddick Doyle for his generosity in interpreting this first lengthy conversation with Michel Serres in Paris.

Notes

1 See Michel Serres, *Times of Crises: what the Financial Crisis Revealed and how to Reinvent Our Lives and Future*, trans. Anne-Marie Feenberg-Dibon (New York: Bloomsbury, 2014).

2 Michel Serres, *The Natural Contract,* trans. Elizabeth MacArthur and William Paulson (Ann Arbor: University of Michigan Press, 1995), p. 1.

3 Michel Serres, *Biogea,* trans. Randolph Burks (Minneapolis: Univocal Press, 2012); idem., *The Natural Contract.*

4 Serres, *The Natural Contract*, p. 37.

5 Michel Serres, *Ecrivains, savants et philosophes font le tour du monde* (Paris: Le Pommier, 2009).

6 Michel Serres, *The Parasite*, trans. Lawrence R. Schehr (Baltimore: Johns Hopkins University Press, 1982).

7 Michel Serres, *Eyes*, trans Anne-Marie Feenberg-Dibon (London: Bloomsbury, 2015).

8 Serres, *Biogea.*

References

Serres, M., *The Parasite*, trans. L. R. Schehr, Baltimore: Johns Hopkins University Press, 1982.

Serres, M., *The Natural Contract*, trans. E. MacArthur and W. Paulson, Ann Arbor: University of Michigan Press, 1995.

Serres, M., *Ecrivains, savants et philosophes font le tour du monde*, Paris: Le Pommier, 2009.

Serres, M., *Biogea*, trans. R. Burks, Minneapolis: Univocal Press, 2012.

Serres, M., *Times of Crises: what the Financial Crisis Revealed and how to Reinvent Our Lives and Future*, trans. A.-M. Feenberg-Dibon, New York: Bloomsbury, 2014.

Serres, M., *Eyes*, trans. A.-M. Feenberg-Dibbon, London: Bloomsbury, 2015.

2

The thinking that is in the world

Alphonso Lingis

FIGURE 2.1 *Copyright: Alphonso Lingis.*

Cogito ergo sum. I think, I affirm, I doubt, I deny. Thinking would be a process or an operation that would be evident in itself, that would produce evidence and first evidence of its own reality. The primary reality of thinking retrospectively makes the 'I' evident. *I* think. *I* perceive, *I* hear, *I* remember. The 'I' now figures as the source, the agent.

Is seeing or hearing a perceptual illusion – a snake in the library, a whisper in my bedroom – an act of the 'I'? Is forgetting? We say: I forget. Nietzsche said that is only a way of speaking. Nietzsche did distinguish an active forgetting – a clearing out of space for new impressions and insights – from passive forgetting, the simple fading out of impressions and representations. But even active forgetting is not an action of the 'I' – as everyone knows who tries to forget something. Forgetting happens. It is a process of screening, of selecting; it is an operation, it proceeds in a certain order. Psychoanalysts have shown a logic, an intelligible system, in the order of things and events forgotten. Freud showed that reawakening one forgotten event – even one forgotten word – brings up a skein connected with it.

Thinking happens. It is not something 'I' produce.

I can decide to think through something. I then let the attention zero in on a problem, a field, pass across objects, waiting for connections to become evident, waiting for relations to form and for insight to happen. I can then appropriate this stretch of mental happening as mine, or not appropriate it.

Logical thinking and mathematical operations do reveal an agency: a focus of attention, a willful combining and connecting, an extraction of a conclusion accompanied with insight – I see that it follows. Because of the exceptional distinctness and clarity of the elements and stages of logical reasoning and mathematical calculation, they take the status of thinking in a paradigmatic sense.

But so much thinking is not logical-mathematical calculation. So much is not the action of an agency that extracts, abstracts, puts together, classifies, connects, relates and combines. Thinking is accomplished in insight. Insight is a mental seeing, evidence shining forth, that the abstraction abstracts the essential, that things are put together by virtue of structural similarities and that things that one thinks to be causally or consequentially related are evidently so. Insight comes as a result of initiatives, a valid deductive reasoning and an empirical observation. It sometimes happens when one is no longer focused at the centre of a problem. Insight comes intermittently, abruptly and unexpectedly. One works long at a mathematical problem or a set of empirical data, and then, upon awakening from sleep, there is insight. What produces insight? Unconscious associations of mental representations? Biochemical, neurological firings? These surely subtend mental acts of focusing, isolating, abstracting and combining, but we do not have an intelligible language to map how insight is produced.

Thinking is not only movement – scanning, leaping from the present to the past and future, or action at a distance – it is also pondering. Thinking is weighing, submitting oneself to the weight of things and events. It is assessing the force of things and events on one another, on the setting, on remote things and events, and on oneself.

Martin Heidegger said that the sense of the environment as a whole affecting us, weighing upon us, is given in mood. We sense the environment as oppressive, suffocating or indifferent, all its points and directions equivalent to any other; or as empowering, surging with forces and possibilities, opening indefinitely in light before us. This evidence of the weight of the world differentiates between things and events that are embedded in the world – in reality – from things and events that our mind fabricates. Thought that thinks in the world is affected, in mood, with the weight of the world as a whole.

Thinking is dwelling with things, in the world. The mind is not a modular unit that has the innate power to take a distance from the whole environment, retreat into itself, and then form a representation of that environment. 'The consciousness of a world is already consciousness in, through, by means of [*à travers*] that world. Something of that world seen is an organ or an essential means of vision: the head, the eye, the eyeglasses, the light, the lamps, the books, the school.'[1] We think about things in the environment and we also think with, through and by means of things in the environment.

We also think with, through and by means of the intelligence of other species. We can understand the intelligence of other species that is so like our own.

We identify things with abstract concepts and identify the visual and musical styles of artworks. Researchers at Harvard University showed one group of pigeons eighty slides of underwater scenes, some with different kinds and colours of fish in them, and some without fish but with turtles or octopuses or divers in them. The pigeons got a treat when they pecked on a button when there were fish in the image. They showed a second group of pigeons the same set of slides, but this time the pigeons got a treat when a particular slide, with fish or not, was shown; so they had to memorize which slides would bring them a treat. The researchers found that pigeons whose task was to pick out the images with fish – fish of any size, shape, or colour – learned twice as fast as those that had to memorize the slides.

Japanese researchers showed pigeons paintings by Claude Monet and Pablo Picasso; the pigeons got a treat each time they selected the painting by Monet. The researchers then showed the pigeons different paintings by Monet and by Picasso. The pigeons quickly learned to choose the Monet, even when the paintings were upside down or in black and white. Next, the researchers showed them paintings by the impressionists Pierre-Auguste Renoir and Paul Cezanne, and the cubists Georges Braque and Henri Matisse. The pigeons that had been rewarded when a Monet painting was shown now selected the Renoir paintings, and not the Braque paintings. The pigeons had learned to recognize the difference between what we have called 'impressionist' and 'cubist' styles of painting. Similar experiments with music showed that pigeons quickly discriminate and classify together different compositions by Johann Sebastian Bach and those by Igor Stravinsky.

We grasp causal connections and execute actions in accordance with an instrumental plan. The malleefowl (*Leipoa ocellata*) is an Australian ground-dwelling bird about the size of a domestic chicken. In winter, the male scrapes out a depression about 3 metres across and 1 metre deep, in sandy soil. He then fills it with leaves, sticks and bark to a height of a half metre above ground level. When the rains begin, he turns and mixes the decomposing compost, and then covers it with a more than 1-metre thick layer of earth or sand. The female arrives and lays up to thirty eggs, four to seven days apart over four or five months. Several times a day, the male digs head deep into the mound, to check the temperature. He keeps the eggs at a constant 33°C by opening and closing air ventilation shafts, and by adding or removing material from the mound. On cold nights, he closes the ventilation shafts. The eggs hatch in the mound after seven weeks. The newborn chicks scratch their way to the surface, and emerge able to run and fly. They fend for themselves without their parents. The scrub turkey, a related species, makes an incubation mound from 35 to 40 feet across and 15 feet high.

We seek to understand the intelligence of species that exceed our abilities. Ethologists have determined that that bees, rats, and birds do not simply find their way back to a site by remembering a succession of landmarks, like Hansel and Gretel following a trail of breadcrumbs. A bird does locate her nest by noting nearby landmarks; if a fountain or doghouse near a nest is moved, the returning bird first looks for her nest near the now-moved fountain or doghouse, before scanning the environs for it. But once she has located it, she readily finds it from any number of different directions. She locates a food source again by any number of different routes. Mental mapping is recalling and combining separate perceptions of spatially extended things and sites, such that their positions relative to one another are grasped.

Migratory birds extend this mental mapping over often enormous distances. Adolescent migratory birds leave the first autumn of their lives and return to the very place where they were born. Lesser Golden Plovers migrate in an ellipse, going from northern Canada south by way of the Eastern United States to South America, returning by way of Mexico and the Western United States. Birds do follow traditional migratory routes, following mountain ranges and rivers, shorelines and forests and, as has recently been shown for pigeons, manmade highways. This, however, is not simply a sequential memory but a genuine mapping; birds blown off course – even hundreds of kilometres – regularly adjust their flight to re-join the route and arrive at their destination. White-crowned sparrows captured in Boston, Massachusetts, were shipped to Baton Rouge, Louisiana; when winter came they flew directly to their wintering grounds in San José, California. Once again they were captured and this time shipped to Maryland, and again they were found in San José at the appropriate time.

To navigate consistently in one direction, it has been shown that birds have an ability to gauge the position of the sun relative to the earth at successive times of day. By studying the restlessness of confined birds during the migratory season, their collective orientations, and by projecting overhead images of stars (which can be rotated), researchers have established that birds also orient themselves by the night sky. Recent research has brought to light a sensitivity in birds to the earth's magnetic field, which can supplement the birds' other navigational procedures when weather conditions curtail them. Minute magnetite crystals sensitive to magnetism have been identified in the heads of pigeons.

Homing pigeons that are carried in closed boxes in airplanes or trains across continents return to find the town and yard from which they were taken. How birds navigate over the open ocean has thus far eluded our understanding. Ruby-throated hummingbirds, doubling their weight from one-tenth to one-fifth of an ounce in preparation, fly 900 kilometres non-stop over the Caribbean. A Manx Shearwater was taken from its home in Wales in the British Isles, put on an airplane and released in Boston, Massachusetts; it had returned to its home in Wales, twelve and a half days later. Bristle-thighed curlews fly 10,000 kilometres from Alaska to Polynesia, making a non-stop flight over 3,200 kilometres of Pacific waters. A Bar-tailed Godwit (tagged and tracked by satellite) flew 11,680 kilometres non-stop over the Pacific, from Western Alaska to New Zealand.

Green sea turtles travel 2,200 kilometres from the coast of Brazil to Ascension Island – an island only 20 kilometres in diameter. Loggerhead turtles travel 8,000 miles solo around the North Atlantic basin for six to twelve years, and then return to the beach where they were born to lay their eggs.

The intelligence most difficult to understand is that of the social insects – ants (about 22,000 species), termites (about 4,000 species), bees (about 600 species) and wasps (about 700 species). However, the effort to understand them may launch a new understanding of our own intelligence. Researchers have identified impressive intelligence in individual honeybees. They understand the concepts of 'sameness' and 'difference',[2] can count from one to four[3] and are able to accurately group visual stimuli into categories.[4] Their 'waggle dances' inform others about the quality and quantity of available food, its distance from the hive, the abundance of other food sources, the colony's current influx of nectar, the weather and time of day, and the presence of dangerous conditions at the food source. Their tremble dance, shaking signal, piping signal, stop signal and buzz run communicate a variety of other information.[5]

However, there is an intelligence in the colony that is not in any single individual. The selection of the new location of a swarming colony and the interior architecture of the hive, the placement and spacing of the combs, the adjustment of the entrance size, and the sealing of crevices and walls exhibit an overall design. The rearing of new queens and the departure of a swarm to a new location is a collective project. In addition, the everyday operation of the colony requires a proportionate and integrated distribution of tasks.

In a colony, worker honeybees perform fifty-nine different tasks, such as building honeycombs, building brood combs – some with bigger cells for drones – feeding baby bees, cleaning vacated brood cells, evaporating water from nectar, capping the cells when the nectar is condensed into honey, foraging for nectar, pollen and gums, etc. By circulating and cooling or heating the air they control the temperature of the hive to within 0.5 degrees.

But there is no planning committee, no politburo and no ruler who governs; there is no executive authority – the 'queen' lays eggs and does not issue orders. There is no 'ego' that thinks.

Mound-building termites are found in Africa, Australia and South America. The termites are blind. Their towers, built of soil and saliva, rise to 6 metres with walls 45 centimetres thick. In arid regions, the termites excavate vertical shafts to the water table – as many as 50 metres below. The queen lives in a small chamber laying up to 30,000 eggs a day, which are then taken away by workers to brood chambers. Their towers include shafts with above-ground chimneys to ventilate the mound and draw off gases. The termites open and close these shafts to maintain the temperature inside at a constant 31°C.

Ants have the greatest brain to body mass ratio of any insects or any living organisms. The leafcutter ants (two genera, *Atta* and *Acromyrmex,* in forty-seven species) are found in South and Central America, and parts of southern North America. They cut pieces of leaves – which they cannot digest – and bring them into chambers in the nest, where they grow *Lepiotaceae* fungus on them with which to feed their larvae. They attend to these fungus gardens constantly, clearing them of pests and moulds, and removing toxic wastes. Young queens depart from established colonies with males. Once mated, the queen excavates a hole in the ground, casts off her wings and eats them. She brings with her a small wad of the fungus. As her fungus garden grows, she lays a few eggs upon it. A month later, hatched worker ants begin to leave the nest and forage for leaves with which to feed the fungus. They take over the work of caring for the fungus and the larvae, and the queen does nothing but lay eggs for the rest of her ten to fifteen-year life. After two or three years, the queen lays eggs that hatch into workers of four different sizes that perform different functions. Colonies increase up to a size of 8 million individuals, in enormous underground nests up to 30 metres across and 8 metres deep.

In the absence of any central planning or executive individuals in a colony of social insects, researchers see that the order and organization of the nest and the distribution of tasks result from self-organization. The overall pattern would emerge from the interactions of individuals responding to only local situations. A flock of birds does not have a leader; the direction of the flock is determined by each bird individually maintaining an optimum distance from the birds about it.

Researchers have explained a few of these patterns. Forager ants leave the nest in the morning. As more of them return more quickly with food, more ants are stimulated to leave to forage. At the start of a termite mound, workers bring clumps of earth and deposit them randomly, marked with their pheromone. More workers leave their loads at the pheromone-marked piles. As a mound gets bigger, its pheromone charge increases and more and more workers add to it. When a swarm of bees has left the hive, it settles on a tree or post and sends out scouts to locate a new hive-site. The scouts return and communicate their finds in a waggle dance. When about fifteen scouts have settled on one site, they return to the swarm, which moves to occupy that site.

But the intelligence in a colony that determines the architecture of a termite mound with all its ventilation shafts (no two termite mounds have the same architecture) and the intelligence that distributes the fifty-nine tasks among the population of worker honeybees has thus far eluded the explanations of researchers.

We also think with, through, by means of the intelligence of plants. At the origin of our species, trees were our homes, our food and our protection. Our ancestors descended from the trees and advanced into the savannah. They freed themselves from the trees by taking on the verticality of the trees. They raised their bodies over the high grass, seeing food plants, waterholes and dangers at a distance.

Our species of primate – standing erect – prizes the upright, equivalent for us to dignity; prizes rectitude, equivalent for us to justice; prizes the elevated; and prizes eyes turned to the skies and the heavens, equivalent for us to the decent, the noble, the sacred and the ideal. Nothing gives us a stronger sense and notion of justice and rectitude than the spectacle of fields and forests, rising upright from the earth to the sun. The branches and the smallest twigs of the branching plants of meadows and of the great trees give us the vision of a veritable architectural order, the ordered distribution of each part in its own place, post and function – the most irresistible everyday vision of justice and harmony.[6]

The stalks, trunks and branches of fields and forests rise up out of roots, which do not have this intricate architecture, and wind, knot and wallow like worms in the wet earth. Our sense of the base – the low, the mean and the vile – designates this kinship of certain behaviours, actions and characteristics in us with dark holes, the dark and dank earth, with doors of rot and decomposition.

We also think with, through, by means of the thinking that is in the world.

Notes

1 Emmanuel Levinas, *Totality and Infinity*, trans. Alphonso Lingis (The Hague: Martinus Nijhoff, 1979), p. 153.

2 M. Giurfa, Zhang, S., Jenett, A., Menzel, R., and M. V. Srinivasan, 'The concepts of "sameness" and "difference" in an insect', *Nature* 410 (2001), pp. 930–33.

3 M. Dacke and M. V. Srinivasan, 'Evidence for counting in insects', *Animal Cognition* 11 (2008), pp. 683–89.

4 Maggie Wray, 'Social Insects and Collective Intelligence' *intelligence.seti.org*, http://intelligence.seti.org/pages/social_insects (accessed 05 October 2013).

5 J. Benard, S. Stach, and M. Giurfa, 'Categorization of visual stimuli in the honeybee Apis mellifera', *Animal Cognition* 9 (2006), pp. 257–70.

6 Georges Bataille, *Visions of Excess: Selected Writings 1927-1939*, trans. Allan Stoekl with Carl R. Lovitt, and Donald M. Leslie, Jr. (Minneapolis: University of Minnesota Press, 1985), p. 13.

References

Bataille, G., *Visions of Excess: Selected Writings 1927–1939*, trans. A. Stoekl with C. R. Lovitt, and D. M. Leslie, Jr., Minneapolis: University of Minnesota Press, 1985.

Benard, J., Stach, S., and M. Giurfa, 'Categorization of visual stimuli in the honeybee Apis mellifera', *Animal Cognition* 9 (2006), pp. 257–70.

Dacke, M. and M. V. Srinivasan, 'Evidence for counting in insects', *Animal Cognition* 11 (2008), pp. 683–89.

Giurfa, M., Zhang, S., Jenett, A., Menzel, R., and M. V. Srinivasan, 'The concepts of "sameness" and "difference" in an insect', *Nature* 410 (2001), pp. 930–33.

Levinas, E., *Totality and Infinity*, trans. A. Lingis, The Hague: Martinus Nijhoff, 1979.

Wray, M., 'Social Insects and Collective Intelligence' *intelligence.seti.org*, http://intelligence.seti.org/pages/social_insects (accessed 05 October 2013).

PART TWO

Senses of place

3

A phenomenology of thinking in place

Edward S. Casey (ESC) in conversation with Jeff Malpas (JM)

In this chapter, Edward S. Casey and Jeff Malpas approach the topic of 'thinking in the world' from their shared position as philosophers of place. Their conversation traces the conceptual trajectories and possibilities of *thinking in place*, through examining, recuperating and rethinking a number of key terms, theorists and texts. Over the course of this conversational essay, they address how an embodied, temporal and poetic understanding of place might allow for a linkage between feeling and thinking, and between place and world.

JM: We've been asked to talk about 'thinking in place'. Here, I think going back to a more fundamental way of thinking – going back to that which is *originary* rather than foundational in the usual sense – is crucial. For me, a key element in such a way of thinking is the idea of place itself. In fact, it seems to me that place is, for both of us, the integrative concept that brings together a range of key ideas around the notion of our singular 'being here' or 'being there', and that this 'being here' is a matter of an embodied being here, a sensuous being here. It's also a thoughtful being here – in the sense of thoughtfulness understood, not as apart from, but as directly connected to a complex sensuous placedness.

ESC: Yes, I certainly agree, please go ahead.

JM: I think this is a vitally important way of thinking about what place is, because place is not mere location or 'site'. I want to also distinguish between 'being here' or 'being there', that is to say, our own placedness and place itself. In this sense, place is not exhausted by our own relation to it. Moreover, this idea of our 'being here', in all of its complexity, is surely also the starting point for any thinking we do as philosophers, and yet, as you say, philosophy seems to have lost sight of that.

ESC: Yes.

JM: So what's the character of this thinking? Because it's not a thinking that begins by trying to first ask after the epistemological foundations of our being here in the world. It's not a mode of thinking that begins with a scepticism casting doubt on that being. Towards the end of *Dreams of a Spirit Seer,* Kant has a line about having folded the 'butterfly wings' of metaphysics and finding ourselves back on the ground of experience, which is after all the only place we can be.[1] It seems to me that that's what both of us have been trying to do as well: to fold the wings of metaphysics and find ourselves back on the ground, back in place, the only place where thinking can begin.

ESC: Yes. Absolutely. I do believe that here our ways are parallel but not the same, in the sense that I think my emphasis on body and the sensuous may be more pronounced or emphatic than yours, and conversely, your emphasis upon thinking place and the thoughtful aspect of place is something that I feel I have neglected, and which I have always admired in your thought. When I first read *Place and Experience*, I was struck at the conceptual elegance of it and how the book itself exemplified *thinking* place, not just thinking about place, but thinking aspects of place that are themselves – if not cognitive, a much abused term – then let's just say *noetic*, searching for a neutral term.[2] I think it's significant that the first step I've taken in that direction is what you may have glanced at last night: 'Thinking on Edge', the introduction to my new book.[3] But edge belongs to place; edges are edges of places for me. Still it's very striking that not until very recently have I really attempted to explore how thinking and place are related: how place provides a domain where thinking is grounded and can operate more creatively than if thinking were located in the human subject alone.

JM: It certainly seems that we have been following a set of parallel tracks, and the reason they are parallel rather than the same is partly a function of the fact that you're much closer to Merleau-Ponty and I'm closer to later Heidegger – the two each opening up different ways of approaching the same topic; namely, place.

ESC: Indeed.

JM: My approach is also much more hermeneutically influenced, so Hans-Georg Gadamer is an important thinker for me. On the point of the sensuous, this is something I have also tried to address, most recently, for instance, in my chapter in *The Intelligence of Place*; there it is taken up through the notion of the *singularity* of place.[4]

ESC: On that last point, I think that singularity and the sensuous go together. That is, I see them as paired concepts: one calls for the other. It's not that you can't generalize, and you can't conceptualize, but nevertheless a sensuous experience itself heads toward the singular, the unique-each-time character of it is very, very striking. I really love your essay on singularity. It links up with the work of Deleuze on singularity, which for him is a very important concept; in *Difference and Repetition*, he contrasts it with particularity, which is subsumable under generals, whereas singularity cannot be so assimilated.[5] And I do believe that the bodily immersion in place through sensuous experience is at least a primary instance – if not the exclusive instance, it's certainly a leading instance – of singularity in our experience. And in particular, the very fact of the localization effected by adverbs like *here* and *there* – if you think about them – are each time singular. I'm here now in Santa Barbara, in a house I know well, in a room I know fairly well; I'm actually at the dining room table because the workmen have driven me out of my study. So I'm in a fairly familiar space, but my being at this table, talking to you on this occasion at this time of day, all of that is radically singular, unprecedented as such in its detail.

JM: Inexhaustible.

ESC: Yes, inexhaustible. It's not only unprecedented, it's not only unique historically, but there's a sense in which I could begin to describe this particular scene – this singular scene, I should say – and I could continue through the afternoon, of course. And I think this is a key to place itself. So there's a paradox of place. It's both grounding, as we said earlier, and, yet, it's indefinitely describable. There's a sense in which it's not any *thing*; it's not any entity that we could sum up in so many traits. It really is bottomless. So here's a ground that's an *Abgrund* – a descriptive *Abgrund*, an abyss, in the sense that the descriptive detail is absolutely endless. And it is always, at each stage, singular as well. So this moment, speaking to you – halfway around the world, as we are doing – is utterly singular. And this will be the case in each successive moment of our talk together, in our respective places. Isn't that amazing, that there is something like the *here* that really refuses to be filled up completely? It's an unending reservoir, I would say.

JM: The sort of language I tend to use here is the language of opening. I guess I would say of the *here* and *there* that they take the form of constant opening – opening that is always opening further. For me, this is also closely connected with the idea of limit, or *the liminal*, in terms of the way in which being in place is always a matter of being at the threshold – it is a constant moving into, a constant opening up – and this is so, even though it is not something to which we always attend.

ESC: Yes.

JM: I take this way of putting things to capture something of the dynamism of place, which I think is extremely important here – its active character, as well as its inexhaustibility – and it also captures something of the inherent spatiality and temporality of place at the same time. That's also something that often gets overlooked. The assumption is all too often made that when we talk about place, we mean something *spatial* as opposed to something *temporal*. I'm always rather surprised about that, because I spend a lot of time trying to make clear that by 'place' I do not mean just 'space'. The idea of place as this constant opening – this constant being at the threshold, this constant moving into – is a way of capturing both of these aspects of place and addressing the inexhaustibility we were talking about before.

ESC: You see now I'm beginning to get a sense of the fact that your sense of limit and mine, although they appear to be very different and they are different, converge in a certain way. Your use of the word 'threshold' is close to what I like to call *boundary*, which means a kind of edge that's comparatively porous and permeable. Whereas my sense of limit is that of formal limit, or an asymptote, or in any case, some type of ideal or even imaginary endpoint that's fiercely stationary. So I'm using that term *limit* in a rather special way in order to contrast it with what I call *boundary*. What you are now calling 'liminality' is for me oxymoronic, since it seems to signify something like an open-ended limit – whereas in my usage of 'limit' there is nothing open-ended: quite the contrary, it's a matter of a definitive closure.

JM: Yes, I think I also saw this in reading your *Thinking on the Edge*.[6] Of course, there is a distinction between the German equivalents of the terms limit and boundary in Kant – the distinction between *Schranke* and *Grenze*[7] – although Kant himself is not always consistent about this. You might argue that both of these terms sometimes have formal elements to them, and certainly the notion of *Grenze* in Kant doesn't imply that there's nothing on the other side of the boundary. There is also an interesting connection between limit and the liminal that goes back to the Latin.

ESC: Yes, through *limen*.

JM: I tend to be less worried about maintaining a strict demarcation between limit and boundary, however, and I'm happy to employ either term depending on the context.

ESC: I think that makes a lot of sense. I think I needed the distinction for the purpose of expanding 'edge'. My whole book is about edges regarded as highly proliferated and proliferating aspects of places and events and things, so I needed this distinction because of the multiple character of edges – some of which I regard as 'borders' and others as 'boundaries'. You see, I'm claiming that the place-world is an edge-world; that places come to us through edges – through many, many kinds of edges, only some of which I can mention in this conversation. And because of the plethora of edges as I have come to explore them over the last ten years, I needed a term that would, as it were, stand over and against the proliferation of edges as something comparatively limitative and restrictive. It's like the theoretical equivalent of a *Schranke* – a *holding in* and *holding back*. So I admit it's an arbitrarily chosen bifurcation that I make here; but I made it in an effort to bring some order into what might otherwise be chaotic.

Your thinking brings us closer to the experience we have of limits as *yielding* in many cases. For example, our energies have what we call limits, but actually those limits are never absolutely quantitative. We find ourselves going on and discovering new resources of energy beyond what we thought was ever possible. So the limits *experientially* – note that here I'm beginning to converge with your thinking – are actually malleable. As such, they are closer to *Grenzen* or bounds, which yield the other side or far side of our energies, indicating what lies over there. So I'm with you phenomenologically in your use of the term 'limit'. I think I was driven by the constraints of a project that had become so extensive that I really needed a limiting term, and that term turned out to be 'limit' itself.

JM: Yes, I can see that. I guess part of what drives my thinking on this too, and maybe this is also part of what underpins my more ambiguous use of *limit* and *bound*, goes back to my reading of Heidegger. One of the ideas in Heidegger that is seldom adequately attended to is his own use of the notions of 'limit' and 'bound' – in his German, the term is mostly *Grenze* – and this comes across in a number of passages in which Heidegger insists on understanding limit or boundary 'in the Greek sense': in terms of the Greek *horismos* as well as *peras* – and so in terms of the boundary as *productive* rather than merely *restrictive*.[8]

ESC: Certainly, yes.

JM: This seems to me an absolutely central idea in Heidegger. It's there very early on, and is already present, for instance, in *Being and Time*.[9] You can't understand that work, and especially the role of being-toward-death, unless you understand this productive sense of boundary or limit. It is also an idea there much later in Heidegger where it also becomes more explicit. I take this emphasis on the productivity of boundary to be an aspect of Heidegger's hermeneutic orientation because it's so much bound up with the focus on the finitude, and hence the boundedness, of human being.

ESC: Yes, yes. I follow you. But we do part ways on this, although not drastically. Since I don't come as much as you from Heidegger, even if I completely agree with your reading of him and especially that passage on *peras* in 'Building Dwelling Thinking'.[10] We both endorse that remarkable passage about productive or *active* boundaries – boundaries that are, precisely, not limits in my sense of this term.

JM: It's surprising, though, how seldom that aspect of Heidegger's work is explicitly taken up. John Sallis picks up on the idea of the productivity of boundary in one of his works, but largely as the starting-point for an exploration of phenomenology and the end of metaphysics[11] – not in such direct relation to place as is so significant for you and I. It's always surprised me that there hasn't been more direct attention paid to this idea as it arises in Heidegger.

ESC: Yes, I agree. I stress it in my teaching if not in my writing.

JM: I take the idea of the boundary as productive to be central to the thinking of place, and it is central to my work, as I think it also is to yours. For me, this idea means that the attempt to think and to attend to place is also about the thinking of and attending to our own finitude – where finitude is understood in its relation to boundary. It is in our finite being that we find the liminal boundary that enables the opening up that we were talking about before – that *is* an opening up – so that rather than seeing our mortality, our fragility, our epistemic or experiential limitation as somehow a handicap, burden, or barrier, it is actually that by which the world is made accessible to us.

ESC: Yes, very nice. This makes me think of someone else who has appreciated this aspect of Heidegger: this is Derrida in his *Aporias* volume.[12] In this work, he is talking about finitude – in particular about death and being toward death – in a way that's completely congenial with your reading of Heidegger.

JM: The other figure that I find exemplifies this for me, and another favourite writer of mine, is Albert Camus. His short essays, especially, have this incredibly strong sense of place – and by 'sense' I mean the *feeling* of place as much as the *thinking* of it – of the way in which the world is only given to us, *can* only be given to us, in a form that is essentially limited, essentially fragile, and therefore essentially human.[13] That seems to me a crucial point. It is also a point that brings an ontology with it: an ontology in which place is at the centre, and in which human being is understood only as it is related to place. The question of the human and the question of place are thus inseparable. Again, I think this is something also central, if not always expressed in quite the same way, to both your work and mine. So the coming back to place is a coming back to what we ourselves are, as the coming back to ourselves is a coming back to place. And all of this, the coming back to place and the human, is in turn tied up with a properly ethical sensibility – a sense of the responsibilities and obligations that come from the placedness in which our own being is embedded.

ESC: Could you say a little more about what Camus means by *feeling* of place? Is 'feeling' meant in the sense of sensuous experience?

JM: Well, I guess, I'm using feeling – and that is my term rather than Camus'– in a way that for me also connects up with something else, though this might seem like an odd connection; namely, the sentimentalist tradition in ethics. 'Feeling' as I am using it refers us to a felt sense of the world and of our relation to it – which means a felt sense of ourselves as well as others. It seems to me, although it is a point that requires argument and explication that something of this sense of feeling is there in Camus – where it does have a sensuous character– but also in the work of someone like Adam Smith, where it involves a sense of the ethical as something felt as much as thought.[14] Since I am being expansive here, I would probably say that I think of this as also present in Levinas, and so as tied up with the sense of the immediate 'felt' presence of 'the Other', and the demand this presence makes.[15] In the case of Smith, I have been struck by the extent to which Smith grounds his account of the moral sentiments – of moral or ethical feeling one might say – in our being with others *here* in this place. I take this idea of moral or ethical feeling as a mode of feeling that is not apart from thinking, but is precisely a felt thinking or a thoughtful feeling that is at the very heart of moral and ethical being. In more Levinasian terms, the encounter with the Other is an encounter with the Other as *here* before us – their very presence in the face-to-face – and thus it's an encounter grounded in our own capacity to feel, to think, to be affected, and to respond. To come back to Camus, I think this sense of feeling, and so of feeling as connected to thinking, is what is powerfully present in his essays.

ESC: Which of these early essays would you recommend to start with?

JM: Well, almost any. There's a collected volume called *Lyrical and Critical Essays*, which contains most of his essay length writings. There is a line I quote from one of the essays, 'Nuptials at Tipasa': 'It is my life I am staking here, a life that tastes of warm stone and the sound of the crickets.'[16] Many of these essays are focused around a very intense evocation of a place. So there is a clear topological or topographic element present in them that I think is central to much of Camus' thinking, and at the same time, just as these essays are bound up with the evocation of place, they are often also meditations on both love and death.

ESC: From what you say here, we'd have to contrast Camus with Sartre, who is rarely preoccupied with place, with the notable exception of *Nausea*.[17] Their sensibilities are so very deeply different. I left Camus back with *The Myth of Sisyphus* too long ago, and I am going to have to return to him, because I'm intrigued by what you say here.

JM: Camus had a somewhat equivocal attitude towards the ideas he sets out in the essay that is titled 'The Myth of Sisyphus',[18] but the volume with that same title also contains another essay that I think is especially valuable and prefigures ideas Camus develops further in *The Rebel*. The essay is called 'Helen's Exile' and in it Camus sets out an argument that is not that far away from Heidegger's on technology, but put in terms of the 'modern' or the 'European'. Camus contrasts 'us' – the moderns, the Europeans – with the Greeks: 'We have exiled beauty; the Greeks took up arms for her', and for him the affirmation of beauty is tied to a recognition of limit in a way that seems to me also to place a real emphasis on the placed and the 'felt' – on 'the beloved face' as he puts it at one point.[19]

ESC: I see. And of course, speaking of face, it's very interesting that Levinas uses the term *proximity* for the face-to-face.[20] I know he means it in his own rather spiritual, metaphysical sense, but still the term proximity cannot be divorced from the sensuous, and is certainly a matter of place. Perhaps neither one of us has adequately explored this direction as such: that between feeling, place and the ethical.

JM: I think you're right; maybe this issue of feeling sort of straddles our two approaches without either of us having done it justice. Perhaps one of the reasons the emphasis on feeling is so important is that it provides a counter to the tendency – especially prevalent in philosophy – to want to treat discussions about our relationship to the world always in terms of the epistemic or the perceptual, or even just in terms of 'sensation', when our *being* in the world is not any of those things taken on its own. Our being in the world is an already being there, an already felt sense of our being in place.

ESC: 'Feeling our way into' – we sometimes use that expression, do we not? You feel your way into something, very much including a particular place. You feel your way into a new place, or you recognize the feeling of that place once you return to it. Or even seeing it in a photograph, you can capture some of that feeling. The only thinker who really does some kind of justice to feeling at this level is Collingwood in his book on art. In *The Principles of Art*, he calls it the psychical level, and he says it's the same as feeling in the generation and appreciation of art.[21] It's quite an extraordinary discussion, and it's not at all foreign to the way that our discussion is now going. He also thinks there is an inner connection between such psychical states, feeling states and thinking. Nevertheless, this discussion remains rather dogmatic and suffers from a preoccupation with stratification that he inherits from Hegel.

JM: My reading of Collingwood has been more from the philosophy of history rather than aesthetics, but I think he is a very insightful thinker in general – even though, perhaps partly because of the context in which he was writing, he can be inclined to some rather dogmatic claims. Still, there is a great deal there. I have always a particularly soft spot for his *An Autobiography*.[22]

ESC: I agree – a wonderful book – and it had great influence on Gadamer; he takes 'the logic of question and answer' straight from *An Autobiography*.[23] I'm pleased to discover our common interest in Collingwood, whose discussion of feeling links up with our discussion of how we feel our way to, and in, place. Once I've finished my tome on edges, I am intending to write a very short book, my first and only such book, on 'feeling'. So I'm intrigued by the way our conversation has moved – organically as it were – into this very topic, because that's the direction my own research is going. I agree with you that feeling cannot be assimilated to sensation; it can't even be assimilated to emotion in my view. It's something else: it's a whole, deep, sensuous layer that has everything to do with being in *place*. It's a primary modality, I would say, of being in place. I think we're probably agreed on this, but what is less clear to me is the relationship between feeling and thinking. Let's ponder that for a moment, because that's something we wanted to get around to – in the form of thinking the world.

JM: Yes, that's right.

ESC: You hinted at that link spontaneously in your own discourse here just a while ago. As I recall, you said that feeling and thinking are not so different; they join up, indeed they're already joined. If so, I would ask, How does this happen? I would think it would require us to rethink thinking itself. It can't be categorical thinking. It can't be top-down thinking. It has to be a different mode of thinking itself. It has to be a kind of thinking that is continuous with feeling; whereas most models of thinking, as you and I know so well, concern abstract thinking, and this is so from at least the time of Parmenides in the West. This is still the case: analytical thinking in the limited sense of parsing out distinct elements is not going to reach feeling, which at every turn features in-distinction. On the contrary, analytical thinking is detached from feeling. So what kind of thinking is this that would be at one with, or in any case overlapping with, feeling? That seems to me to be a very major conundrum of our time, and I believe that the work of both of us is leading us there; that's what I'm sensing from this conversation, where we hadn't even intended to speak about feeling and thinking, but now it has emerged to our own surprise.

JM: Yes. I've already invoked later Heidegger a few times, but of course almost all of late Heidegger's work is about thinking in just this sense. He says that the greatest question for thinking now is the fact that we are still not thinking. One of the questions is what he might mean by that, but it is a question to which he has already given an answer in *What Is Called Thinking?*[24]

ESC: Indeed. This is what makes this book – this lecture course – one of his most significant later works.

JM: Having said that, I don't want to separate thinking from feeling; I do think there is something more to say about thinking and place – especially if we pay attention to Heidegger. The question of thinking is, in an important sense, a question about place, about how we find ourselves in place and about how place gives rise to thinking. Just as it is not separate from feeling, so the thinking at issue here is not a matter of any, as you imply, linear, analytic thinking, top-down thinking, categorical thinking. It's an attending to, and also a listening and responding. The question about the relation of thinking to place comes up in a strange but interesting way in Hannah Arendt's *The Life of the Mind*. At the end of the first volume, she puts the question 'where are we when we think?' Her answer is 'nowhere'.[25] On the face of it, this is one of those occasions in Arendt's work when she seems to open up a radical line of questioning, apparently to lapse into what seems a more conventional conclusion. Arendt argues for a notion of thinking as standing in a particular relation to time rather than place, but the notion of time that she invokes actually seems to bring a set of topological notions with it – it is time as the event of the opening up of the world. Thinking is tied to just such an event – is itself an event of opening and emergence, of attunement and attentiveness. So, I would argue that even in this supposedly temporalized conception, thinking nevertheless appears as tied to place, since that is what these notions of opening, emergence and even event imply. This leads me on to the idea of thinking as a mode of active *orientation* – and this is an idea that, of course, also appears in Kant, notably in the essay 'What Is Orientation in Thinking?'[26]

ESC: I know that essay very well, and I was just thinking that that title is very cleverly chosen, because its exact wording in the German ('Was Heist: Sich im Denken Orientieren?') directs attention to the way in which orientation – which is always placial – occurs *in* thinking, *by* thinking, *through* thinking. That's quite uncanny. And this essay was rather late in Kant's oeuvre, after 1780; you would not expect him to be that speculative and open in that post-critical moment. His earlier, 1768 essay on the material regions of space is also rife with implications for place, but it is not pitched in terms of thinking.[27]

All this points to the need for rethinking orientation – something I have undertaken in my book *The World at a Glance*.[28]

JM: That's right.

ESC: Thinking in this direction – about the relationship between thinking and place via the experience of orientation in space – moves us away from a preoccupation with world space, and thus from geographical concerns of an abstract sort.

JM: It moves us back to *felt* space.

ESC: Exactly so.

JM: That's the interesting thing here. So, if thinking is about orientation, then it's orientation in the sense of a certain felt being there. Again, if you go back to that earlier essay of Kant's, he says that orientation – having a sense of the differentiation between the regions of space – has to be connected back to the sense of differentiation in one's own body.[29] So it is literally a *felt* sense, and, by this route, we come back to the connection between thinking and feeling again.

ESC: So the question becomes: Is such thinking really an altogether different form of thinking, or is it only a different *mode* of thinking? How would you construe this?

JM: Well, I guess I just want to say that this is what thinking genuinely is – *it is orientation*. My claim is that just as being in place comes first, so too must this sense of thinking in relation to place – thinking as orientation. Moreover, this is not just one mode of thinking among others, since it is only on the basis of such orientation that any other mode of thinking is even possible. Yet, at the same time, thinking tends to obscure its own orientational grounding. So, it tends to constantly move itself back to an analytical, or linear or a displaced mode. And that's a misrepresentation of the character of thinking to which thinking itself gives rise. What this means is that genuine thinking – and here we come back to Heidegger again – genuine thinking is always an attempt at remembrance, that is, a return to its already given, and felt, orientational ground.

ESC: Orientational ground is another word for place, is it not? At this very moment when Heidegger is being reviled across the globe for his *Black Notebooks*,[30] you are insisting that, in his later years, there is an absolutely original thought going on – paradoxical as this conjunction may be – which we cannot afford to neglect, in particular in matters of place. In the United States, it's very difficult to talk about Heidegger, or to *teach* Heidegger at this point, because of the cloud that's come over him. So, I appreciate your effort to retrieve and keep valid what is extraordinary in his thought – late as well as early. My dissertation was very close to the late Heidegger – titled *Being and Poetry in Heidegger and Bachelard* – so I started my career situating myself very close to late Heidegger.

JM: That is very interesting, and I wonder if this isn't something that once again brings us very close together. Part of the reason why I'm so close to late Heidegger – and the reason why I also like Camus so much – is that in the end, I'm not terribly interested in philosophy, or at least not in conventional academic philosophy. I'm interested in what Heidegger calls 'poetic thinking'. This doesn't just mean the thinking of poetry, of course, but it does bring poetry into the picture. I've had an ongoing conversation with Kenneth White, who has his own very idiosyncratic way of approaching the questions of place and world that interests both of us; and what attracted me to Kenneth's work, his essays as well is his poetry, is the strong sense of poetic engagement that is related to place.[31] Maybe it is a felt thoughtfulness that belongs to both poetry and genuine philosophy, even as the two nevertheless differ. In that case, what is at issue is again fundamentally about feeling, and yet not a feeling apart from thinking; it's an attempt to thoughtfully feel, to think in this felt way.

ESC: I think that's why I was drawn to Bachelard, and why I've just edited (with two others) a volume on Bachelard in philosophy,[32] hoping to induce a better appreciation of this more sober side of Bachelard. But it is also about poetic language and its relationship to place.

JM: Well, the beginning of *The Poetics of Space* has a very interesting discussion about poetic language,[33] and this is an especially important topic since it concerns the very language of place itself, and the intimacy of the relation between language and place – something captured in Heidegger's talk of language as 'the house of being'.[34] The tendency is always to read this Heideggerian phrase, as with many other topological ideas and images, as metaphorical; but Heidegger is quite clear that it is not.[35] In fact, he seems to insist at several places that his thinking cannot be understood in metaphorical terms – and that one cannot understand Hölderlin that way either. This raises an issue about language, and especially poetic language – about poetic thinking and poetic speaking. It now also raises for me a question about what we have been calling 'felt thinking' or 'thinking feeling', because it seems to me that this is one way of starting to approach what poetic thinking is. Moreover, thinking itself often has something like the character of an encounter with – of a finding oneself somewhere – which is why we can talk about orientation, but this is not to be construed metaphorically, and the thinking itself, and the way it might proceed orientationally, is not a thinking *in metaphors*. That remains so, even though such thinking may draw upon spatial and topographic images and ideas. Having said this, I would want to acknowledge that this suspicion or rejection of metaphor is really about a specific sense or use of metaphor – maybe close to the one Heidegger criticizes. One can also think of metaphor differently, and more fundamentally; and in this sense, metaphor may itself be fundamental. There is, for instance, a tradition of thinking that begins with Coleridge and includes people like Owen Barfield, in which metaphor is a much more alive and fundamental notion, and is not merely to be contrasted with the literal.

ESC: Yes, absolutely. Metaphor takes us into the real – in unique ways.

JM: I think that within a lot of discourses, in philosophy and elsewhere, metaphor becomes an easy way of describing a mode of thinking that we're not quite sure about and which perhaps we don't completely trust. And often the assertion that something is a metaphor becomes a way of not having to take it seriously, having to give our attention to what we have been calling its 'felt' character.

ESC: Heidegger is rather dogmatic on metaphor and its misleading character. I discussed that as long ago as 1967.[36] I think that what Bachelard encourages us to try out – and it draws together this part of our argument – is the felt thinking in which he's been engaged when thinking through the material elements. Material elements are, after all, really *factors of place*, and the way by which the early pre-Socratics single out the elements is at one with your notion that the first philosophy was philosophy of place. And you can see that Bachelard, although he wasn't thinking of the history of philosophy or the pre-Socratics, is, in a certain way, actually saying that poetizing about the elements *is* really thinking in and about place. And to call it topoanalysis, as he does in the introduction to *The Poetics of Space*, is rather uncanny.[37] In fact, he doesn't even follow up on it; it's just a brilliant comet in the sky of his mind that occurs to him as he writes that book in the 1950s. And, I think that his work on the elements can be said to be about the poetry of place *primarily* – specialized into the elements, of course – and to indicate that these are various modalities of place; but as a poet would be in touch with them, through feeling and thinking alike. I do think that Bachelard, like late Heidegger, is another resource that not enough philosophers are really going to, or taking seriously.

JM: Almost *no* philosophers! Bachelard is himself almost entirely neglected by philosophers. Even outside of philosophy, he's almost never directly engaged. And I wonder if that's because this idea of poetic thinking that we're talking about – which is also topological or topographic thinking, that is thinking in, with and through place – is a thinking that is quite difficult for most people, even though it is also very simple. And of course such thinking is made even harder in a world where the dominant mode of thinking (or of not thinking) is a mode that is oriented to the pragmatic, the linear and so on.

ESC: Yes, absolutely. So, here we come around to a concern of this conversation, that is, thinking the *world,* differently. And I do completely agree with you: the calculative way of thinking, in Heidegger's term, is to be radically contrasted with the poetic thinking and feeling, or feeling-thinking. I think we have to put those terms together – properly – and hyphenate them in some fashion: *Fühlen-Denken* or *Fühlen des Denkens.* We should really create a new notion here, as a serious alternative to the calculative, conventional, global and other ways by which thinking has become, as it were, wholly abstracted from the poetics of place. Also, language figures into this, for obviously the poet is doing his thinking and feeling through an extraordinary use of language called poetic language. So we'd have to explore this; not at the level of metaphor but probably image. Notice that in this way we're coming back to the realm of *feeling place.*

JM: It's interesting that Heidegger seems to focus on image as well. If one looks at 'Poetically Man Dwells', one finds a whole discussion of the image and the role of the image in poetic thinking.[38] But I also think that just as we are talking about *Fühlen-Denken* – felt thinking or feeling thinking – part of what this is leading us to is a conception of language as itself felt. Something like this appears in Heidegger in *On the Way to Language.*[39] Language is not something abstract, but concrete; it is that which beckons us, which we do indeed feel and hear. And again, just as the tendency is always to misconstrue, to allow thought to lead us away from its own felt character, so too constantly language seems to lead us away from its own felt character. One has to attend closely to language if one is going to stay with it and stay with its own felt character. This is what poetry tries to do.

ESC: Yes, this is Heidegger's view. I have a friend, a poet, George Quasha, who has a series of books that are all called *preverbs*[40] – a very suggestive phrase. In these poems Quasha shows an uncanny sense of how language takes us both to earth and to the elements, as well as to image. These works go *under* concepts by way of earth-based imagery that is insistently place-specific. Part of going *under* is going into feeling, of course. I do believe that poets like Quasha are a fertile source for the kind of direction we're taking now: a direction which indicates that there is something about place that calls for poetry (and doubtless poetry for place), for poetic expression in which feeling and image invoke place. Poetry of this sort is a kind of first among equals, you might say, of modes of expression: such poetry is not exclusively powerful, but it is especially powerful.

JM: Well that was partly why that essay of mine on singularity focuses so much on engaging with a poem – one by the New Zealand poet C. K. Stead, 'After the Wedding'.[41] I wanted to do it that way partly because I've long had an admiration for C. K. Stead's poetry, but also because of the issues we have just been talking about. Stead is an interesting figure in his own right. There has always been a strong attentiveness to place in his work, and it seems to me that this particular poem itself has a very strong sense of the singularity of place – and of a very specific place – at work in it. I can't see how one could get a sense of that – convey a sense of that – other than through poetry or poetic writing. Only the poetic gives the sort of linguistic articulation that is at issue here, and that allows a sense of the felt character of place to emerge.

ESC: Yes, I think it actually *induces* feeling in the reader from out of the feeling of the poet, expressing that feeling in language that's concretely imagistic – that has a specific gravity that's very sensitive to the particularities of place – and from there entering into the reader's sensibility and imagination; not mimetically, rather in somehow inspiring a correlative state of mind that possesses poetic feeling or sensibility not otherwise available in the course of everyday life. Such feeling is usually excluded in the course of everyday life precisely because of the calculative thinking that dominates daily doings. Still, given that we live halfway around the earth from each other, much of our own contact would not be possible without contemporary electronic communication.

JM: Yes, there certainly are compensations that come from what might be thought the products of 'calculative thinking'! But there are so many things that are coming up now in this conversation, including, for instance, the character and the role of the image. There's a lot more to say about that. And here, I think I would also want to note that what seems to bedevil much thinking about language, and its relation to the image, is a tendency not to think language and thinking itself essentially enough, so that often it's assumed that the image is somehow to be understood as somehow apart from language: as non-linguistic or even pre-linguistic. But of course, in the very way we're talking, language and image are bound up together.

ESC: They certainly are.

JM: One of the things that's sometimes said is that there are too many images nowadays –for instance, the director Wim Wenders has talked about a problematic proliferation of images[42] – and I think there is actually a sense in which such a *proliferation* also involves a *loss* of the image. Perhaps this means that we need to distinguish between the image as it is multiplied through cinema, television the Internet, and so on – the image that is constantly being replaced by other images, so that the image is itself barely seen or attended to – and the image as that which remains as the focus of attention, that is not merely one in a succession of images, but rather opens up before us, *as singular*, almost as a place into which we can step; perhaps the image here appears as a place. So now it seems that we have been led to draw together the thinking or rethinking of the image along with the thinking of place, as well as the thinking and rethinking of thinking. All of these are brought together, and I think this is characteristic of the sort of topological or topographic thinking that we have been talking about.

ESC: Absolutely. They're all parallel projects, and deeply connected. As you were talking about image in the non-proliferating sense, this phrase was coming to my mind: *felt image*. The tradition of separating imagination from feeling, which is often allied with sensation classically, is exactly where we're not going with this conversation. Feeling and imaging belong together; and they belong together, I would say, because each and both are rooted in place, so that we can almost regard image and feeling as dimensions of place. Or shall we say 'feathers of place', as if they form a headdress poised on place itself. In any case, we can agree that feeling and imaging are both indispensable in poetic language.

JM: And more generally in speaking, or 'saying', as Heidegger would put it.

ESC: Yes, absolutely. Images and feelings really feather the nest of place. Now we're really getting into images ourselves! Nevertheless, how do we keep our eye on place as somehow subtending and pervading these other terms that have now arisen spontaneously in this talk? Feeling, thinking, image, word – I think those are the four primary terms that have been coming forth. Would we want to say that place somehow is indeed the *sub rosa* substructure of these very particular ways by which poetry modalizes place, as well as expresses it?

JM: I'm not sure I would say that 'substructure' is the right term here. That doesn't seem to me to quite capture what's at issue. Place gathers things together, and yet each also gathers the others in place. I'm not sure we can talk about it other than in that sort of way – so maybe to talk about place as substructure is too simplifying or reductive here.

ESC: I do follow you, and I do like gathering, in Heidegger's sense of *Versammlung* – that is loose assemblage.

JM: Yes, exactly.

ESC: I agree that this is a better way of putting things. I was suddenly carried away by the image of structure, which suggests a stratification that is not always in play in poetry. You're right that gathering is much more adequate, given that it doesn't lend itself to any discrete or single image, least of all structure or substructure.

JM: And of course there's one term that we've left out there, but that has been in the background of our discussion – and only occasionally surfacing – and that is 'world'.

ESC: Indeed. Let's talk a little bit more about world because that's where we wanted to come to. So what do you think about my term 'place-world'*?* My claim has been that every world that matters, or every experiential world at least, is a place-world. I came across that, of course, way back in my first foray into place, in *Getting Back Into Place*, first published in 1993.[43]

JM: It's a term that I'm a little uncomfortable with, simply because it seems to imply a mode of world that belongs to place. And I'm not sure I want to use either of those terms in that way. I don't see *place* as allowing a mode of world, and I don't think I see *world* such that it can properly have modes. I guess I see place and world as always tied together, so the world always and only ever opens up in and through the singularity of place.

ESC: And of course, I agree with that. I'd only want to add that my claim is as much ontological as phenomenological: every world occurs as place – place of some specific sort. A placeless world is not any kind of world. So I hold that every world is first, and finally, a place-world.

JM: I had more or less assumed that was what you meant, without being quite sure if I was reading you correctly. But the worry I have is that the way the term 'place-world' is constructed lends itself to the sort of construal that I would want to avoid.

ESC: I will admit that my term has strong ontological implications that you may not want to accept. My sense is that for you 'world' is not only about place, or place-specific. Here we part ways even as we agree on the phenomenological priority of place: a priority of place at the level of feeling and image. Perhaps we can agree that 'world' is a capacious word – a kind of floating signifier – and yet that nevertheless, every time 'world' occurs, place is at stake, however indirectly?

JM: I think that something like that is right. And I would also add that, throughout all of our discussions, we seem always to be involved in a rethinking, a retrieval, a recuperation of terms from everyday use that we take for granted: terms such as 'world' and 'place', 'image' and 'feeling'. Heidegger says in *The Basic Concepts of Phenomenology* that the elucidation of the concept of world is the central task of philosophy and yet also that the concept of world has not yet been recognized by philosophy.[44] One might think that there's something odd about that, because surely almost every philosopher has had something to say about world. Yet part of what is at issue here is the very notion of world itself. The sense in which Heidegger uses it is indeed a sense almost entirely neglected, and it is a sense that is closely related to his own eventual notion of gathering.

ESC: Yes, I think so. Being in the world, for example, even that very basic term of *Being and Time*, if you think about it, involves a loose collection of equiprimordial existential structures; so that every way in which *Dasein* is in the world involves a group of loosely affiliated set of existentials, and that these existentials imply place – despite Heidegger's muteness on 'place' at this early point. Still, he's already on the way to place, don't you think?

JM: Definitely. I think the problem with Heidegger's *Being and Time* is that he's essentially doing topology, but doesn't yet have the language to understand that this is what he's doing.

ESC: That's beautifully put. He's place-bound without acknowledging it to himself or to his reader.

JM: Exactly. In fact, that is pretty much what Joe Fell argues in his *Heidegger and Sartre* with respect to both the early and late Heidegger: that Heidegger is indeed doing topology, and was doing so from the beginning.[45] My *Heidegger's Topology* is, in this sense, an elaboration of the work that Joe had done.[46]

We haven't talked much about memory yet. And yet memory, for both of us, really stands in a central relationship to place. It's no accident that very often the most topological thinkers and poets are those who are also preoccupied or concerned with the issue of memory. Proust is the obvious example. It seems to me that the way you first addressed the issue of place was in relation to place memory. The famous madeleine passage in Proust was also an important starting point for me.[47] But the connection to memory isn't just about Proust – it reflects something essential about memory itself. Maybe the connection to the image and to feeling is also at issue in their intimate relation to thinking as remembrance. There's another whole area of the conversation that opens up here.

ESC: Yes, exactly that. My claim was that 'secondary memory' – or ordinary recollection – requires a scene, as we call it; the scene of memory. I insisted that every such remembered scene happens in some kind of a place.

JM: Yes.

ESC: But we'd have to push this further, to now consider thinking in relation to memory, and thus to place – I mean, one would move backwards in this respect. My original project was to write four books: on imagination, memory, and then thinking and feeling. I abandoned the latter two because place took over. Place obsessed me for fully a quarter of a century – and still does. But it's interesting; I feel like maybe I'll return to it, now from a different direction. Our conversation is encouraging me to do this, via the very topics of feeling and thinking. If I go in this direction, I assure you that I will not pursue a formal phenomenology – an eidetic – of feeling and thinking. Here we are ending in a quite comparable or at least compatible place: which is rather extraordinary. I refer to our agreement that any of the major terms we've been discussing – thinking, remembering, imaging, feeling –are all place terms. This is a pretty radical way of doing philosophy that the majority of philosophers do not appreciate. They must think we have fallen off the edge of the earth.

JM: We're always on the edge anyway – always at the threshold.

ESC: Yes, exactly, we live on the edge. This is somewhat uncanny. You and I come to our current edges from our very different points of origin. Unlike you, I did not have analytical philosophy in my background – I held it at arm's length. I was at schools where it was barely taught; you had analytical philosophy as a major element of your earlier education, particularly through Donald Davidson. Yet we each found our way to place from our quite different origins, our philosophical set of origins. I find that very confirming.

JM: And yet it also does place us both on the edges of philosophy, but also in one sense at the centre of philosophy, too. Institutionally, in my case, I am definitely at the edge, so much so that my office – by choice, in fact – is currently in the geography department.

ESC: You and I are treading on the edges of the field of philosophy; there is no question about it. I don't regret it – I'm very happy that I never aspired to be in the centre of that field. It's a precarious perch that I feel I've put myself on, and I'm sure you feel the same way. By indirection, we found out the direction of place – and direction is a term of orientation – so, we got oriented in philosophy through place, we *re*-oriented ourselves through place. We found our way in and by place. In contrast, most of analytical philosophy and formal or eidetic phenomenology is place-deaf.

JM: Well if, as we both think, place is so fundamental, then it's fundamental for philosophy too. You've done a history of place *in* philosophy: showing the way philosophy has neglected place, or forgotten place. And yet there is also, if you like, a sort of history to be written about the way in which place constantly re-emerges in philosophy, even on those occasions when it seems to be denied or forgotten. This is there, for instance, in terms of the ever-present images of place that constantly occur in even the most abstruse philosophical writing. And yet those images are never really taken seriously or interrogated. So, place is constantly there – rather like a shadow – even in the most conceptually abstract thinking. What we've been doing has, on the one hand, been on the margins of philosophy, and yet on the other hand, has been going back to its hidden centre, if you like, at the place where philosophy begins – which is the place in which we find ourselves – in a felt as well as a thought way.

ESC: Absolutely, and in all those ways, we are placial creatures from head to toe, and we are also placial as philosophers. That's the extraordinary thing, as both of us have just been saying. Even the philosophers who deny this importance will nevertheless from time to time make remarks that are place-saturated. It is a matter of the recrudescence of place – the spontaneous rediscovery of its importance of place – right where you wouldn't expect it to happen. It's a matter of *topos noetos* in a phrase in the *De Anima*, where Aristotle says very explicitly: there's a place of thought.[48] And yet he dismisses it as if it were a mere analogy or metaphor. But – as you were saying earlier in relation to Heidegger's use of the term – no metaphor is idle, and particularly not this one, I would say.

JM: I think that's very true. Before we finish, there is one thing I want to mention that we haven't yet touched upon, but nevertheless seems to me quite important, and that is the idea of *surface*. You talk about this, and it connects with things I've been thinking about as well. I don't use the notion of edge so much, but certainly I do use surface, and it seems to me that surface is again a central concept for us both. Indeed, I would want to say that our engagement with the world, our thinking in the world as well as our being in the world, is, in an important sense, always at the surfaces of things.

ESC: Yes, literally so. J. J. Gibson says the surface is where the action of perception is to be found.[49]

JM: Yes, of course, and there's also that connection between surface and *topos*. *Topos* is itself a surface – a bounding surface.

ESC: I think there's a world of work to be done with surface. I just went to the edge. And yet edge and surface are obviously covalent, co-necessary; you can't have one without the other, and you can't have either without place.

Notes

1 Immanuel Kant, *Dreams of a Spirit Seer*, trans. E. Goerwitz (London: S. Sonnenschein & Co., 1900), p. 114.

2 Jeff Malpas, *Place and Experience: A Philosophical Topography* (Cambridge and New York: Cambridge University Press, 2009).

3 See Edward S. Casey, 'Thinking on the Edge', in *The World on Edge* (Indiana: Indiana University Press, forthcoming 2017), appendix.

4 Jeff Malpas, 'Place and Singularity', in *The Intelligence of Place*, ed. Jeff Malpas (London: Bloomsbury, 2015), pp. 65–92.

5 Gilles Deleuze, *Difference and Repetition,* trans. Paul Patton (London and New York: Continuum, 1994 [1968]), pp. 1–5.

6 Casey, 'Thinking on the Edge'.

7 Immanuel Kant, *Prolegomena to Any Future Metaphysics that Will Be Able to Come Forth as Science*, trans. Gary Hatfield, in *Theoretical Philosophy after 1781, The Cambridge Edition of the Works of Immanuel Kant* (Cambridge: Cambridge University Press, 2002), pp. 142 and 144.

8 See e.g. Martin Heidegger, 'Building Dwelling Thinking', in *Poetry, Language, Thought,* trans. Albert Hofstadter (New York: Harper & Row, 1971), p. 154.

9 Martin Heidegger, *Being and Time,* trans. John Macquarrie and Edward Robinson (New York: Harper and Row, 1962).

10 Heidegger, *Poetry, Language, Thought,* p. 154.

11 John Sallis, *Delimitations: Phenomenology and the End of Metaphysics* (Bloomington: Indiana University Press, 1995).

12 Jacques Derrida, *Aporias,* trans. Thomas Dutoit (Stanford: Stanford University Press, 1995).

13 See Albert Camus, *Lyrical and Critical Essays,* ed. Philip Thody, trans. Ellen Conroy Kennedy (New York: Vintage, 1970).

14 Adam Smith, *The Theory of Moral Sentiments,* ed. Knud Haakonssen (Cambridge: Cambridge University Press, 1992).

15 Emmanuel Levinas, *Violence and Metaphysics*, trans. A. Lingis (Pittsburgh: Duquesne University Press, 1969), pp. 78–80.

16 Camus, *Lyrical and Critical Essays*, p. 16.

17 Jean-Paul Sartre, *Nausea*, trans. Robert Baldick (London: Penguin, 2000).

18 See Albert Camus, *The Myth of Sisyphus,* trans. Justin O'Brien (London: Hamish Hamilton, 1955), Preface.

19 'Helen's Exile', in Camus, *The Myth of Sisyphus,* pp. 147–51 (the quoted line is from p. 147); see also the version of 'Helen's Exile', in *Lyrical and Critical Essays,* pp. 148–53. The essay was first written in 1948.

20 See the discussion in Edward S. Casey, 'The Ethics of the Face to Face Encounter: Schroeder, Levinas, and the Glance', *The Pluralist* 1 (2006), pp. 74–97.

21 Robin George Collingwood, *The Principles of Art* (Oxford: Clarendon Press, 1938).

22 Robin George Collingwood, *An Autobiography* (London and New York: Oxford University Press, 1939).

23 See Hans-Georg Gadamer, *Truth and Method,* trans. Rev. Joel Weinsheimer and Donald G. Marshall (New York: Crossroads, 2nd rev. ed., 1992), pp. 70–373.

24 Martin Heidegger, *What Is Called Thinking?,* trans. J. Glenn Gray (New York: Harper and Row, 1968).

25 Hannah Arendt, *The Life of the Mind,* one-volume edn (San Diego: Harcourt Brace and Co., 1978, 1977), I, pp. 200–1.

26 Immanuel Kant, 'What Is Orientation in Thinking?' in *Kant: Political Writings,* ed. Hans Siegbert Riess, trans. Hugh Barr Nisbet (Cambridge: Cambridge University, 1991).

27 Immanuel Kant, 'Concerning the Ultimate Ground of the Differentiation of Directions in Space', in David Walford and Ralf Meerbote (eds), *The Cambridge Edition of the Works of Immanuel Kant. Theoretical Philosophy, 1755–1770* (Cambridge: Cambridge University Press, 1992), pp. 365–72.

28 Edward S. Casey, *The World at a Glance* (Bloomington: Indiana University Press, 2007).

29 Kant, 'Concerning the Ultimate Ground of the Differentiation of Directions in Space', pp. 366–8.

30 Heidegger kept a series of black-bound Notebooks for much of his academic life, which are now being published in separate volumes of the Heidegger *Complete Works* (*Gesamtausgabe*) by Klostermann in Frankfurt (beginning in 2014). They are known collectively as the *Black Notebooks,* with individual volumes having their own titles. The first of the individual volumes (the first three of which are each titled *Überlegungen*), has appeared in English as *Ponderings II–VI*, and *Ponderings VII–XI,* trans. Richard Rojcewicz (Bloomington: Indiana University Press, 2016/2017).

31 See, for instance, Kenneth White, *The Wanderer and His Charts* (Edinburgh: Polygon, 2004); also *Open World: Collected Poems 1960–2000* (Edinburgh: Polygon, 2003); see also White's essay in Malpas (ed.), *The Intelligence of Place*, pp. 221–52.

32 *Gaston Bachelard: Adventures in Phenomenology,* ed. Eileen Rizo-Patron, Edward Casey, Jason Wirth (Albany: SUNY Press, 2017).

33 Gaston Bachelard, *The Poetics of Space,* trans. Maria Jolas (Boston: Beacon Press, 1959).

34 Heidegger, 'Letter on "Humanism"', trans. Frank A. Capuzzi, in *Pathmarks,* ed. William McNeill (Cambridge: Cambridge University Press, 1998), p. 239.

35 'Letter on "Humanism"', p. 272. See also Jeff Malpas, '"The House of Being": Poetry, Language, Place', in Günter Figal et al. (eds), *Pathways to Heidegger's Later Thinking* (Bloomington: Indiana University Press, forthcoming, 2017).

36 Edward S. Casey, *Poetry and Ontology: Bachelard and Heidegger on Poetic Language*: dissertation (Northwestern University, 1967).

37 Bachelard, *The Poetics of Space*, pp. xxxii, 8, 10, 226.

38 Martin Heidegger, 'Poetically Man Dwells', in *Poetry Language, Thought,* trans. Albert Hofstadter (New York: HarperCollins, 1971), pp. 211–29.

39 Martin Heidegger, *On the Way to Language,* trans. Peter D. Hertz (New York: Harper and Row, 1971).

40 The 'preverb' series begins with George Quasha, *Verbal Paradise* (La Laguna: Zasterle Press, 2010) and continues with a series of other volumes.

41 C. K. Stead, 'After the Wedding', in *Between* (Auckland: Auckland University Press, 1988), pp. 9–10.

42 Wim Wenders 'Talk About Germany', in *Wim Wenders: On Film. Essays and Conversations* (London: Faber & Faber, 2001), p. 442; see also 'In Defence of Places', *Director's Guild of America Magazine*, 28–4 (2003), http://www.dga.org./news/v28_4/craft_wendersplaces.php3 (accessed 01 January 2017).

43 Edward S. Casey, *Getting Back into Place,* 2nd edn (Bloomington: Indiana University Press, 2009).

44 Martin Heidegger, *The Basic Concepts of Phenomenology*, trans. Albert Hofstadter, (Bloomington and Indianapolis: Indiana University Press, 1982), p. 165.

45 Joseph P. Fell, *Heidegger and Sartre: An Essay on Being and Place* (New York: Columbia University Press, 1979).

46 Jeff Malpas, *Heidegger's Topology: Being, Place, World* (Cambridge, MA and London: MIT Press, 2006).

47 Marcel Proust, *In Search of Lost Time*, Vol I, *Swann's Way*, trans. C. K. Scott Moncrieff and Terence Kilmartin, Rev. D. J. Enright (New York: Modern Library, 1983), pp. 60–4.

48 Aristotle, *On the Soul. Parva Naturalia. On Breath*, trans. W. S. Hett, Loeb Classical Library (Cambridge, MA: Harvard University Press, 1957), p. 32.

49 "The surface is where most of the action is" (James J. Gibson, *The Ecological Approach to Visual Perception* [Hillsdale, NJ: Erlbaum, 1986], p. 23). See also Avrum Stroll, *Surfaces* (Minneapolis: University of Minnesota Press, 1988).

References

Arendt, H., *The Life of the Mind* (one-volume Edition), San Diego: Harcourt Brace and Co., 1978, 1977.

Aristotle, *On the Soul. Parva Naturalia.* On Breath, trans. W. S. Hett, Loeb Classical Library, Cambridge, MA: Harvard University Press, 1957.

Bachelard, G., *The Poetics of Space*, trans. Maria Jolas, Boston: Beacon Press, 1959.

Camus, A., *The Myth of Sisyphus*, trans. Justin O'Brien, London: Hamish Hamilton, 1955.

Casey, E. S., 'Thinking on the Edge', in *The World on Edge*, Bloomington, IN: Indiana University Press, forthcoming 2017.

Casey, E. S., *Getting Back into Place* (2nd Edition), Bloomington: Indiana University Press, 2009.

Casey, E. S., *The World at a Glance*, Bloomington: Indiana University Press, 2007.

Casey, E. S., 'The Ethics of the Face to Face Encounter: Schroeder, Levinas, and the Glance', *The Pluralist* 1(1), 2006, pp. 74–97.

Casey, E. S., *Poetry and Ontology: Bachelard and Heidegger on Poetic Language: dissertation*, Northwestern University, 1967.

Collingwood, R. G., *An Autobiography*, London and New York: Oxford University Press, 1939.

Collingwood, R. G., *The Principles of Art*, Oxford: Clarendon Press, 1938.

Deleuze, G., *Difference and Repetition*, trans. Paul Patton, London and New York: Continuum, 1994 [1968].

Derrida, J., *Aporias*, trans. Thomas Dutoit, Stanford: Stanford University Press, 1995.

Fell, J. P., *Heidegger and Sartre: An Essay on Being and Place*, New York: Columbia University Press, 1979.

Gadamer, H.-G., *Truth and Method* (2nd rev. Edition), trans. Rev. Joel Weinsheimer and Donald G. Marshall, New York: Crossroads, 1992.

Gibson, J. J., *The Ecological Approach to Visual Perception*, Hillsdale, NJ: Erlbaum, 1986.

Heidegger, M., *Ponderings II–VI*, and *Ponderings VII–XI*, trans. Richard Rojcewicz, Bloomington: Indiana University Press, 2016/2017.

Heidegger, M., 'Letter on "Humanism"', in *Pathmarks*, ed. William McNeill, trans. Frank A. Capuzzi, Cambridge: Cambridge University Press, 1998.

Heidegger, M., *The Basic Concepts of Phenomenology*, trans. Albert Hofstadter, Bloomington and Indianapolis: Indiana University Press, 1982.

Heidegger, M., *On the Way to Language*, trans. Peter D. Hertz, New York: Harper and Row, 1971.

Heidegger, M., *Poetry Language, Thought*, trans. Albert Hofstadter, New York: HarperCollins, 1971.

Heidegger, M., *What is Called Thinking?*, trans. J. Glenn Gray, New York: Harper and Row, 1968.

Heidegger, M., *Being and Time*, trans. John Macquarrie and Edward Robinson, New York: Harper and Row, 1962.

Kant, I., *Prolegomena to any future metaphysics that will be able to come forth as science*, trans. Gary Hatfield, in *Theoretical Philosophy after 1781, The Cambridge Edition of the Works of Immanuel Kant*, Cambridge: Cambridge University Press, 2002.

Kant, I., 'Concerning the Ultimate Ground of the Differentiation of Directions in Space', in David Walford and Ralf Meerbote (eds), *The Cambridge Edition of the Works of Immanuel Kant. Theoretical Philosophy, 1755–1770*, Cambridge: Cambridge University Press, 1992.

Kant, I., 'What is Orientation in Thinking?' in *Kant: Political Writings*, ed. Hans Siegbert Riess, trans. Hugh Barr Nisbet, Cambridge: Cambridge University, 1991.

Kant, I., *Dreams of a Spirit Seer*, trans. E. Goerwitz, London: S. Sonnenschein & Co., 1900.

Levinas, E., *Violence and Metaphysics*, trans. A. Lingis, Pittsburgh: Duquesne University Press, 1969.

Malpas, J., '"The House of Being": Poetry, Language, Place', in Günter Figal et al. (eds), *Pathways to Heidegger's Later Thinking*, Bloomington: Indiana University Press, forthcoming, 2017.

Malpas, J., 'Place and Singularity', in *The Intelligence of Place*, ed. Jeff Malpas, London: Bloomsbury, 2015, pp. 65–92.
Malpas, J., *Place and Experience: A Philosophical Topography*, Cambridge and New York: Cambridge University Press, 2009.
Malpas, J., *Heidegger's Topology: Being, Place, World*, Cambridge, MA and London: MIT Press, 2006.
Proust, M., *In Search of Lost Time*, Vol I, *Swann's Way*, trans. C. K. Scott Moncrieff and Terence Kilmartin, rev. D. J. Enright, New York: Modern Library, 1983.
Quasha, G., *Verbal Paradise*, La Laguna: Zasterle Press, 2010.
Rizo-Patron, E., Casey, E., and J. Wirth (eds), *Gaston Bachelard: Adventures in Phenomenology*, Albany: SUNY Press, 2017.
Sallis, J. *Delimitations: Phenomenology and the End of Metaphysics*, Bloomington: Indiana University Press, 1995.
Sartre, J.-P., *Nausea*, trans. Robert Baldick, London: Penguin, 2000.
Smith, A., *The Theory of Moral Sentiments*, ed. Knud Haakonssen, Cambridge: Cambridge University Press, 1992.
Stead, C. K., 'After the Wedding', in *Between*, Auckland: Auckland University Press, 1988, pp. 9–10.
Stroll, A., *Surfaces*, Minneapolis: University of Minnesota Press, 1988.
Wenders, W., 'Talk About Germany', in *Wim Wenders: On Film. Essays and Conversations*, London: Faber & Faber, 2001, pp. 434–44.
Wenders, W., 'In Defence of Places', *Director's Guild of America Magazine*, 28–4 (2003), http://www.dga.org./news/v28_4/craft_wendersplaces.php3 (accessed 01 January 2017).
White, K., *The Wanderer and His Charts*, Edinburgh: Polygon, 2004.
White, K., *Open World: Collected Poems 1960–2000*, Edinburgh: Polygon, 2003.

4

Attunement as architectural meaning

Alberto Pérez-Gómez

Contemporary buildings designed by architects are unquestionably diverse and often novel, even seductive. Yet I would argue that, in general, the true cultural relevance of architecture in our complex world remains unclear. Pursuing a tendency that can be dated back to the early nineteenth century, architecture has sought its justification in a logic associated with either the sciences and engineering or the fine arts; today it has resulted in two major positions, one that champions endless – often striking, yet mostly gratuitous – formal innovation, and the other that obsessively seeks technical sustainability while still presupposing 'development' and perennial economic growth. Flaunting its supposedly unshakable nature as an autonomous act of creation or engineering, it ignores the meanings present in the social environment that appear from the bottom-up, through the customs and habits of the cultures that inhabit our planet. Architecture remains mostly detached from the places in which it should be rooted, and disconnected from both the ways of life of its inhabitants and the stories that should be foundational to it. Whether seductive formal gestures attract tourist dollars, or bankrupt municipalities through their cost overruns – as they have famously done in Spain – they ultimately make little sense to the average citizen and contribute almost nothing to his or her psychosomatic health.

Starting during the European nineteenth century, contemporary humans have disregarded the crucial importance of the environment for life and psychosomatic well-being, reducing nature – previously regarded as living, and often sacred – to a vast repository of 'natural resources', and thus exposing it to exploitation by nation states and corporations. Urban contexts have been subjected to more benevolent, yet equally real, indifference – brought about by our culture of privatization, distraction and telecommunications, and compounded today by our use of sophisticated technology and mapping techniques such as GPS, which themselves propitiate the apparently growing meaninglessness of the environments in which we conduct our lives, thus exacerbating our nihilistic propensities.[1] It is in view of such critical questions that we should emphasize *the crucial role of the physical environment, of cities and their architecture, for human consciousness itself.*[2]

Mistakenly identifying consciousness with attention, we may think that we live in our screens, that we truly *are* our avatars in social media and that telecommunication is truly communication. It is not so. Human communication is primarily oral, gestural, erotic and embodied; other modes, like writing and digital codes, render information but can never fully reduce such communication. We may think all that matters is what we can represent, verbally or instrumentally. And yet, this is hardly the case: representational consciousness is like the tip of an iceberg. About 80 per cent of our consciousness when we are awake is not subconscious or unconscious, but pre-reflective.[3] And consciousness is enactive, never passive; even visual perception is not like the generation of a photographic image in the back of the retina: we see in high definition because our body, acting in the world, is enabled by motor and conceptual skills to contemplate such a world, which otherwise would appear sadly vague, full of holes and (literally) pixelated.[4]

We actually dwell amidst an overwhelmingly constructed landscape and built environment, pervasive for the majority of the world's population. Contemporary cognitive science and neurobiology now recognize what has long been an insight in phenomenology during the twentieth century: that the environment is a constitutive part of animal and human consciousness. Just like each animal has its own world that emerges from their organic morphology, their biology and the way the environment appears through such conditions; the same is true for humans. The world of the fly and the world of the monkey, for example, have little in common, if anything at all: they co-emerge for each organism as it acts out its own life, seeking its particular modes of homeostasis; the equilibrium that allows the organism to prevail in life and which is its own modality of meaning.[5] In other words, our personal consciousness is not our brain, it is both *embodied* – the entire sensorium of our nervous system with our particular bodily morphology and orientation, bipedal, with a distinct front and back, left and right, and up and down, frontal vision, and the ability to contemplate the regular motions of the stars – and, equally importantly, always in *place*. Despite the popular assumptions about the supposed interiority of consciousness, there is no human consciousness without place. Moods and emotions are effectively *in the world*: a seeming paradox that has been carefully explained by philosophers such as Maurice Merleau-Ponty and more recently Nick Crossley, establishing the primacy of the social body in the constitution of human reality.[6] The internal and external components of consciousness are always interacting through bodily motility; they constitute non-representational knowledge in the form of cultural habits, for example, long before things come to our attention. Thus, internal and external components condition each other, *evolving* as they deploy themselves in time, along the path that is life.[7]

An unfeeling, intentionally neutral or merely distracting built environment qualifies our thoughts and feelings, and either contributes to our well-being or – as I would argue in the case of our present dysfunctional architectural and urbanistic practices – to our collective psychopathologies. In this connection, it is important to recall the work of the distinguished neuroscientist Antonio Damasio, who has argued for the importance of emotions and feelings as essential building blocks of cognition; supporting human survival and enabling the spirit's greatest creations.[8] Recovering Baruch Spinoza's (and later phenomenology's) critique of Descartes' dualism, refusing to separate the mind and body, Damasio has shown the continuity between emotions and appetites, feelings and concepts. He points out that every emotion is a variation of pleasure and pain, a condition of consciousness at the cellular level, always seeking homeostatic equilibrium. Furthermore, he has carefully observed how patients who are incapable of feeling as a result of neurological disorders are also incapable of clear thought.

Given the crucial importance of the environment as a place for embodied cognition – literally a constitutive part of consciousness that demands attuned emotions to be productive, and potentially revealing of purpose through human action – I have argued for an urgent need to consider alternatives to banal formalism or aestheticism, and to the rhetoric of sustainability in both architecture and urban design. These efforts must recognize the problematic conditions and inevitable responsibilities for the architectural imagination that the end of traditions (in the form of cohesive mytho-poetic cultural structures) imposed upon contemporary modernity, after about 1800. The primary referential frameworks for artistic symbolization, such as the cosmological images associated with hegemonic religions, have been inoperative since early modernity. However, abdicating the personal, embodied and linguistic imagination (in favour of rational consensus, design by committee or even algorithmic fabrication, for example) is not an option. Modernity demands that architects 'experiment', enabling a productive imagination to promise a better world for future dwelling. However, I would add that to be significant, this mode of invention must necessarily engage a humble, cultured and hermeneutically open attitude to given reality, and its values.

Despite the seeming solidity of a world that stays put when we are not looking, matter does not have ontological precedence over consciousness: quantum mechanics provides simple, if bewildering, evidence of this fact. From this, it would appear to follow that architectural meaning cannot simply arise from an object-oriented ontology and be dependent on formal geometries imposed from the top-down, whether invented *a priori* by 'starchitects' or generated by algorithmic software. Challenging assumptions that appear to be justified by historical practices going back to Ancient Egyptian architecture, the understanding of this problem – particular to modernity – was the topic of my first book, *Architecture and the Crisis of Modern Science*.[9] Put simply: geometry, a fabrication of the human mind, was profoundly significant for architectural practices in contexts that assumed the world of experience to be in perennial change and transformation, while the Euclidean forms and commensurate organization of buildings referenced the only modes of stability present to perception, epitomized by the geometry of the heavenly vault and the mathematically determined motions of the stars and planets, given to the naked eye. This resulted, particularly after Hellenistic times, in an architecture mimetic of the cosmos through its symbolic geometry. Yet as this geometry became instrumentalized in the early nineteenth century, challenging its Euclidean axioms and limits based on the priority of tactile multi-sensory experience to enable the modes of production common since the Industrial Revolution, it cannot longer be assumed to possess inherent meaning. Identifying with other contemporary architects and writers such as Peter Zumthor and Juhani Pallasmaa, who believe that architectural meaning has more to do with the creation of *atmospheres* than with specific formal vocabularies, my recent work contributes to this position through an original interdisciplinary approach, avoiding the understanding of atmosphere as a mere orchestration of effects, but rather grasping its importance as the expression of moods in lived situations, occurring in habitual human action. Understood as atmosphere, architecture is revealed as a communicative setting for human life, *both cognitive and emotive* – beyond its common, yet failed definition as decorated building, issuing from the misunderstandings of eighteenth-century aesthetics.

The concept of atmosphere has the advantage of immediately enabling a critique of objectivist aesthetics: the common misunderstanding of aesthetic experience as aesthetic judgement.[10] Yet this concept is complex, and can be misleading. It is obvious, for example, that atmospheres and moods can be changed by users: if I light a few candles in a typical motel room, I can transform it, at least to some extent, into the abode of Venus, making it propitious for romance. An angry speech, on the other hand, can obliterate the sacred mood of a church. Arguably, atmosphere is perceived immediately, and it affects us not only intellectually but also at a pre-reflective level, as we act. For atmosphere to function as architectural meaning, however, there must be some degree of fixity, and certainly, forms, materials and details play a very important role. It is therefore crucial to grasp the roots of the concept in architectural history and its theories, and closer to us, the affinity of atmosphere with the concept of character in European eighteenth-century architectural theories.

The concern for properly attuned physical environments can be traced back to the historical origins of European architecture and its musical analogy in Greco-Roman culture. This analogy appears in all traditional architectural treatises, and even today is the subject of scholarly papers, student projects and competition briefs – usually evoking Goethe's famous phrase: *architecture is frozen music*. However, this analogy is commonly misunderstood and treated in formal terms – by following the reasoning that, since music deals with proportions and mathematics for its harmonic effects and to produce beautiful sounds, this must be transposable in some way to architectural form; in effect, seeking a congruity of the parts of a building, and its whole, through proportional ratios. In fact, a careful study of the Western theoretical tradition reveals that the musical analogy, since its inception, has involved far more than such formal transpositions. The central issue has been the design of human situations contributing to a 'good life': one that is in harmony and balance, properly tempered. The spatial experience of architecture was therefore like that of music, capable of conveying cognitive, poetic moods through primary emotional sentience. Curiously, however, the attunement thought to be brought about by an atmosphere today is generally understood as a matter of subjectivity, in stark contrast with the objectivity of mathematics evoked in traditional literature. This differing emphasis is the result of diverging cultural conditions too complex to elaborate here; yet it speaks about the intertwining between intellectual and emotional cognition present in place, which as I mentioned above, is now better understood (in opposition to Cartesian assumptions) through phenomenology and neuroscience.

This analogy of music and architecture for the sake of a good life is very clear in the first text of architectural theory available to us: *The Ten Books* by Vitruvius.[11] Architecture operates as a communicative setting for societies: *its beauty is, in fact, it's meaning as it contributes to human health and self-understanding*. For Vitruvius, there is no concern for innovation or efficient design. If parts of buildings must be in proportional relations according to mathematical ratios, this is not a question of mere formal composition. The same numbers were believed to govern musical and cosmic orders, and to operate to further the harmonious and well-tempered city – an attuned environment that operates in both time and space like music, as the original foundation and necessary precondition for good architecture: the setting of a good and healthy life. Harmony and temperance remained the core values in architectural theory throughout the Renaissance and well until the end of the Baroque period in seventeenth-century Europe.

An interesting example from the Renaissance is Palladio's Basilica in Vicenza. In Palladio's treatise, the *Quattro Libri*, proportionality is taken for the first time in the history of Western architecture in 'three dimensions', coordinating the dimensions of rooms – their depth, length and height – so that they convey a symphonic experience, following trends in the theory of musical polyphony of its time.[12] Palladio notates his architectural ideas in this way, appearing as drawings of his work in his own book. He proposes a perfectly regular and harmonic Basilica for Vicenza, one that nevertheless is *not* imposed on reality by demolishing the pre-existing medieval buildings on the site, as one might imagine a modern architect would normally do. When one visits Vicenza, if one is not aware of the care taken by the architect, one may easily suppose that the building built is exactly the one drawn – I certainly thought so when I first visited, having at the time not much more than cursory knowledge of Renaissance history. And yet this is not the case; Palladio did not raze the old buildings – literally frozen habits embodying the wisdom of the present culture – to build his ideal project. The ideal music is present, carefully embedded in the new and existing fabric, but not imposed; it qualifies everyday life to make it more temperate. The harmonic form has a transformative effect on the complex and contradictory functions that were housed by the building, at the very centre of the Renaissance city, including brothels, taverns, courts of law and ceremonial spaces for city governance.

The meaning of architecture as a cosmic analogy through musical proportions began to be questioned in the late seventeenth and eighteenth centuries, eventually weakening the possibilities of employing geometry as a transcendental symbol in architecture. Architects then began to focus on the importance of narrative language to preserve the communicative function of architecture. While still emphasizing the prominence of harmony as a goal, eighteenth-century character theory adopted a linguistic analogy, to take the place of the older mathematical one. A good example from the last part of the eighteenth century is the treatise by Nicolas Le Camus de Mezières, *The Genius of Architecture*.[13] Le Camus believes that harmony can be sought in the analogy between proportions and human sensations, yet it cannot be attained by theoretical prescription or mathematical ratios, only through expressive fictions, engaged through narratives. His book presents the earliest ever qualitative description of architectural 'space' in human dwelling; moods are characterized through literary language and metaphor, as they are deemed appropriate for the diverse rooms of a prototypical house, which are experienced in a crescendo reminiscent of erotic tension.

This development culminated in Romantic philosophy, in the formulation of *Stimmung* – the original German term for atmosphere and, more properly, attunement – as central to artistic expression. *Stimmung* describes both the effect and the knowledge art provide, far more crucial for our cultural sustainability than the partial, if precise, truths of instrumental science. Therefore, the work of art allows us to recognize ourselves as complete and purposeful, in order to abide in life. This is the aim of excellent architecture.

The etymological origins of *Stimmung* are important for understanding the potential of this concept in contemporary architectural and environmental design. Indeed, it is crucial to observe that – over and above its connotations as internal or subjective mood – *Stimmung's* philological roots include word families related to both *harmony* and *temperance*, the key terms in traditional architectural theories. Let me emphasize that there is no contradiction here. Romantic philosophy had recognized, like phenomenology and poets like Rainer-Maria Rilke did much later, that 'the inner is the outer': my joy or sadness is in fact the joy or sadness of the environment, dwelling in the atmosphere. Furthermore, *Stimmung* preserved its musical aspirations, while being formulated not through proportional or geometrical relationships, but through poetic language, in lyrical forms and novelistic narratives.

Significantly, the novel became, at the time, the central form of cultural expression, later to be adopted by almost all world cultures and rendered into movies and television: the telling of stories that deal with human issues, the true modern heir to a practical philosophy in the tradition of Aristotle, leading to *phronésis:* wisdom, articulating human, situated truths and enabling a good life. Grasping the primary importance of poetic language for artistic expression thus appears as a central issue to be explored in relation to the enactment of *Stimmung* in modernity after the nineteenth century, and up the contemporary era.[14]

To understand the full scope of *Stimmung* for contemporary design practices, it is also crucial to grasp the precedence of embodied *place* over geometric *space* throughout the long history of Western philosophy and architecture.[15] Architects never verbalized *concepts of space* – qualitative or geometrical – before the time of Le Camus. Surprising as it may seem today, it must be noted that space was never theorized as the so-called artistic material of architecture prior to the late nineteenth century. It had always been accepted that intersubjective cultural significance was present in architectural sites, constituting a fundamental dimension of the meaning that buildings might convey. There exist inveterate relations between place and narrative throughout history, and the manner in which architecture builds upon autochthonous meanings to generate its own frameworks for significant human action is instructive for the generation of attuned architecture. In other words: what characterizes *place* is, first and foremost, the cultural narratives related to topography, and *place* is primary in the manifestation of *being consciousness.* While scientific space, starting with Galileo, may have become our placement in a technological, universal world-village, autochthonous *places* abide in hiding. They are present, and it is the task of good architecture to bring them back to collective awareness. A fundamental dimension of architectural atmospheres is their capacity to unveil *place*.

Romantic *Stimmung* was aimed at the emotional heart: *Gemüt* was considered the true seat of consciousness. This mode of understanding is multi-sensory, *aesthetic* in the original Greek sense of the term; as real knowledge that is fundamentally sensory (αισθήσεις), not as an inferior kind of intellectual knowledge, such as defined by Baumgarten and followed by Kant in the eighteenth century. Such genuine aesthetic knowledge is primary, neither exclusively internal nor external; it is always situated, or as we might say today, distributed. It is at odds with the intellectual pure judgement of Descartes and subsequent science, presumed to be constructed by an emancipated subjectivity (the *ego cogitans*). The Romantic recovery of *aesthesis* made explicit the implicit, multi-sensory nature of artistic meaning at work in the Western tradition, which had been taken for granted in architecture before the popularization of Cartesian psychology in the late seventeenth century, with its belief – still unfortunately common today – in independent mechanistic senses; and in the hegemony of disembodied vision and its associationist explanations of meaning, as if it were a conceptual construction in the brain. The Romantics perception is, on the contrary, always meaningful, at its inception. The primacy of synaesthesia in perception intuited by Romantic philosophy was eventually clearly postulated by the phenomenological philosophers of the twentieth century – namely, Husserl and Merleau-Ponty – and has been recently buttressed by neuroscience and so-called third-generation *enactive* cognitive theory. This is the way that architectural meanings are first *given* to our embodied consciousness, of which, as I already suggested, 80 per cent is pre-reflective, and in continuity with reflective attention and judgement. It is in this way that architectural meaning is understood through phenomenology and that we can assert that architecture cannot be reduced to pictures, or merely 'objective' formal products. Atmosphere is given as a whole and, in a sense, at the very moment of one's physical, embodied and multi-sensory encounter with a place, as one *acts* framed by the architectural environment. A poetic image – the often-identified aesthetic effect of good architecture – is a second-order meaning, in continuity with the first.

For enactive cognitive theory and phenomenology, perception and consciousness are not passive, like digestion, or the impression of a photographic image; they are *always an action*. Only by unpacking this insight is it possible to grasp how architecture conveys its meanings both in the emotional immediacy of presence and as a cognition of order through the poetic image. Indeed, Edmund Husserl's phenomenological studies on the nature of temporality – today substantiated by neuroscience and biology, as explained in a recent book by Evan Thompson on the intertwining of mind and life – show how the present is not merely a non-existent point between past and future, but how, in our experience (as exemplified by our perception of music) the present has a thickness or dimension, with an immediate past and future, and a mediate history and project.[16] The present, therefore, can be said to have a structural and permanent dimensionality. Grasping the true nature of human temporality is important to understand how architecture as atmosphere can communicate both emotional and cognitive meaning, and not be reduced to some inconsequential or subjective orchestration of effects.

An attuned architecture for the future might therefore offer societies a place for existential orientation. This is its primary, perhaps its only, essential function. It allows us to feel – with our inner touch – complete and meaningful as we participate in action, and yet leaves open a space for wonderment and meditation, encompassing harmony and temperance, which includes ecological homeostasis. When successful, architecture allows for *participation* in meaningful actions, conveying to the participant an understanding of his or her place in the world. In other words, it opens up a clearing for the individual's experience of purpose through participation in cultural institutions. It is, however, not possible to paraphrase the order it conveys. It is radical orientation in *experience*, beyond words, and experiencing what appears as 'given' is analogous to the experience of beauty, in nature or in works of art. So while its theoretical roots may have shifted historically between mythic and poetic stories, philosophy, theology or science, architecture is none of these but is a spatiotemporal event (like music): its meaning is experienced through action in attuned atmospheres. As such, it is ephemeral, yet it has the capacity to change one's life in the vivid present. Thus, it can be said to embody knowledge, but rather than clear logic – it is aesthetic knowledge in the original Greek sense of the term as sensuous, emotional and multi-sensory, or even carnal, in the Biblical sense: a sexual experience of truth. For this reason, its 'meaning' can never be objectified, reduced to functions, ideological programmes, or formal or stylistic formulas. Likewise, its technical media are open rather than specific (like, say, building typologies), including all artefacts that enable human dwelling 'at the limits of language': a most important alternative once modernity co-opts most building to serve the aims of technology, fashion or consumerism.

Indeed, recognizing how attuned environments become a comprehensive alternative to merely ecological and sustainable cities reveals another surprising possibility: the potential contribution of the physical environment, beyond the conflicts of religious sectarianism, to furthering the spiritual dimensions of human existence, and to a genuine human brotherhood. Architecture, to be truly what it should be, must concern itself with psychosomatic health, with the spiritual (literally 'atmospheric') dimensions of life. In order to address life as lived, a life always and already possessed of sensorimotor skills afforded by the body and structured by cultures, architecture must create appropriate transformative atmospheres that both accommodate habit and bring about productive (poetic and ethical) change. This architectural power emulates that of the classical gods in the physical realm, already present in the meanings and uses of the Greek word *atmós*.

In ancient Greek, *atmós* doubled as both vapour and steam, and was sometimes associated with breath; it could be poisonous, like that of the Furies in Aeschylus' *Eumenides*, or beneficial, like the divine vapours emanating from the ground in Delphi that inspired the Oracle.[17] Tracing the roots of the term back to Sanskrit we find *Atman*, meaning 'inner self' (or soul – in a non-dualistic sense), the 'first principle' or true self of the individual before identification with phenomena. In Hinduism, in order to be liberated, the individual must realize that one's true self (*Atman*) is identical to the transcendent self. According to Plutarch, the *atmós* of moving water or foggy air is capable of bearing fleeting images – like the imagination of the inner self (or soul):[18] it can bear words like human breath. From Latin we inherit *spiritus* (breath), in words such as 'spirit' and 'spiritual'. In architecture, pre-reflective transformative atmospheres can indeed give place to reflective poetic images, completing architecture's cognitive and communicative, affective and intellectual function. This is, in essence, its spiritual function.

Notes

1 See Hubert Dreyfus and Sean D. Kelly, *All Things Shining: Reading the Western Classics to Find Meaning in a Secular Age* (New York: Free Press, 2011).

2 I examine the consequences of embodied and sited cognition for architectural meaning in my recent book, *Attunement: Architectural Meaning after the Crisis of Modern Science* (Cambridge, MA: MIT Press, 2016).

3 See Evan Thompson, *Mind in Life: Biology, Phenomenology and the Science of the Mind* (Cambridge, MA: Harvard University Press, 2010).

4 A growing number of philosophers and cognitive scientists espouse this view. See, for example, Alva Noë, *Action in Perception* (Cambridge, MA: MIT Press, 2004).

5 See Louise Barrett, *Beyond the Brain: How Body and Environment Shape Animal and Human Brains* (Princeton, NJ: Princeton University Press, 2011).

6 Merleau-Ponty's seminal thesis, *The Phenomenology of Perception*, in a recent new translation by Donald Landes (New York: Routledge, 2012), is a cornerstone of this position. See also Nick Crossley, *The Social Body: Habit, Identity and Desire* (London, UK: Sage, 2001).

7 This condition, which is even applicable more generally to account for biological evolution, has been beautifully captured by Antonio Machado, a remarkable Spanish poet of the so-called 'Generation of 1898' when he writes: 'Wanderer, there is no path, the path is made by walking…' Antonio Machado, 'Proverbios y Cantares XXIX', *Campos de Castilla* (Madrid, 1912).

8 See Antonio Damasio, *Descartes' Error* (Toronto, ON: Penguin Books, 2005); and *Looking for Spinoza: Joy, Sorrow, and the Feeling Brain* (Toronto, ON: Harcourt, 2003).

9 Alberto Pérez-Gómez, *Architecture and the Crisis of Modern Science* (Cambridge, MA: MIT Press, 1984).

10 A number of European philosophers, most importantly Gernot Böhme and Tonino Griffero, have tackled the issue of atmosphere as the subject of aesthetics. Their work is slowly being translated into English. See *Architecture and Atmosphere,* ed. Philip Tidwell (Helsinki: Peripheral Projects, 2015).

11 Vitruvius M. P., *Ten Books of Architecture* (Cambridge, UK: Cambridge University Press, 2001), see especially Book 1.

12 Andrea Palladio, *The Four Books of Architecture* (Cambridge, MA: MIT Press, 1997).

13 Nicolas Le Camus de Mezières, *The Genius of Architecture; or The Analogy of That Art with Our Sensations* (Los Angeles: Getty Center, 1992).

14 This topic, as well as other architectural references in this essay, is extensively developed in Pérez-Gómez, *Attunement.*

15 See Alberto Pérez-Gómez, 'Place and Architectural Space', in *Timely Meditations*, 2 vols (Montreal: RightAngle International, 2016), vol. 2, pp. 143–70.

16 Thompson, *Mind in Life*, p. 312 *f.*

17 See Aeschylus' *Eumenides*, line 138, and Pausanias, *Description of Greece*, 10.5.7. I am grateful to Dr Lisa Landrum from the University of Winnipeg for these references.

18 Available at http://www.perseus.tufts.edu/hopper/text?doc=Perseus:text:2008.01.0392:section=47&highlight=a%29tmoi%3Ds (accessed 1 January 2017).

References

Aeschylus, 'Eumenides', in *Aeschylus* 3 vol., trans. A. H. Sommerstein, Cambridge, MA: Harvard University Press, 2008 [458 BCE].

Barrett, L., *Beyond the Brain: How Body and Environment Shape Animal and Human Brains*, Princeton, NJ: Princeton University Press, 2011.

Crossley, N., *The Social Body: Habit, Identity and Desire*, London, UK: Sage, 2001.

Damasio, A., *Looking for Spinoza: Joy, Sorrow, and the Feeling Brain*, Toronto, ON: Harcourt, 2003.

Damasio, A., *Descartes' Error*, Toronto, ON: Penguin Books, 2005.

Dreyfus, H. and S.D. Kelly, *All Things Shining: Reading the Western Classics to find Meaning in a Secular Age*, New York: Free Press, 2011.

Le Camus de Mezières, N., *The Genius of Architecture; or The Analogy of That Art with Our Sensations*, Los Angeles: Getty Center, 1992.

Machado, M., 'Proverbios y Cantares XXIX', *Campos de Castilla*, Madrid, 1912.

Merleau-Ponty, M., *The Phenomenology of Perception*, trans. D. Landes, New York: Routledge, 2012.

Noë, A., *Action in Perception*, Cambridge, MA: MIT Press, 2004.

Palladio, A., *The Four Books of Architecture*, Cambridge, MA: MIT Press, 1997.

Pausanias, *Description of Greece*, trans. W. H. S. Jones, Cambridge, MA: Harvard University Press, 1969.

Pérez-Gómez, A., *Architecture and the Crisis of Modern Science*, Cambridge, MA: MIT Press, 1984.

Pérez-Gómez, A., *Attunement: Architectural Meaning after the Crisis of Modern Science*, Cambridge, MA: MIT Press, 2016.

Pérez-Gómez, A., 'Place and Architectural Space', in *Timely Meditations*, 2 vols., Montreal: RightAngle International, 2016.

Plutarch, *Plutarch's Morals*, trans. W. W. Goodwin, Cambridge: John Wilson and Son, 1874, http://www.perseus.tufts.edu/hopper/text?doc=Perseus:text:2008.01.0392:section=47&highlight=a%29tmoi%3Ds (accessed 01 January 2017).

Thompson, E., *Mind in Life: Biology, Phenomenology and the Science of the Mind*, Cambridge, MA: Harvard University Press, 2010.

Tidwell, P (ed.), *Architecture and Atmosphere*, Helsinki: Peripheral Projects, 2015.

Vitruvius, M. P., *Ten Books of Architecture*, Cambridge, UK: Cambridge University Press, 2001.

PART THREE

Extended minds and bodies

5

Embodying thought in skilful action

John Sutton, Doris McIlwain, Wayne Christensen and Andrew Geeves

Introduction

The baseball great Yogi Berra notoriously asked, 'Think? How can you hit and think at the same time?'[1] Because practitioners in many skilled movement domains know that self-conscious thought can disrupt well-practised actions, they like to entrust grooved action sequences to the body, to the habitual routines of kinaesthetic memory. But because they also know that open-ended, flexible performance is context-sensitive and, in the ideal, exquisitely responsive to subtle changes in a situation, they also want to bring all of their experience to bear in the moment, to bring memory and movement together, with thought and action cooperating instead of competing. An elite cricketer, for example, with less than half a second to execute an ambitious cover drive to a hard ball homing directly in at 140 kmh, draws not only on smoothly practised strokeplay but somehow also on experience of playing *this* fast bowler in *these* conditions, and on dynamically updated awareness of the current state of the match and of the opposition's deployments, to thread an elegant shot with extraordinary precision through a slim gap in the field.[2] It's fast enough to be a reflex, yet it is *perfectly* context-sensitive.

This kind of context-sensitivity, we suggest, requires some forms of mindedness. We are interested in the interpenetration of thought and action exemplified in such open skills, where salient features of the environment are tracked and accommodated in an ongoing manner. Dynamic skilful action is constantly embodying thinking, in unique worlds and contexts. In the improvisatory intelligence of experts in sport or music or dance, for example, the old mind-body problem comes to practical life, or is relocated in rich cognitive ecologies. The complex settings of such mindful thinking in the world incorporate technological, material, cultural, affective and collaborative resources, in shifting balances. An expert skier may monitor the freezing of the powder snow as the sun goes off the slope in a late evening run, accommodating the manner of turning to those subtle changes in conditions. Likewise, the apparently effortless way in which musicians together adapt their performance every night of a long tour reflects not just the direct or immediate drawing-forth of specific styles and forms of musical comportment by a unique constellation of audience and venue but also a much broader and temporally embedded set of contextual factors mediated by collaborative cognition. In different ways, our everyday habitual actions too retain comparable, genuine context-sensitivity when, for example, we are driving in changing conditions or cooking for a particular occasion. Even in more frequently repeated everyday behavioural sequences, like brushing our teeth or gathering together our keys and belongings before leaving home in the morning, we can remain more or less open and responsive to any peculiarities of today's unique constellation of moods and events.

Philosophers could take more account of the nature of intelligence in action by attending to the practices and conceptions of the specialist participants, teachers, critics and enthusiasts who devote vast portions of their lives to sport, dance, yoga, jazz, circus or other forms of embodied performance in what are often dynamic and affectively saturated environments, and who collectively develop their own peculiar ways of communicating, thinking and talking about their activities, often 'beyond the easy flow of everyday speech'.[3] These are often highly collaborative activities, more like stealing horses together than driving to work alone or playing chess against a single determined opponent. Understanding them requires us to draw critically on joint action research in the cognitive sciences.[4] Working phenomenologically but also in conjunction with students of sports psychology, choreographic cognition, ethnomusicology and the like, a richer applied philosophy of mind might tap key dimensions of variation on which distinctive skilled practices differ.[5] Likewise, with regard to more widely shared habits, phenomenologists, for example, could help forge new hybrid, experience-near approaches to everyday coping alongside theorists of material culture and cognitive ethnographers of habit.[6] In this chapter, we stick to the general theoretical landscape in examining broad views on how we influence ourselves.

I Habits and skills in phenomenology and embodied cognition

Philosophers of many different persuasions query Ryle's sharp distinction between habits and intelligent capacities, by which habits are single-track dispositions more akin to bare reflexes than to complex tendencies like skills.[7] As conceptions of agency expand further beyond the momentary, occurrent reasoner, we loosen the association between habit and rigid automaticity, and suggest that habits can be flexible and adaptive as well as idiosyncratic.[8] Habits are thus fruitfully seen, in certain contexts, as more like immersed embodied skills: in both cases, as explicit and conscious deliberation is set within a broader picture of the non-conscious and relational constitution and maintenance of agency, we can treat both mundane and unique, both expert and ordinary socially situated activities as among the central ways that we express, create and transform our selves.

In seeking to develop such a richer picture of both habits and skills, phenomenologists from Merleau-Ponty onwards have often sought a middle ground between rationalist or ultra-cognitivist intellectualism, on the one hand, and mechanistic forms of pure empiricism on the other. Although there are dramatic variations, too often neglected by philosophers, in individual style and across distinctive activities, embodied activities are neither in general the outcome of detailed prior internal planning and calculation, nor stereotyped and fossilized, mechanically invariant in every exercise. While there are genuine targets at each of these two extremes in contemporary philosophy and science, the alternatives are sometimes caricatured. We prefer to see the two poles as distinctive, if sparsely populated regions of a multidimensional space of possibilities: we query the standard historical narrative by which they are the twin legacies of Descartes' dualism (Section II), and more importantly argue that the spaces between have not been adequately described and explored in recent phenomenology. Roughly, our concern is that some attempted syntheses or resolutions of the putative Cartesian impasse about embodied action still overreact to the intellectualist prong of the alleged theoretical dilemma by taking habit and embodied skill out of the psychological realm entirely. We deny that any invocation of intelligence must be intrinsically intellectualist or rationalist, and argue that there is a rich, under-explored space between deliberative calculation and 'mindless' intuition.

Further, we worry that the forms of evidence brought to bear in discussions of habit and embodied skill by phenomenologists, analytic philosophers and cognitive scientists alike are often unnecessarily thin and abstract. It is not easy to understand the meaning and role of terms like 'minded' or 'mindful', let alone 'conceptual', in the debate between Hubert Dreyfus and

John McDowell.[9] Phenomenological and cognitive philosophers alike invoke embodied skills primarily as intuitively compelling examples. In explaining the nature of continuous reciprocal causation within coupled dynamical systems, Andy Clark writes:

> The players in a jazz trio, when improvising, are immersed in a web of causal complexity. Each member's playing is continually responsive to the others' and at the same time exerts its own modulatory force. Dancing, playing interactive sports, and even having a group conversation all sometimes exhibit this kind of mutually modulatory dynamics.[10]

Susan Hurley introduced her account of embodied human beings as dynamic singularities in the causal flow, 'characterized through time by a tangle of multiple feedback loops of varying orbits', by way of the following example:

> Consider the circus performer who puts the handle of a dagger in her mouth, tips her head back, balances a sword by its point on the point of the dagger, and with the whole kit balanced above her head magisterially climbs a ladder, swings her legs over the top rung, and climbs back down the other side of the ladder. Each move she makes is both the source of and exquisitely dependent on multiple, internal and external, channels of sensory and motor-signal feedback, the complex calibrations of which have been honed by years of practice.[11]

Clark and Hurley were in a sense recapitulating the Cambridge psychologist F.C. Bartlett's attempt in 1932, attending to social, cultural, bodily, affective and neural factors at once, to model all cognitive activity on skilled movement:

> Suppose I am making a stroke in a quick game, such as tennis or cricket ... when I make the stroke I do not, as a matter of fact, produce something absolutely new, and I never merely repeat something old. The stroke is literally manufactured out of the living visual and postural 'schemata' of the movement and their interrelations. I may say, I may think that I reproduce exactly a set of textbook movements, but demonstrably I do not; just as, under other circumstances, I may say and think that I reproduce exactly some isolated event which I want to remember, and again demonstrably I do not.[12]

Here the rich, context-sensitive variability of embodied activity characterizes remembering, thinking and decision-making too, with physiology by no means a source of rigidity.

Reference to such cases was still striking in the late 1990s, a necessary intervention before the '4E cognition' ('embodied, embedded, extended and enactive') movements had taken off, when an early writer in those movements could be ridiculed in a top philosophy journal for offering a definition of cognition on which 'it would seem that climbing the stairs in the dark is a cognitive process'.[13] But now, with the embodied and active nature of cognition accepted as a live research programme with many weaker and stronger variants in mainstream cognitive science, we can aim to supplement and build on such anecdotal evidence, seeking firmer and mutually informative links between philosophy and relevant applied fields of enquiry. Building on Bartlett, Clark and Hurley, theorists' attention could be directed to a wider array of the ordinary and extraordinary skills on show around us every day. Let us return to the apparent source of the twin bogeymen of dualism and mechanism.

II Reinterpreting the Cartesian cyborg

When Dreyfus suggests that 'mindedness is the enemy of embodied coping', McDowell charges him with 'a dualism of embodiment and mindedness that is reminiscent of Descartes': even though Dreyfus is not taking the body to be merely mechanical, by evacuating mindedness from 'egoless' absorbed activity, he too is engineering an 'awkward separation of me from my body'.[14] We suggest that mainstream Cartesian scholarship goes wrong precisely in ascribing to Descartes a fundamental dichotomy between true action and brute reflex automatism. In addition to the historical interest of this richer Cartesian account of how we influence ourselves as unified embodied beings, it also highlights the telling theoretical need for a more differentiated picture of the dimensions and varying characteristics of embodied responses. Some critics who defend a more exuberant and visceral form of contemporary materialism than was visible in mainstream cognitive philosophy until recently do so still by contrasting it with a deadening mechanism based on tight analogies between brain and machine.[15] But arguably, that form of mechanism is itself little more than a ghoul, and we need instead, as Catherine Malabou puts it, 'an approach to the machine that thinks of it not as a control centre but as an organ with multiple and adaptable structures – a future-producing organization, susceptible to an always-accruing functional differentiation'.[16] This shift is dramatically supported when we realize that the body depicted even in 'Cartesian mechanism', that dreich imposition of order on barren matter by which Descartes allegedly sought to bypass 'the concrete life of feeling',[17] is in fact itself a richly baroque system precisely structured on plasticity. In briefly summarizing here the case for such a reinterpretation, which the current first author has developed elsewhere, building on a swathe of revisionary Cartesian scholarship from the 1980s onwards by historians of the passions and of natural philosophy, we focus on the neurophilosophy of *L'homme,* the *Treatise of Man,* in which Descartes delineates in detail a vision of animal spirits roaming through the pores and traces of body and brain, which is entirely consistent with his scattered remarks elsewhere, through to *The Passions of the Soul,* on corporeal memory and the dynamics of embodied cognition.[18]

We can take as representative Owen Flanagan's account of the 'Cartesian automaton', restricted to reflex behaviour in its impoverished world, just because it is only body:

> The complete system of wired-in reflex arcs exhausts its behavioural potential. What a particular automaton does, how it in fact behaves, is the inevitable result of the interaction between the environment and the wired-in arcs. Such a system is deterministic in the sense that, barring mechanical failure, there is one and only one response for each stimulus.[19]

On this standard interpretation, this is why Cartesian natural philosophy could exclude the contingencies of individual experience: the point of Descartes' fables of automata is to demonstrate that only initial wiring and the immediate environmental input drive the (body-) machinery. For Timothy Reiss, these automata are 'endlessly repeatable, and by definition not particular, not the subjects of a specific history'.[20] In the case of a human being, who has an incorporeal soul conjoined to the body-machine, flexibility and genuine action arise solely through the mediation of the rational soul.

But this is a mistaken interpretation of the functioning of a Cartesian 'automaton', which Descartes clearly and consistently describes as capable of (corporeal but entirely genuine) learning. There's no reason to accept that hardwiring or biology, on the one hand, and current stimuli, on the other, must be the sole determinants of machine behaviour. The example of memory, discussed at length in *L'homme* and rehearsed again in *The Passions of the Soul,* makes this easy to see. Figures transmitted by or in the incessant motions of animal spirits or nervous fluids are 'imprinted in the internal part of the brain, which is the seat of Memory'.[21] This is achieved through bending or rearranging brain filaments so as to alter the intervals between pores through which the spirits will flow in future. The spirits 'trace figures in these gaps': with stronger or more frequent patterns of input, more enduring changes are made in the pores, so that the figures can be more easily formed again, in the absence of the specific stimulus.[22] The pattern of the pores, which constrains the patterned flow of spirits, is itself altered over time by the differing motions of the spirits. These patterned motions are not themselves stored, but are merely 'retained in such a way that' previous figures can be recreated. Even if a particular input is only partially represented, recognition may still occur if the connected pores have been disposed so as to open together more easily.[23]

So as Hall notes, for Descartes, 'memory traces ... consist in residual patterns of openness among the interstices of the filamentous brain substance'.[24] Only physical factors need be involved in reconstruction: the soul may play a part, when united to the machine, but it is not necessary for memory operation. It 'usually happens', according to Descartes, that 'several different figures are traced in the same region of the brain'; thus, 'the spirits will acquire a combined impression of them all'.[25] So memories are motions, rather than separate atomic items, and representation in memory does not operate by resemblance. Every trace in a brain region affects any episode of processing, so every memory is composite, just as every sensation dangerously carries the perceptual history of the perceiver. This is how 'chimeras and hypogryphs are formed in the imaginations of those who daydream', who neglect the twin direction offered by external objects and by reason.[26] The basic mechanisms of memory, therefore, are mechanisms of creation and effacement simultaneously, as the history-dependent processes by which the nervous spirits restructure the pores of the brain constantly involve both the annihilation of certain prior patterns and possibilities, and the upsurge of new ones.[27]

So in the memory processes of the Cartesian automaton, the effects of experience are transmitted over long temporal gaps, and are causally involved in behaviour mediated by complex internal processes. The determinism involved is not a simple stimulus/response link, for the corporeal causes act holistically. To put it another way, the case of memory shows that an automaton's physiology changes over time. Automata with different histories, different 'experiences' marking their brains and bodies, will (*contra* Flanagan) respond differently, and one automaton will respond differently to the same stimulus at different times after a new experience has modified the pores and folds of its brain. So if 'automatic' just *means* 'responding identically to the same stimulus', then these Cartesian machines (which, after all, operate as they do because of the disposition of their *living* organs) are not automata. Genuine (unconditioned) reflexes like sneezing, blinking and withdrawing the foot from the fire are the exceptions, *not* the model for all action produced without the soul. There are even distinct neural bases suggested in Descartes' fantastical neurophilosophy. Despite persistent misinterpretation of the famous image of a boy's reflex withdrawal from the fire in the first French edition of *L'homme,* the pineal gland is *not* involved in genuine, basic reflexes, whereas it *does* mediate equally corporeal but complex and adaptive responses.[28]

Because Descartes' physiology is explicitly modelled on fluid dynamics, the internal operations of the permeable, fluid-filled body in his natural philosophy are in ceaseless, circulatory, holistic exchange with the fluid-filled cosmos.[29] The passions are linked by 'nature or habit' with particular movements of animal spirits and fluids in the body and the brain. Those connections set by 'institutions of nature', which are initially set by our temperament and nature but are sometimes still alterable, are sometimes seen as the main threat to the good life.[30] On this understanding of Cartesian ethics, Descartes 'offers the hope that by careful training, and the resolute exercise of our will, we can become not the slaves but the masters of our biological inheritance'.[31]

This gives the impression that Descartes took the enemy, in moral life, to be the fixity of biology, the rigidity of the machine's programming, which it is the task of the will to overcome. But in fact, the institutions of nature don't reach all that deeply: by themselves they are neither the main problem, nor the major hope. What Descartes sees as the problem is not fixity, but our tendency to uncontrolled plasticity. Not nature, but *habitude* is the moral key. The term covers various kinds of *variable* connections between bodily motions and thoughts or passions. Habits are grounded in dispositions, which in turn are grounded in the complex dynamical arrangements of physical parts.[32] *Habitude* reaches further beyond the individual than does the English 'habit'. All the teachings of childhood are sedimented in associations, the route by which culture intrudes into the soul. Descartes thus has a physiological basis for his concern about our pre-reflective views of the world. He does not hold the intellectualist view that everything implicit in our forms of life must be explicitly encoded in the brain. This would require the equally implausible separate rooting out and challenging of each and every belief.[33] Memories do not have to be stored independently or discretely to be causally active: there are no independent storage boxes which can be either full or empty – only the sets of folding pores in the net of the brain. Our bodies thus hold cultural forms of life not as quasi-theoretical axioms but as nested sets of causal tendencies, realized differently in each brain and body. Descartes' psychophysiology makes quite incoherent the kind of total epistemological re-evaluation and wholesale destruction of false beliefs that mainstream interpretations attribute to him. We should reject these interpretations, and acknowledge instead that Descartes accepts the inevitability of working with our pre-reflective cognitive equilibrium, while seeking also to home in on the more damaging of the inconsistencies and anomalies, accretions of the (social and individual) past, which we have internalized.

Understanding the passions then, for Descartes, is not the simple reprogramming of a rigid body-machine by an authoritative but entirely external soul.[34] Rather, it requires *industrie* – artifice, or (psychological) work – the laborious and interminable acquisition of knowledge of our own *habitudes* and their dispositional bases. Moral life is not based on the old dualist diatribe against the body, but consists, in part, in the knowing use of habit and association in body and brain, inhabiting them more fully as we slowly apply intelligence to the reflexes and (fallibly, interminably) re-colonize the body.[35] Standard Cartesian scholarship, scarred by the inability to think outside a dichotomy between self-conscious rational thought and mere reflex, wrongly relegates all ordinary corporeal cognition to the agent's exterior, whereas in fact Descartes saw the unique history of each embodied organic creature as grounding a much wider array of flexible responses and activities than just those mediated directly by reason.[36]

This reinterpretation of Cartesian accounts of memory and the body unsettles, both historically and conceptually, the very idea of reducing complex embodied action to mere reflex, so much so that that reduction need no longer retain its grip as the historical shadow against which phenomenological philosophy defines itself. The plasticity in play at the heart of this paradigmatic version of mechanism confirms the non-repeatable 'eventlike dimension of the mechanical'.[37] As we return to consideration of skilful action, we can see that a multiplicity of parameters inevitably influence the respective contributions of sedimented history and present input: the degree of openness of the skill, the rate and familiarity of change of the current environment, the risk/benefit trade-off of improvisation, and whether it is one person interacting with a quiescent environment or also co-acting with others in a changing world, as in stealing horses together. In refusing the separation of embodied activity from psychology, we need to develop a feel for the shapes and complexities of this multidimensional space where the parameters are yet to be fully discovered.

III Habit and skill without psychology: Overreacting to intellectualism

We suggest that some phenomenological accounts of embodied activity are built on overreactions to ultra-cognitivist intellectualist or rationalist theories. Intellectualist views in the psychology of expert systems or in classical motor control theory have two broad characteristics or commitments: action involves the application of explicit rules, and the agent builds up and draws directly on a rich and relatively stable domain-specific knowledge base composed of causally active explicit representations. In some versions, this process might be consciously accessible, whereas on other views, access to that expert knowledge has been wholly proceduralized. These views, which have been effectively and persuasively criticized by Dreyfus and others, are not our targets here.[38] We note, as has Dreyfus, that fast and rapidly changing dynamic domains like open-skill sports or improvisatory jazz make intellectualist approaches particularly hard to credit. There is no complete specification of the task domain available to be internalized, and even if there was, it couldn't be searched and applied in time: with little more than half a second to react before the cricket ball reaches you, how could you think first, then act?

Any intellectualist requirement of a deliberate, pre-planned, explicit blueprint which is merely executed in the expression of embodied action would, we agree, impose an overly static psychology on actions which are often sculpted on the fly, to the needs of the moment and on the basis of a dynamic implicit repertoire of tendencies and potential responses. Our concern is not with the phenomenological critique of ultra-cognitivism, but with the constructive alternatives available. In particular, we think it unhelpful to discard psychology entirely in the process of discarding an overly static psychology. It is too simple just to decentre conscious, effortful, controlled responses in favour of intuitive, attuned, flowing responses, because this merely reverses the values of an unnecessarily dichotomous scheme. We address first habit, then skill and absorbed coping.

Bill Pollard argues that habits are central to agency: identifying someone's action as habitual can, in certain circumstances, be an effective explanation of that action, locating it 'in one pattern in the agent's career'. Compared to compulsions and addictions, habitual actions are more open to simultaneous, online influence: even though they do not require 'any preceding deliberation', they are still unlike mere reflexes in that the agent retains some direct power to intervene and control.[39] But Pollard thinks that this link between habit and agency requires a severing of the link between habit and psychology, where he treats 'psychology' as the realm of beliefs, desires, intentions and reasons, and as requiring 'that the agent has some privileged perspective on her own psychological condition'. Given these assumptions about psychology, he recommends placing it at the margins of the philosophy of action, and he invokes much the same line of thought as Yogi Berra or Dreyfus:

> For whilst thought is very helpful when we are in novel or important circumstances, the rest of the time it rather gets in the way. In a slogan we might say: we only think when our habits give out.[40]

So Pollard is assuming that when habits are in play, there is no thinking. We query this background assumption that thought is or requires 'preceding deliberation', and the corresponding sharp line between psychology and embodied action. In contrast, we agree with Brett and Sheets-Johnstone that even in the most habitual activities – brushing teeth, washing hands and weaving through a crowd – we often retain significant levels of care, attention and kinetic awareness. Even if the initiation of the habitual action is now outside our sphere of attention, the exercise of many habits intrinsically involves certain kinds of monitoring. No matter how effectively we have grooved and routinized our expertise as drivers or ball-players, as Brett points out, 'the habit of paying attention to the road is one of the necessary ingredients in being a good driver, just as the habit of keeping one's eye on the ball is essential to being a good ball-player': there is, therefore, in habitual action no inevitable lack of care or attention.[41] Likewise, Sheets-Johnstone cautions that

> When Luria speaks of the *automatization* of movement, it is important to point out that he is describing the way in which a single impulse is sufficient to activate a kinetic melody, and not asserting that one is unaware of writing one's name, that one is unconscious of doing so, or that one can nod off while the process continues by itself.[42]

So it's an unnecessary constriction on the dynamics of thought to assume that what's done from force of habit must be done without thinking: as Brett argues, a 'continuum of cases' will range from more channelled and stereotyped responses to nearly identical situations, 'to those in which attentiveness and variation are an essential part'.[43] As well as offering a more complex picture of habitual actions, this perspective also points to a common framework for habits and skills, in which different cases may vary on a range of distinctive dimensions.

Turning then to skill, we can pick out features of the work of Dreyfus, Elizabeth Ennen and Michael Wheeler as exhibiting related overreactions to intellectualism.[44] Our concern, again, is that these theorists tend to evacuate psychology entirely from action, running the risk of thus neglecting the complex interplay between embodied dynamical factors and cognitive factors. In finding 'no place' for mindfulness in 'the phenomenology of fully absorbed coping', Dreyfus retains and underlines a fundamental dichotomy between what he elsewhere calls 'two distinct kinds of intentional behaviour: deliberative, planned action, and spontaneous, transparent coping'.[45] This spontaneous, attuned responsiveness or intuitive coping is entirely dominant at high levels of expertise, whether in sport, chess, nursing or driving. At the highest stage in the 'Dreyfus model' of skill acquisition, action management and decision-making do not even appear as problems for the expert practitioner. As a result of a long history of engagement with a complex domain, 'an immense library of distinguishable situations is built up on the basis of experience', allowing fresh 'experience-based holistic recognition of similarity' in the present.[46] When emotionally engaged and immersively achieving a maximal grip on a complex situation, context-sensitivity is simply built in as part of an ongoing activity:

> With enough experience in a variety of situations, all seen from the same perspective but requiring different tactical decisions, the brain of the

> expert gradually decomposes this class of situations into subclasses, each of which requires a specific response. This allows the immediate intuitive situational response that is characteristic of expertise.[47]

Practical experience is thus immeasurably more valuable than mere factual knowledge of a domain. Aligning themselves with the scorn for critics exhibited by practitioners in some domains of embodied expertise, Dreyfus and colleagues forcefully and negatively compare professional political commentators to 'articulate chess kibitzers, who have an opinion on every move, and an array of principles to invoke, but who have not committed themselves to the stress and risks of tournament chess and so have no expertise'.[48] Only when one is involved, and gets a lot of practice, will the body take over and do the rest.[49] There is then neither thinking nor awareness, neither attention nor choice: at this level of fluid performance, 'an expert's skill has become so much a part of him that he need be no more aware of it than he is of his own body'.[50] On this account then there is no interplay of automatic and controlled factors when all is going well in an expert's attuned embodied activity, no dynamic interaction of cognition and reaction or of strategy and skill.

In an impressive extension of Dreyfus's phenomenology, Elizabeth Ennen maps this picture of absorbed skilful coping on to a neuroscientific account of skill memory, under which label she addresses habit memory and sequence memory. The non-conscious fluidity of expert activity, Ennen argues, is grounded in the 'non-representational mechanisms of the striatal system', involving in particular highly context-dependent and non-transferable dispositions to respond readily in complex but specific ways.[51] Such 'smooth and unobtrusive responsiveness to circumstances' does not require any conscious or online knitting together of distinct stored items, because that work has already been done in the course of experience: perceptual-motor chunks 'lose their individual identities and become, in a sense, inaccessible', and thus 'not de-coupleable from their sources'.[52] For these reasons, responses based on skill memory are fast and fluid, quite unlike slow, conscious decision-making processes which draw explicitly on declarative knowledge. Once a sequence has been successfully proceduralized, its activation is non-conscious, involving no awareness, attention, anticipation, accessibility or articulability. For Ennen, this account vindicates Dreyfus's phenomenology of 'mindless' everyday coping skills.[53]

Although phenomenological views like these have many subtleties and complications, on these central points, the picture is clear and in firm agreement with a range of views elsewhere in the philosophy of mind. Despite their other differences, for example, Dreyfus and Searle agree broadly that as skill develops, the verbalizable rules on which novices rely are not wired-in, internalized or memorized; instead, 'repeated practice enables the body to take over'.[54] Likewise, Fred Dretske argues that 'in the case of all skilled actions, whether it be tying your shoelaces, playing a musical instrument or dribbling a basketball – the mind goes elsewhere while the body performs'.[55]

Despite their many differing views on other matters, we suggest that all these philosophers successfully avoid ultra-cognitivist intellectualism in the theory of skilful embodied action only at the cost of entrenching the core intellectualist (and pseudo-Cartesian) dichotomy, even if reversing the values attached to its twin poles. If the intellectualist privileges slow, controlled, effortful planning, and sees cognitively permeable, verbalizable conscious thought as the root of skilful action, the anti-intellectualist overreaction is to privilege fast, effortless, intuitive and entirely non-cognitive responses which are merely the flip side of the same dichotomy.[56] Such privileging of intuition is both culturally and intuitively appealing, as attested by the popularity of Gladwell's theory of 'thin-slicing', by which we unconsciously find the right patterns in situations faster and more effectively than we would by conscious and deliberate thinking.[57] The pressure to see mindfulness or mindedness as the enemy of embodied coping is also powerful in practitioners' lore in sport, music and dance. Top sportspeople say that 'when you're playing well you don't think about *anything*', and one leading sports psychologist recommends that 'you absorb yourself in the moment', while musicians typically downplay knowledge and conceptual memory, wanting to entrust performance to the hands or to motor processes.[58] Introspection and reflection are sometimes viewed with suspicion, as potentially disruptive influences, and it is not a compliment to say that someone talks a good game.

In addition to the dynamical neuroscience on which Dreyfus occasionally draws, there is also empirical research in these applied domains that could be put to service in the attack on mindedness, of which we mention just one example here in lieu of fuller discussions on other occasions.[59] Visual neuroscientists have discovered that elite players in a high-speed ball sport like cricket actually look *away* from the ball (to the predicted bounce point on the pitch) significantly earlier than novices.[60] It might appear then that the entrenched verbal maxim 'watch the ball' is, as Dreyfus might put it, a mere training wheel, an awkward linguistic residue of early practice, a beginner's tag which is now severed from the expert's intuitive responses, or a semantic intrusion which the engaged body no longer needs.[61]

Before sketching an alternative interpretation of some of these lines of thought and evidence, we note finally the impressive synthesis of phenomenology and cognitive science developed in the recent work of Michael Wheeler. Fusing Heidegger and embodied, embedded cognitive science in the quest for 'a land beyond Cartesianism', Wheeler offers the most sophisticated account yet of absorbed coping without mindedness, in which personal and sub-personal levels of description are mutually constraining.[62] We are 'thrown machines', always already embedded in a context, and we don't have reflectively to match a representation of our current situation against a library of stored, context-free representations. Instead, smooth practical activity, whether in habitual behaviour or embodied skill, is our basic mode of interaction. When equipment 'becomes a *transparent* feature of the human agent's phenomenal world', the agent 'has no self-referential awareness of herself as a subject over and against a world of objects': there is no need to *recognize* the doorknob as a doorknob as it turns. But Wheeler's treatment of hitch-free coping stresses two points which are not always highlighted by Dreyfus. First, there is still 'a form of awareness' in play, which Wheeler explains on the basis of Heidegger's 'circumspection' as an action-oriented form of embodied knowledge of how to use equipment in accordance with normatively constrained public practices.[63] The neural mechanisms underpinning this kind of smooth coping, Wheeler argues, are likely to exhibit 'extreme nontrivial causal spread', rather than any localizable or repeatable programme driving the motor processes. In sport, for example, Wheeler therefore suggests that 'the neural contribution may be more a matter of nudges and triggers than specification and control, with the real intelligence residing in bodily (e.g. muscular) adaptations and dynamics'.[64] Second, Wheeler acknowledges the diversity and online complexity of practical activity, following Heidegger in noting a number of ways in which smooth coping can be disturbed as equipment breaks, malfunctions or gets in the way, and when the agent must take a step away from absorbed circumspection, for example, 'by calling a temporary halt to her activity, and by engaging, instead, in practical thinking'.[65]

So Wheeler does see fluid, adaptive embodied cognition as a form of online intelligence, and also rightly encourages us to examine a spectrum of subtly different intermediate cases between absorbed coping and entirely detached theoretical reflection, in which the '*pure* circumspective know-how' characteristic of entirely hitch-free coping might actually be 'somewhat rare'.[66] Yet he still paints 'thinking' as something that happens only in breakdown, and not when the expert is simply adjusting to minor variations in dynamic task constraints. This point lies at the heart of the diverse views we have canvassed in this section, which for all their differences in method and emphasis converge on a rejection of all forms of 'mindedness' within both habitual and skilful embodied coping. Although they start from a plausible rejection of the idea that action is driven by explicit rules or inner blueprints accessed by way of conscious reflective deliberation, both philosophers and scientists go too far in the other direction by treating expertise as *entirely* intuitive, the sole product (as Dreyfus put it) of 'attractive and repulsive forces drawing appropriate activity out of an active body'. Thus in taking embodied activity right out of the psychological realm, these theories paradoxically reinforce dichotomies between doing and knowing, or acting and thinking, which we might have hoped to overcome.

IV Habit and skill in expanded psychologies: Applying intelligence to the reflexes

If we want to bring embodied skills within the realm of an enriched and expanded psychology, and to suggest that the body which takes over in engaged practice might itself be minded, we need to respond to applied, empirical and phenomenological concerns alike. We start with the case of verbal maxims or cue words like 'watch the ball', or tags for improvisational jazz pianists such as 'sing while you're playing' or 'jazz hands'.[67] In both cases, it does seem that such linguistic tags and nudges are not used only by beginners, as Dreyfus might expect. The most experienced elite cricketer in our pilot series of interviews told us 'I personally say "watch the ball, play straight", before every single ball that's bowled': this isn't simply a preparatory tactic in the quiescent peacetime between periods of online activity, because 'I usually say that just as the bowler's heading up into his delivery stride. So that's at the point of delivery'.[68] It's true that 'watch the ball' is not an instruction sent from a detached mind to an obedient body, the top-down (re-)programming of the body-machine. The function of the verbal maxim is not exhausted (perhaps even no longer significantly affected) by its semantic content; rather, it operates in real time as a *material* symbol, an iterated and interactive self-stimulatory loop.[69] The role of 'instructional nudges' like 'watch the ball' or 'jazz hands', as Wheeler suggested, need not be precise control of the microstructure of action; yet the expert performer is using these verbal components of multimodal embodied routines to distribute intelligence, coordinating or often resetting and re-chunking patterns of movement or affect or mood, as one among many forms of scaffolding that support the embodied rebuilding of action sequences from the inside. The mind does not only intrude during offline strategic rehearsal or at moments of breakdown. Rather, thought, talk or memory can interact with practised embodied skill at a range of timescales, both in real time at the height of performance and in temporally complex feedback loops.

This line of thought, we submit, should not be surprising. Where Dreyfus pictures the context-sensitivity of expert performance as having all been set up in advance, the simple drawing forth of the appropriate option from the experienced and attuned body, we argue that genuine expertise often requires the rapid switching of modes and styles *within* the performance context. Grooved embodied action must thus be open, under certain circumstances, to the influence of explicit knowledge, specific memories, or particular decisions. Admittedly, these influences cannot operate simply as top-down triggers of fully structured motor programmes; rather, expertise is in part the training up of the right indirect links *between* thought and action, not the evacuation of thought from action.[70] We don't need to *oppose* mindfulness to 'attractive and repulsive forces', for mindfulness is itself a complex and dynamic field of embodied forces.

In a series of papers which combine internal critique within phenomenology with the development of a new constructive approach to embodiment, Elizabeth Behnke offers a very different picture of the complexity of kinaesthetic awareness. Phenomenologists, she argues, have too often exclusively and damagingly concentrated only on the alienating and disruptive roles of attention and thought. Where Dreyfus, in seeking to overcome the twin evils of intellectualism and mechanism, sees the expert as equally unaware of his skill and of his body, Behnke complains that 'in attempting to save the Body from being regarded as a mere thing or object that is other than "me", existential phenomenology tends to emphasize the completely tacit, anonymous, pre-reflective Body, and even to privilege a state in which we do not feel or notice our own Body "in the act" at all'. Although, as Behnke notes, there are also more positive and detailed accounts available of 'the experientially absent Body in its intertwining with its environment', her characterization here does fit the views of Dreyfus and others which we discussed in the previous section. We concur with her diagnosis that thus 'not sensing one's Body', as the Dreyfusian expert does not, 'is cause for concern', a potentially damaging form of 'sensory-motor amnesia'. Behnke acknowledges that becoming aware of my own *body* may sometimes bring 'alienation and rupture', as those hostile to mindedness point out: but this is not inevitable, for 'there are also ways to feel myself Bodily from within, in lucid awareness, without necessarily making my own Body into a separate object over and against "me"'. [71]

In both habitual action and skilled movement, on this alternative perspective, neither attention nor awareness is the enemy of embodied coping. Kinaesthetic awareness is indeed fully experiential, and many skilled practitioners in embodied disciplines actively cultivate 'the very event of undergoing sensuous affection in a thoroughly bodily way, directly sensing this undergoing itself as a streaming moment of subjective bodily life'.[72] Here, somatic education and re-education is entirely within the realm of an expanded psychology, as by way of somatic *perception* we can inhabit movements from within, exploring nuances of bodily possibilities that are otherwise often simply taken for granted.[73] The kind of awareness and subjectivity at stake here is clearly not solipsistic or intellectualist, for it is always actually or potentially dispersed and shared across an uneven world of equipment and other bodies rather than hidden in some unified private realm; sometimes, when in the company of others, for example,

> In experiencing shared movement kinaesthetically … I am neither walled off from the other nor kept at a spectator's distance; rather, I participate from within, whether I am caught up in an ongoing movement, or resist it, or initiate a new move in which another mover is caught up, and so on. Thus kinaesthetic awareness permits an encounter with alterity in which kinaesthetic autonomy and interkinaesthetic connectivity coexist.[74]

In her extraordinary essay 'Ghost Gestures: Phenomenological Investigations of Bodily Micromovements and their Intercorporeal Implications', Behnke catalogues a diversity of the 'ongoing kinaesthetic patterns and processes' of everyday life 'not as observed from the outside, but as experienced from within'.[75] At different timescales, 'ghost gestures' are tendencies towards movement, schematic or barely perceptible ghostly micromovements that can persist in the body even when the implied or virtual larger-scale gesture or bodily pattern is not actually performed. I still feel the movements of digging in the garden today, or on a longer scale my movement styles hold traces of specific historical patterns of comportment due to long-vanished material constraints, cultural expectations or moral norms. For our current purposes, the significance of such 'ghost gestures as one example of bodily "sedimentation" as the effective presence of the past' lies in Behnke's account of the ways in which we can reactivate this sediment and retrieve the tacit choreography of everyday life. Although ghost gestures are usually an 'inadvertent isometrics', in that they are both unplanned and not sensed, by coming to notice them or bringing them to awareness, I can come, more or less successfully, to inhabit them, rather than letting that sediment simply play out anonymously within me. Awareness plays a key role here in the attempt to open up or counter sensory-motor amnesia, as in certain yoga traditions with approaches to embodiment quite different from sport or Western dance. Not only specific movement patterns, but also silent zones and signature patterns of tension may be for the first time accessed or matched, less as passive parts of a static body that is 'mine' than as ongoing kinaesthetic acts.

In such sedimented bodily patterns, as well as in the recalcitrance of things, the competitiveness of opponents, and the general opacity of the world, we see further limits to smooth embodied coping. But perhaps awareness and attention play useful roles only in such situations when the habitual or expert performer meets with resistances or disruption, or finds unexpected constraints on previously hitch-free practices. The enemy of mindfulness might retreat to such a position, agreeing that thought can play a variety of important roles not in performance but in practice, when the practitioner has time to employ it, either under the pressure of trouble or the luxury of peacetime. But such a theorist might then hold firm to their central claim that active, smooth online coping in real time does not and should not itself involve any psychological processes. At the right time, the idea would run, apprenticeship must end, and the body must take over, leaving thought entirely out of the picture.

Again, we disagree with this understanding of the nature and role of mindedness and thought in embodied action. Skill is not a matter of bypassing explicit thought, to let habitual or grooved actions run entirely on their own, but of building and accessing flexible links between knowing and doing. The forms of thinking and remembering which can, in some circumstances, reach in to animate the subtle kinaesthetic mechanisms of skilled performance must themselves be re-described as active and dynamic. Thought, again, is not an inner realm *behind* practical skill, but an intrinsic and worldly aspect of our real-time engagement in complex physical and cultural activities.

In many distinctive domains, elite practitioners specifically resist the kind of automation which Dreyfus ascribes to the highest levels of expertise, worrying that trusting the body alone to take over will lead to arrested development. Just as they challenge themselves constantly and deliberately in practice, they know that in performance they will be constantly opened up to new limits. As Rietveld argues, 'every situation contains perturbing influences', with new affective influences always potentially altering our evaluations of significance.[76] So expert performers precisely 'counteract automaticity' because it limits their ability to make specific adjustments on the fly.[77] We agree with Jack Reynolds that because experts must avoid 'ignoring and downplaying all that is surprising and traumatic', they remain open to the ongoing trauma of learning so as always to be able to mobilize their capacities afresh in a previously unanticipated 'world of radically differentiated possibilities'.[78] Again, the knowledge which is thus accessed in action need not be – indeed, cannot be – a stable stock of discrete items because it emerges in real time, and often collaboratively, in the interaction between brain, body and (both social and physical) world. But, again, just because skilful action is usually pre-reflective, it does not have to be mindless. Once we cut the instinctive links many philosophers make between thought and conscious rational deliberation, we remember that a sinuous and sensuous intelligence can indeed animate the skilful body.

By the notion of 'applying intelligence to the reflexes', then, we mean that certain patterns of behaviour which might appear stably chunked, automated and thus inflexible are in skilled performance already and continually open to current contingency and mood, past meanings and changing goals. Experts have opened their 'reflexes' up into acquired adaptive patterns, and constructed over time not a set array of clever moves, but dynamic repertoires of potential action sequences, which can be accessed, redeployed and transformed appropriately. This process can be enacted at different timescales, and it can be undertaken either deliberately, with the opening up of habits as an end in itself as in yoga, or when innovative choreographers seek to put 'the implicit properties of the motor system … under conscious control',[79] or, as in competitive sports, it can flow into action from skilled coaching or arduous effort in the service of other ends. There are many different ways in which embodied coping is minded or mindful in ways like these, varying dramatically across individuals, task domains and cultures. We recommend the search for forms of mid-level, experience-near theorizing, which highlight such differences by focusing on what actually happens to practitioners as they direct attention to kinaesthetic cues in increasingly skilful ways.

Acknowledgements

This is a revised version of a paper previously published as 'Applying Intelligence to the Reflexes: Embodied Skills and Habits between Dreyfus and Descartes' in the *Journal of the British Society for Phenomenology 42* (1), 2011, 78–103. Ed Cooke, Greg Downey, Beth Preston and Kate Stevens have each contributed greatly to our thinking on these topics, and influenced our take substantially. Earlier versions of parts of this material were presented at seminars at Monash University, Macquarie University and Lewis and Clark College, to the annual conference of the Australasian Association of Philosophy, and to the Skill Acquisition Research Group at the Australian Institute of Sport. We're grateful to our audiences on those occasions for many helpful suggestions.

Notes

1 Sian L. Beilock, Sarah A. Wierenga and Thomas H. Carr, 'Expertise, Attention, and Memory in Sensorimotor Skill Execution', *Quarterly Journal of Experimental Psychology 55* (2002), 1211–40, p. 1236.

2 Sean Müller and Bruce Abernethy, 'Skill Learning from an Expertise Perspective: Issues and Implications for Practice and Coaching in Cricket', in *The Sport Psychologist's Handbook*, ed. J. Dosil (Chichester: John Wiley, 2006), pp. 245–61; John Sutton, 'Batting, Habit, and Memory: The Embodied Mind and the Nature of Skill', *Sport in Society* 10 (2007), pp. 763–86.

3 Maxine Sheets-Johnstone, 'What Are We Naming?', in *The Corporeal Turn: An Interdisciplinary Reader* (Exeter: Imprint Academic, 2009), pp. 328–49, p. 336 [first published 2005]. For effective critique of the thin and overly metaphorical conceptions of 'embodiment' in recent 'enactivist' philosophy of cognitive science, see also Sheets-Johnstone, 'Animation: The Fundamental, Essential, and Properly Descriptive Concept', *Continental Philosophy Review* 42 (2009), pp. 375–400. While cultural stereotypes often depict the sportsperson or rock musician as inarticulate, both verbal and multimodal communication between expert practitioners can of course be much richer than either journalists or researchers can easily access. See also Sheets-Johnstone, 'On the Challenge of Languaging Experience', in *The Corporeal Turn*, pp. 362–81.

4 Natalie Sebanz, Harold Bekkering, and Günther Knoblich, 'Joint Action: Bodies and Minds Moving Together', *Trends in Cognitive Sciences* 10 (2006), pp. 70–6; Bruno Galantucci and Natalie Sebanz, 'Joint Action: Current Perspectives', *Topics in Cognitive Science* 1 (2009), pp. 255–9; R. Keith Sawyer, *Group Creativity: Music, Theatre, Collaboration* (Philadelphia, PA: Psychology Press, 2003).

5 On dance, Catherine Stevens et al., 'Choreographic Cognition: The Time-Course and Phenomenology of Creating a Dance', *Pragmatics and Cognition* 11 (2003), pp. 299–329, and David Kirsh, 'Thinking with the Body', *Proceedings of the 32nd Annual Meeting of the Cognitive Science Society* (2010), http://adrenaline.ucsd.edu/kirsh/articles/interaction/thinkingwithbody.pdf (accessed 6 November 2010); on music, Paul F. Berliner, *Thinking in Jazz: The Infinite Art of Improvisation* (Chicago: University of Chicago Press, 1994); Ingrid Monson, *Saying Something: Jazz Improvisation As Interaction* (Chicago: University of Chicago Press, 1996); Andrew Geeves, Doris J. F. McIlwain, John Sutton, and Wayne Christensen, 'To Think or Not to Think: The Apparent Paradox of Expert Skill in Music Performance', *Educational Philosophy and Theory 46* (2014), pp. 674–91; on embodied disciplines, Loïc Wacquant, *Body and Soul: Notebooks of an Apprentice Boxer* (Oxford: Oxford University Press, 2003); Greg Downey, *Learning Capoeira* (Oxford: Oxford University Press, 2005); Jaida Kim Samudra, 'Memory in Our Body: Thick Participation and the Translation of Kinesthetic Experience', *American Ethnologist 35* (2008), pp. 665–81; Doris J. F. McIlwain and John Sutton, 'Yoga from the Mat Up: How Words Alight on Bodies', *Educational Philosophy and Theory 46* (2014), pp. 655–73.

6 Charles Goodwin, 'Professional Vision', *American Anthropologist 96* (1994), pp. 606–33; Jean-Pierre Warnier, 'A Praxeological Approach to Subjectivation in a Material World', *Journal of Material Culture 6* (2001), pp. 5–24; Christina Grasseni, 'Skilled Vision: An Apprenticeship in Breeding Aesthetics', *Social Anthropology 12* (2004), pp. 41–55; David Kirsh, 'Distributed Cognition: A Methodological Note', *Pragmatics & Cognition 14* (2006), pp. 249–62; David de Leon, 'The Cognitive Biographies of Things', in *Doing Things with Things*, eds A. Costall and O. Dreier (Farnham: Ashgate, 2006), pp. 113–30; Lambros Malafouris and Colin Renfrew (eds), *The Cognitive Life of Things: Recasting the Boundaries of the Mind* (Cambridge: McDonald Institute for Archaeological Research, 2010); Ed Hutchins and Saeko Nomura, 'Collaborative Construction of Multimodal Utterances', in *Embodied Interaction: Language and Body in the Material World, eds* J. Streek,

C. Goodwin, and C. LeBaron (Cambridge: Cambridge University Press, 2011), pp. 29-43.

7 Gilbert Ryle, *The Concept of Mind* (Harmondsworth: Penguin, 1963 [first published 1949]), pp. 41–50, 126–30. But for a sophisticated recent taxonomy in which habits are again deliberately yoked to innate propensities, see Tamar Szabo Gendler, 'Alief in Action (and Reaction)', *Mind & Language 23* (2008), pp. 552–85.

8 Nathan Brett, 'Human Habits', *Canadian Journal of Philosophy 11* (1981), pp. 357–76; Edward Casey, 'The Ghost of Embodiment: On Bodily Habitudes and Schemata', in *Body and Flesh*, ed. D. Welton (Oxford: Blackwell, 2000), pp. 207–25; Bill Pollard, 'Explaining Actions with Habits', *American Philosophical Quarterly 43* (2006), pp. 57–68; Nancy Snow, 'Habitual Virtuous Actions and Automaticity', *Ethical Theory and Moral Practice 9* (2006), pp. 545–61; Ezio di Nucci, *Mind Out of Action* (Saarbrücken: VDM Verlag, 2008); Clare Carlisle, 'Between Freedom and Necessity: Félix Ravaisson on Habit and the Moral Life', *Inquiry 53* (2010), pp. 123–45. For Carlisle, 'a person's habit – her posture, her walk, her gestures, the incline of her head; in short, the way she holds herself – may be what most approximates to her essence': 'Creatures of Habit: The Problem and the Practice of Liberation', *Continental Philosophy Review 38* (2006), 19–39, p. 22.

9 Indeed, the terms of this debate reinforce the unfortunate implication that 'mindedness' or 'mindfulness' is some relatively unified domain. In contrast, we suggest that there are independent anthropological, historical, and conceptual grounds to deny that 'mind' or 'mindedness' is a useful category in such contexts. See for example Anna Wierzbicka, *Semantics, Culture, and Cognition: Universal Human Concepts in Culture-Specific Configurations* (Oxford: Oxford University Press, 1992); Paul S. Macdonald, *History of the Concept of Mind: Speculations About Soul, Mind and Spirit from Homer to Hume* (Aldershot: Ashgate, 2003); Amelie Rorty, *Mind in Action* (Boston: Beacon, 1988), especially p. 5; Ian Hunter, 'Mind Games and Body Techniques', *Southern Review: Literary and Interdisciplinary Essays 26* (1993), pp. 172–85.

10 Andy Clark, *Being There: Putting Brain, Body, and World Together Again* (Cambridge, MA: MIT Press, 1997), p. 165.

11 Susan Hurley, *Consciousness in Action* (Cambridge, MA: Harvard University Press, 1998), p. 2.

12 F. C. Bartlett, *Remembering: A Study in Experimental and Social Psychology* (Cambridge, MA: Cambridge University Press, 1932), pp. 201–2. Compare Maxine Sheets-Johnstone, 'Kinesthetic Memory', *Theoria et Historia Scientiarum 7* (2003), 69–92, p. 71: 'a kinetic dynamics unfolds that is at once both familiar and yet quintessentially tailored kinetically to the particular situation at hand' (the essay is reprinted in Sheets-Johnstone, *The Corporeal Turn*, pp. 253–77).

13 Lynne Rudder Baker, review of *The Body in Mind* by Mark Rowlands, Mind *109 (2000)*, pp. 644–7, 646. This is what gave Clark's summary characterization, in *Being There*, of cognitive systems like us as being 'good at Frisbee, bad at logic' (p. 60), its rhetorical force as cognitive scientists began to catch up with the phenomenology of embodiment.

14 John McDowell, 'Response to Dreyfus', *Inquiry 50* (2007), pp. 366–70, 369; compare Dreyfus, 'Response to McDowell', *Inquiry 50* (2007), pp. 371–7, 376.

15 Carlisle, 'Between Freedom and Necessity', p. 131; Charles T. Wolfe, 'De-ontologizing the Brain: From the Fictional Self to the Social Brain', *C-Theory 30* (2007), http://www.ctheory.net/articles.aspx?id=572 (accessed 10 November 2010).

16 Catherine Malabou, *What Should We Do with Our Brain?*, trans. S. Rand (New York: Fordham University Press, 2008), p. 38.

17 Marjorie Grene, *Descartes* (Brighton: Harvester Press, 1985), p. 52. Likewise, laments Jonathan Rée, Descartes made the body just another object in a world 'not of meaning and love and laughter and tears ... but of material particles going about their lonely business' – it was inevitable that the person would subsequently disappear from medical theory, since this 'materialization' of flesh 'takes the juice out of animate bodies, leaving only bare bones and pulp': Rée, 'Subjectivity in the Twentieth Century', *New Literary History 26* (1995), pp. 205–17.

18 René Descartes, *L'homme*, in *Oeuvres de Descartes*, eds C. Adam and P. Tannery (Paris: Vrin, 1996), vol. xi; T. S. Hall (trans.), *René Descartes: Treatise of Man* (Cambridge, MA: Harvard University Press, 1972). For more detail on this interpretation, and contrast with standard readings, see John Sutton, *Philosophy and Memory Traces: Descartes to Connectionism* (Cambridge, MA: Cambridge University Press, 1998), pp. 50–106; Sutton, 'The Body and the Brain', in *Descartes' Natural Philosophy*, eds S. Gaukroger, J. Schuster, and J. Sutton (London: Routledge, 2000), pp. 697–722. For other revisionary work in the same vein, see Desmond Clarke, *Descartes' Philosophy of Science* (Manchester: Manchester University Press, 1982); Richard B. Carter, *Descartes' Medical Philosophy: The Organic Solution to the Mind-body Problem* (Baltimore: Johns Hopkins University Press, 1983); T. M. Brown, 'Descartes, Dualism, and Psychosomatic Medicine', in *The Anatomy of Madness*, eds W. F. Bynum, R. Porter, and M. Shepherd (London, 1985), vol. 1, pp. 40–62; Peter Schouls, *Descartes and the Enlightenment* (Kingston and Montreal: McGill-Queens University Press, 1989), pp. 144–72; Amelie Rorty, 'Descartes on Thinking with the Body', in *The Cambridge Companion to Descartes*, ed. J. Cottingham (Cambridge: Cambridge University Press), pp. 371–92; Susan James, *Passion and Action: The Emotions in Seventeenth-Century Philosophy* (Oxford: Oxford University Press, 1997). A few other scholars see the depth and ramifications of Descartes' reliance on self-organizing dynamical and non-linear feedback mechanisms in his biological, physiological, and medical psychology, but instead of jettisoning the assumption that he was aiming at a linear biophysics of barren matter, convict him of inconsistency: see especially Emily Grosholz, *Cartesian Method and the Problem of Reduction* (Oxford: Clarendon Press, 1991); Steven Shapin, 'Descartes the Doctor: Rationalism and its Therapies', *British Journal for the History of Science 33* (2000), pp. 131–54; Dennis Des Chene, *Spirits and Clocks: Machine and Organism in Descartes* (Ithaca: Cornell University Press, 2001).

19 Owen Flanagan, *The Science of the Mind,* 2nd edition (Cambridge, MA: MIT Press, 1991), p. 3.

20 Timothy J. Reiss, 'Denying the Body? Memory and the Dilemmas of History in Descartes', *Journal of the History of Ideas 57* (1996), pp. 587–607, 604; compare Peter Dear, 'A Mechanical Microcosm: Bodily Passions, Good Manners, and Cartesian Mechanism', in *Science Incarnate*, eds C. Lawrence and S. Shapin (Chicago: University of Chicago Press, 1998), pp. 51–82, 76–7.

21 Descartes, *L'homme*, vol. xi., p. 177.

22 Ibid., p. 178.

23 Ibid., pp. 178–9.

24 Hall, René Descartes: Treatise of Man, 96, n. p. 145.

25 Descartes, *L'homme*, vol. xi., p. 185.

26 Ibid., p. 185.

27 Compare Malabou, *What Should We Do with Our Brain?*, pp. 70–2.

28 Sutton, *Philosophy and Memory Traces*, pp. 74–81.

29 Stephen Gaukroger, *Descartes: An Intellectual Biography* (Oxford: Oxford University Press, 1995), especially pp. 241–56 and pp. 375–7; Sutton, *Philosophy and Memory Traces,* pp. 83–97. On the holistic background in humoural materialism, see Gail Kern Paster, 'Nervous Tension: Networks of Blood and Spirit in the Early Modern Body', in *The Body in Parts*, eds D. Hillman and C. Mazzio (London: Routledge, 1997), pp. 107–25; Paster, *Humoring the Body* (Chicago: Chicago University Press, 2004); Sutton, 'Spongy Brains and Material Memories', in *Environment and Embodiment in Early Modern England,* eds M. Floyd-Wilson and G. Sullivan (London: Palgrave Macmillan, 2007), pp. 14–34.

30 René Descartes, 'The Passions of the Soul', in *Oeuvres des Descartes* xi, pp. 394–5.

31 John Cottingham, 'The Self and the Body: Alienation and Integration in Cartesian Ethics', *Seventeenth-Century French Studies 17* (1995), pp. 1–13, 11.

32 See the entries for 'disposition' and 'habitude' in Stephen Voss' outstanding lexicon, in his edition of *The Passions of the Soul* (Indianapolis: Hackett, 1989), p. 138 and 140; Sutton, 'The Body and the Brain', pp. 712–14.

33 See Reiss, 'Denying the Body?'

34 Compare Adam Phillips, 'Minds', in *Terrors and Experts* (Cambridge, MA: Harvard University Press, 1995), pp. 93–104, on the Cartesian soul as 'a kind of enraged bureaucrat, a master of circumstances' (p. 99).

35 Sutton, 'The Body and the Brain'. For something of the subsequent uptake and history of related ideas in British philosophy, see Sutton, 'Carelessness and Inattention: mind-wandering and the physiology of fantasy from Locke to Hume', in *The Body as Object and Instrument of Knowledge: Embodied Empiricism in Early Modern Science*, eds C. T. Wolfe and O. Gal (Springer, 2010), pp. 243–63.

36 In arguing recently that we are now fulfilling a 'Cartesian vision' by which our bodies are 'just machines in space' and 'something other than ourselves',

Ian Hacking discusses many intriguing cases of the apparent transferability and alienability of body parts, but not a single example of skilful embodied activity: see Hacking, 'The Cartesian Vision Fulfilled: Analogue Bodies and Digital Minds', *Interdisciplinary Science Reviews 30* (2005), pp. 153–66, and 'Our Neo-Cartesian Bodies in Parts', *Critical Inquiry 34* (2007), pp. 78–105. Hacking's neo-Cartesian future, a reader of Malabou might note, is one in which mere flexibility has won out over the richer forms of plasticity which have resistance inbuilt.

37 Compare Malabou, *What Should We Do with Our Brain*? p. 38.

38 But here is one dramatic statement of intellectualism in practice: 'Sir Isaac Newton laid the foundation for modern skiing with several basic laws of motion. Violations of these laws are the cause of problems. Anyone attempting to thoroughly understand skiing should know these laws and the terms used in their proper, intended meaning' – John Howe, *Skiing Mechanics* (Boulder, CO: Poudre Press, 1982), p. 9, as quoted in Sigmund Loland, 'The Mechanics and Meaning of Alpine Skiing: methodological and epistemological notes on the study of sport technique', *Journal of the Philosophy of Sport 19* (1992), pp. 55–77, 58. A particularly effective critique of such views is Hubert L. Dreyfus and Stuart E. Dreyfus, 'Making a Mind versus Modelling the Brain', in *The Artificial Intelligence Debate*, ed. S. R. Graubard (Cambridge, MA: MIT Press, 1988), pp. 15–41. An influential defence of the priority of 'knowing-that' over 'knowing-how' in recent analytic philosophy is Jason Stanley and Timothy Williamson, 'Knowing How', *Journal of Philosophy 98* (2001), pp. 411–44: for responses see Alva Noë, 'Against Intellectualism', *Analysis 65* (2005), pp. 278–90, and Josefa Toribio, 'How do we know how?' *Philosophical Explorations 11* (2008), pp. 39–52. It is harder to assess whether more moderate, empirically anchored theoretical views in contemporary cognitive psychology remain recognizably intellectualist in these respects. We have previously put such charges to Roger Chaffin's impressive account of memory in music performance: see Geeves, Christensen, Sutton, and McIlwain, 'Critical Review of *Practicing Perfection*', *Empirical Musicology Review 3* (2008), pp. 163–72. Likewise, dynamically oriented sports psychologists charge Anders Ericsson's impressive 'deliberate practice' framework with residual intellectualism: see for example Bruce Abernethy, Damian Farrow, and Jason Berry, 'Constraints and Issues in the Development of a General Theory of Expert Perceptual-Motor Performance', in *Expert Performance in Sports*, eds J. L. Starkes and K. A. Ericsson (Champaign, IL: Human Kinetics, 2003).

39 Pollard, 'Explaining Actions with Habits', pp. 58, 67. See also Pollard, 'The Rationality of Habitual Action', *Proceedings of the Durham-Bergen Philosophy Conference 1* (2005), pp. 39–50.

40 Ibid., p. 67.

41 Brett, 'Human Habits', pp. 365–6.

42 Sheets-Johnstone, 'Kinesthetic Memory', 75; 'Animation', pp. 390–4.

43 Brett, 'Human Habits', p. 369.

44 Again, because we're not here doing detailed exegesis, our discussion here neglects important subtleties in and differences between these theories: in simplifying and highlighting certain key shared assumptions, however, we seek to capture recognizable views across these theorists.

45 Dreyfus, 'Refocusing the Question: Can There Be Skillful Coping Without Propositional Representations or Brain Representations?', *Phenomenology and the Cognitive Sciences 1* (2002), pp. 413–25, 417.

46 Dreyfus and Dreyfus, *Mind Over Machine: The Power of Human Intuition and Expertise in the Era of the Computer* (New York: Free Press, 1986), p. 32.

47 Dreyfus, 'Overcoming the Myth of the Mental', *Topoi 25* (2006), pp. 43–9, 47. Compare Dreyfus, 'A Phenomenological Account of the Development of Ethical Expertise and Mastery', in *Moving Bodies*, vol. 4, ed. E. Jespersen (Oslo: The Norwegian School of Sport Sciences, 2006), pp. 15–30, especially p. 20: the genuine expert has gradually learned 'to decompose … situations into subclasses, each of which share the same decision, single action or tactic. This allows an immediate response to each situation'. In this and other more recent versions of his model of the stages of skill acquisition, Dreyfus does allow for further development beyond expertise, towards 'mastery' and 'practical wisdom', but the key points under discussion here are not affected.

48 Charles Spinosa, Fernando Flores, and Hubert L. Dreyfus, *Disclosing New Worlds: Entrepreneurship, Democratic Action, and the Cultivation of Solidarity* (Cambridge, MA: MIT Press, 1997), p. 87. I owe this quotation to the excellent critical discussion of the Dreyfus model by Evan M. Selinger and Robert P. Crease, 'Dreyfus on Expertise: The Limits of Phenomenological Analysis', *Continental Philosophy Review 35* (2002), pp. 245–79.

49 Dreyfus, 'Intelligence without Representation: Merleau-Ponty's Critique of Mental Representation', *Phenomenology and the Cognitive Sciences 1* (2002), pp. 367–83, 379.

50 Dreyfus and Dreyfus, *Mind Over Machine*, p. 30.

51 Elizabeth Ennen, 'Phenomenological Coping Skills and the Striatal Memory System', *Phenomenology and the Cognitive Sciences 2* (2003), pp. 299–325.

52 Ibid., p. 314, relying especially on Ann Graybiel, 'The Basal Ganglia and Chunking of Action Repertoires', *Neurobiology of Learning and Memory 70* (1998), pp. 119–36. There are difficult questions about the unity of the category of 'memory', given the unique properties of the procedural memory systems: see Danièle Moyal-Sharrock, 'Wittgenstein and the Memory Debate', *New Ideas in Psychology 27* (2009), pp. 213–27; Kirk Michaelian, 'Is Memory a Natural Kind?', *Memory Studies 4* (2011), pp. 170–89. As we read it, however, recent neuroscientific research increasingly underlines the dynamic interactivity of procedural and declarative memory processes, to such an extent that the distinction might come under some pressure. See Graybiel, 'The Basal Ganglia: learning new tricks and loving it', *Current Opinion in Neurobiology 15* (2005), pp. 638–44; Henry H. Yin and Barbara J. Knowlton, 'The Role of the Basal Ganglia in Habit Formation', *Nature Reviews Neuroscience 7* (2006), pp. 464–76.

53 Ennen, 'Phenomenological Coping Skills', p. 321, quoting Dreyfus, *Being-in-the-World: A Commentary on Heidegger's Being and Time, Division I* (Cambridge, MA: MIT Press, 1991), p. 3.

54 John Searle, *Intentionality* (Cambridge: Cambridge University Press, 1983), p. 150. Searle goes on to say that the rules 'recede into the Background', which is a much harder doctrine to interpret: see especially the discussion of Searle's views on this point by Dreyfus in 'Responses', in *Heidegger, Coping, and Cognitive Science*, eds M. Wrathall and J. Malpas (Cambridge, MA: MIT Press, 2000), pp. 324–6. But Dreyfus there accepts that he and Searle agree on the fact that the body takes over.

55 Fred Dretske, 'Where is the Mind when the Body Performs?', *Stanford Humanities Review 6* (1998), http://www.stanford.edu/group/SHR/6-2/html/dretske.html (accessed 6 November 2010). Dretske does, however, argue that even though consciousness is withdrawn, 'intelligence' is delegated or dispersed, and that the skilful routines thus delegated to the body 'bear the marks of genuine intelligence'. We think that this last point is spot on, a version of our idea of applying intelligence to the reflexes. Dretske also does allow a range of roles for psychology in attending to higher-order objectives, although from our perspective he retains an unnecessarily hierarchical or managerial picture of the control of skilled action.

56 In these respects, our critique of the phenomenologists' response to intellectualism could be connected with a discussion of currently influential 'dual process' theories in psychology and moral philosophy, which also entrench such an extreme dichotomy between two entirely opposed modes of response. For the link to theories of memory see Eliot R. Smith and Jamie DeCoster, 'Dual-Process Models in Social and Cognitive Psychology: Conceptual Integration and Links to Underlying Memory Systems', *Personality and Social Psychology Review 4* (2000), pp. 108–31, and for an entry into current controversies about dual process theories and social intuitionism in moral psychology see Joshua D. Greene, 'Dual-Process Morality and the Personal/ Impersonal Distinction: A Reply to McGuire, Langdon, Coltheart, and Mackenzie', *Journal of Experimental Social Psychology 45* (2009), pp. 581–4. We don't have space here to make the connections with theories of skilful coping more explicit. There are clear statements and critical evaluations of dual process theories in J. Evans and K. Frankish (eds), *In Two Minds: Dual Processes and Beyond* (Oxford: Oxford University Press, 2009).

57 Malcolm Gladwell, *Blink: The Power of Thinking Without Thinking* (London: Penguin, 2005), pp. 18–47.

58 The sporting quotations are from Ken Barrington and Sandy Gordon: for references and discussion see Sutton, 'Batting, Habit, and Memory', p. 767. Contemporary sports scientists are heavily influenced by J. J. Gibson's ecological psychology and by dynamical systems theories in cognitive science, in each case reinforcing the tendency to distrust mindedness: see for example Ian Renshaw, Keith Davids, Rick Shuttleworth and Jia Yi Chow, 'Insights from Ecological Psychology and Dynamical Systems Theory can Underpin a Philosophy of Coaching', *International Journal of Sport Psychology 40* (2009), pp. 580–602; Renshaw, Davids, and Geert J. P. Savelsbergh (eds), *Motor Learning in Practice: A Constraints-led Approach* (London: Routledge, 2010). For musicians' assumptions and pedagogical traditions, see Roger Chaffin, Gabriela Imreh and Mary Crawford, *Practicing*

Perfection: Memory and Piano Performance (Mahwah, NJ: Erlbaum, 2002), especially, pp. xii–xiii and 26–65.

59 Erik Rietveld and colleagues argue for an analogous pluralism in understanding embodied cognition and skilful action, with cognitive and abnormal psychology joining theories of affect and dynamical neuroscience to supplement phenomenological and philosophical investigations. While we draw on Rietveld's constructive theoretical proposals below, he does not canvas the kind of work with known groups in the cognitive neuroscience and psychology of dance and sport which we are recommending. On pluralism see Pim Klaassen, Erik Rietveld, and Julien Topal, 'Inviting Complementary Perspectives on Situated Normativity in Everyday Life', *Phenomenology and the Cognitive Sciences 9* (2010), pp. 53–73. Dreyfus, however, draws constructively neither on psychological research, stressing instead occasionally the anti-cognitivist neuroscience of Walter Freeman, nor on the sport sciences, which remain an enormous, often conceptually sophisticated, almost entirely untapped resource for philosophical exploration.

60 Michael F. Land and Peter McLeod, 'From Eye Movements to Actions: How Batsmen Hit the Ball', *Nature Neuroscience 3* (2000), pp. 1340–5; Land and Benjamin W. Tatler, *Looking and Acting: Vision and Eye Movements in Natural Behaviour* (Oxford: Oxford University Press, 2009), pp. 153–60; see Sutton, 'Batting, Habit, and Memory', pp. 770–4.

61 We can briefly mention two further intriguing examples of the kind of research in dance and sport with which studies of absorbed coping and embodied skill could be dealing. Beatriz Calvo-Merino and colleagues argue that our response to dance sequences, for example in ballet or capoeira, is driven not by abstract knowledge of an action repertoire, but only on the basis of individual movement experience in a specific movement style: our understanding of action is by motor simulation and is tuned to an individual motor repertoire (B. Calvo-Merino, D. E. Glaser, J. Grezes, R. E. Passingham, and P. Haggard, 'Action Observation and Acquired Motor Skills: An fMRI Study with Expert Dancers', *Cerebral Cortex 15* (2005), pp. 1243–9. Meanwhile, Sian Beilock and colleagues suggest that expert performance in motor skills requires little attention, operates largely outside of working memory, and is substantially closed to introspection: therefore, they argue, highly skilled practitioners in movement domains exhibit a surprising 'expertise-induced amnesia', by which their recollections of real-time performance are 'impoverished' compared to novices (Sian L. Beilock and Thomas H. Carr, 'On the Fragility of Skilled Performance: What Governs Choking Under Pressure?', *Journal of Experimental Psychology: General 130* (2001), pp. 701–25; Sian L. Beilock, Sarah A. Wierenga, and Thomas H. Carr, 'Memory and Expertise: What Do Experienced Athletes Remember?', in *Expert Performance in Sports,* eds Starkes and Ericsson, especially pp. 315–16). See also now Wayne Christensen, Kath Bicknell, Doris J. F. McIlwain and John Sutton, 'The Sense of Agency and its Role in Strategic Control for Expert Mountain Bikes', *Psychology of Consciousness: Theory, Research, and Practice 2* (2015), pp. 340–53; Christensen, Sutton and McIlwain, 'Putting Pressure on Theories of Choking: Towards an Expanded Perspective on Breakdown in Skilled Performance', *Phenomenology and the Cognitive Sciences 14* (2015), pp. 253–93.

62 Michael Wheeler, *Reconstructing the Cognitive World: The Next Step* (Cambridge, MA: MIT Press, 2005), p. 120; Wheeler, 'Cognition in Context: phenomenology, situated robotics, and the frame problem', *International Journal of Philosophical Studies 16* (2008), pp. 323–49.

63 Wheeler, *Reconstructing the Cognitive World,* pp. 131–2; 'Cognition in Context', p. 338.

64 Ibid., p. 229.

65 Ibid., p. 139.

66 Ibid., pp.,142–3. Dreyfus, in contrast, often appears somewhat uninterested in dimensions of variation within expert performance, or across distinctive expert domains: for recent critiques along these lines see for example Barbara Montero, 'Does Bodily Awareness Interfere with Highly Skilled Movement?', *Inquiry 53* (2010), pp. 105–22; Jørgen W. Eriksen, 'Mindless Coping in Competitive Sport: Some Implications and Consequences', *Sport, Ethics, & Philosophy 4* (2010), pp. 66–86. Dreyfus, meanwhile, accuses Wheeler of a 'cognitivist misreading of Heidegger': 'Why Heideggerian AI Failed and How Fixing it Would Require Making it More Heideggerian', *Philosophical Psychology 20* (2007), pp. 247–68, 254.

67 David Sudnow, *Ways of the Hand: A Rewritten Account* (Cambridge, MA: MIT Press, 2001), from whom we borrow and extend the notion of 'instructional nudges'.

68 These interviews were conducted by Ed Cooke. Likewise, in a more formal study by Juanita Weissensteiner, one of the best Australian cricketers of recent times reports that his multimodal routine includes essential verbalized components: 'Well, in the lead-up, I mark my crease, I turn towards the stumps, I mark my crease, I tap my right foot about three or four times on the toe, then I turn around and I tell myself to have my arms either as loose as possible or whatever I've actually been working on at the time. ... I get that right to start off, then I tell myself "play straight, play straight" or the other one I might use is "be sharp, be sharp". I do this until it gets to the point of delivery where all my intention, all my focus goes on him letting go of the ball': Juanita Weissensteiner, Bruce Abernethy and Damian Farrow, 'Towards the Development of a Conceptual Model of Expertise in Cricket Batting', *Journal of Applied Sport Psychology 21* (2009), pp. 276–92, 288.

69 On self-talk and the non-semantic looping roles of verbal tags and maxims, see Andy Clark, 'Magic Words: How Language Augments Human Computation', in *Language and Thought: interdisciplinary themes*, eds P. Carruthers and J. Boucher (Cambridge: Cambridge University Press, 1998), pp. 162–83; Clark, 'Material Symbols', *Philosophical Psychology 19* (2006), pp. 291–307; Clark, *Supersizing the Mind: Embodiment, Action, and Cognitive Extension* (Oxford: Oxford University Press, 2008), pp. 129–33.

70 Compare concert pianist Gabriela Imreh's comment, while learning Bach's extraordinarily demanding *Italian Concerto (Presto)* that 'the practice I needed was in my head': Roger Chaffin and Gabriela Imreh, 'Practicing Perfection: Piano Performance as Expert Memory', *Psychological Science 13* (2002), pp. 342–9, 344. See also John Sutton and Kellie Williamson, 'Embodied Remembering', in *The Routledge Handbook of Embodied Cognition*, ed. L. Shapiro (London: Routledge, 2014), pp. 315–25.

71 Elizabeth A. Behnke, 'Edmund Husserl's Contribution to Phenomenology of the Body in *Ideas II*', in *Issues in Husserl's Ideas II*, eds T. Nenon and L. E. Embree (Dordrecht: Kluwer, 1996), pp. 135–60, 154. Behnke acknowledges the Sartrean mode of embodied experience which Dreyfus celebrates, the body 'passed over in silence, transcended toward the task, pre-reflectively geared in with the situation, ... utterly undisturbed either by the visibility of this comportment to others, or by one's own reflective glance; one is oblivious to oneself, completely caught up in whatever one is doing': but she notes that this mode of bodily 'self-effacement' is for Sartre only one possible ontological dimension of the body, and identifies it as a potential 'locus of crisis in need of a critique of corporeal experience', to be supplemented (if not replaced) with other modes in which distinctive fields of experiential possibility can be accessed. See Behnke, 'The Socially Shaped Body and the Critique of Corporeal Experience', in *Sartre on the Body*, ed. K. J. Morris (Basingstoke: Palgrave, 2010), pp. 231–55, 235–6.

72 Elizabeth A. Behnke, 'Interkinaesthetic Affectivity: A Phenomenological Approach', *Continental Philosophy Review 41* (2008), pp. 143–61, 146.

73 Elizabeth A. Behnke, 'Matching', in *Bone, Breath, and Gesture*, ed. D. H. Johnson (North Atlantic Books, 1995), pp. 317–37. (First published 1988).

74 Elizabeth A. Behnke, 'Contact Improvisation and the Lived World', in M. Diaconu (ed.), *Kunst und Wahrheit* (Bucharest: Humanitas, 2003), p. 49.

75 Elizabeth A. Behnke, 'Ghost Gestures: Phenomenological Investigations of Bodily Micromovements and Their Intercorporeal Implications', *Human Studies 20* (1997), pp. 181–201.

76 Erik Rietveld, 'The Skillful Body as a Concernful System of Possible Actions', *Theory & Psychology 18* (2008), pp. 341–63, especially pp. 350–1; Wayne Christensen, John Sutton and Doris J. F. McIlwain, 'Cognition in Skilled Action: Meshed Control and the Varieties of Skill Experience', *Mind & Language 31* (2016), pp. 37–66.

77 K. Anders Ericsson, 'Development of Elite Performance and Deliberate Practice', in *Expert Performance in Sports*, pp. 64–5.

78 Jack Reynolds, 'Dreyfus and Deleuze on *l'habitude*, Coping, and Trauma in Skill Acquisition', *International Journal of Philosophical Studies 14*, pp. 539–59.

79 Ivar Hagendoorn, 'Cognitive Dance Improvisation: How Study of the Motor System Can Inspire Dance (and Vice Versa)', *Leonardo 36* (2003), pp. 221–7.

References

Abernethy, B., D. Farrow and J. Berry, 'Constraints and Issues in the Development of a General Theory of Expert Perceptual-Motor Performance', in J. L. Starkes and K. A. Ericsson (eds) *Expert Performance in Sports*, Champaign, IL: Human Kinetics, 2003, pp. 349–370.

Bartlett, F. C., *Remembering: A Study in Experimental and Social Psychology*, Cambridge, MA: Cambridge University Press, 1932.

Behnke, E. A., 'Matching', in D. H. Johnson (ed.) *Bone, Breath, and Gesture*, North Atlantic Books, 1995 [1988], pp. 317–37.
Behnke, E. A., 'Edmund Husserl's Contribution to Phenomenology of the Body in *Ideas II*', in T. Nenon and L. E. Embree (eds) *Issues in Husserl's Ideas II*, Dordrecht: Kluwer, 1996, pp. 135–60.
Behnke, E. A., 'Ghost Gestures: Phenomenological Investigations of Bodily Micromovements and Their Intercorporeal Implications', *Human Studies 20* (1997), pp. 181–201.
Behnke, E. A., 'Contact Improvisation and the Lived World', in M. Diaconu (ed.), *Kunst und Wahrheit*, Bucharest: Humanitas, 2003, p. 49.
Behnke, E. A., 'Interkinaesthetic Affectivity: A Phenomenological Approach', *Continental Philosophy Review 41* (2008), pp. 143–61, 146.
Behnke, E. A., 'The Socially Shaped Body and the Critique of Corporeal Experience', in K. J. Morris (ed.), *Sartre on the Body*, Basingstoke: Palgrave Macmillan, 2010, pp. 231–55.
Beilock, S. L. and T. H. Carr, 'On the Fragility of Skilled Performance: What Governs Choking Under Pressure?' *Journal of Experimental Psychology: General 130* (2001), pp. 701–25.
Beilock, S. L., Wierenga, S. A. and T. H. Carr, 'Expertise, Attention, and Memory in Sensorimotor Skill Execution', *Quarterly Journal of Experimental Psychology 55* (2002), pp. 1211–40.
Beilock, S. L., Wierenga, S. A. and T. H. Carr, 'Memory and Expertise: What Do Experienced Athletes Remember?' in J. Starkes and K. A. Ericsson (eds), *Expert Performance in Sports*, Champaign: Human Kinetics, 2003, pp. 295–320.
Berliner, P. F., *Thinking in Jazz: The Infinite Art of Improvisation*, Chicago: University of Chicago Press, 1994.
Brett, N., 'Human Habits', *Canadian Journal of Philosophy 11* (1981), pp. 357–76.
Brown, T. M., 'Descartes, Dualism, and Psychosomatic Medicine', in W. F. Bynum, R. Porter and M. Shepherd (eds), *The Anatomy of Madness*, London: Tavistock, 1985, vol. 1.
Calvo-Merino, B., D. E. Glaser, J. Grezes, R. E. Passingham and P. Haggard, 'Action Observation and Acquired Motor Skills: An fMRI Study with Expert Dancers', *Cerebral Cortex 15* (2005), pp. 1243–9.
Carlisle, C., 'Creatures of Habit: The Problem and the Practice Of Liberation', *Continental Philosophy Review 38* (2006), pp. 19–39.
Carlisle, C., 'Between Freedom and Necessity: Félix Ravaisson on Habit and the Moral Life', *Inquiry 53* (2010), pp. 123–45.
Carter, R. B., *Descartes' Medical Philosophy: The Organic Solution to the Mind-body Problem*, Baltimore: Johns Hopkins University Press, 1983.
Casey, E., 'The Ghost of Embodiment: On Bodily Habitudes and Schemata', in D. Welton (ed.), *Body and Flesh*, Oxford: Blackwell, 2000, pp. 207–25.
Chaffin, R. and G. Imreh, 'Practicing Perfection: Piano Performance as Expert Memory', *Psychological Science 13* (2002), pp. 342–9.
Chaffin, R., G. Imreh and M. Crawford, *Practicing Perfection: Memory and Piano Performance*, Mahwah, NJ: Erlbaum, 2002.
Christensen, W., K. Bicknell, D. J. F. McIlwain and J. Sutton, 'The Sense of Agency and its Role in Strategic Control for Expert Mountain Bikes',

Psychology of Consciousness: Theory, Research, and Practice 2 (2015), pp. 340–53.

Christensen, W., J. Sutton and D. J. F. McIlwain, 'Cognition in Skilled Action: Meshed Control and the Varieties of Skill Experience', *Mind & Language 31* (2016), pp. 37–66.

Christensen, W., J. Sutton and D. J. F. McIlwain, 'Putting Pressure on Theories of Choking: Towards an Expanded Perspective on Breakdown in Skilled Performance', *Phenomenology and the Cognitive Sciences 14* (2015), pp. 253–93.

Clark, A., *Being There: Putting Brain, Body, and World Together Again*, Cambridge, MA: MIT Press, 1997.

Clark, A., 'Magic Words: How Language Augments Human Computation', in P. Carruthers and J. Boucher (eds), *Language and Thought: Interdisciplinary Themes*, Cambridge: Cambridge University Press, 1998, pp. 162–83.

Clark, A., 'Material Symbols', *Philosophical Psychology 19* (2006), pp. 291–307.

Clark, A., *Supersizing the Mind: Embodiment, Action, and Cognitive Extension*, Oxford: Oxford University Press, 2008, pp. 129–33.

Clarke, D., *Descartes' Philosophy of Science*, Manchester: Manchester University Press, 1982.

Cottingham, J., 'The Self and the Body: Alienation and Integration in Cartesian Ethics', *Seventeenth-Century French Studies 17* (1995), pp. 1–13.

de Leon, D., 'The Cognitive Biographies of Things', in A. Costall and O. Dreier (eds), *Doing Things with Things*, Farnham: Ashgate, 2006, pp. 113–30.

Dear, P., 'A Mechanical Microcosm: Bodily Passions, Good Manners, and Cartesian Mechanism', in C. Lawrence and S. Shapin (eds), *Science Incarnate*, Chicago: University of Chicago Press, 1998, pp. 51–82.

Des Chene, D., *Spirits and Clocks: Machine and Organism in Descartes*, Ithaca: Cornell University Press, 2001.

Descartes, R., *L'homme*, in C. Adam and P. Tannery (eds), *Oeuvres de Descartes*, Paris: Vrin, 1996, vol. xi.

di Nucci, E., *Mind Out of Action*, Saarbrücken: VDM Verlag, 2008.

Downey, G., *Learning Capoeira*, Oxford: Oxford University Press, 2005.

Dretske, F., 'Where is the Mind when the Body Performs?', *Stanford Humanities Review 6* (1998), http://www.stanford.edu/group/SHR/6-2/html/dretske.html (accessed 6 November 2010).

Dreyfus, H. L., *Being-in-the-World: A Commentary on Heidegger's Being and Time, Division I*, Cambridge, MA: MIT Press, 1991.

Dreyfus H. L., 'Responses', in M. Wrathall and J. Malpas (eds), *Heidegger, Coping, and Cognitive Science*, Cambridge, MA: MIT Press, 2000, pp. 324–6.

Dreyfus, H. L., 'Intelligence without Representation: Merleau-Ponty's Critique of Mental Representation', *Phenomenology and the Cognitive Sciences 1* (2002), pp. 367–83.

Dreyfus, H. L., 'Refocusing the Question: Can There be Skillful Coping Without Propositional Representations or Brain Representations?', *Phenomenology and the Cognitive Sciences 1* (2002), pp. 413–25.

Dreyfus, H. L., 'Overcoming the Myth of the Mental', *Topoi 25* (2006), pp. 43–9.

Dreyfus, H. L., 'A Phenomenological Account of the Development of Ethical Expertise and Mastery', in E. Jespersen (ed.) *Moving Bodies* vol. 4, Oslo: The Norwegian School of Sport Sciences, 2006, pp. 15–30.

Dreyfus, H. L., 'Why Heideggerian AI Failed and How Fixing it Would Require Making it More Heideggerian', *Philosophical Psychology 20* (2007), pp. 247–68.

Dreyfus, H. L., 'Response to McDowell', *Inquiry 50* (2007), pp. 371–7.

Dreyfus, H. L. and S. E. Dreyfus, *Mind Over Machine: The Power of Human Intuition and Expertise in the Era of the Computer*, New York: Free Press, 1986.

Dreyfus, H. L. and S. E. Dreyfus, 'Making a Mind versus Modelling the Brain', in S. R. Graubard (ed.), *The Artificial Intelligence Debate*, Cambridge, MA: MIT Press, 1988, pp. 15–41.

Ennen, E., 'Phenomenological Coping Skills and the Striatal Memory System', *Phenomenology and the Cognitive Sciences 2* (2003), pp. 299–325.

Ericsson, K. A., 'Development of Elite Performance and Deliberate Practice', in J. L. Starkes and K. A. Ericsson (eds), *Expert Performance in Sports*, Champaign, IL: Human Kinetics, 2003, pp. 64–5.

Eriksen, J. W., 'Mindless Coping in Competitive Sport: Some Implications and Consequences', *Sport, Ethics, & Philosophy* 4 (2010), pp. 66–86.

Evans, J. and K. Frankish (eds), *In Two Minds: Dual Processes and Beyond*, Oxford: Oxford University Press, 2009.

Flanagan, O., *The Science of the Mind*, 2nd edition, Cambridge, MA: MIT Press, 1991.

Galantucci, B. and N. Sebanz, 'Joint Action: Current Perspectives', *Topics in Cognitive Science 1* (2009), pp. 255–9.

Gaukroger, S., *Descartes: An Intellectual Biography*, Oxford: Oxford University Press, 1995.

Geeves, A., W. Christensen, J. Sutton, and D. J. F. McIlwain, 'Critical Review of *Practicing Perfection*', *Empirical Musicology Review 3* (2008), pp. 163–72.

Geeves, A., D. J. F. McIlwain, J. Sutton and W. Christensen, 'To Think or not to Think: The Apparent Paradox of Expert Skill in Music Performance', *Educational Philosophy and Theory 46* (2014), pp. 674–91.

Gladwell, M., *Blink: The Power of Thinking Without Thinking*, London: Penguin, 2005.

Goodwin, C., 'Professional Vision', *American Anthropologist 96* (1994), pp. 606–33.

Grasseni, C., 'Skilled Vision: An Apprenticeship in Breeding Aesthetics', *Social Anthropology 12* (2004), pp. 41–55.

Graybiel, A., 'The Basal Ganglia and Chunking of Action Repertoires', *Neurobiology of Learning and Memory 70* (1998), pp. 119–36.

Graybiel, A., 'The Basal Ganglia: Learning New Tricks and Loving It', *Current Opinion in Neurobiology 15* (2005), pp. 638–44.

Greene, J. D., 'Dual-Process Morality and the Personal/ Impersonal Distinction: A Reply to McGuire, Langdon, Coltheart, and Mackenzie', *Journal of Experimental Social Psychology 45* (2009), pp. 581–4.

Grene, M., *Descartes*, Brighton: Harvester Press, 1985.

Grosholz, E., *Cartesian Method and the Problem of Reduction*, Oxford: Clarendon Press, 1991.

Hacking, I., 'The Cartesian Vision Fulfilled: Analogue Bodies and Digital Minds', *Interdisciplinary Science Reviews 30* (2005), pp. 153–66.

Hagendoorn, I., 'Cognitive Dance Improvisation: How Study of the Motor System can Inspire Dance (and Vice Versa)', *Leonardo* 36 (2003), pp. 221–7.

Hall, T. S. (trans.), *René Descartes: Treatise of Man*, Cambridge, MA: Harvard University Press, 1972.

Howe, J., *Skiing Mechanics*, Boulder, CO: Poudre Press, 1982.

Hunter, I., 'Mind Games and Body Techniques', *Southern Review: Literary and Interdisciplinary Essays 26* (1993), pp. 172–85.

Hurley, S. *Consciousness in Action*, Cambridge, MA: Harvard University Press, 1998.

Hutchins, E. and S. Nomura, 'Collaborative Construction of Multimodal Utterances', in J. Streek, C. Goodwin, and C. LeBaron (eds), *Embodied Interaction: Language and Body in the Material World*, Cambridge, MA: Cambridge University Press, 2011, pp. 29–43.

James, S., *Passion and Action: The Emotions in Seventeenth-Century Philosophy*, Oxford: Oxford University Press, 1997.

Kirsh, D., 'Distributed Cognition: A Methodological Note', *Pragmatics & Cognition 14* (2006), pp. 249–62.

Kirsh, D., 'Thinking with the Body', *Proceedings of the 32nd Annual Meeting of the Cognitive Science Society* (2010), http://adrenaline.ucsd.edu/kirsh/articles/interaction/thinkingwithbody.pdf (accessed 6 November 2010).

Klaassen, P., E. Rietveld and J. Topal, 'Inviting Complementary Perspectives on Situated Normativity in Everyday Life', *Phenomenology and the Cognitive Sciences 9* (2010), pp. 53–73.

Land, M. F. and P. McLeod, 'From Eye Movements to Actions: How Batsmen Hit the Ball', *Nature Neuroscience 3* (2000), pp. 1340–5.

Land, M. F. and B. W. Tatler, *Looking and Acting: Vision and Eye Movements in Natural Behaviour*, Oxford: Oxford University Press, 2009, pp. 153–60.

Loland, S., 'The Mechanics and Meaning of Alpine Skiing: Methodological and Epistemological Notes on the Study of Sport Technique', *Journal of the Philosophy of Sport 19* (1992), pp. 55–77.

Malabou, C., *What Should We Do with Our Brain?*, trans. S. Rand, New York: Fordham University Press, 2008.

Malafouris, L. and C. Renfrew (eds), *The Cognitive Life of Things: Recasting the Boundaries of the Mind*, Cambridge: McDonald Institute for Archaeological Research, 2010.

Macdonald, P. S., *History of the Concept of Mind: Speculations About Soul, Mind and Spirit from Homer to Hume*, Aldershot: Ashgate, 2003.

McDowell, J., 'Response to Dreyfus', *Inquiry 50* (2007), pp. 366–70.

McIlwain, D. J. F. and J. Sutton, 'Yoga from the Mat Up: How Words Alight on Bodies', *Educational Philosophy and Theory 46* (2014), pp. 655–73.

Michaelian, K., 'Is Memory a Natural Kind?', *Memory Studies 4* (2011), pp. 170–89.

Monson, I., *Saying Something: Jazz Improvisation As Interaction*, Chicago: University of Chicago Press, 1996.

Montero, B., 'Does Bodily Awareness Interfere with Highly Skilled Movement?', *Inquiry 53* (2010), pp. 105–22.

Moyal-Sharrock, D., 'Wittgenstein and the Memory Debate', *New Ideas in Psychology 27* (2009), pp. 213–27.

Müller, S. and B. Abernethy, 'Skill Learning from an Expertise Perspective: Issues and Implications for Practice and Coaching in Cricket', in J. Dosil (ed.), *The Sport Psychologist's Handbook*, Chichester: John Wiley, 2006, pp. 245–61.

Noë, A., 'Against Intellectualism', *Analysis 65* (2005), pp. 278–90.
Paster, G. K., 'Nervous Tension: Networks of Blood and Spirit in the Early Modern Body', in D. Hillman and C. Mazzio (eds), *The Body in Parts*, London: Routledge, 1997, pp. 107–25.
Paster, G. K., *Humoring the Body*, Chicago: Chicago University Press, 2004.
Phillips, A., 'Minds', in *Phillips, Terrors and Experts*, Cambridge, MA: Harvard University Press, 1995, pp. 93–104.
Pollard, B., 'The Rationality of Habitual Action', *Proceedings of the Durham-Bergen Philosophy Conference 1* (2005), pp. 39–50.
Pollard, B., 'Explaining Actions with Habits', *American Philosophical Quarterly 43* (2006), pp. 57–68.
Rée, J., 'Subjectivity in the Twentieth Century', *New Literary History 26* (1995), pp. 205–217.
Reiss, T. J., 'Denying the Body? Memory and the dilemmas of history in Descartes', *Journal of the History of Ideas 57* (1996), pp. 587–607.
Renshaw, I., K. Davids and G. J. P. Savelsbergh (eds), *Motor Learning in Practice: A Constraints-Led Approach*, London: Routledge, 2010.
Renshaw, I., K. Davids, R. Shuttleworth and J. Y. Chow, 'Insights from Ecological Psychology and Dynamical Systems Theory can Underpin a Philosophy of Coaching', *International Journal of Sport Psychology 40* (2009), pp. 580–602.
Reynolds, J., 'Dreyfus and Deleuze on l'habitude, Coping, and Trauma in Skill Acquisition', *International Journal of Philosophical Studies 14* (2006), pp. 539–59.
Rietveld, E., 'The Skillful Body as a Concernful System of Possible Actions', *Theory & Psychology 18* (2008), pp. 341–63.
Rorty, A., *Mind in Action*, Boston: Beacon, 1988.
Rorty, A., 'Descartes on Thinking with the Body', in J. Cottingham (ed.), *The Cambridge Companion to Descartes*, Cambridge: Cambridge University Press, 2006, pp. 371–92.
Rudder Baker, L., Review of *The Body in Mind* by Mark Rowlands, *Mind 109 (2000)*, pp. 644–7.
Ryle, G., *The Concept of Mind*, Harmondsworth: Penguin, 1963 [1949].
Samudra, J. K., 'Memory in Our Body: Thick Participation and the Translation of Kinesthetic Experience', *American Ethnologist 35* (2008), pp. 665–81.
Sawyer, R. K., *Group Creativity: Music, Theatre, Collaboration*, Philadelphia, PA: Psychology Press, 2003.
Schouls, P., *Descartes and the Enlightenment*, Kingston and Montreal: McGill-Queens University Press, 1989.
Searle, J., *Intentionality*, Cambridge: Cambridge University Press, 1983.
Sebanz, N., H. Bekkering, and G. Knoblich, 'Joint Action: Bodies and Minds Moving Together', *Trends in Cognitive Sciences 10* (2006), pp. 70–6.
Selinger, E. M. and R. P. Crease, 'Dreyfus on Expertise: The Limits of Phenomenological Analysis', *Continental Philosophy Review 35* (2002), pp. 245–79.
Shapin, S., 'Descartes the Doctor: Rationalism and Its Therapies', *British Journal for the History of Science 33* (2000), pp. 131–54.
Sheets-Johnstone, M., 'Kinesthetic Memory', *Theoria et Historia Scientiarum 7* (2003), pp. 69–92.
Sheets-Johnstone, M., *The Corporeal Turn: An Interdisciplinary Reader*, Exeter: Imprint Academic, 2009 [2005].

Sheets-Johnstone, M., 'Animation: The Fundamental, Essential, and Properly Descriptive Concept', *Continental Philosophy Review 42* (2009), pp. 375–400.

Smith, E. R. and J. DeCoster, 'Dual-Process Models in Social and Cognitive Psychology: Conceptual Integration and Links to Underlying Memory Systems', *Personality and Social Psychology Review 4* (2000), pp. 108–31.

Snow, N., 'Habitual Virtuous Actions and Automaticity', *Ethical Theory and Moral Practice 9* (2006), pp. 545–61.

Spinosa, C., F. Flores and H. L. Dreyfus, *Disclosing New Worlds: Entrepreneurship, Democratic Action, and the Cultivation of Solidarity*, Cambridge, MA: MIT Press, 1997.

Stanley, J. and T. Williamson, 'Knowing How', *Journal of Philosophy 98* (2001), pp. 411–44.

Stevens, C., S. Malloch, S. McKechnie, and N. Steven, 'Choreographic Cognition: The Time-Course and Phenomenology of Creating a Dance', *Pragmatics and Cognition 11* (2003), pp. 299–329.

Sudnow, D., *Ways of the Hand: A Rewritten Account*, Cambridge, MA: MIT Press, 2001.

Sutton, J., *Philosophy and Memory Traces: Descartes to Connectionism*, Cambridge, MA: Cambridge University Press, 1998.

Sutton, J., 'The Body and the Brain', in S. Gaukroger, J. Schuster, and J. Sutton (eds), *Descartes' Natural Philosophy*, London: Routledge, 2000, pp. 697–722.

Sutton, J. 'Batting, Habit, and Memory: The Embodied Mind and the Nature of Skill', *Sport in Society* 10 (2007), pp. 763–86.

Sutton, J., 'Spongy Brains and Material Memories', in M. Floyd-Wilson and G. Sullivan (eds), *Environment and Embodiment in Early Modern England*, London: Palgrave Macmillan, 2007, pp. 14–34.

Sutton, J., 'Carelessness and Inattention: Mind-wandering and the Physiology of Fantasy from Locke to Hume', in C. T. Wolfe and O. Gal (eds), *The Body as Object and Instrument of Knowledge: Embodied Empiricism in Early Modern Science*, Springer, 2010, pp. 243–63.

Sutton, J. and K. Williamson, 'Embodied Remembering', in L. Shapiro (ed.), *The Routledge Handbook of Embodied Cognition*, New York: Routledge, 2014, pp. 315–25.

Szabo Gendler, T., 'Alief in Action (and Reaction)', *Mind & Language 23* (2008), pp. 552–85.

Toribio, J., 'How do we know how?' *Philosophical Explorations 11* (2008), pp. 39–52.

Voss, S., *The Passions of the Soul*, Indianapolis: Hackett, 1989.

Wacquant, L., *Body and Soul: Notebooks of an Apprentice Boxer*, Oxford: Oxford University Press, 2003.

Warnier, J-P., 'A Praxeological Approach to Subjectivation in a Material World', *Journal of Material Culture 6* (2001), pp. 5–24.

Weissensteiner, J., B. Abernethy and D. Farrow, 'Towards the Development of a Conceptual Model of Expertise in Cricket Batting', *Journal of Applied Sport Psychology 21* (2009), pp. 276–92.

Wheeler, M., *Reconstructing the Cognitive World: The Next Step*, Cambridge, MA: MIT Press, 2005.

Wheeler, M., 'Cognition in Context: Phenomenology, Situated Robotics, and the Frame Problem', *International Journal of Philosophical Studies 16* (2008), pp. 323–49.

Wierzbicka, A., *Semantics, Culture, and Cognition: Universal Human Concepts in Culture-specific Configurations*, Oxford: Oxford University Press, 1992.

Wolfe, C. T., 'De-ontologizing the Brain: From the Fictional Self to the Social Brain', *C-Theory 30* (2007), http://www.ctheory.net/articles.aspx?id=572 (accessed 10 November 2010).

Yin, H. H. and B. J. Knowlton, 'The Role of the Basal Ganglia in Habit Formation', *Nature Reviews Neuroscience 7* (2006), pp. 464–76.

6

What does the stick do for the blind?

Lambros Malafouris

Introduction

The boundaries of what we call the mind have always been problematic; however, they have never been so problematic as they are today. New theoretical and empirical work on enactive, situated, distributed, embodied and extended cognition clearly suggests that, in a variety of ways and to different degrees, what is outside the head may not necessarily be outside the mind. Of course, there is nothing especially new about that premise. The basic idea of a mind that is not limited by the skin is at the centre of various intellectual traditions, from the process philosophy of C. S. Peirce, H. L. Bergson and A. N. Whitehead, the pragmatism of J. Dewey, the phenomenology of M. Merleau-Ponty, and the more recent work in ecological psychology of J. Gibson and G. Bateson to the embodied cognitive science of F. Varela. Throughout the twentieth century, there have been continuous reactions against the oppressive separatist logic of the dominant modernist mind-set, and of the capitalist ethos of fabrication that sought to alienate mind from matter.

Today, the debate continues more intensely than ever, given the advent of cognitive science in the sixties and the rapid development of brain sciences in the last few decades. Still, the basic question concerning how to understand the relationship between mind, brain and the world remains the same: productively unsettled. Our sense of reality and our modes of acting, creating and imagining depend on the way that we understand this question, and make sense of the continuities or discontinuities between mind and matter. It is these questions about how we *think in* and *with* the world, and of how the world *thinks with* and *in* us, that Jill Bennett and Mary Zournazi see as the main thread that runs through this volume (see editorial introduction).

Understanding the process of material engagement

What is the mind? The question remains open; nothing about it has been resolved, or has lost its freshness. Anthropology and archaeology have kept a close eye on this question. Understanding human becoming and ways of thinking remains a central concern, both in relation to the long-term question of human cognitive origins and in relation to the comparative question about the unity and diversity of the human mind – questions that anthropologists and archaeologists see as their own 'hard' problems. This concern has become even more explicit as a result of recent interest in the study of material culture and the cognitive life of things.[1] At the point of intersection between cognition, affect and materiality, there is a knot that still waits to be untangled and understood.

This is exactly where the challenge for cognitive archaeology and anthropology lies: to explore how human intelligence emerges out of situated interactions among people and between people and things. Meeting this challenge demands reconnecting the brain with the body and the material world. One approach to this issue is to consider material culture as a kind of cognition-enhancing or grounding device. To give an example: by constructing a material symbol, we can materialize an abstract idea, and thus we transform something intangible and elusive into something concrete and manipulable. Objects of thought can therefore become objects of attention and perception – tangible things to engage with and use to construct meaning and store information. This kind of thought-enabling role for material culture has become a central tenet in much of the recent thinking in embodied and situated cognition. But to solely take this perspective is to leave out much of value. I say this not because I wish to deny that material culture extends the human cognitive niche by providing persisting and flexible scaffolding that supports the growth and development of human mind. Rather, my intention is to stress the importance of turning our attention to the specific historically and culturally constituted ways that the structural affordances, materials and functions of this scaffolding become realized. I argue that it is primarily by looking at the changing scaffolding 'process' of material engagement – rather than the static scaffolding 'structure' – that we might be able to overcome the limits of 'internalism' in the study of mind.[2]

The blind man's stick hypothesis

The classical example of the blind man with a stick can help us navigate this conceptual path of material engagement and follow the enactive threads that it embodies. Where does the blind man's self end and the rest of the world begin? A simple answer could be that the blind man is simply using a tool to overcome a perceptual deficiency, by substituting vision with touch. To a certain extent, this is precisely what happens: cortical areas normally underlying vision are recruited for other sensory modalities. What about the stick? Does the stick play some causal role in the above processes of cross-modal plasticity, and if it does, just what role might that be? *What does the stick do for the blind?*

From a phenomenological perspective it can be argued that the blind man using a stick does not sense the stick but the presence or the absence of objects in the outside environment. Although the stick offers the actual means for this exploration, it is itself forgotten. As Merleau-Ponty describes:

> The blind man's stick has ceased to be an object for him, and is no longer perceived for itself; its point has become an area of sensitivity, extending the scope and active radius of touch, and providing a parallel to sight. In the exploration of things, the length of the stick does not enter expressly as a middle term: the blind man is rather aware of it through the position of objects than of the position of objects through it. The position of things is immediately given through the extent of the reach that carries him to it, which comprises, besides the arm's reach, the stick's range of action.[3]

As with many other examples of prosthetic 'phenomenological osmosis',[4] with time and practice, the stick becomes incorporated, and thus transparent. Tactile sensation is somehow projected onto the point of contact between the tip of the stick and the outside environment. In short, on the one hand, the body schema extends to incorporate the stick, and on the other hand, the brain treats the stick as if it were part of the body. Does this mean that the biological boundary of the skin remains intact in the case of the blind?

Theories of extended and distributed cognition add an interesting twist to these questions by means of the so-called parity principle. When a part of the world – like the blind man's stick (BMS) in our case – 'functions as a process which, were it to go on in the head, we would have no hesitation in accepting as part of the cognitive process, then that part of the world is (for that time) part of the cognitive process'.[5] The implication of removing or damaging that part of the world is equal to that of removing or damaging part of the brain. The question can thus be put as follows: By removing the BMS, are we not preventing him from seeing? Or, more specifically, are we not preventing the world from touching his visual cortex?

Those questions become even more pronounced from a comparative anthropological or evolutionary perspective, raising a simple but powerful challenge against the legitimacy of the traditional boundaries of skin and skull. Some of the most persistent questions about the emergence and evolution of human intelligence depend on precisely where one decides, implicitly or explicitly, to draw the line between the mind and the material world, and infer the direction of causality between biology and culture. From such long-term perspectives, the stick is no longer a mere abstraction for any 'pathway along which differences are transmitted under transformation',[6] but is instead a *difference* in itself.

Interestingly, whatever actual form the 'stick' might have taken in the history of our species, its primary function was that of helping us to find our way and make sense of the world. Through the 'stick', the human species – much like the blind man in our example – feels, discovers and enacts the way forward. We should not think of this process as one where the purified mind of a pre-formed subject projects meaning and order onto the world. Rather, the analogy of the stick refers to the thoroughly relational and sensuous prosthetic becoming by which humans learn to identify, attend to and transform their world. Let's not forget that from an evolutionary point of view, the main reason we have a brain is to *move,* and not to entertain mental states like beliefs and desires. To begin with, moving was thinking. I mean this not in the computational sense of developing a brain able to produce and control adaptable complex movement. Rather, I mean it in the enactive sense of developing a mind which is 'inextricably linked to histories that are lived, much like paths that exist only as they are laid down in walking'.[7] And it seems fair to say that the reason we came to develop sophisticated capacities for meta-cognition, imagination and language is that – unlike other animal species – we gave our movement conscious purpose, direction and collective meaning. We had to use a stick to accomplish this – something concrete, a material sign to think through, with and about.

However, the question of the ontological status of the stick remains vague, even for those of us willing to subscribe to some of the current relational models of embodiment that recognize that differentiations between 'inside' and 'outside' often do not apply in the context of mediated activity and material engagement. Can things made of wood, stone, clay, metal or plastic really be parts of human thought?

Our inherent difficulty in conceptualizing the ontology of the stick stems, I believe, from the still-dominant representational habit of imagining the mind as a brain-bound computational device. The example of the blind man with a stick aims to help us break away from that habit, and redraw the line that separates brains, bodies and things. More than a mere thought experiment, this example has been employed in the context of material engagement theory as a working hypothesis, stating that the functional anatomy of human intelligence (brain and body) is a dynamic construct remodelled in detail by behaviourally important experiences, which are mediated – and often constituted – by the use of material objects, which, for that reason, should be seen as continuous, integral parts of the human mind.[8]

I proposed the BMS hypothesis as a simple but effective heuristic to overcome the inherited, unproductive conceptual split between the mind and the material world that constrains and imposes limits on our *thinking about the process of thinking* – in archaeology, anthropology and beyond. The aim is not necessarily to abandon boundaries altogether; rather, it is to question the authority of fixed boundaries, and assist us in rediscovering their border-like ontology. Boundaries, as Richard Sennett proposes using an example from natural ecology, are like cell walls.[9] Borders, in contrast, resemble the cell membrane. A boundary is 'simply an edge where things end'; a border, by contrast, is a site of exchange and interaction. A sensible objective towards a new ecology of mind would be to turn boundaries into borders, specifically into life pathways of a sort, and to use this transformation as a method for studying the mind as a situated process.

In particular, the BMS hypothesis embodies the spirit of 'material engagement theory'[10] in a double sense:

In one sense, the example of the blind man and the stick asserts that material things *matter*. Things matter, as means of dynamic and perturbatory mediation. The presence of the simplest artefact has the potential to alter relationships between humans, and between humans and their environments. Tool-making and use is one of a number of examples of such prosthetic gestures and material signs in the evolutionary history of our species.

In another sense, the blindness of the person reminds us of a very important universal feature of the human mind that many tend to forget, or prefer to ignore: namely, its 'incomplete' nature. Incompleteness[11] is not how we are inclined to think about the mind. Quite the contrary; the human mind is seen as a fully evolved, brain-bound biological entity, well-equipped with a superior computational intelligence in comparison with other animals, and ready to receive input from, and to impose structure upon, the 'external' world. There are many variations in the myth of human cognitive modernity, but the basic idea is the same: the mind is what the brain does, and what the brain does is predetermined by the evolved genetic makeup of our species –

which was largely established between 100,000 and 200,000 years ago. The underlying assumption is that all humans are naturally equipped (born with) with a set of potential capacities, which may be realized with some variation in different cultural settings. This human potential is genetically fixed and pre-given (innate), and nothing that an organism does or experiences in its life is capable of changing it.

In contrast to this obsolete myth of the 'modern' mind as an isolated, long-evolved and genetically fixed entity, the material engagement approach and the BMS hypothesis allow us to see the human mind as an incomplete and unfinished process – in some sense – 'blind' – and thus potentially in a permanent state of ongoing evolution. Human intelligence can now be seen not as a genetic set-up or an evolutionary stage but as an ongoing, co-evolutionary entanglement of people, materials and things. There is no moment in the history of human becoming where biology (in the sense of an essential human nature engineered by natural selection) gave way to culture.[12] Culture is not a separate, added layer of complexity but is a compound of material forces and energies that mingle and assemble, allowing us to become what we are in different historical contexts.

I believe that such a view, which draws on recent post-genomic and enactive perspectives, is better attuned to the remarkable plastic qualities and prosthetic abilities of our species. From a material engagement perspective, no human is ever complete; all humans are prosthetic sites of self-transformation. That brings us to the issue of 'metaplasticity'.[13]

Metaplasticity

In recent decades there have been drastic advances in knowledge about the ability of the developing brain to modify its organization to sensory input – and thus escape the restrictions of its own genome.[14] Not only is neuroscience now able to provide new insights into the mechanisms of experience-dependent plasticity – as demonstrated by D. Hebb's experiments, comparing rats that were allowed to roam freely in his home with those that had been left in laboratory cages[15] – but it is now possible to delay the onset and progression of brain disorders (e.g. Huntington's disease, Parkinson's disease, Down's syndrome) and various forms of brain injury in transgenic mice, by manipulating 'environmental enrichment'.[16] Moreover, it has been demonstrated that material enrichment enhances learning and memory, reduces memory decline in aged animals, decreases anxiety and increases exploratory activity.[17] Even more impressive are findings in primate studies, which edge closer to our own species. An exemplar of current progress in this area is the neuroanatomical study by Hihara and colleagues, in which two weeks of tool-use training was shown to forge a novel connection (linking the intraparietal area and temporoparietal junction) in the adult monkey cerebral cortex.[18]

Equally important are recent findings in human studies, where cognitive and social neuroscience have begun to offer an entirely new approach for exploring the effect of culture on the human brain, and the mechanisms of activity-dependent plasticity underlying the reorganization of cortical representations during learning. We now know that plasticity is not an occasional event but is the normal and ongoing state of the nervous system throughout the human lifespan. Not only do the human cortical maps exhibit strong plasticity during the early developmental period – in which synaptic densities (the number of synapses per unit volume of brain tissue) in most brain regions are at their maximum, but these maps show that the cortex retains a significant degree of plasticity into adulthood.[19]

Furthermore, new evidence is emerging for learning-induced alterations in the brain's macroscopic structure – which, among other things, contradict the traditionally held view that cortical plasticity is associated with functional rather than anatomical changes. Two well-studied examples can be found in musical training and in navigation expertise. In the first case, comparison of the brain anatomy of skilled musicians with that of non-musicians indicates that prolonged instrument practice leads to an enlargement of the hand area in the motor cortex.[20] Similar plastic effects have been observed in professional pianists and violinists with respect to the size of the *corpus callosum*.[21] In the second case, a study of the navigation-related changes observed in the hippocampi of London taxi drivers is revealing.[22] A comparison of the structural magnetic resonance imaging (MRI) scans obtained from both taxi drivers and control subjects revealed that the posterior hippocampi of taxi drivers were significantly larger due to their extensive training and experience in navigating the city of London and that the hippocampal volume correlated with the amount of time the individual had worked as a taxi driver (positively in the posterior and negatively in the anterior hippocampus).

Better understanding the plasticity of the mind has important implications for our conventional understanding of human cognitive becoming. Although neural plasticity is not the whole story, it certainly points us in the right direction – encouraging new hypotheses and offering a useful analytic bridge between brain, body and culture. For indeed, if the volume of the hippocampus of a taxi driver and the *corpus callosum* of a pianist can be positively correlated with the time spent taxi-driving or practising the piano, then the evolutionary significance of many long-term practices in human brain anatomy, structure and function needs extensive rethinking. Stone knapping is an obvious example here. Researchers Stout and Chaminade[23] have already offered concrete imaging evidence about the neural correlates of changing lithic technologies and their possible implications for long-standing evolutionary questions, such as the relationship between tool use and language. Clearly, the questions raised by these findings extend beyond the domain of stone tools. They also relate to more recent processes and practices that appear well after the appearance of *Homo sapiens*, between 200,000 and 70,000 years ago, arguably with major implications for our conventional archaeological understanding of the origins, development and varieties of human intelligence. Long-standing anthropological questions about the role of embodiment and technique in evolution and culture, or about the effects of different forms of enskilment and enculturation in the human cognitive system, can now be seen in a new light.

Naturally, exploring the effects of culture on the brain (and vice versa) over the long-term is a far more difficult task. The link between ontogeny and evolution is not as straightforward as the aforementioned parallels between taxi-driving and tool-making might imply. At present, learning- and practice-related developmental plasticity appear as the most promising areas of research for building analytic bridges between the short-term and long-term aspects of human cognitive becoming. To this end, theories of neural reuse,[24] cultural reconversion,[25] neuroconstructivism[26] and niche construction[27] may offer some additional guidelines in our attempt to understand the nature and varieties of human plasticity.

Needless to say, we should resist the temptation to use these rapidly accumulating neuroscientific resources to firmly situate the human mind inside the head. The real challenge lies in reconciling and integrating this new knowledge about the functional networks of the developing human brain (and their possible culture-specific patterns of activity) with the accumulating evidence for the extended, distributed, embodied and mediated character of human cognition. The objective is not to translate or reduce a cultural story into a biological one, but instead to integrate the two stories. The key question to ask, as philosopher Andy Clark has proposed, is how do we put brain, body and the world back together again?[28] I propose that the study of material culture can offer important contributions in address to this question.

More specifically, the challenge for anthropology lies in determining how our plastic brains and the associated patterns of *reorganization, redistribution* and *scaffolding* can be understood within the wider sociomaterial networks of somatic enskilment and mediated action that historically delineate the boundaries of human consciousness. As we saw, there are many parameters (that can be argued to be) strongly associated with neuroplasticity, and many different levels on which plastic changes can be understood. But the key question, both from an archaeological long-term perspective and from an anthropological comparative perspective, should concern the mechanisms that might mediate plastic changes – not at the individual level, but at the broader level of the human entanglement with the material world. At this broader level of material engagement, new forms of material culture compete equally with any other brain region for cortical space and connectivity. It should be noted that there is, at present, no evidence to suggest that processes of neural plasticity are radically different, or operate independently, from processes of extra-neural plasticity. In fact, from the perspective of archaeology, anthropology and material culture studies it makes sense to assume the continuity and inseparability of brain and culture, and to explore cultural change as a form of extra-neural plasticity.

Seen from such an angle, it is not enough to simply ask *how* and *why* a taxi driver's 'grey matter' might enlarge in order to store a mental map of the city of London. From a material engagement perspective, the significant question is not about brain size, neural connectivity or the changes in cerebral blood flow. Rather, the question is about the extensiveness, the leakages and the possible transubstantiations of this flow, where it meets the external world of human action and interaction. This 'natural' capacity for reconfiguring our cognitive ecologies or assemblies I describe using the term 'metaplasticity'.[29] In particular, metaplasticity denotes the processes by which the plasticity of the mind is embedded and inextricably enfolded within the plasticity of culture. The extraordinary plasticity of human extensiveness, and its openness to creative evolution by way of making and learning, becomes a distinctive feature of our species. Notions of neuronal and cultural plasticity offer a bridge between human ontogeny and evolution, and a useful means for understanding the role of embodiment as a powerful link between mind, brain and culture.

Minding the world

One approach commonly used in philosophy and embodied cognitive science to address questions of this relational nature is to extend the conventional boundaries of the mind into the world. Another approach, better suited to the epistemic demands of material engagement, would be to abandon once and for all the logic of 'boundaries' and 'delimiting lines'. The purity of delimiting lines, or of any concomitant neat analytical or metaphysical distinction, cannot accommodate the situated and transactional character of our everyday bodily engagement with the material world. In our thinking and living inside the world, no specific connection or demarcation is eternal or definitive.

The example of the BMS offers an intuitive way of doing this, by helping shift our attention from the distinction of 'mind' and 'matter' or 'in' and 'out' towards developing common, relational ways of thinking about the complex interactions among brain, body and world. The transactional character of the relation between the blind man and the stick provides a diachronic point of reference for advocating an ontological continuity between mind and matter. It also helps us to re-conceptualize the profound embodiment, ecology and plasticity of the human mind.

Acknowledgements

The writing of this essay was assisted by the John Templeton Foundation (JTF) Grant, *Self-Bound: The Making of Human Consciousness* (ID 60652). I am very grateful to the JTF for its support.

Notes

1 Lambros Malafouris and Colin Renfrew, 'The Cognitive Life of Things: Archaeology, Material Engagement and the Extended Mind', in *The Cognitive Life of Things: Recasting the Boundaries of the Mind*, eds Lambros Malafouris and Colin Renfrew (Cambridge: McDonald Institute Monographs, 2010), pp. 1–12. See also John Sutton, 'Porous memory and the cognitive life of things', in *Prefiguring Cyberculture: An Intellectual History*, eds Darren Tofts, Annemarie Jonson and Alessio Cavallaro (Cambridge, MA, and Sydney: MIT Press and Power Publications, 2004), pp. 130–41.

2 Lambros Malafouris, *How Things Shape the Mind: A Theory of Material Engagement* (Cambridge, MA: MIT Press, 2013).

3 Maurice Merleau-Ponty, *Phenomenology of Perception*, trans. C. Smith (London: Routledge & Kegan Paul, 1962), p. 143.

4 Drew Leder, *The Absent Body* (Chicago: University of Chicago Press, 1990).

5 Andy Clark and David Chalmers. 'The extended mind', *Analysis* 58:1 (1998), pp. 7–19.

6 Gregory Bateson, *Steps to an Ecology of Mind* (New York: Granada, 1973).

7 Francisco J. Varela, Evan Thompson and Eleanor Rosch (eds), *The Embodied Mind: Cognitive Science and Human Experience* (Cambridge, MA: MIT Press, 1991).

8 Lambros Malafouris, 'Beads for a plastic mind: the 'Blind Man's Stick' (BMS) hypothesis and the active nature of material culture', *Cambridge Archaeological Journal* 18 (2008), pp. 401–14.

9 Richard Sennett, *The Craftsman* (New Haven: Yale University Press, 2008), p. 227.

10 Malafouris, *How Things Shape the Mind.*

11 Lambros Malafouris, 'On human becoming and incompleteness: a material engagement approach to the study of embodiment in evolution and culture', in *Embodiment in Evolution and Culture*, eds Gregor Etzelmüller and Christian Tewes (Tübingen, Germany: Mohr Siebeck, 2016), pp. 289–306.

12 Daniel Lord Smail, *On Deep History and the Brain* (California: University of California Press, 2007), p. 144.

13 Lambros Malafouris, 'Metaplasticity and the human becoming: principles of neuroarchaeology', *Journal of Anthropological Sciences* 88 (2010), pp. 49–72. Lambros Malafouris, 'Metaplasticity and the primacy of material engagement', *Time and Mind* 8:4 (2016), pp. 351–71.

14 For summary review and references see Malafouris 'Beads for a plastic mind'; Idem., 'Metaplasticity and the human becoming'.

15 Donald Olding Hebb, *The Organization of Behavior: A Neuropsychological Theory* (Psychology Press, 1949).

16 Jess Nithianantharajah and Anthony J. Hannan, 'Enriched environments, experience-dependent plasticity and disorders of the nervous system', *Nature Reviews Neuroscience* 7 (2006), pp. 697–709.

17 Ibid.

18 Sayaka Hihara, Tomonori Notoya, Michio Tanaka, Shizuko Ichinose, Hisayuki Ojima, Shigeru Obayashi, Naotaka Fujii and Atsushi Iriki, 'Extension of corticocortical afferents into the anterior bank of the intraparietal sulcus by tool-use training in adult monkeys', *Neuropsychologia* 44:13 (2006), pp. 2636–46.

19 Dean Buonomano and Michael M. Merzenich, 'Cortical plasticity: from synapses to maps', *Annual Review of Neuroscience* 21 (1998), pp. 149–86. Steven Quartz and Terrence J. Sejnowski, 'The neural basis of cognitive development: a constructivist manifesto', *Behavioral and Brain Sciences* 20 (1997), pp. 537–56. Daniel Feldman, 'Synaptic mechanisms for plasticity in neocortex', *Annual Review of Neuroscience* 32 (2009), pp. 33–55. Clare Kelly and Hugh Garavan, 'Human functional neuroimaging of brain changes associated with practice', *Cerebral Cortex* 15 (2005), pp. 1089–1102. Anthony Holtmaat and Karel Svoboda, 'Experience-dependent structural synaptic plasticity in the mammalian brain', *Nature Reviews Neuroscience* 10:9 (2009), pp. 647–58. Janina Boyke, Joenna Driemeyer, Christian Gaser, Christian Büchel and Arne May, 'Training-induced brain structure changes in the elderly', *Journal of Neuroscience* 28 (2008), pp. 7031–5.

20 Katrin Amunts, Gottfried Schlaug, Lutz Jäncke, Helmuth Steinmetz, Axel Schleicher, Andreas Dabringhaus and Karl Zilles, 'Motor cortex and hand motor skills: structural compliance in the human brain', *Human Brain Mapping* 5:3 (1997), pp. 206–15.

21 Gottfried Schlaug, Lutz Jäncke, Yanxiong Huang, Jochen F. Staiger and Helmuth Steinmetz, 'Increased corpus callosum size in musicians', *Neuropsychologia* 33:8 (1995), pp. 1047–55. For a good review see: Thomas Münte, Eckart Altenmüller and Lutz Jäncke, 'The musician's brain as a model of neuroplasticity', *Nature Reviews Neuroscience* 3:6 (2002), pp. 473–8.

22 Eleanor Maguire, David G. Gadian, Ingrid S. Johnsrude, Catriona D. Good, John Ashburner, Richard SJ Frackowiak and Christopher D. Frith,

'Navigation-related structural change in the hippocampi of taxi drivers', *Proceedings of the National Academy of Sciences* 97:8 (2000), pp. 4398–4403.

23 Dietrich Stout and Thierry Chaminade, 'The evolutionary neuroscience of tool making', *Neuropsychologia* 45:5 (2007), pp. 1091–1100.

24 Michael L Anderson, 'Neural reuse: a fundamental organizational principle of the brain', *Behavioral and Brain Sciences* 33:4 (2010), pp. 245–66.

25 The hypothesis of cultural reconversion or 'neuronal recycling' refers to the capacity of human cerebral architecture to transform what was initially a useful function in our evolutionary past into another function, more useful in the present cultural context. Stanislas Dehaene and Laurent Cohen, 'Cultural recycling of cortical maps', *Neuron* 56:2 (2007), pp. 384–98.

26 Steven R. Quartz and Terrence J. Sejnowski, 'The neural basis of cognitive development: a constructivist manifesto', *Behavioral and Brain Sciences* 20 (1997).

27 John Odling-Smee, Kevin N. Laland and Marcus W. Feldman, *Niche Construction: The Neglected Process in Evolution* (Princeton, NJ: Princeton University Press, 2003).

28 Andy Clark, *Being There: Putting Brain, Body and World Together Again* (Cambridge, MA: MIT Press, 1997).

29 Malafouris, 'Metaplasticity and the human becoming'; Idem., 'Metaplasticity and the primacy of material engagement'.

References

Anderson, M., 'Neural reuse: a fundamental organizational principle of the brain', *Behavioral and Brain Sciences* 33:4 (2010), pp. 245–66.

Amunts, K., Schlaug, G., Jäncke, L., Steinmetz, H., Schleicher, A., Dabringhaus, A. and K. Zilles, 'Motor cortex and hand motor skills: structural compliance in the human brain', *Human Brain Mapping* 5:3 (1997), pp. 206–15.

Bateson, G., *Steps to an Ecology of Mind*, New York: Granada, 1973.

Boyke, J., Driemeyer, J., Gaser, C., Büchel, C. and A. May, 'Training-induced brain structure changes in the elderly', *Journal of Neuroscience* 28 (2008), pp. 7031–5.

Buonomano, D. V. and M. M. Merzenich, 'Cortical plasticity: from synapses to maps', *Annual Review of Neuroscience* 21 (1998), pp. 149–86.

Clark, A., *Being There: Putting Brain, Body and World Together Again*, Cambridge (MA): MIT Press, 1997.

Clark, A. and D. Chalmers. 'The extended mind', *Analysis* 58:1 (1998), pp. 7–19.

Dehaene, S. and L. Cohen, 'Cultural recycling of cortical maps' *Neuron* 56:2 (2007), pp. 384–98.

Hebb, D. O., *The Organization of Behaviour: A Neuropsychological Theory*, New York: Wiley, 1949.

Hihara, S., Notoya, T., Tanaka, M., Ichinose, S., Ojima, H., Obayashi, S. and A. Iriki, 'Extension of corticocortical afferents into the anterior bank of the intraparietal sulcus by tool-use training in adult monkeys', *Neuropsychologia* 44:13 (2006), pp. 2636–46.

Holtmaat, A. and K. Svoboda, 'Experience-dependent structural synaptic plasticity in the mammalian brain', *Nature Reviews Neuroscience* 10:9 (2009), pp. 647–58.

Feldman, D., 'Synaptic mechanisms for plasticity in neocortex', *Annual Review of Neuroscience* 32 (2009), pp. 33–55.

Kelly, A. C., and H. Garavan, 'Human functional neuroimaging of brain changes associated with practice', *Cerebral Cortex* 15 (2005), pp. 1089–1102.

Leder, D., *The Absent Body*, Chicago: University of Chicago Press, 1990.

Maguire, E. A., Gadian, D. G., Johnsrude, I. S., Good, C. D., Ashburner, J., Frackowiak, R. S. and C. D. Frith, 'Navigation-related structural change in the hippocampi of taxi drivers', *Proceedings of the National Academy of Sciences* 97:8 (2000), pp. 4398–4403.

Malafouris, L., 'Beads for a plastic mind: The 'Blind Man's Stick' (BMS) hypothesis and the active nature of material culture', *Cambridge Archaeological Journal* 18 (2008), pp. 401–14.

Malafouris, L., 'Metaplasticity and the human becoming: principles of neuroarchaeology', *Journal of Anthropological Sciences* 88 (2010), pp. 49–72.

Malafouris, L., *How Things Shape the Mind: A Theory of Material Engagement*, Cambridge, MA: MIT Press, 2013.

Malafouris, L., 'Metaplasticity and the primacy of material engagement', *Time and Mind* 8:4 (2015), pp. 351–71.

Malafouris, L., 'On human becoming and incompleteness: a material engagement approach to the study of embodiment in evolution and culture', in Gregor Etzelmüller and Christian Tewes, eds., *Embodiment in Evolution and Culture*, Tübingen, Germany: Mohr Siebeck, 2016, pp. 289–306.

Malafouris, L., and C. Renfrew, 'The cognitive life of things: archaeology, material engagement and the extended mind', in Lambros Malafouris and Colin Renfrew, eds., *The Cognitive Life of Things: Recasting the Boundaries of the Mind*, Cambridge: McDonald Institute Monographs, 2010, pp. 1–12.

Merleau-Ponty, M., *Phenomenology of Perception*, trans. C. Smith, London: Routledge and Kegan Paul, 1962.

Münte, T. F., Altenmüller, E. and L. Jäncke, 'The musician's brain as a model of neuroplasticity', *Nature Reviews Neuroscience* 3:6 (2002), pp. 473–8.

Nithianantharajah, J., and A. J. Hannan, 'Enriched environments, experience-dependent plasticity and disorders of the nervous system', *Nature Reviews Neuroscience* 7 (2006), pp. 697–709.

Odling-Smee, F. John, K. N. Laland and M. W. Feldman. *Niche Construction: The Neglected Process in Evolution*, Princeton, NJ: Princeton University Press, 2003.

Schlaug, G., Jäncke, L., Huang, Y., Staiger, J. F. and H. Steinmetz, 'Increased corpus callosum size in musicians', *Neuropsychologia* 33: 8 (1995), pp. 1047–55.

Sennett, R., *The Craftsman*, New Haven: Yale University Press, 2008.

Smail, D. L., *On Deep History and the Brain*, Berkeley: University of California Press, 2008.

Stout, D., and T. Chaminade, 'The evolutionary neuroscience of tool making' *Neuropsychologia* 45:5 (2007), pp. 1091–1100.

Sutton, J., 'Porous memory and the cognitive life of things', in Darren Tofts, Annemarie Jonson, and Alessio Cavallaro, eds., *Prefiguring Cyberculture: An Intellectual History*, Cambridge, MA, and Sydney: MIT Press and Power Publications, 2004, pp. 130–41.

Quartz, S. R., and T. J. Sejnowski, 'The neural basis of cognitive development: a constructivist manifesto, *Behavioral and Brain Sciences* 20 (1997), pp. 537–56.

Varela, F. J., Thompson, E. and E. Rosch, *The Embodied Mind: Cognitive Science and Human Experience*, Cambridge, MA: MIT Press, 1991.

PART FOUR

Technologies

7

The distributed-centred subject

Hélène Mialet

Rethinking the knowing subject in an intellectual landscape where the death of the subject has been collectively embraced is the goal of this essay. The knowing subject I describe, especially in 'its distributed dimension', is akin to the paradigm of distributed cognition, which shows that cognition is not only the product of the mind but also distributed in its environment.[1] In other words, cognition is conceived as being in part inside the mind of the subject and in part outside of it, inscribed for example in the instruments s/he manipulates. However new distributed cognition is, cognition, as with the classical model, is still conceived as the product of the manipulation of representations, though they are not only internal, but also external. Likewise, the distinction between humans and non-humans, and in particular, humans and machines, is clearly defined. I want to go further, however. The subject I depict is attached to instruments and machines (*and* humans) that are not only an extension of him or her; s/he is, in a real sense, I argue, constituted through them. Moreover, the instruments, devices and machines (*and* humans) are as much constitutive of knowledge production as disturbing factors that can reorganize and trouble the interaction; non-humans also have agency, so to speak. The frontier between machines and humans is blurred. Finally, distribution is relevant not only to think about the world of cognition but also, in my view, to understand how identity and presence are constituted through the actions of humans and non-humans. In this sense, this subject echoes certain aspects of Actor Network Theory (ANT). However, it turns on an important distinction from these two theoretical frameworks (ANT and distributed cognition), insofar as I'm trying to recuperate and flesh out a form of singularity that has been lost in these phenomena of distribution and collectivization. This is why this subject is called the distributed-centred subject.

Stephen Hawking is the focus of my study and of my book *Hawking Incorporated* upon which this essay is based. Hawking epitomizes the perfect Cartesian subject, the myth of our modernity, 'the brain in the vat', as it were. He is a liminal figure or case, so revered in our society, which proved bluntly – each time he made an appearance or a move – that everything science and technology studies (STS) has taught us was wrong. He is the ultimate test of falsification for STS. Unable to move his hands, arms and legs, unable to write or speak, he was, however, able to give talks, write, think, publish, 'chat' and be a genius. He was, it appears, living the life of the mind. His very presence, his performances and his accomplishments seemed to put into question or offer limits to the field of STS that has repeatedly shown us that knowledge is materially, socially or collectively made. Indeed, how are we supposed to study 'an individual', 'a mind', 'cognition' and 'abstraction', if no visible traces of their immediate activity are there to be seen? What is the ethnographer expected to follow 'if the hands, the eyes and the context, of [the one who] knows' are not there to be 'followed'? Was everything in Hawking's mind (the genius – the ideas – the science) as the press has tended to portray him?

To avoid the 'too easy' conundrum that makes us jostle back and forth between 'his genius resides in his brain', 'he is a social construct' or 'please, look at the networks!'[2] I attuned my ethnographic probes to grasp the reality of my subject: sometimes in the presence of the man, sometimes far away from him, sometimes hanging on his words – or lack of them for that matter – sometimes being carried by the speech and deeds of those who had met or worked with him, sometimes being moved by face-to-face encounters with him and sometimes travelling into his world through the words of others, whether in the flesh, or in newspapers, articles or movies. It was by following the traces left by his presence – through practices, daily events and activities, or digitized and printed words and images – that I tried to forge the tools and concepts that would help me rethink the knowing subject in the making.[3] Zooming in and out, up close and far away, I tried to grasp the locus of agency, inverting the naïve idea that the closer we are, the better we know. Indeed, the identity of the man was more tangible in texts than in person. I opened black boxes like Russian dolls, peeling off the numerous layers that constitute the great HAWKING, making visible the thin and intricate ramifications that made the genius. I looked at the different facets of the man: the performer, the writer, the thinker, the interlocutor, the author and the icon. I followed what happened between the moment he said 'yes' to give a talk, write an article, meet with a journalist, become a memory, or be artistically represented, and the moment where the word 'yes', so little and so ephemeral, gained weight and materiality to become a visible and tangible product: a talk, an article, an interview, an archive or a statue. And not, 'any' talk, but 'his' talk, article, interview, archive and statue. I discovered that a sentence (and a statement) such as 'he gave a talk' or 'his talk' is an easy shortcut for what is on the tip of the tongue: a process of attribution, a condensation that by-passes, forgets, and hides six months of complex collective work which the supposedly main actor is (not always) a part; and simultaneously, fifty pages of ethnographic description, which, of course, are another form of reduction or condensation, I agree.[4] And this is true as well when one says 'he thinks', 'he writes', 'he acts', 'he represents' and so on.

Surprised, then, I discovered that what seemed entirely encompassed by Hawking's mind was, for the most part, outside of it – already inscribed in the competences and organization of the machines and the assistants who had been trained to attune to him.[5] Indeed, unable to do anything by himself (or so little, a twitch of an eyebrow or a movement of his cheek), he had to delegate competences to machines and humans that were transforming what they were interpreting as a yes or no into HAWKING the thinker, the writer, the actor, the author, the icon and so on. Contrary to the way he was portrayed in the media, Hawking was not a pure brain; he had a flesh and blood body that was crucial to the activation of this environment. Around him, machines and human beings were acting synchronically, trained (in part) to interact with, act and respond to the little signals of his face; they were also, as in any social interaction, interpreting, completing, making mistakes, projecting and attributing (a lot) to him. This is perhaps where the difference between machines and human beings resides. This collective work of interpretation, completion, and sometimes messiness, was participating in the construction of words, sentences, paragraphs, articles, papers, conferences, books and more. I was observing, in fact, a pioneer, as Hawking was among the first to use the devices upon which our iPads, iPhones, androids and computers work today – these devices that complete words and sentences. If this description seems mechanical, it is not! Hawking's body was not just reduced to a twitch of an eyebrow; he was married twice, had children and had an important – some might say, charismatic – presence. Hawking had a flesh and blood body then, but he also had what I call a multiplicity of collective or extended bodies (composed of machines and human beings), of which he was at once an element and a product – HAWKING the genius.

Each collective body was in charge of one aspect of his being, that is, his intelligence, his physical body and his public persona. I will here provide a quick overview of their different ramifications.

Body I was composed of his computer, without which he would have been unable to speak or give conferences (though Hawking also communicated through body language with people who were familiar with him). Equipped with special software that facilitated the process of writing – thanks to specific interfaces or choice and organization of vocabulary, ways of saving complete paragraphs, and ways of retrieving them at will – this machine was constantly updated according to the modification of Hawking's body. When I met him, he was still able to move his fingers and click and select words on his computer via a hand-held interface. By 2005, he began to use his cheek muscle to move his glasses, which commanded an infrared beam that selected words on his computer. At around this time, a team from Intel spent months with him trying to observe his ways of interacting with his computer to design a better interface and a faster machine. Moreover, if the computer was in charge of giving him words by learning the patterns of its user, the synthesizer allowed him to have a voice, which became part of his identity, even though it had an American accent, as he liked to point out. His personal assistant took care of public requests, the media and the conferences. The world, which was supposed to receive HAWKING the genius, would thus be brought 'into the lab' in such a way that it would be able to receive the man after he had been briefed and prepared for his performance. The graduate assistant, in turn, worked with his computers, ensuring they were up-to-date and functioning, taking care of every aspect of his travel (organizing it from start to finish, down to the slightest detail, as well as the transportation and coordination of Hawking, his synthesizer and his computer). Finally, his nurses took care of his physical needs. As with his computer, assistants and nurses also learnt the patterns of their 'user'.

Body II was composed of his computer (which was in charge of giving him the possibility of writing and accessing information and scientific articles), his selected graduate students (to whom he assigned different subjects to pursue, 'extend', re-contextualize, transform into calculus and eventually articles) and the department and the university in charge of providing symbolic, financial and material resources.

Body III was composed of special diagrams, drawn by his graduate assistants, through which Hawking could travel in space and time. Indeed, Hawking's use and memorization of diagrams to think and elaborate new questions as a technique of visualization and imagination were made possible by the back and forth between the concrete labour of his students and collaborators, who 'thought/saw' with, and on behalf of, Hawking, and constructed for him the visual universe within which he could move and think. This operation could be seen as a form of gift of an image and counter gift of a thought made possible through the labour of mentorship, friendship and collaboration.

Body IV was composed of another collective, the media that transformed Hawking into a genius without a body, and into a stable identity, through the manipulation, use and re-contextualization of written artefacts such as his quotations or similar stories about him (his smile, his jokes, his geometrical way of thinking, etc.).

Body V was composed of the ethnographer (myself), Body I, and his sacred body, 'the Lucasian Professor of Mathematics'. We see how all the narratives that participated in the stabilization of his identity broke down when one entered in contact with him. It became difficult to read Hawking in the absence of body language, the presence of the machines that reconfigured the spatial arrangement necessary for a smooth conversation and the intervention of his assistants that constantly appeared and recalibrated the interaction caused by medical problems or machine malfunction.[6]

Body VI was composed of the archivists in Cambridge who are still collecting today what has been written by and about him, accumulating the material through which Hawking's presence has been and will continue to be reconstructed.

Body VII was composed of the artist and a statue that was supposed to represent him in the garden of the Department of Applied Mathematics and Theoretical Physics (DAMTP), another way to extend his presence, and the first encounter between the mock-up of the statue in plaster and Hawking in his office. In this particular context, in which his colleagues were invited to comment on the statue, we see how the statue became a catalyst, that made the qualities of one and the other appear in words, and visually, to the extent that we were assisting in an exchange of properties between the two – to the point of being lost in a hall of mirrors, bouncing between copies and originals.

Thus, throughout my book, *Hawking Incorporated*, I describe the movement, operation and deployment of the multiplicity of these extended bodies, each of which can be glimpsed through its workings and/or through its arrangements: bodies sometimes connected and sometimes divergent, bodies that become apparent or disappear, that exemplify or differentiate, anchor or abstract.

Hawking's mind, body and identity were made and remade through the translation and actions of these/his (collective) bodies. The mind was connected to machines and human beings that selected, translated, acted and offered a materiality thanks to whom and through which he could think. The flesh and blood body was connected to machines and human beings that allowed Hawking to be, move and speak. Identity was connected to machines and human beings that produced it. Indeed, his mind, his body and his identity were not only connected to humans and non-humans, they were also distributed through (and via) them – the intelligence, through the students, machines and diagrams; the body, through the assistants (who made travel possible), the nurses, the mechanical voice, the wheelchair; and the identity, through the assistants (who briefed the media and prepared the performance), the machines that allowed him to express himself or that became him, such as the tone of his voice, the colour of the words and the visible organization of the vocabulary. It is like we were 'stretching' an envelope that constituted an individual by making apparent the functioning of his mind, body and identity through permanent acts of translation and distribution by and through other beings, whether humans or machines (i.e. they were interpreting, reformulating, re-appropriating, selecting, transforming, adding or acting upon). In other words, the interiority, privacy and invisibility of the intellectual, corporeal and agential processes that constituted an individual became exteriorized, public and visible through acts of delegation.[7] The individual has become a collective (composed of different materialities). The individual *is* a collective.

The coalescence of this multiplicity into a whole is a complex endeavour, however, insofar as these collective bodies, as independent units and/or together, must be coordinated in such a way that 'an individual'[8] and a persona can emerge in the same movement. Sometimes things go wrong, like a frozen image on Skype, where the persona and 'the individual' are not superimposed or synchronized anymore, as, for example, when Hawking's computer broke down and he couldn't give a performance; or worse, when 'the individual' vanishes (e.g. as in my interview with him, where (1) his discourse was on the screen in front of him, (2) his 'voice' was near him, (3) his flesh and blood body flashed across the computer to alert the collective that it was 'broken', (4) his capacity to write (and speak) stopped as the machine stopped and (5) his body language was absent). Unable 'to read' him, we didn't know where he was anymore; reminding us that agency is related to synchronicity – a perfect synchronization between time (responses follow questions) and space (if our interaction is not mediated, reconfigured and muddled by the presence of the computer, then we can read each other), and between 'spoken', written and body language.[9]

Sometimes the boundary between himself and the actors (humans and non-humans) to which he was attached became so thin that they started to melt into one another: his mechanical voice became his identity (in his eyes and those of others), his assistants started completing his words and responding for him, or were perceived to be an extension of him (people would send emails to them instead of Hawking), his nurses would see him walking in their dreams, his assistant would say 'we' when he talked about Hawking's wishes and the statue became Hawking and allowed his colleagues who were talking about the statue to compare both of them, and through this comparison to speak about him.[10] We are thus dealing with an exchange of properties, a form of plasticity, that allows beings made of different physical, material or psychological qualities to become (in part) one another, to absorb traits of those with whom they are in contact (physically, or in spirit), to modify them or add properties to them at the same time as they are modified by them – another act of translation.[11]

Does this mean that what constitutes the essence of an individual is the equivalent of the addition of those who compose him/her? Can we still say that we are dealing with the same individual if one of those elements disappears, and stops being part of what constitutes him/her? Are the mechanical or material bodies and human beings to which a man or a woman is attached *just* an extension of him or her, then? Or do they do more than this? Are we assisting in processes of identification or transfer? Is the flesh and blood body 'real' while the other bodies – mechanical, extended or collective – are only 'metaphorical?' Are these extended bodies spatial, as the figure of the knowing subject they are producing tends to become? Is the distribution of action and presence so extreme that we lose the central actor, in this case Hawking, in this collective? How are asymmetries constructed? How does one become the centre of action? Is there one centre? Or, are there a multitude of centres appearing at different moments in time and space that are linked to each other to create what we call an individual?

These collective bodies were much more than an extension of the man. They were not 'extending' or transmitting some form of intentionality from the centre to the periphery. These collectives were making it possible for Hawking to be, act and work and to become the centre of action, through constant translations and disruptions (indeed, they didn't just transmit, they sometimes made mistakes, disturbed or redirected the action). Thus, we don't want to focus on what appears to be at the centre to comprehend how power is extended; rather, we want to start by looking at what appears to be at the periphery to understand how the centre is made. In this case, trained students translated problems into calculations and drew visible and material diagrams through which Hawking could project himself and think. Attentive nurses and collaborators allowed his flesh and blood body to live; he became enmeshed in a collective that took care of him, so much so that his own body became part flesh and part machine. Assistants, computer and synthesizer allowed an identity to be produced and maintained such that his identity became the equivalent of this collective.

In other words, the one who seemed to have the most agency didn't 'do' more than others; on the contrary, the others did more than him. They were doing what he couldn't do. Trained to adapt to anyone who might have 'a similar profile' or some aspects of it ('scientist', 'disabled' etc.), they were also attuning to him in particular, and in a particular way. By doing, working and performing, they were materializing, collectivizing and distributing 'his' competences. 'It is they' who were doing the work. His students were his hands, legs and words, becoming his intelligence, in the same way as his assistants were making his identity, or the machines were becoming his body. Hawking, because of his disability, was thus more distributed than anyone else insofar as, for him, language, *his* intellectual competences, *his* identity and even *his* own body, became the property of a human-machine network rather than the individual himself. But paradoxically, it was because he was the most distributed (competences *had to* be delegated), collectivized (others were doing the work) and materialized (his competences were incorporated in humans and non-humans) that he became the centre of this particular association and dissociation between collectives whose totality was (and is) called HAWKING. He was what I call a distributed-centred subject. Thus, he was not the most singular because – as we tend to portray him – he was outside the social and material world (the brain in the vat or the disembodied mind), but because he was the most materialized, collectivized and distributed. And it is also for the same reason that he made visible what we normally don't see. In this sense, he was not an exception; rather, he was an exemplum.[12] Like him, movie stars rely on complex collectives that allow them to perform; top notch scientists rely on machines or students who, for example, do the work of calculation; or scientists, who think in geometrical ways, rely (as he did) on the manipulation of diagrams; we see also, thanks to or through him, how journalists work, recycling similar quotations and stories around prominent figures; what a smooth communication implies through the breakdown and glitches characteristic of the complex system that surrounded him; and how archivists rethink the author in the digital age; and finally, what objects do in and to our social fabric.

He, she, we or the individual is produced by the collectives to which she is attached. She *is* a collective or the addition of the multiplicity of these collectives (all these actors/actants are becoming part of him/her). In my study, Hawking stands out because he was also more distributed, materialized and collectivized than anybody else; this is why he was the most singular. Moreover, because he was the most distributed, materialized and collectivized, he made visible invisible (and similar) processes without which anyone might be able to think, produce science, publish, give talks and so on. In other words, we see emerging different processes in the constitution of a knowing subject: distribution, singularization and exemplification.

Thus, Hawking's case problematizes the question of 'ability'. Like Harold Garfinkel, who was using 'the breach' in social interactions to see the norms, I describe how Hawking's configuration – a disabled man permanently attached to machines – modifies, accentuates and makes visible the invisible elements that are present in phenomena as diverse as 'starization'; scientific practices and scientific thinking; communication; ways of memorizing, archiving and constructing the author; and phenomena of encounter that allow the unconscious to talk. In other words, *this* individual makes visible how *other* individuals in similar situations – whether scientists, stars (in politics, art, industry or sport) – or for that matter all individuals, that is, any of us, are made.[13]

The movement I describe resembles the movement of a wave that inflates, breaks down, and rolls up onto itself again. We started with the assumption that a body, however frail it might be, contains in itself the essence of the person, of his identity and of his intelligence. Slowly I reconstructed and made visible the thin attachments, corporal or intellectual equipment or props out of which the flesh and blood body, the intelligence and the identity are made, and showed how this extension, distribution, redistribution, delegation, mediation, translation and projection in and through other beings, allows a body, mind and identity to function and be. A movement from inside to outside and from outside to inside again – and then outside again. The most extended, the most singular; the most singular, the most generalizable.

In other words, it is through these movements of distribution and redistribution and these processes of singularization that a particular figure emerges as a centre from which everything spreads out: intelligence, science and ideas. By processes of singularization, I am referring, for example, to processes of attribution, as when the students do most of the work, but still attribute their production to the insights of the professor, or to intentional processes of effacement of the collective bodies, where the assistants and the machines that participate in the construction of a particular performance disappear during this performance.[14] At another level, another form of singularity appears in different localizations of these networks or collectives through the ways in which the man resists and refuses to enter into (or engage with) the desires of others, something that I will call 'life' or 'will power'; or conversely, his singularity appears in the ways in which he becomes a participant in the construction of his persona. His singularity, here taken as what is not de-constructible, emerges when he goes against the collective and resists it, or when he works with it to construct himself at its centre.

Here is the beginning of an answer to the question with which I started this essay: how can we explain why one actor seems to have more agency than others, when agency has become the privilege of everyone else or everything else – that is, it is shared and distributed through associations? In other words, how does one explain that some seem to have more agency than others, if everything has agency? The properties of a subject are made by and through the actions of others: they add properties to her; they multiply her agency. Yet her singularity is not the only result of their actions, the actor does something that makes people act in a certain way. In the same way, the scientist can't make an object do whatever she wants, the subject of the social scientist resists. But the movement, the wave that she creates, is made possible, rendered audible, because of the specific arrangement, configuration and attunement to this particular entity. As Nigel Thrift points out, 'The world is being continually animated by actors who never work individually, always in concert, in a space that is in-between. Indeed, we might go so far as writers as various as Shotter or Sloterdijk and argue that the in-between of shared situations, and an accompanying art of orientation and tuning, is what there is and all there is.'[15] This may explain why sometimes an action, if not well connected to this specific configuration, falls flat. This may also explain the importance of ethnography in registering the infinite subtleties of reality so often lost in the march of our big categories.

Borrowing from the literary scientist Algirdas Julien Greimas the tools of semiotics, ANT portrays an actor (or an actant) as constantly moving; the actant, in this case, projects herself into different places and times through complex scripts that gain in materiality through the work of others. The configuration of an actor depends on the configuration of the network. If the network changes (as it constantly does, the main problem is its stabilization, not its movement), the definition of the actor changes with it, as does the definition of the actors to which s/he is attached. In other words, we are dealing with spatiotemporal envelopes that move and fluctuate, similar to the distributed-centred subject I have just described. There is a sense in which the subject I describe *is* an actor network. I show and make visible and tangible the multiplicity of spatiotemporal envelopes that constitute Hawking, while at the same time fleshing out and making visible what an actor network is. Again, his intelligence is distributed, but also his identity and his presence. In the same way as I get an email from Bernie Sanders – who obviously didn't write it or even conceive it – I believe it is him and not a representation of him, insofar as this email is a part of what constitutes him. It *is* him. This email is part of Sander's essence. The identity of Sanders is the equivalent of the collective, in the same way as Hawking's identity is the equivalent of this multiplicity of collectives, though in the case of Hawking, even his flesh and blood body was distributed – part machine/part human. All the properties – intelligence, identity and the body – that constitute the person or the self are outside, distributed and replayed. But if they stop, and if certain crucial elements stop, does this reality called HAWKING disappear?

The distributed-centred subject reintegrates a form of singularity that has been erased in these phenomena of distribution and collectivization. Indeed, in ANT, the subject fluctuates and is insatiable, unstable, moving and always rewritten by others. Or it is in the process of changing its definition by being attached to other actors that, depending on whether or not they want to pursue the subject's desires (as a means of fulfilling their own), gives the subject a form of reality, or not. It is an ontology that makes 'the other' the possibility for any existence.[16] Again this 'other' can take on different materiality. In ANT, the human actor is endowed with certain competences that are a strategy or a capacity to convince others; however, in this model, the human actor doesn't have any psychological probability – this is what makes it function.[17] The distributed-centred subject I propose is an envelope grounded in a specific body. The competences of the man were distributed, more than others, and thus he emerged as this singular figure called HAWKING (and this figure/persona was sometimes inscribed in the body of the man, sometimes not).[18] But the singularity of the man appeared at different localizations of the network, and this addition of points of resistance or amplification appeared like the thread left by a needle in a piece of fabric. Finally, knowledge production is not only made through manipulation of representations, but also through processes of projection, identification and exchange of properties. For example, in my first book, I showed how a scientist who was simulating petroleum fluid was becoming the object he was working on.[19] In the same way, Hawking – though he could not manipulate things with his hands – could project himself into the universe through the use of diagrams (something at which he became an expert).[20] Thus, we don't have one individual + machines + other human beings, but rather intelligence is the equivalence of this collective, and sometimes – though made possible by this collective (thanks to a phenomenon of exchange of properties) – entirely detached from it. Or again how, when Hawking was presented with a version of the statue that was supposed to represent him and would be displayed in the garden of the DAMTP (and sitting next to each other in his office), one became the other by a phenomenon of juxtaposition. Indeed, his colleagues, who had been invited to evaluate the statue, started to see him through the statue, and the statue at his side began to live a kind of life on its own.[21] In his book, *Par-delà Nature and Culture*, Philippe Descola talks about the ways in which the hunter becomes the jaguar.[22] There is also here, one could say, an exchange of properties between humans and non-humans, between humans and humans. In the case of Hawking, acolytes learned the patterns of their master and responded for him – they were becoming him, and were perceived as being him – thus the complex training that occurred when the assistants had to be replaced. In a similar way, Hawking started inhabiting the dreams of others. We are assisting, I argue, in different forms of an exchange of properties.[23]

Of course, all the elements we are dealing with are specific and singular, starting with Hawking, his field of research, those who worked with him, the intellectual tools he used and so on, but at the same time he gave us access to a form of reality, a construct, an intellectual tool or a concept that we can use to describe other subjects in other domains.[24] The concept of the distributed-centred subject allows us to reorganize and think about differences differently; we don't have an individual versus a collective, we have an individual that is a collective and sometimes, though always connected, is able to retrieve and construct himself against it or with it. It is different to say that an individual emerges (only) from the association of these collectives constituted of humans and non-humans than to say, as I do, that an individual (body, mind and identity) *is* a collective singularized. Agency, in the latter case, becomes distributed, spatialized *and* singularized. In other words, we are dealing with an individual as a product of processes of individuation, where the relation is always ontologically and epistemologically primordial.[25] In this sense, the distributed-centred subject echoes and resonates with other concepts such as the monad,[26] bubbles and spheres,[27] rhizomes[28] and networks,[29] though it makes them visible and tangible through the skin (definitely stretched) of a particular individual. The concept of the distributed-centred subject also helps us rethink the place, the role and the texture of human agency that too often has been dissolved in these sociomaterial-semiotic ontologies.

It has become generally accepted that we have to leave behind the dichotomies upon which we have been used to understanding the world, such as subject/object, nature/culture and so on and so forth, as they were the product of an area called 'modernity'. The work of STS scholars has been important in offering the possibility of questioning 'scientific knowledge'. By doing this, they have shaken the edifice upon which our modernity is constructed: science versus everything else. It has shaken the dichotomy between natural and physical sciences versus the humanities or social sciences and so on. Most importantly, in the present context, by deconstructing the scientific object, they have also destabilized the role and the status of the knowing subject, which, I argue, is in need of being rethought. Indeed, scientific knowledge has become the product (in part) of humans that are perfectible. Attempts to contain 'irrationality' by philosophers (e.g. Popper), sociologists (e.g. Merton) and historians (e.g. Kuhn) – by creating artificial barriers between, respectively, the context of discovery versus the context of justification, technical versus social norms, or normal science versus revolutionary science and so on – gave way to observations that have allowed us to understand the heterogeneity of entities (belonging to what we thought were incompatible ontologies) that make knowledge on the ground while at the same time presenting it as detached from it (i.e. as being the product of the rational disembodied mind). By reintroducing non-humans, ANT has destabilized the distinction between the material and the social. It has transformed the knowing subject into a collective. In other words, the knowing subject corresponds, maps or mirrors the collective process of knowledge production from which it emerges.[30] Thus, on the one hand, ANT has given a certain amount of agency to any actor that make the world (gods included), while on the other, it has lost the specificity of the human and everything that goes with it, such as the interiority, the psyche, subjectivity, self-reflexivity and the locus of knowledge production.[31] Those properties have become a product (a historical, sociological or collective construction of the Moderns) that can always be undone. Indeed, the reattribution of agency to non-humans – the fact that the subject/object dichotomy is a result of processes, and not the starting point – makes the place, the role and the specificity of human agency difficult to think about. Do we need to go back and reaffirm the original power of the human being with which we started this essay? No. But we still need to understand how asymmetries are constructed, why certain individuals are more creative than others, what subjectivity and interiority are made of and how intelligence and imagination function. ANT does not help us in this regard. We need to rethink how differentiation is created in an ontology where difference prevails in the first place, where everything is made flat and equivalent in its difference.[32] We are still very much obsessed with individuality, powerful figures, stars, geniuses and human specificity and so on. The necessity and possibility of rethinking this in the light – and at the limits – of these new socio-material-semiotic ontologies is what I propose. In this sense, I'm not claiming that we have to return to the disembodied individual rational actor that transforms the world based on the sole strength of her mind (this is precisely what I have questioned by using Hawking's case), nor that we have to go back to a subject that is construed as determined by invisible social forces that are only accessible to the analysts (the critic).[33] Rather, I have followed the humans and non-humans that, through the traces they have left, construct a mind, a body and an identity that we call a knowing subject. Sometimes we see a collective, sometimes we see an individual (that can be a collective), sometimes we see a man, sometimes we see a person and sometimes we see a collection of acts resembling a thread left by a needle in the collective fabric that makes the presence and contour of an individual tangible. Thinking about a subject that is distributed, but also centred (by centred I mean not as placed in the middle, but as localized) is a way of reintroducing the question of singularity in a new way.[34] We are all more or less distributed or centred, and we are distributed and centred in different ways. This is a programme of research I propose that has to be understood and tested on the ground by following other beings (human and non-human), geniuses or not, belonging to different collectives (art, science, politics, sport or literature).

The implications of adding or substituting another account to the ways in which we have traditionally thought about the knowing subject (i.e. the disembodied rational mind) by offering the concept of the distributed-centred subject could have consequential performative effects. The mind/body dichotomy has had interesting (if not dreadful) repercussions insofar as it has allowed us to construct ourselves as being different from (and superior to) other cultures and allowed us to colonize them. In our society, it has allowed us to create a distinction between the theoreticians (and intellectuals) who work with their mind and the workers who work with their hands; in our laboratories, between the chief as 'the visionary mind' and the assistants as 'hands that execute' and humans as 'the mind' and non-humans as 'bodies and matter'. Thinking about a distributed-centred subject that is constituted through, and equivalent to, a multiplicity of overlapping and interconnecting collectivities (when at the same time detached from them through collective processes of singularization of which s/he plays a part) can help us rethink all these dichotomies. It will change our way of thinking about ourselves and of presenting ourselves to others, of thinking about the distinction between theory and practice, leaders and assistants, and humans and non-humans. It could also help us understand how heroic figures are constituted in fields as diverse as art, politics, science, industry, literature and sport. It could also have implications for how we think about authorship, how we distribute resources or salaries and so on. Multiplying accounts opens up new possibilities. In the same way as Vinciane Despret tells us that she prefers to live with intelligent animals by constructing devices that allow them to be intelligent,[35] or Emilie Hache reminds us that another account of the ways in which we interact with nature could have important consequences for the ways we relate to it,[36] this new account could help us move forward in the ways in which we understand and represent ourselves, engage and present ourselves to 'others', and rethink the organization of a society that is becoming more and more distributed through media, machines and non-humans.

Notes

1 Edwin Hutchins, *Cognition in the Wild* (Cambridge, MA: MIT Press, 1995), and Andy Clark, *Being There: Putting Brain, Body and World Together Again* (Cambridge, MA: MIT Press, 1997).

2 I have in mind the analysis of Pasteur by Latour who is a semiotic actor; see Bruno Latour, *The Pasteurisation of France* (Cambridge, MA: Harvard University Press, 1988).

3 I also developed the theoretical framework I had elaborated in my previous book; Hélène Mialet, *L'Entreprise Créatrice, Le rôle des récits, des objets et de l'acteur dans l'invention* (Paris: Hermès-Lavoisier, 2008).

4 It is more a condensation than a reduction in so far as we are adding knowledge, more than reducing a reality to existing categories.

5 This notion of attunement is crucial in this entire enterprise. See also Vinciane Despret, 'The body we care for, Figures of anthropo-zoo-genesis', in *Body and Society: Special Issue on « Bodies on Trial »*, M. Akrich and M. Berg (eds), Vol. 10:2/3 (2004), pp. 111–34.

6 Thus, the idea that the farther we are, the better we know him.

7 In other words, because Hawking had to delegate all these operations, they became visible for the ethnographer.

8 I use quotations marks here to illustrate the fact that I'm talking about the individual in the traditional sense, that is as being the opposite of the collective.

9 Hélène Mialet, 'Reading Hawking's presence: an interview with a self-effacing man', *Critical Inquiry* 29 (2003), pp. 571–98.

10 Hélène Mialet, *Hawking Incorporated: Stephen Hawking and The Anthropology of the Knowing Subject* (Chicago: University of Chicago Press, 2012).

I show that Identity does not stop at the boundary of the flesh, but those we are interacting with routinely, physically or in spirit, become part of ourselves, of our sense of the self as much as we start inhabiting their selves or sense of the self. We panic, as they do, when these ties break, when our machines stop functioning, when our loved ones disappear. How do we create a boundary between what belongs to the other and what belongs to us?

11 Mialet, *L'Entreprise Créatrice*; idem, 'making a difference by becoming the same', *The International Journal of Entrepreneurship and Innovation* 10:4 (2009), pp. 257–65; idem, *Hawking Incorporated*; idem, 'The pugilist and the cosmologist: a response to *Homines in Extremis*: what fighting scholars teach us about Habitus by Loic Wacquant', *Body and Society* 20:2 (2014), pp. 91–9; idem, 'Les Pratiques de l'Invention', in Robert Prost (ed.), *Concevoir, Créer, Inventer* (Paris: L'Harmattan, 1995), pp. 283–300. The examples proposed by Evelyn Fox Keller, *A Feeling for the Organism* (San Francisco: W.H. Freeman, 1983), Natasha Myers, 'Molecular embodiments and the body-work of modeling in protein crystallography', *Social Studies of Science* 38:2 (2008), pp. 163–99, Janet Vertersi, 'Seeing like a Rover: visualization, embodiment, and interaction on the mars exploration rover mission', *Social Studies of Science* 42:3 (2015), pp. 393–414, and Bruno Latour, 'Mixing humans and non-humans together: the sociology of a door-closer', *Social Problems* 35 (1988), pp. 298–310, might fit well with the model that I am developing here.

12 Or his exceptionality resided in the fact that he was the most distributed and not the least, as we tend to portray him, i.e. 'the brain in the vat' outside the social and material world.

13 However, there is a difference that has to be explored through other ethnographies between what constitutes a political subject, a religious subject, a loving subject, etc.

14 See the structure of the stage and how the star is made visible; for example, the light is focused on the person, the background is black and so on. I follow as well the mechanisms used by the press such as repetition, recontextualization, etc., that participate in the processes of singularization of the person. See Mialet, *Hawking Incorporated* for a more detailed account of these processes of singularization.

15 Nigel Thrift, 'I just don't know what got into me: where is the subject?' *Subjectivity* 22 (2008), p. 85.

16 Bruno Latour, *An Inquiry into Modes of Existence* (Cambridge, MA: Harvard University Press, 2013).

17 Mialet, *L'Entreprise;* idem, 'Do Angels have bodies: two stories about subjectivity in science, the cases of William X and Mr. H', in E. Selinger and R. P. Crease (eds), *The Philosophy of Expertise* (New York: Columbia University Press, 2006), pp. 246–79.

18 By this is, I mean, the man and the persona are perfectly synchronized or not.

19 Mialet, *L'Entreprise* and Mialet, 'Making a Difference by Becoming the Same'.

20 Mialet, *Hawking*, chapter 3.

21 Mialet, *Hawking*, chapter 7.

22 Philippe Descola, *Beyond Nature and Culture*, trans. J. Lloyd (Chicago: University of Chicago Press, 2013).

23 This is what I'm pursuing in my new book, tentatively entitled, *The Thinking Person's Disease: An Ethnographic Study of the Senses*.

24 This is why *Hawking Incorporated* is not a biography, but a work of empirical philosophy.

25 Gilbert Simondon, *L'individuation psychique et collective* (Paris: Aubier, 1989), p. 54. 'The relation can never be conceived as a relation among preexisting terms, but rather as a reciprocal regime of the exchange of information and of causality in a system that individuates itself. The relation exists physically, biologically, psychologically, collectively as internal resonance of the individuated being; the relation expresses individuation and is at the heart of being.' Quoted in Bernard Stiegler, 'The theater of individuation: phase-shift and resolution in Simondon and Heidegger', trans. K. Lebedeva, *Parrhesia*, 7 (2009), pp. 46–57. See also Bernard Stiegler, *La technique et le temps 2. La désorientation* (Paris: Galilée, 1996).

26 Gottfried Liebniz, *Monadology and other philosophical essays*, trans. P. Schrecker and A. M. Schreker (Indianapolis: Bobbs-Merill Co: 1965); Gabriel Tarde, *Monadology and Sociology*, trans. and ed., T. Lorenc (Melbourne: re-press, 2012); see also Didier Debaise, 'Une Métaphysique des possessions, Puissances et Sociétés chez G. Tarde', *Revue de Métaphysique et de Morale* 4 (2008), pp. 447–60.

27 Peter Sloterdijk, *Bubbles*, Spheres Vol. 1, trans. W. Hoban (Cambridge, MA: MIT, 2011).

28 Gilles Deleuze and Félix Guattari, *A Thousand Plateaus: Capitalism and Schizophrenia,* trans. and forward by Brian Massumi (Minneapolis: University of Minnesota Press, 1987).

29 See for example Michel Callon, 'Some elements of a sociology of translation: domestication of the scallops and the fishermen of St Brieuc Bay', in J. Law (ed.), *Power, Action and Belief: A New Sociology of Knowledge?* (London: Routledge, 1986), pp. 196–233; Bruno Latour, *Reassembling the Social, An Introduction to Actor Network Theory* (Oxford: Oxford University Press, 2005); John Law, and Michel Callon 'on the construction of sociotechnical networks: content and context revisited', *Knowledge and Society* 9 (1989), pp. 57–83; Antoine Hennion, 'From ANT to pragmatism: a journey with Bruno Latour at the CSI', *New Literary History* 47/2/3 (2016).

30 In brief, we seem to be returning to the figure of the knowing subject floating above the ground, a figure against which, strangely, ANT and STS had constructed themselves in the first place. See Hélène Mialet, 'Reincarnating the knowing subject: scientific rationality and the situated body' *Qui Parle*? 18:1 (2009), pp. 53–73 and Hélène Mialet, 'Where would STS Be without Latour? What would be missing?' *Social Studies of Science* 42:3 (2012), pp. 456–61.

31 The only thing we can study is the materiality of the traces left by the actors; or if we assume that everything is externalized, how can interiority become possible becomes the question.

32 If the answer is located in the processes of associations, we need to understand, I argue, the materiality and the texture of associations. We have to refuse to qualify elements from the start. In other words, we have to refuse to create distinction between the 'psychological,' 'the sociological' and 'the political.' We have to follow what actors do, how they give agency to others and borrow agency from them to understand how these boundaries are created. This is why it is so important to go into the details of the description; see Mialet, *Hawking Incorporated.*

33 Hélène Mialet. 'The "Righteous Wrath" of Pierre Bourdieu', essay review of Pierre Bourdieu's *Science de la science et réflexivité, Social Studies of Science* 33:4 (2003), pp. 613–21.

34 In other words, the question is not who was Hawking, but where was he.

35 Vinciane Despret, 'Sheep Do Have Opinions', in B. Latour and P. Weibel (eds), *Making Things Public, Atmospheres of Democracy* (Cambridge, MA: MIT Press, 2005), pp. 360–8.

36 Emilie Hache, 'Tremblez, tremblez, les sorcières sont de retour! Ecrivaines, philosophes, activists et Sorcières écoféministes face au dérèglement climatique. Récit écoféministe de l'anthropocène', *Colloque: Comment penser l'Anthropocène?*, 5–6 November 2015.

References

Callon, M., 'Some elements of a sociology of translation: domestication of the scallops and the fishermen of St Brieuc Bay', in J. Law (ed.), *Power, Action and Belief: A New Sociology of Knowledge?*, London: Routledge, 1986, pp. 196–233.

Clark, A., *Being There: Putting Brain, Body and World Together Again*, Cambridge, MA: MIT Press, 1997.

Debaise, D., 'Une Métaphysique des possessions, Puissances et Sociétés chez G. Tarde', *Revue de Métaphysique et de Morale* 4 (2008), pp. 447–60.

Deleuze, G. and F. Guattari, *A Thousand Plateaus: Capitalism and Schizophrenia*, trans. and forward by B. Massumi, Minneapolis: University of Minnesota Press, 1987.

Descola, P., *Beyond Nature and Culture*, trans. J. Lloyd, Chicago: University of Chicago Press, 2013.

Despret, V., 'The body we care for, Figures of anthropo-zoo-genesis', *Body and Society: Special Issue on « Bodies on Trial »*, M. Akrich and M. Berg (eds), Vol. 10:2/3 (2004), pp. 111–34.

Despret, V., 'Sheep do have opinions', in B. Latour and P. Weibel (eds), *Making Things Public, Atmospheres of Democracy*, Cambridge, MA: MIT Press, 2005, pp. 360–8.

Hache, E., 'Tremblez, tremblez, les sorcières sont de retour! Ecrivaines, philosophes, activists et Sorcières écoféministes face au dérèglement climatique. Récit écoféministe de l'anthropocène', *Colloque: Comment penser l'Anthropocène?*, 5–6 November 2015.

Hennion, A., 'From ANT to pragmatism: a journey with Bruno Latour at the CSI', *New Literary History* 47/2/3 (2016), pp. 289–308.
Hutchins, E., *Cognition in the Wild*, Cambridge, MA: MIT Press, 1995.
Keller, E.F., *A Feeling for the Organism*, San Francisco: W.H. Freeman, 1983.
Latour, B., 'Mixing humans and non-humans together: the sociology of a door-closer', *Social Problems* 35 (1988), pp. 298–310.
Latour, B., *The Pasteurisation of France*, Cambridge, MA: Harvard University Press, 1988.
Latour, B., *Reassembling the Social, an Introduction to Actor Network Theory*, Oxford: Oxford University Press, 2005.
Latour, B. *An Inquiry into Modes of Existence*, Cambridge, MA: Harvard University Press, 2013.
Law, J. and M. Callon, 'On the construction of sociotechnical networks: content and context revisited', *Knowledge and Society* 9 (1989), pp. 57–83.
Liebniz, G., *Monadology and other Philosophical Essays*, trans. P. Schrecker and A. M. Schreker, Indianapolis: Bobbs-Merill Co, 1965.
Mialet, H., 'Les Pratiques de l'Invention', in R. Prost (ed.), *Concevoir, Créer, Inventer*, Paris: L'Harmattan, 1995, pp. 283–300.
Mialet, H., 'The "Righteous Wrath" of Pierre Bourdieu', essay review of Pierre Bourdieu's *Science de la science et réflexivité, Social Studies of Science* 33:4 (2003), pp. 613–21.
Mialet, H., 'Reading Hawking's presence: an interview with a self-effacing man', *Critical Inquiry* 29 (2003), pp. 571–98.
Mialet, H., 'Do Angels have bodies: two stories about subjectivity in science, the cases of William X and Mr. H', in E. Selinger and R. P. Crease (eds), *The Philosophy of Expertise*, New York: Columbia University Press, 2006, pp. 246–79.
Mialet, H., *L'Entreprise Créatrice, Le rôle des récits, des objets et de l'acteur dans l'invention*, Paris: Hermès-Lavoisier, 2008.
Mialet, H., 'Reincarnating the knowing subject: scientific rationality and the situated body', *Qui Parle?* 18:1 (2009), pp. 53–73.
Mialet, H., 'Making a difference by becoming the same', *The International Journal of Entrepreneurship and Innovation* 10:4 (2009), pp. 257–65.
Mialet, H., 'Where would STS be without Latour? What would be missing?' *Social Studies of Science* 42:3 (2012), pp. 456–61.
Mialet, H., *Hawking Incorporated: Stephen Hawking and The Anthropology of the Knowing Subject*, Chicago: University of Chicago Press, 2012.
Mialet, H., 'The pugilist and the cosmologist: a response to *Homines in Extremis*: what fighting scholars teach us about habitus by Loic Wacquant', *Body and Society* 20:2 (2014), pp. 91–9.
Mialet, H., *The Thinking Person's Disease: An Ethnographic Study of the Senses* (forthcoming).
Myers, N., 'Molecular embodiments and the body-work of modeling in protein crystallography', *Social Studies of Science* 38:2 (2008), pp. 163–99.
Simondon, G., *L'individuation psychique et collective*, Paris: Aubier, 1989.
Sloterdijk, P., *Bubbles*, Spheres Vol. 1, trans. W. Hoban, Cambridge, MA: MIT, 2011.
Stiegler, B., *La technique et le temps 2. La désorientation*, Paris: Galilée, 1996.

Stiegler, B., 'The theater of individuation: phase-shift and resolution in Simondon and Heidegger', trans. K. Lebedeva, *Parrhesia* 7 (2009).

Tarde, G., *Monadology and Sociology*, trans. and ed. T. Lorenc, Melbourne: Re-press, 2012.

Thrift, N., 'I just don't know what got into me: where is the subject?', *Subjectivity* 22 (2008), p.82–89.

Vertersi, J., 'Seeing like a Rover: visualization, embodiment, and interaction on the mars exploration rover mission', *Social Studies of Science* 42:3 (2015), pp. 393–414.

8

Dancing with the non-human

Petra Gemeinboeck

This essay explores alternative notions of thinking to re-imagine the non-human, and with it, our relationship with machines. Thinking is an act of shaping the world – so much so that we tend to forget that it is not separate from us. It could be argued that in traditional Western thought, thinking is akin to forging the world, which is always external, but fully knowable. But what if, instead, thinking is a delicate, mutual reconfiguring *with* the world, which we can only ever partially know? The distinction between the two viewpoints implies a radically different subject position: the first places the human at the 'top of the world', from where it is constructed and controlled, while the latter places us inside the world, amidst its unfolding mess of relations, and in constant, even if only partial, connection to it. Andrew Pickering states that 'if the world is knowable, command and control follow'.[1] Interestingly, a world that is knowable can be known entirely without a body as it can be 'thought up', fabricated according to one's beliefs and assumptions. Attempting to 'grasp' a world that is continuously being reconfigured and continually 'still to know', however, requires active, bodily engagement. Thinking here is not about moulding and controlling the world, but a more humble, entangled pursuit, more akin to negotiating while being transformed in the process; a thinking *with* the world is always situated, relational and materially anchored.

Bodily engagement with a messy, unknowable world sets the tone for my inquiry into an arena, which, traditionally, has been blind to this entanglement. Built on a strong Cartesian foundation, beliefs in an inherent and fixed difference between subject and object and a 'Cartesian separation of intelligibility and materiality'[2] still shape the sociomaterial practices of artificial intelligence (AI) and robotics, and with it, visions of our technologically enhanced future. Rolf Pfeifer, former director of University of Zurich's Artificial Intelligence Lab, really says it all: '[o]nce you are caught up in this Cartesian world view that thinking is algorithms or a computer programme, it is enormously difficult to free yourself from that. It just seems so obvious: there is input, processing, output – how else could it be?'[3] Yet it seems that there's more at stake than ever, as we might face a near future with autonomous battlefield robots,[4] and we already encounter mechanical assistants, carers and companions – smart, friendly, gendered and supposedly able to understand a person's feelings.[5]

This essay aims to intervene into the practices of situated and social robotics, and their material concerns with embodiment, situatedness and interaction, by exploring how feminist post-human perspectives and dancers' bodily ways of thinking can offer an alternative pathway to imagining and materially enacting human-machine-environment configurations. Thinking as a material enactment not only bounds the ways we conceive these configurations but, as we will see, also opens up alternative, non-human ways of 'bodily thinking' and intelligibility. First, I discuss some of the dominant practices in situated and social robotics, and the humanist views they manifest, in tandem with feminist counterviews. This follows a material account of – what I hope to be – a more radical post-humanist approach to robotic design: a research project I lead titled *Machine Movement Labs*, spanning experimental art, performance and engineering to explore the relational and performative potential of movement.

Situatedness by proxy

Situated and social robotics communities do not often mingle, although they both share situated, embodied interactions as one of their core engineering challenges. In a nutshell, situated robotics 'deals with embodied machines in complex, challenging, often dynamically changing environments',[6] whereas social robotics is concerned with situating embodied machines in complex (human) social environments. Hence, 'social robots' engage in social interactions,[7] while for 'situated robots,' the environment is commonly considered only in physical terms, devoid of the social.

The foundations for situated robotics were laid in the late 1980s, when a movement in AI, often referred to as 'New AI', 'rediscovered the body and the environment as major causal forces in the shaping of intelligent behavior'.[8] Motor control and 'smooth real-time behavior',[9] it was argued, could be achieved by exploiting the physical properties of materials and embodied interactions with the world. Previous complex and unreliable 'symbolic' models of the world were replaced by notions of embodied agency, situating the agent in the environment, and exploiting emergent behaviours.[10] AI had finally rediscovered the body, after it had forgotten about its predecessor, cybernetics and its open-ended, embodied engagements situated within the material world,[11] thirty years earlier. Unlike cybernetics, however, New AI's material world is bereft of the social.

The term 'situated' in AI and robotics is 'usually intended to mean that [a robot's] behaviour and cognitive processes first and foremost are the outcome of a close coupling between agent and environment'.[12] Yet the world brought forth in the robot's history of structural coupling[13] is a very limited and conveniently pragmatic one, and 'interacting' with the environment, in Lucy Suchman's words, 'comprise[s] variations of conditioned response, however tightly coupled the mechanisms or emergent the effects'.[14] Also, the nature of this coupling rarely acknowledges the involvement of the human designer, which seems absurd, given that the robot is designed by a human and trained to adapt to an environment to solve a task, both of which are specified by the designer, and success or failure are defined by, and only matter to, the human designer.[15] Conceptions of embodied cognition in these material enactments are equally pragmatic, and lay open the designers' computationalist/functionalist views.[16] The body of the robot is 'typically viewed as some kind of input and output device that provides physical grounding to the internal computational mechanisms', reducing it to a physical container 'that allows the computational mind to interact with its environment through sensors and actuators'.[17] Seen through my critical lens, we are thus presented with artificial agents that are granted their own agency thanks to an independent computational mind that feeds from and acts through a body container. Although coupled to the environment, they remain separate from the world.

My lens is shaped by Lucy Suchman's radical reworkings of human-machine configurations,[18] and Karen Barad's concept of 'agential realism'.[19] The latter offers a post-humanist understanding of how the world, subjects and objects are reconfigured in our material-discursive practices, such as robotics, and how these continuous 'agential intra-actions' enact specific boundaries and meanings. Agency, in this performative understanding, is not a property that someone or something can have or be granted with; rather, 'agency is a matter of intra-acting … an enactment'.[20] What makes this philosophical account so appealing is that the world is no longer fixed, waiting for us to 'be known'. Any fixed relations, boundaries and meanings are our doings and result from our re-configurings of the world, which makes us, and our sociomaterial practices, accountable. Particularly relevant for this discussion is that subject–object difference also is a matter of intra-action, 'aris[ing] from the material-discursive practices through which boundaries and associated entities are made'.[21] This is not to say that it is a world potentially without differences, but rather that boundaries and related entities are not given; they are produced and continuously reaffirmed and reproduced.

Robotics through the looking glass

Social robotics as a material-discursive practice is, one could argue, all about reconfiguring subject–object boundaries. In contrast to situated robotics, social robotics places and explores robots within a social environment; however, they are not situated by means of structural coupling, as their social capacities, most commonly, are neither dynamically produced nor continually conditioned by their social environment. In social robotics, the robot is still considered an electro-mechanical artefact rather than a sociomaterial phenomenon; hence, the robot needs to be implanted with the 'social', like embellishing an alien other with etiquette. This still-young field is currently preoccupied, it seems, with robots' social acceptability, and it thus focuses on questions of appearance and social behaviour as it is perceived and accepted, rather than exploring how a robot becomes a social entity in its intra-actions and re-configurings of the social environment. Most research has directed its attention to 'the application of 'benign' social behaviour. Thus, social robots are usually designed as assistants, companions or pets, in addition to the more traditional role of servants'.[22] As robots are assigned their social role – roles that already exist in our society – and are made to fit them, it is crucial that we recognize the active production of boundaries as part of this material practice. Particularly since the objective of 'fitting' these roles and for people to accept them in these roles seemingly justifies the assumption that humanlike or humanoid physical features are the best approach.[23] And, having *enacted* robots as companions and servants in our own image, 'dominant discourses in robotics are quick to grant subjecthood to the humanoid machine', and with it, 'to embrace the erasure of human/machine difference'.[24] Robots mimicking humans or pets – often in cute, caricatured ways – deliberately blur the difference between organic and mechanical bodies, as well as human and machine cognition, to elicit human investment based on superficial, and often fake, social cues. Suchman argues that 'the figure of the humanoid robot sits provocatively on the boundary of subjects and objects, threatening its breakdown at the same time that it reiterates its founding identities and differences'.[25] In practice, it needs to be said, the current limitations of robotics technology and AI quickly cause this façade to crumble and break, and interacting with these humanlike machines is often frustrating and disappointing.[26] But this only buys us time; it doesn't seem to weaken the foundations of the humanist assumptions this charade is built on. It is as if we were looking for a robotic counterpart, to look into a mirror: a mirror, which is predictable, programmable and replaceable.

What we see in current robotics – particularly in social robotics, which has in recent years attracted the majority of funding in robotics – is the jarring paradox of a quest for increasing (social) intelligence and autonomy, while clinging to our human high ground that separates us from our machines and 'safely' putting them into their place of servitude.[27] It is the conservative politics of the upstairs–downstairs scenario, whereas we're pouring millions into the 'education' of downstairs to become a more productive workforce (here, the 'sociable' robot only reflects the expansion from industrial production into social services; it is not to join the upstairs). In this paradoxical humanist narrative, we seek to inscribe into robots the superior position of cognitive entities – making them in our image – to serve us and fulfil our wishes so that we can more effectively maintain and expand our superior position in the world. It is an age-old narrative, of course, that now promises to have a ubiquitous material effect. Ironically, this humanist view also requires engineers and collaborating psychologists to define 'what human is',[28] so that the machine can recognize these 'parameters' in humans, and/or re-perform them. This, for instance, leads to grotesquely simplified models of human emotion, suitable to be translated into rules and algorithms. Non-humanlike machines, on the other hand, are usually seen as 'functional'[29] and rarely graced with social behaviours or (apparently) human-level intelligence. Intelligence, in particular social intelligence or intelligent machines embedded in our social milieu, seems to be inseparably linked to humanlike appearance.

Perhaps, what we currently see in social robotics is a phenomenon similar to the one in early AI, driven by overly ambitious, unachievable goals based on arrogant, humanist assumptions. Referred to as the 'top down' approach, it was thought that AI could be 'solved' through symbolic representations, including the explicit formalization of 'human common-sense knowledge',[30] that is 'the millions of abstractions, models, facts, rules of thumb, representations, etc., that we all possess and that we assume everyone else does'.[31] Needless to say, this goal was bound to fail, but imagine if it hadn't. Looking at the current development of androids in Japan, and how they manifest our humanist desires for replicating human life and common-sense assumptions about sex and gender roles,[32] it seems that the ultimate goal for social robotics is to literally embody the vision of a perfect(able) human. One can't help seeing the parallel to early AI's presumptuous desires to replicate human intelligence. The assumptions and desires that allow for human intelligence to be equated to a disembodied algorithm are the very same that allow for the human to be re-enacted as a humanoid mechanism.

Dancing with the non-human: Machine Movement Lab

We can also find critical voices within the robotics field, questioning the focused attention on the reproduction of human bodies and behaviours. Rolf

Pfeifer and Josh Bongard argue that 'we have to develop an understanding of the robot's own embodiment because it is this embodiment that will ultimately determine the grounding and thus the level of understanding and communication that is possible between humans and robots'.[33] The following introduces our research project *Machine Movement Lab*,[34] which aims to develop an understanding of the robot's own embodiment, albeit not only to ground itself but also to explore human-machine configurations that can offer, in Suchman's words, 'more radical reworkings of the figures of both'.[35] Rather than turning machines into 'social actors', this material practice challenges the dominant assumptions of subject–object difference and develops a relational, performative approach that investigates how human and machine co-constitute each other, by materially exploring the 'folding of humans and nonhumans'.[36] As we will see, movement generates the trajectory along which this folding occurs. In a nutshell, the project's enactive approach harnesses dancers' movement expertise to design the robot's non-anthropomorphic body, its potential to move and capacity to learn. Collaborating with (human) choreographers and dancers, our aim is not to render the robot more humanoid, but rather to investigate the micro-ecologies of a robot becoming entangled with other bodies and the world. That is, how sociomaterial relations and dynamics get produced and activated, and furthermore, how alternative, post-humanist notions of intelligence are spawned from these always material interdependencies. The project puts forward the proposition that movement and its connection-making, knowledge-generating potential is key to both the 'bodying'[37] of a machine and its capacity to 'intra-act'[38] with other bodies and the world. This becoming of agency promises to be the more transformative the more we recognize and embrace the difference of machinic embodiment and cognition. Here is where movement's capacity of bodying, worlding and eliciting responses can be exploited to bring about interesting relations without relying on human likeness or the familiarity of pets. Let me unfold this idea in more detail.

Thinking with the body

Leach and deLahunta have argued that 'movement, "thinking with the body", is a way of exploring the world'.[39] Movement is the core medium of contemporary dance, where it is 'deliberately and systematically cultivated for its own sake'.[40] To explore the potential of movement to relate beyond the human, we collaborate with the De Quincey Company, and its Artistic Director and choreographer Tess de Quincey. Training in BodyWeather, founded on Butoh dance and drawing from both Eastern and Western dance, martial arts and theatre practice, De Quincey Co's practice is already well-attuned to our relational, performative approach. BodyWeather practitioners are extremely skilled in tuning into 'the *how* of the movement as it is being embodied moment by moment'.[41] To shift the body out of its known, habitual pathways,[42] the dancers often respond to imagery while skilfully attending to the becoming of movement and how it transforms their bodies. Using images, for example, of external forces like wind or a pressure cooker, for the body to work from allows them to escape the habitual, and 'find' new movements to bodily explore the imagined forces, tensions and connections evoked by these images; the forces and trajectories produced by their movements, in turn, reconfigure their body.

According to deLahunta et al., this bodily sensibility allows 'the movement to become "thought-filled", itself the instrument of cognition'.[43] Perhaps more than 'thought-filled', this continuous becoming of movement actively propels and gives form to thought in the making. In many ways, the bodily relations continuously made and unmade by the dancers lay open the embeddedness and situatedness of cognition. Albeit here, the world not only provides the external scaffoldings[44] that extend the dancers' cognition but rather co-constitutes and co-shapes the body and its unfolding movement. Because the BodyWeather practice always positions and experiences the body in relation to space, other bodies and things, Barad's notion of intra-action[45] deeply aligns with the dancers' co-emerging with the world, moment by moment. In this sense, their bodily thinking also evokes the ecological approach of distributed cognition,[46] however, not, as it is often understood in robotics, in the form of a collective of networked, separate agents, but rather as an entanglement –a thinking *with* the world. Hence, the moving body in space generates new knowledge by actively creating new connections and reconfiguring the world. Doing so requires rejecting our habitual pathways: being in the present, and actively engaging with forces within and (apparently) outside – a re-recognition of bodies and things beyond their existing labels.

Neither situated robotics nor social robotics currently explore the potential of relational, kinaesthetic intelligence and how it could expand our human-machine configurations. Situated robotics aims for artificial, embodied agents that exhibit intelligent behaviour compared to living 'role models', while social robotics is invested in developing sociable agents that people *perceive* as intelligent. In both cases, judgement of the agent's intelligence is actively located in the human observer, who is placed outside – separated from this entanglement. Yet in favouring the human viewpoint, separated from the world and 'equipped' with its own autonomous agency, we are starting with a problematic set of epistemological and ontological assumptions.[47] More than simply reaffirming these assumptions, they reproduce a 'humanist preoccupation, with the individual actor living in a world of separate things',[48] and with it, a functionalist stance to understanding intelligence. In contrast, movement and bodily thinking makes itself part of the world, promoting a post-humanist world view in the sense that it shifts the focus from representation to performativity, and opens up notions of the body as always being entangled with other bodies, things and the world. Laying open the co-constitution of bodies and phenomena, it also destabilizes the differential boundaries between human and non-human bodies and their intelligence, without simply equating the two. Notions of bodily intelligence can thus open up a 'third' path for our interactions with machines, one that doesn't reconstruct or mimic existing post-humanist desires of human likeness and humanlike models of intelligence. Rather, such a *relational* approach suggests that we can open up mutual intelligibilities between humans and machines by exploring what gets activated and emerges 'through and as part of their entangled intra-relating'.[49] Robots are then no longer positioned outside the social, and it is no longer necessary to 'imbue' them with artificial social attributes. Movement – and how it makes itself part of the world – thus opens up a productive path to better understanding subject–object entanglement, and to explore notions of sociality, agency and intelligibility beyond their human conceptions.

It is messy

Before I continue, it is worth noting that the relational approach discussed here is a practice still in the making, and it seeks to open up and to explore questions rather than presenting a solution (if there is such a thing). Entanglements of bodies are messy, and our material practice, without doubt, continuously defines and produces boundaries.[50] The challenge is to give into this continuous becoming – and I would like to say here 'without assuming control''; however, this would not accurately reflect how our material practice evolves in the lab, 'on the ground' as it were. There are many moments in which we feel that we need to 'make a decision', excluding ideas, materials and potential relations in favour of others; where we actively channel a path forward as we feel the pressure to move the project along. An important part of this material practice, then, is to acknowledge these lines drawn, but also to record a large amount of context, conversations and seemingly small details to – in a way – capture (at least a slice of) the sociomaterial environment that they emerged from. This allows us to reflect on the relations that we had previously carved out against a set of excluded potential relations, and for this evolving practice – and its 'measurable' results – to not be cut off from the complex, productive mess that they brought about, and emanated from. This is what Donna Haraway has talked about as the 'world of immeasurable results',[51] which, unsurprisingly, is where all the relations happen.

There is one particular exclusion in our project, however, that is very deliberate: attributes of (organic) lifelikeness. Counter to most current assumptions in robotics, we are exploring how far we can push the relationship between abstract, simple machine morphologies and their potential to become a body by moving in relational, performative ways. Rather than attributing the quality of relationality, and with it, the capacity for eliciting responses to the body,[52] we look to the relational potential of movement to generate meaning and intelligibility. This performative understanding undermines dominant humanist-representationalist assumptions in robotics, and opens up interesting configurations with abstract, non-anthropomorphic machines.

When a 'thing' becomes a body

How then can bodily thinking be harnessed to develop a relational, performative approach, to assist with the bodying of a robot and its learning to move and interact with the world? Our material exploration revolves around the development of a new method, called Performative Body Mapping (PBM), which currently comprises four stages: bodying, grounding, imitation and improvisation. Future stages will also include a performative approach to learning and improvising in social situations, beyond the sociomaterial environment of the lab. In the following, I will take a closer look at the first stage – bodying – then briefly outline our relational machine learning approach and, finally, cycle back to movement's relational potential to discuss how our performative approach draws on the social phenomenon already built into the encounter.

The first stage of PBM involves a machine 'costume' to be inhabited and activated by a dancer. Costume here refers to a wearable object, standing in for a potential machine body, that is, the machine to be bodied. The shape of the costume is not fixed but changes – evolves, if you will – in response to what kind of movements and bodily relations the dancer can activate. Once we find a costume shape that, when activated, allows for interesting 'bodying', motion captures of the activated costume inform the design of a mechanical prototype. From a technical viewpoint, the costume is a full-size, non-mechanical prototype of a robot design in process. Yet, involving the sensibilities and bodily imagination of a choreographer and a dancer, it becomes an instrument for mapping between two different body morphologies, and for the dancer to embody and skilfully tune into this strange object: to explore how it 'bodies' in movement. The dancer's movements, in turn, are co-shaped by the material forces and affordances of the machine costume, so that their distinct direction, speed, and rhythm[53] emerge from the entanglement of the two. The use of costumes to literally co-shape performers' movements is not new. For his 1993 production of *Tristan and Isolde*, Heiner Mueller asked Yohji Yamamoto to design costumes for the performers 'that would impede the movement they are used to'.[54] Rather than impeding the dancer's movement, however, we are looking for a productive intermeshing. BodyWeather practitioners, trained to bodily explore the 'beyond human', are well-attuned to the challenging task of bodily thinking with the costumes. As Tess de Quincey put it, 'the whole point about BodyWeather is to go beyond the biomechanics through images, [that is] we recruit the biomechanics to find ways to move, which are not normally positioned as human movements'.[55]

Let me take a closer look at the process of bodily negotiating between these two – the dancer's body and the materiality of the costume – and the emerging transformation. It's the process of the 'thing' becoming an interesting, affective body as it moves, relates, and takes on a presence of its own. In other words, movement produces and propels the becoming-body (bodying) of the machine costume. We found that the costume becomes a body as soon as the dancer enters it and begins exploring how she can respond to its material tensions and forces, and 'find' movements *with* them. Our task, then, was to find material properties for the making of interesting bodyings, which to us are bodies whose becoming does not rely on human or lifelike qualities, but emerge from the entanglement and the movements and relations it produces. In practice, finding this 'interesting bodying' occurred in approximation, step-by-step. At the start, we asked the dancers to inhabit a wide range of materials, shapes and objects, only to narrow the scope of possible paths and filter out those whose resulting body, when activated, relied too much on the dancer's own morphology. We favoured simple, abstract shapes – similar to a blank canvas – without a front or back, head or face, or limb-like structures, to heighten the bodying ability of movement and elude the distractions of physical appearance, tempting us to make analogies to known or living 'things'.

Rather than moving the costume, dancers learned to move *with* the strange morphology, and the inherent material tensions and forces it afforded. Sometimes the dancers would improvise, however, most of the negotiations emerged from the dialogue between choreographer and dancer, extending the material entanglement and process of bodying beyond the physical confines of the costume. In these negotiations, the choreographer developed her ideas based on an external perspective of the costume-becoming-body, and the dancer responded from within, based on the material experience, to which only she had access. The choreographer would articulate an image or find a word 'that bridge[s] the distance between the intellectually understood and the range of feelings'[56] elicited. In one session, for instance, Tess de Quincey asked the dancer, inhabiting a plain cardboard box, to express a question mark.

When the dancer responded to the prompt, we witnessed the box performing a shape, seemingly positing layers of hesitation, inquiry and alertness along its movement trajectory. To be precise, rather than a positing, we experienced the *finding* of a movement, starting off with a hesitating twist that accelerated upwards, with a slight inclination, before it came to a sudden halt. This was not a visual representation of a question mark, but rather the bodily processing of what a question mark *does*. Indeed, the box-becoming-body emerged from the 'movement subtleties and qualities, contrasts between tension and relaxation, and between high degrees of physicality and absolute stillness'.[57]

Once we found an 'interesting bodying', the activated costume is recorded using motion capture, which in the next project stage informs the design of a mechanical prototype that resembles the costume and its capacities to move as closely as possible. This is the stage, where the dancer's bodily thinking becomes a movement 'apparatus', that is, where the movement emerging from this entanglement becomes the diagram for the robotic mechanism, and with it, its ability to learn to move based on its machinic relations with the world. It is also where we focus on the machine's own embodiment and its grounding,[58] and bodily potential to learn and relate. While this robot-making stage clearly introduces new boundaries and material entanglements, we must take great care to not undo the productive effects of the human-non-human entanglement that produced the body in the first place.

Towards machinic bodily intelligence

Although the robot's mechanical design is shaped by the costume's movements – resulting from a human-non-human enmeshment – recognizing and tapping into the difference of the machine's embodiment and how it can relate to the world is at the very core of our project. Our performative, relational approach thus also materializes in the methods we adopt and adapt for the robot's machine learning. Our aim is for the robot's movements to continue to 'body' its otherwise abstract, simple morphology. That is to say, the moving object becomes a body as it assumes a presence, senses and relates to the environment and its affordances, and elicits responses from other bodies. Doing so, our aim is not for the body to reproduce behaviours from living organisms, which significantly differs from common situated robotics approaches. Our motivation is to experiment with new, non-organic forms of embodied couplings (producing and produced by movement), and with it, to move into a non-organic realm of body-environment couplings. We are thus not interested in giving lifelike characteristics to the robot,[59] although people may project them, but rather seek to explore the micro-ecologies of a robot body becoming entangled, and how its movements produce and activate relations and sensations. Eluding subject–object binaries, this machine-becoming-body takes on a position in the middle; neither subject nor object.

Movement shapes the way the robot perceives, learns about and relates to its world, producing material, mutual relationships with other bodies and the environment as a form of machinic bodily intelligence. This potential to relate is further mobilized and enhanced by the robot's ability to learn and adapt. Rather than looking at the robot's body as a mobile container, a relational approach to machine learning is developed in tandem with the robot's embodiment and capacity to move, that is, its potential to relate to and reconfigure its environment. To explore this interdependency in more detail, the following briefly outlines the first three relational machine learning phases: *grounding, imitation* and *improvisation*. Later learning phases will engage choreographers and dancers to develop performance scenarios for the machine to learn and improvise in more complex sociomaterial environments beyond the lab.

In the *grounding* phase, the robot learns how it can move in relation to its environment through trial-and-error, to ground its movements and relations, and any future learning, in its own specific embodiment. In both situated and social robotics, mind (control system) and (robot) body are still considered separate; that is, the artificial nervous system operates 'largely independent of the body it is carried out in'.[60] Both intelligence and intelligibility are decoupled from the body 'substrate', which also lays the ground for human intelligence to be transferable into a machinic body, and a machinic body being intelligible if it 'carries' humanlike intelligence. Our approach, in contrast, develops the robot's intrinsically machinic intelligence, and potential to be intelligible, from its unique bodily capacity to move. It deploys the developmental robotics[61] method of 'motor babbling',[62] which allows for the robot to 'discover' its own body and possible kinaesthetic relations in response to environmental affordances. Through this active self-exploration, the robot gradually generates a body map, which is unique to its own material body and intricately couples it with the control system, developed in response to the body's capacity to move. In the *imitation* phase, the robot learns to imitate the movements of its dancer-activated costume twin, as closely as its own body map allows. This is the phase in which the bodying of the robot and its ability to relate through movement come full circle. Learning by imitation is a popular social learning method in social robotics,[63] where, commonly, robots learn to imitate human movements, limited to narrowly defined tasks. Given the enormous difference between human and machinic embodiments, regardless of how humanlike the machine appears, the translation between the two usually proves quite difficult. Perhaps even more problematic, however, this required translation between human and machinic bodies fuels the desire for robots to look and behave similarly to humans.[64] In contrast, motion captures of our dancer-activated robot costume allow the robot to learn from its own mirror image. As it learns to imitate the costume's movements, the goal is for the robot to learn the constraints that produce the movement qualities and subtleties, which emerged from the dancer-costume enmeshment. Hence, rather than only knowing a specific set of movements, the robot gradually learns patterns of movement – that is, 'the systematic way patterns are structured, sequenced and related to one another'[65] – based on its own machinic body sense (see *grounding*). The final phase is *improvisation*, where the robot learns to adapt its previously learned patterns of movement to invent new movements, in dialogue with the choreographer. Drawing on methods from computational creativity,[66] the machine learns to play with the given movement material to develop movements that are unique to its own machinic body and its relations to the environment.

A new playground

Bodily intelligence and the moving body's potential to sense, relate to, reconfigure and tune into other bodies not only inform our enactive design approach but also constitute the common ground from which mutual relations between humans and machines can unfold. 'We literally discover ourselves in movement',[67] and we make sense of the world and other bodies based on our kinaesthetic understanding and sensibilities. Bodies in movement – human and non-human – thus elicit responses in other bodies. Leach and deLahunta describe the affective reach of movement as 'an extension of feeling, knowing, and sensing into the world with, and of, other bodies'.[68] Knowing here is about the ongoing active, bodily engagement, 'a matter of intra-acting',[69] which I touched upon at the very beginning of this chapter. Thinking and knowing as an ongoing reach into and with the world – a movement that is always becoming and never fully complete – are melding together. Movement, and how it bodies a 'thing', is thus, I believe, key to an intrinsically machinic notion of intelligence, a machine's potential to be intelligible, and furthermore, is at the core of the complex relationships we can develop with a machine.

It is important to reiterate, however, that a thing becoming a body does not mean it becomes a subject. While the potential of our relational approach stems from a post-humanist world view in which subjects and objects (humans and artefacts) mutually constitute each other, Suchman reminds us that mutualities are not necessarily symmetries. Her own analysis suggests 'that persons and artefacts do not constitute each other *in the same way*'.[70] The sensations and agencies that are enacted in this encounter naturally have different values and effects for people and robot. For a start, the robot only has a limited access to our 'culturally and historically constituted resources for meaning making'.[71] Rather, my argument is that thinking relationally opens up approaches to machinic design that allow for already always-emerging relations to unfold and be recognized, without undermining this potential by presenting robots 'as if they had feelings'.[72] As mentioned earlier, a machine moving to relate based on its own machinic embodiment, rather than mimicking other bodies' behaviours, destabilizes subject–object boundaries and instead opens up a space in-between.

There is much research on a moving body's capacity to resonate with the observer,[73] arguing that observed movement literally moves and bodily affects us.[74] This resonance also fuels our engagement with moving bodies, as we are compelled to anticipate the trajectory of movements.[75] This is also interesting in relation to human-machine configurations and a machine's potential to 'make sense' to other (human) bodies with regard to its potential for action.[76]

However, the external position of the 'observer' is problematic here, as it still locates agency and affect within each separate body. Rather, it is only through the encounter that agency and affect are enacted across bodies. What is referred to as resonance here is the relation made felt between the two bodies. The other encountering body positioned as an external observer creates what Barad calls 'an *agential cut*'[77] that effects a separation between the two bodies, rendering the observing body cut off and passive.

In contrast, a relational approach foregrounds the encounter of subjects and objects; indeed, according to Barad,[78] subjects and objects emerge in the encounter. This intra-action is also where the social is enacted; thus, robots not only are specific material configurations but also become specific social entities in the process of negotiating these configurations, both in the making (the design process) and enacting (as we encounter and engage with them). Counter to dominant assumptions in social robotics, agency, sociality and intelligibility are not human characteristics that can be bestowed on a humanoid robot but are a matter of intra-acting.[79] Sensation, too, is enacted in the encounter, as it constitutes (in Elizabeth Grosz's words) a 'zone of indeterminacy between subject and object, the bloc that erupts from the encounter of the one with the other'.[80] Meaning can thus emerge from a flow of agency and affect, enacted in the encounter through movement, rather than from specific humanlike embodiments or behaviours. This opens up a notion of thinking with the machine and 'machinic intelligence' that is quite different from that of importing humanlike intelligent behaviour into a machinic body, one that is, however, well-aligned with understanding the machine's potential for action[81] in terms of its situatedness. In tandem with and inseparable from agency and affect, thinking here is intimately tied to our entanglement with the world, and an ongoing process of mutual reconfiguring

– a material, bodily enactment. Granted, as we learn to dance with the non-human, this entanglement does not offer people an easy, effortless mirror image, pretending to have eliminated or sufficiently blurred the boundary in-between. Rather, it seeks to complicate subject–object difference, rendering the boundary relational and dynamic, and by doing so, opening up a new playground for humans and machines.

Notes

1. Andrew Pickering, 'The Next Macy Conference: A New Interdisciplinary Synthesis. Keynote', *IEEE Technology and Society Magazine* 34 (2014), p. 38.
2. Karen Barad, *Meeting the Universe Halfway: Quantum Physics and the Entanglement of Matter and Meaning* (Durham: Duke University Press, 2007), p. 175.
3. Rolf Pfeifer quoted in Katrin Weigmann, 'Does intelligence require a body?' *EMBO Reports* 13 (2013), p. 1067.
4. Noel Sharkey, 'The evitability of autonomous robot warfare', *International Review of the Red Cross* 94 (2012).
5. Judy Wajcman, 'Automation, robotics and the promise of an easier life' (Lecture at Oxford Martin School, University of Oxford, 02 March 2016). <http://www.oxfordmartin.ox.ac.uk/event/2268> [accessed 01 November 2016].
6. Maja J. Matarić and Francois Michaud, 'Behavior-Based Robotics' in *Handbook of Robotics,* eds Bruno Siciliano and Oussama Khatib, (Springer, 2008), p. 891.
7. Terrence Fong, Illah Nourbakhsh and Kerstin Dautenhahn, 'A survey of socially interactive robots', *Robotics and Autonomous Systems* 42 (2003).
8. Luc Steels, 'Fifty Years of AI: From Symbols to Embodiment – and Back' in *50 Years of Artificial Intelligence: Essays Dedicated to the 50th Anniversary of Artificial Intelligence*, eds M. Lungarella, F. Iida, J. Bongard, R. Pfeifer (Berlin and Heidelberg: Springer, 2007), p. 23.
9. Ibid.
10. Ibid.
11. See Andrew Pickering, 'Cybernetics and the Mangle: Ashby, Beer and Pask', *Social Studies of Science* 32 (2002).
12. Tom Ziemke, 'The Construction of 'Reality' in the Robot: Constructivist Perspectives on Situated Artificial Intelligence and Adaptive Robotics', Special issue on 'The Impact of Radical Constructivism on Science', ed. A. Riegler, *Foundations of Science* 6 (2001), p. 164.
13. See Francisco J. Varela, Evan Thompson and Eleanor Rosch, *The embodied mind: Cognitive science and human experience* (Cambridge: MIT Press, 1991).

14 Lucy Suchman, *Human-Machine Reconfigurations: Plans and Situated Actions* (Cambridge: Cambridge University Press, 2007), p. 15.

15 See Ziemke, 'The Construction of "Reality" in the Robot: Constructivist Perspectives on Situated Artificial Intelligence and Adaptive Robotics'.

16 Tom Ziemke, 'The body of knowledge: On the role of the living body in grounding embodied cognition', *BioSystems* 148 (2016).

17 Ibid., p. 7.

18 Suchman, *Human-Machine Reconfigurations.*

19 Barad, *Meeting the Universe Halfway.*

20 Ibid., p. 826.

21 Lucy Suchman, 'Subject Objects' in *Feminist Theory* 12 (2011), p.121.

22 Fong et al, 'A survey of socially interactive robots', p. 145.

23 Kerstin Dautenhahn, 'Human–robot interaction' in *Encyclopedia of Human-Computer Interaction*, eds M. Soegaard & R.F. Dam (Aarhus: Interaction Design Foundation, 2nd ed.), 2013.

24 Suchman, 'Subject Objects', p. 122.

25 Ibid., p. 133.

26 Dautenhahn, 'Human–robot interaction'.

27 Also see Suchman's argument on 'technological imaginaries' in *Human-Machine Reconfigurations,* p. 213-214.

28 See Wajcman, 'Automation, robotics and the promise of an easier life', and Suchman, *Human-Machine Reconfigurations.*

29 Wajcman, 'Automation, robotics and the promise of an easier life'; Fong et al, 'A survey of socially interactive robots'.

30 Ziemke, 'The Construction of 'Reality' in the Robot: Constructivist Perspectives on Situated Artificial Intelligence and Adaptive Robotics', p. 180.

31 Doug Lenat and Edward, P. Feigenbaum, 'On the Thresholds of Knowledge', *Artificial Intelligence* 47 (1991), p.216.

32 Jennifer Robertson, 'Gendering Humanoid Robots: Robo-Sexism in Japan', *Body Society 16* (2010).

33 Rolf Pfeifer and Josh Bongard, *How The Body Shapes The Way We Think: A New View Of Intelligence* (Cambridge: MIT Press, 2007), p. 348.

34 This project is supported under the Australian Research Council's *Discovery Projects* funding scheme (DP160104706), with Lead Chief Investigator Petra Gemeinboeck, Chief Investigator Rob Saunders, and Partner Investigators Maaike Bleeker and Ben Robins.

35 Suchman, *Human-Machine Reconfigurations,* p. 243.

36 Bruno Latour, *Pandora's Hope: Essays on the Reality of Science Studies* (Cambridge: Harvard University Press, 1999), p. 193.

37 Erin Manning and Brian Massumi, 'Just Like That: William Forsythe, Between Movement and Language' in *Touching and to Be Touched. Kinesthesia and Empathy in Dance and Movement*, eds. G. Brandstetter, G. Egert, and S. Zubarik (Berlin: DeGruyter, 2013).

38 Karen Barad, 'Posthumanist Performativity: Toward an Understanding of How Matter Comes to Matter', *Signs: Journal of Women in Culture and Society* 28 (2003).

39 James Leach and Scott deLahunta, 'Dance 'Becoming' Knowledge', *Leonardo* (accepted for publication, April 13, 2015), p. 8.

40 Catherine Stevens and Shirley McKechnie, 'Thinking in action: thought made visible in contemporary dance', *Cognitive Processing* 6 (2005), p. 243.

41 Scott deLahunta, Gill Clarke, Phil Barnard, 'A conversation about choreographic thinking tools', *Journal of Dance & Somatic Practices* 3 (2012), p. 247.

42 Tess De Quincey, video recording (26 March 2015), unpublished.

43 deLahunta et al, 'A conversation about choreographic thinking tools', p. 248.

44 Andy Clark, *Being There: Putting Brain, Body, and World Together Again* (Cambridge: MIT Press, 1997).

45 Barad, 'Posthumanist Performativity'.

46 Edwin Hutchins, 'Cognitive Ecology', *Topics in Cognitive Science* 2 (2010).

47 See Barad, *Meeting the Universe Halfway.*

48 Lucy Suchman, 'Agencies in technology design: Feminist reconfigurations', Online Proceedings of the *5th European Symposium on Gender and ICT. Digital Cultures. Participation – Empowerment – Diversity* (University of Bremen, March 5-7, 2009), p. 2.

49 Barad, *Meeting the Universe Halfway,* p. ix.

50 Ibid.

51 Donna Haraway, Donna, *Modest_Witness@Second_Millenium.FemaleMan_Meets_Oncomouse, Feminism and Technosciemce* (New York and London: Routledge, 1997), p. xiii.

52 See Leach and deLahunta, 'Dance 'Becoming' Knowledge'.

53 See Carrie Noland, *Agency and embodiment: Performing gestures/producing culture* (Cambridge: Harvard University Press, 2010).

54 Stephan Suschke, *Müller macht Theater: Zehn Inszenierungen und ein Epilog* (Berlin: Theater der Zeit, 2003), p. 205 (author's own translation).

55 De Quincey, video recording (unpublished).

56 Stevens and McKechnie, 'Thinking in action', p. 245.

57 Ibid., p. 246.

58 Pfeifer and Bongard, *How The Body Shapes The Way We Think.*

59 See Jackie Stacey and Lucy Suchman, 'Animation and Automation: The liveliness and labours of bodies and machines', *Body and Society 18* (2012).

60 Ziemke, 'The Construction of "Reality" in the Robot', p. 220.

61 Pierre-Yves Oudeyer, 'On the impact of robotics in behavioral and cognitive sciences: from insect navigation to human cognitive development', *IEEE Transactions on Autonomous Mental Development,* 2 (2010).

62 Ryo Saegusa, Giorgio Metta, Giulio Sandini and Sophie Sakka, 'Active motor babbling for sensorimotor learning', *Proceedings of the IEEE International Conference on Robotics and Biomimetics* (2008).

63 Fong et al., 'A survey of socially interactive robots'.

64 Ibid.

65 Stevens and McKechnie, 'Thinking in action', p. 248.

66 Rob Saunders, 'Towards autonomous creative systems: A computational approach', Special issue on 'Computational Creativity, Intelligence and Autonomy', *Cognitive Computation* 4 (2012).

67 Maxine Sheets-Johnstone, *The primacy of movement* (Amsterdam and Philadelphia: John Benjamins Publishing, 2011), p. 136.

68 Leach and deLahunta, 'Dance "Becoming" Knowledge', p. 6.

69 Barad, *Meeting the Universe Halfway*, p. 149.

70 Suchman, *Human-Machine Reconfigurations*, p. 269, original emphasis.

71 Ibid., p. 15.

72 Wajcman, 'Automation, robotics and the promise of an easier life'.

73 Susan Leigh Foster, 'Movement's Contagion: The Kinesthetic Impact of Performance' in *The Cambridge Companion to Performance Studies*, ed. Tracy C. Davis (Cambridge: Cambridge University Press, 2008); Ivar Hagendoorn, 'Some Speculative Hypotheses about the Nature and Perception of Dance and Choreography', *Journal of Consciousness Studies* 11 (2004); Stevens and McKechnie, 'Thinking in action'.

74 See Foster, 'Movement's Contagion'.

75 Hagendoorn, 'Some Speculative Hypotheses about the Nature and Perception of Dance and Choreography'.

76 Varela et al, *The embodied mind.*

77 Barad, 'Posthumanist Performativity', p. 815, original emphasis.

78 Ibid.

79 See Karen Barad 'Nature's queer performativity', *Qui Parle: Critical Humanities and Social Sciences 19* (2011), and *Meeting the Universe Halfway.*

80 Elisabeth Grosz, *Chaos, Territory, Art: Deleuze and the Framing of the Earth* (New York: Columbia University Press, 2008), p. 73.

81 Varela et al, *The embodied mind.*

References

Barad, K., 'Posthumanist Performativity: Toward an Understanding of How Matter Comes to Matter', *Signs: Journal of Women in Culture and Society* 28:3(2003), pp. 801–31.

Barad, K., *Meeting the Universe Halfway: Quantum Physics and the Entanglement of Matter and Meaning*, Durham: Duke University Press, 2007.

Barad, K., 'Nature's queer performativity', *Qui Parle: Critical Humanities and Social Sciences*, 19:2 (2011), pp. 121–58.

Clancey, W.J., 'A boy scout, Toto, and a bird: How situated cognition is different from situated robotics', in L. Steels and R. Brooks (eds), *The 'Artificial Life' Route to 'Artificial Intelligence': Building Situated Embodied Agents*, Hillsdale: Lawrence Erlbaum Associates, 1995, pp. 227–36.

Clark, A., *Being There: Putting Brain, Body, and World Together Again*, Cambridge: MIT Press, 1997.

Dautenhahn, K., 'Human–robot interaction', in M. Soegaard and R.F. Dam (eds), *Encyclopedia of Human-Computer Interaction* (2nd ed.), Aarhus: Interaction Design Foundation, 2013, pp. 2283–366.

deLahunta, S., Clarke, G., and P. Barnard, 'A conversation about choreographic thinking tools', *Journal of Dance & Somatic Practices* 3:1-2 (2012), pp. 243–59.

De Quincey, T., video recording, unpublished, 26 March 2015.

Fong, T., Nourbakhsh, I. and K. Dautenhahn, 'A survey of socially interactive robots', *Robotics and Autonomous Systems* 42 (2003), pp. 143–66.

Foster, S. L., 'Movement's Contagion: The Kinesthetic Impact of Performance', in T.C. Davis (ed.), *The Cambridge Companion to Performance Studies*, Cambridge: Cambridge University Press, 2008, pp. 46–59.

Grosz, E., *Chaos, Territory, Art: Deleuze and the Framing of the Earth*, New York: Columbia University Press, 2008.

Hagendoorn, I., 'Some Speculative Hypotheses about the Nature and Perception of Dance and Choreography', *Journal of Consciousness Studies* 11 (2004), pp. 79–110.

Haraway, D., *Modest_Witness@Second_Millenium.FemaleMan_Meets_On comouse, Feminism and Technosciemce*, New York and London: Routledge, 1997.

Hutchins, E., 'Cognitive Ecology', *Topics in Cognitive Science 2* (2010), pp. 705–715.

Latour, B., *Pandora's Hope: Essays on the Reality of Science Studies*, Cambridge: Harvard University Press, 1999.

Leach, J. and S. deLahunta, 'Dance 'Becoming' Knowledge', *Leonardo*, Cambridge: MIT Press, accepted for publication, April 13, 2015. https://curve.coventry.ac.uk/open/file/cce782d9-6cde-4726-819a-92b58f6b2489/1/becomingcomb.pdf [accessed 12 October 2016].

Lenat, D. and E.P. Feigenbaum, 'On the Thresholds of Knowledge', *Artificial Intelligence* 47:1-3 (1991), pp. 185–250.

Manning, E. and B. Massumi, 'Just Like That: William Forsythe, Between Movement and Language', in G. Brandstetter, G. Egert and S. Zubarik (eds), *Touching and to Be Touched: Kinesthesia and Empathy in Dance and Movement*, Berlin: DeGruyter, 2013, pp. 35–62.

Matarić, M.J. and F. Michaud, 'Behavior-Based Systems', in B. Siciliano and O. Khatib, *Handbook of Robotics*, Berlin, Heidelberg: Springer, 2008, pp. 891–909.

Noland, C., *Agency and embodiment: Performing gestures/producing culture*, Cambridge: Harvard University Press, 2010.

Oudeyer, P.-Y., 'On the impact of robotics in behavioral and cognitive sciences: from insect navigation to human cognitive development', *IEEE Transactions on Autonomous Mental Development*, 2:1(2010), pp. 2–16.

Pickering, A., 'Cybernetics and the Mangle: Ashby, Beer and Pask', *Social Studies of Science* 32 (2002), pp. 413–37.

Pickering, A., 'The Next Macy Conference: A New Interdisciplinary Synthesis. Keynote', *IEEE Technology and Society Magazine* 34:3 (2014), pp. 37–8.

Pfeifer, R. and J. Bongard, *How The Body Shapes The Way We Think: A New View Of Intelligence*, Cambridge: MIT Press, 2007.

Robertson, J., 'Gendering Humanoid Robots: Robo-Sexism in Japan', in *Body Society* 16:2 (2010), pp. 1–36.

Saegusa, R., Metta, G., Sandini, G. and S. Sakka, 'Active motor babbling for sensorimotor learning', *Proceedings of the IEEE International Conference on Robotics and Biomimetics* (2008), pp. 794–9.

Saunders, R., 'Towards autonomous creative systems: A computational approach', in Special issue on 'Computational Creativity, Intelligence and Autonomy', *Cognitive Computation* 4:3 (2012), pp. 216–25.

Sharkey, N., 'The evitability of autonomous robot warfare', in *International Review of the Red Cross* 94 (2012), pp. 787–99.

Sheets-Johnstone, M., *The primacy of movement*, Amsterdam and Philadelphia: John Benjamins Publishing, 2011.

Steels, L., 'Fifty Years of AI: From Symbols to Embodiment – and Back', in M. Lungarella, F. Iida, J. Bongard and R. Pfeifer (eds), *50 Years of Artificial Intelligence: Essays Dedicated to the 50th Anniversary of Artificial Intelligence* (Lecture Notes in Computer Science 4850), Berlin and Heidelberg: Springer, 2007, pp. 18–28.

Stacey, J. and L. Suchman, 'Animation and Automation: The liveliness and labours of bodies and machines', *Body and Society* 18:1 (2012), pp. 1–46.

Suchman, L., *Human-Machine Reconfigurations: Plans and Situated Actions*, Cambridge: Cambridge University Press, 2007.

Suchman, L., 'Agencies in technology design: Feminist reconfigurations', *Online Proceedings of the 5th European Symposium on Gender and ICT. Digital Cultures: Participation – Empowerment – Diversity*, 5–7 March (2009) University of Bremen. http://www.informatik.uni-bremen.de/soteg/gict2009/proceedings/GICT2009_Suchman.pdf [accessed 10 October 2016].

Suchman, L., 'Subject Objects', in *Feminist Theory* 12:2 (2011), pp. 119–45.

Suschke, S., *Müller macht Theater. Zehn Inszenierungen und ein Epilog*, Berlin: Theater der Zeit, 2003.

Stevens, C. and S. McKechnie, 'Thinking in action: thought made visible in contemporary dance', in *Cognitive Processing* 6 (2005), pp. 243–52.

Wajcman, J., 'Automation, robotics and the promise of an easier life', Lecture at Oxford Martin School, University of Oxford, 2 March 2016. http://www.oxfordmartin.ox.ac.uk/event/2268 [accessed 21 September 2016].

Varela, F.J., Thompson, E. and E. Rosch, *The embodied mind: Cognitive science and human experience*, Cambridge: MIT Press, 1991.

Weigmann, K., 'Does intelligence require a body?', *EMBO Reports* 13:12 (2013), pp. 1066–9.

Ziemke, T., 'The body of knowledge: On the role of the living body in grounding embodied cognition', in *BioSystems* 148 (2016), pp. 4–11.

Ziemke, T., 'The Construction of 'Reality' in the Robot: Constructivist Perspectives on Situated Artificial Intelligence and Adaptive Robotics', in A. Riegler (ed), Special issue on 'The Impact of Radical Constructivism on Science', *Foundations of Science* 6:1–3 (2001), pp. 163–233.

PART FIVE

Creativity

9

Thinking in film

Mieke Bal

Introduction: Thinking as art

Forget the study, the books and the armchair. Whatever is claimed or imagined, thinking is not a lone, individual act but a social process, embedded in what I have called, apropos of the artist Doris Salcedo, 'the social buzz': the constant implicit discussion – agreement, disagreement, qualification and passionate thinking – of ideas by the people constituting the social environment of the thinker. Three aspects can be derived from that collective nature of thought. These are the aspects that, in my view, are most central in that activity. They are, respectively, and bound in implication: performativity, theorizing and 'anachronizing'. I argue that thinking is neither individual nor particular. Nor is it bound to the time of articulating the ideas. The life of thoughts is like that of images: both are enduring, as well as constantly changing, and collectively sustained. They are subject to debate, and thus entice people to do the thinking *with*, *through* and *in*, more than *about* the world, including its visual manifestations. We do not 'read' the content of thought in an image but make, construct it, in interaction with it.[1]

As a result, at any given time, what each of us sees when considering an idea is a new idea, fresh from the thought-act the viewer and what his/her baggage of thoughts brings to bear on it. This is not, not ever, our own thinking power only but primarily the idea, or the word, metaphor or image we encounter that persuades us in the interaction. This is how ideas themselves can be said to participate in the thinking that produces them: in interaction (performatively), in theoretically relevant ways (as theoretical object) and across time (anachronistically). This thinking power of ideas – which does not mean that they think – makes thinking with, rather than about, the ideas of others an important contribution to the understanding of the social world. That is, for me, the process, the activity of what is called 'philosophy'. In these respects, thought is quite like art. I find it useful to keep thought and art in each other's company. Creativity and the imagination are essential to both.

It is also what we try to do as academics; in my case, in the humanities. Thinking, when it is in touch with the world in a rather strong sense of that expression 'in touch', is a form of analysing. And since it is largely based on what we see around us, it is anchored in visuality. This essay concerns not thought about art but art about thought, and practice as a form of theory. I consider the task of the humanities to be understanding, analysing and explaining the importance of art for the contemporary world. This has made my work interdisciplinary, simply because I could never believe in the delimitations of fields – literature also contains images; paintings don't stop at the edge of their frames; and, as I realized at some point, images move, if only because people move in relation to them when visiting museums or flipping pages in books. I have termed it 'cultural analysis' and co-founded in 1994, with Hent de Vries (philosophy) and Peter van der Veer (cultural anthropology), the research institute ASCA (Amsterdam School for Cultural Analysis) to promote interdisciplinary activity. When working on visual art, the movement of images was and is my starting point. Images move in ways that philosophers, especially Henri Bergson and, in his wake, Gilles Deleuze have attempted to grasp. I was interested in movement as an integration of physical and emotional movement; the trajectories of affect and perception. Thinking, for me, belongs in the same category.[2]

Due to this interest, and to some more anecdotal reasons, I have begun to integrate – a verb to be taken in the strongest possible sense – cultural analysis as an academic activity with art-making as an artistic one, and thus deepen my thinking. I felt compelled to explore these imbricated aspects of images as moving, in experiments in film-making. My desire was to understand the culture I was studying on a more profound, 'lived' level that was, also, more complexly *contemporary*. I wanted to understand how culture works in the present. This has led to a body of experimental documentaries. With some young artists, we started a collective called Cinema Suitcase. Its members seek to facilitate the self-narration of their subjects, always encountered on the basis of a great intimacy, rather than constructing their stories for them. This approach enhances the performative quality of film-making as a collective process. Our films characteristically refrain from deploying narrative voice-over, and only contain set sound. Stories are not chronological but emerge from associative links, constituting a kind of 'free indirect style'.[3]

When these videos were mainly exhibited in art contexts I had to adjust my academic self-image. Once I accepted that I was not only analysing culture but also producing things others saw as art, I began to think about how I could deploy such 'artistic expression' to understand more, and in more depth and nuances, what it means to be a participant in, yet also analyse, *contemporary* culture. And at some point, thinking about contemporaneity, Flaubert's novel *Madame Bovary* – my long-time favourite – insinuated itself.[4]

In the course of this project, I understood more and more how Flaubert, while committed to create beauty, was (also) an exceptionally smart thinker, 'inventing' hysteria before Freud and capitalist exploitation before Marx. The making of the images compelled us to integrate 'beauty' with the ideas that we termed, after Eva Illouz, 'emotional capitalism'. Today, with the economic crisis and its worldwide consequences for individuals and families – and, related, the resurgence of feminism because, after laying to rest what we thought was a won struggle, the renewed need for activism in this regard becomes clearer every day – it became more and more obvious that visual thinking is important, specifically, 'thinking in film'. The need for activism calls on performativity; learning from Flaubert about Freudian and Marxist ideas requires anachronism. This together leads to theorizing film as a form of thinking.[5]

And when I was pondering, in the aftermath of the *Madame B* project, how powerful this combination of the three elements of thinking is, and searching for philosophical support, Descartes, the classic master of Western thought, came along. This happened when in my various readings I encountered the empty qualifier 'post-Cartesian' one time too many, without any further explanation and specification. I felt disconsolate about the lack of thinking in texts supposed to be thoughtful and exemplars of thinking, and I decided to go back to my roots in French Studies and look again at the work of this master of thought. I was interested less in his ideas than in the way he did his thinking, and with my three elements in mind, in the question of how to visualize that process. I wondered if it is possible to show thought-as-process visually, to make it accessible for everyone. I took up the project to show, in film, how thinking happens, and at the same time, to do that through thinking 'in' film, as a foreign language. In this essay I present a number of instances of how thinking in the film I attempt, each time differently, to unfold what thinking in film is, and how thinking is, in a sense, filmic.

Thinking about thinking, in film

With its visualizing, moving images, sounds, voices and gestures, and its appeal to active acts of looking, 'film' as a site of social interaction – a site where the 'social buzz' can concentrate itself – is so common in contemporary culture that it bears comparison with language – that means of communicating we consider so normal as to be unnoticeable as a medium. With 'film,' I mean moving images, no matter whether analogue or digital. And as we think in language, we also think in images. And 'film' is that synaesthetic medium we can 'think in' – as, for example, when engaged in intensive learning of a foreign language, we sometimes dream 'in' that language. 'Thinking' is what the artworks and their viewers do in interaction with each other. 'In' refers both to an otherness that comes with a certain familiarity – as, for instance, the phrase 'in a foreign language' intimates. It also alludes to the spatial situation, physical and relational, of video installation as an art form. Which is why both *Madame B* and the film project I will discuss here, *Reasonable Doubt: Scenes from two lives,* exist both as feature films and as video installations. And what better subject for an exploration of 'thinking *in* film' than the making a film *on* thinking, namely, the activity of thinking of a master of thought? [6]

The wish to make a film on, through and with Descartes' thinking immediately compelled me to consider that primary aspect of thinking: that no one does it alone. The need for a story, however tenuous, diffused the individualistic myth that surrounds philosophy and its practitioners. We speak of influence, but not about the need to be with others for thought to be even possible. Also, it seemed obvious that thinking is not done in one single way, or mode. Moreover, thinking – in spite of the alleged but misconstrued meaning of the *cogito* – does involve the body, and moods. It also needs places where the process can happen. All these considerations, even before embarking on it, led to the project. The project consists of a feature film (ninety-eight minutes) and five installation pieces (thirty minutes each) on the lives and works of René Descartes and Kristina, Queen of Sweden. Both film and exhibition premiered in Kraków, Poland, on April 23 (film) and 24 (exhibition), 2016. [7]

As an experiment to audio-visualize thought – in other words, to think 'in film' about thinking – this project stages scenes from two lives of thinking people, briefly crossing in an intellectual (thinking) friendship. The encounter led to the death of Descartes and influenced the abdication, conversion and expatriation of Kristina. The work is not a biography; it does not produce a proper narrative, but a series of scenes that constitute a non-coherent double portrait. Some scenes are historical, some are my fictionalizing way of doing justice to historical ideas relevant for today and my imaginative imaging of what thinking looks like. The combination as I present it in this essay is an example of 'thinking in film'. [8]

The installation pieces qualify the notion and experience of film. They have been made to accommodate visitor's interest, moods, endurance and, if it so happens, impatience, as a complex and embodied way of absorbing thought in process. The possibility to see them in installation – either sculpturally dispersed throughout a space, or simultaneously projected on a wall – makes the idea of 'thinking *in* film' spatially concrete, and precludes attempts to turn the pieces into a (linear) biography. Wherever in the scenes one is focusing, what one has seen before becomes an amalgamation of memories. Thought, I propose, works that way, rather than in linear fashion. The pieces, which I term *scenes*, present moods rather than events, while biographical moments appear a bit more than in the feature film. Some of these are semi-ironic allusions to historical research. In exhibition, seating should be provided to encourage immersive looking. Sound must be calibrated carefully; there is quite a bit of on-set music, embodying the 'noise' that is always also part of the thinking process. Each scene experiments differently with expressing the inexpressible, the subtleties and ambivalences of reason and emotion together, outside of the narrative impulse, in the process of thinking.[9]

The feature film, in contrast, has a fixed duration, over which the viewer has no say. Compared to the installation pieces, it is barer of events and mostly limited to presenting the thought process intensely. And, as a feature film, it has an underlying story, tenuous as it is: after a relationship by correspondence, philosopher René Descartes (1596–1650) met and briefly interacted with Queen Kristina (1626–89) in Stockholm, where he died six weeks after arriving, due to the cold. Once Descartes had reached Sweden, the two didn't see each other much. Kristina's philosophical interest was genuine enough. But he was there in a more or less decorative function, to adorn Kristina's ambitious project of creating an academy that would put Sweden's intellectual elite on the European map.[10]

Descartes left Western thought with a burden, and a treasure. The burden: a misconstrued dualistic tradition. In my view, he accepted the dualism of the Catholic Church, but fought against it all his life – torn by doubt, because it is not reasonable. The treasure: a decisive advance in rational thought that, precisely, did not excise the body, nor religion for that matter. The (in)famous *cogito* can be interpreted in the opposite direction from the clichéd dismissal of it, as an attempt to embody and subjectify thought. This is especially clear when we look back from his last book, *The Passions of the Soul,* and see the ongoing struggle against dualism in different episodes of his life.[11]

Moreover, I speculate that he left a more specific treasure. Descartes dedicated that book to another woman friend-by-correspondence, Princess Elisabeth of Bohemia. This woman had been traumatized by childhood events of a political and economic order. As she writes in her letters, Descartes truly helped her overcome a chronic affliction caused by the trauma. Although they never met as a trio, Descartes at some point asked Kristina to help Elisabeth. I use that anecdote for the far-reaching claim that through his mode of thinking, specifically thinking *with* the other person, he 'invented' psychoanalysis, in a post-Freudian form that returns this theory to re-becoming a true social science. This theory that so eminently integrates body and mind, as it was later developed, emerged not only from Descartes' thoughts about the interaction between body and mind as exposed in his book but also from the solidarity with Elisabeth that he, as one who was also traumatized in childhood, felt and demonstrated. This also has implications for a contemporary feminism that makes us too easily consider gender relations in the past as hopelessly exclusive. The two women who thought *with* Descartes, and helped him think with them, stand for the aspect of thinking that counters the myth of the thinker as loner.[12]

Descartes' struggle to integrate what religion had separated is of concern to me because, among the many tenacious dualisms we continue to use (whereas merging the issues would be beneficial to all) are those between cultural and economic values, and between academic and artistic – in other words, intellectual and sense-based – expressive thought, analysis, and reasoning. In these and other dualisms I live and work; they hamper me. I see Descartes' thinking process in the cracks between the certainties he also proffered when bracketing his doubt in his reasoning. In order to help overcome them, I look at the discrepancies between the Descartes we have abused and the one who was the point of origin of the struggle for a non-dualistic mode of thinking. Conversely, Queen Kristina, on her part, is not only capricious but also philosophical, constantly thinking about life, and the bearer of the after-effects of this different Descartes. And, as a conversation partner, she asks the questions the philosopher needs to ponder to make headway in his process.

My interest in doing this project focuses on the complexity of the rationalism these figures represent. The productivity of the dialectical relationship between reason and a certain kind of madness in both Descartes and Kristina was never fully recognized. Through this project, I want to suggest that reason and 'madness' – meaning the form doubt takes when it is cut off from the social bonds based on respect and dialogue – can go very well together. The persistent deceptive and arrogant progressivism in our thinking is fond of the qualifier 'post-Cartesian', as something we have happily left behind. But it is that 'post-' thinking itself that betrays us as, I'd say, pre-Cartesian; as failing to integrate doubt in reason. Caught in a world where dogma ruled and disbelieving it was severely punishable, Descartes spent his life doubting dualism and attempting to overcome it, rationally as well as in his capricious behaviour. Had we really listened to and looked at him, that vexed preposition 'post-' itself would be used with more (Cartesian) doubt. Using audio-visual images to put this on the table is my attempt to bring thought and images together in supporting each other.

Why imaging and/of thinking move

The most characteristic image of thinking as a process is a sequence where Descartes (played by Thomas Germaine) is walking alone in the dunes, or along a busy highway, clearly thinking. Descartes was famous for his long walks. The first scene – solely on Descartes – integrates the sense of avid learning, curiosity and ambition, and his walking and moving about are the physical condition of this learning. It also includes the obstacles that emotional combination sometimes mounts in a young person unaware of what makes things difficult for him. The mood is eagerness and insecurity. In this scene we also get a glimpse of the young philosopher's economically easy, but emotionally difficult, everyday life, where caring men surround him. Beginning with a preface that puts all relevant ideas on the table, the scene ends on a non-narrative cliff hanger of sorts.

Energetically walking towards an unknown place, in the preface a still insecure Descartes visits an art exhibition on emotions in the seventeenth century (curated by Gary Schwartz for the Frans Hals Museum, Haarlem). He wants to explain his views on the human as an integration of body and mind to a friend, hoping to get confirmation. Asking his friend questions, he seeks to understand the bond between body and soul, and its visibility in painting. Asking questions is the first mode of thinking we get to see; it couldn't be more clearly social. The harp music his sister played when the two were little lingers in his head.[13]

This connects the preface to the childhood scenes that follow. Waking him by tentative harp music, his sister Jeanne (Olympe Lefèbvre) playfully teaches the little boy (Ambroise Lefèbvre) about the senses, their deceptive nature and the need to understand the world through them, in combination with thinking. After asking her about the absence of their parents, the little boy walks off alone into the woods, metaphorically standing for the great wide world, and continues walking when he turns into a young man who makes walking outside into his substitute armchair: this is his method of thinking. Music, the sister and walking together constitute the *conditio sine qua non* of the thinking. Film is the language, the only one, in which this can be articulated and shown.[14]

Each scene contains an artwork by someone else, to make the point that thinking in film cannot be done alone any more than thinking in general. After dreaming about making choices, he turns to intellectual work, without ever sitting at a desk. As avid a learner as he was in childhood, after thinking and exploring botany in his own garden, we see him walk endlessly through nature, thinking about the mineral world in a dunes landscape – the microscopic images of minerals filmed from the inside of a fragment from the artwork *A Thing Among Things* by Giovanni Giaretta (2015). The thinker asks a butcher's help to understand anatomy in a meat workshop, for he believed in the usefulness of studying in practice. He studies plants in his garden, with the help of a young valet (Simon Ferdinand). Hunting for a house – the grandeur of which is never good enough – he meets the mathematician Isaac Beeckman (Ilja Nieuwland),

FIGURE 9.1 *Descartes talks to his friend Chanut about body and soul. Photo: Margreet Vermeulen. Copyright: Mieke Bal.**

with whom he strikes up a friendship. The new friend becomes the recipient of his first writing: a treatise on music. For Beckman's eyes only! This will lead to his first serious break-up. The events and situations are based on historical evidence, but the weaving together in an audio-visual creation of thinking-in-process needed film as its language of expression.[15]

But the fictional imaging kicks in when I give Descartes another friend to test his social clumsiness along with the social anchoring of thought. Among his practice-based learning experiences is his search for a dialogue with the lens makers of Amsterdam, when he was studying 'dioptrics' – the science of the refraction of light. Descartes writes about this wish at the beginning of the treatise. That opening suggests that he sought to be 'democratic' in his writing, wanting it to be accessible to the men of practice even if they had no scientific background. What if one of the men of practice – the artisans working for a living around him – happened to be called Baruch Spinoza, the next of the world's most brilliant philosophers, about twenty years his junior? There is no historical impossibility, nor is there evidence that they ever met. But they *could* have, and what would have happened then? This question required 'thinking in film'. Testing Descartes' democratic mind-set, I staged a meeting of the two in a lens shop. Descartes solicits the young man's help.

They agree to meet at the end of the scene. What will happen when they do? That is the breathtaking question; the intellectual cliff hanger that ends the first scene, with the word 'intellectual' emphatically not limited to the mind alone.[16]

The bond between movement and the image is not limited to the moving image of film, although the latter is an over-determined instance of it. I stage the scene at the museum in the beginning as a preface of sorts, to bind the moving image to the still one of painting. To understand why and how I can claim that still images also move, the best resource is the work of Henri Bergson (1859–1941). Particularly, Bergson's book *Matter and Memory* is vital to my quest (1991 [1896]). This 'essay on the relationship between body and mind', as its subtitle has it, is inspirational to anachronistically understand Descartes' search for such a relationship. It starts with the thesis that perception is not a construction but a *selection* that the subject makes in view of her own interests. Perception, in Bergson's view, is an act *of* the body and *for* the body. The selection that perception is takes place in the present. It is motivated not only by the interests of the perceiver but also by her memories. '(M)emory [images], laden with the whole of the past, responds to the appeal of the present state', Bergson writes.[17]

At the end of the book, Bergson sums it up in these words:

> In concrete perception memory intervenes, and the subjectivity of sensible qualities is due precisely to the fact that our consciousness, which begins by being only memory, prolongs a plurality of moments into each other, contracting them into a single intuition.[18]

FIGURE 9.2 *Descartes meeting Spinoza. Photo: Margreet Vermeulen.*

That coexistence of different moments (or memories) has a spatial aspect to it. This timespace is given shape in video installation in the simultaneous presence of – and, hence, the simultaneous movement on – multiple screens. This was one of the reasons I examined Eija-Liisa Ahtila's work in an earlier study. I have learned an enormous amount from it – about space, for example.[19]

According to Bergson, space is not geometrical, as in the Renaissance perspective; consequently, it is neither measurable nor identical for everyone who perceives it. Instead, our sense of space develops according to what Bergson calls a 'natural feeling'. This natural feeling is heterogeneous and different for everyone, depending on wherever they are. This comes to the fore in the images of Descartes, armed with a magnifying glass, roaming around the world – whether the small portion of it that is his garden, the tiny world of a slaughtered pig in the butcher shop or the larger one of the dune landscape. The multiple screens of video installation exemplify heterogeneity with their non-synchronously moving images. In video installations, space is precisely that: heterogeneous, multiple, both fictional and real, both subjective and 'extensive', or deictic. The story may be fictional; the contact with it is real.

Reminiscent of Descartes' unsettlement in *The Passions of the Soul,* Bergson considers the body to be a material entity, and he consequently sees perception as a material practice. This makes Bergson's conception of the image synonymous with the moving image. This is a deeper level on which images move; it comes closer to affect. The image itself – not its support – is both moving and material. It implies that it is plural and functional; it *does* something. Today, we call it *performative*. In 1907, Bergson coined the term 'creative evolution' to account for yet another aspect of movement in the image: the *readiness to act*, which occurs when the perception image, as Deleuze called it, morphs into an affect-image and makes the perceiver develop the *readiness to act*. This readiness – not the potentially resulting actualization – lies at the heart of the political potential of the (figurative) image, film and video installation. The combination of these kinds or forms of movement is the possibility film offers when we try to 'think in film'.[20]

Mastery, in doubt

While never happening in isolation, even when the thinker is a bit of a recluse, thinking is also subjected to the dialogic relation within the self. In the second scene, the mood is the difficult-to-live combination of pride and fear. What might seem a weakness of Descartes turns out his primary strength: he dares to doubt, fear and panic. This scene begins with the discussion with Spinoza (Abel Streefland). The passionate plea of the young man converges with the mature thinker's conception; it is as if they repeat each other's ideas. Throughout the scene, Descartes enacts his status of the famous master of thought he had become in his lifetime, and simultaneously runs into his personality problems. The philosophical doubt of his somewhat-sceptical leanings converges with his paranoid tendency and his suspicion of others. In a series of short episodes, I merge the many friends and correspondents of his social buzz into one, named – after the loyal and long-standing one – Hector-Pierre Chanut (Florent Houdu), French ambassador to Kristina's court. This friend regularly appears.

The meeting with Spinoza shows that Descartes' attempts to consider the ideas and lives of others – his democratic statement at the beginning of the *Dioptrique* – as shipwreck on his sense of superiority. When he pontificates to the young man about the interaction of light and colour – for which I inserted a fragment from the fabulous abstract artwork of colour, *Deep Orange* by Ann Veronica Janssens (2010) – the future master of ethics interrupts him with challenges. He puts forward the need of the imagination, and of the togetherness of people in the present. This insistence has turned Spinoza into an anachronistic master of contemporary social thought. Spinoza, here, articulates the elements of thought that sustain the need for the humanities, and the study of images, as serious 'theoretical objects' with thought of their own. Slightly flabbergasted, Descartes' understanding dawns. Who is this young craftsman? He sounds like a philosopher![21]

After challenging Descartes' class prejudice, Spinoza disappears. A symbolic expression of a lonely Descartes' ambition is enacted when he (fictionally) visits the Royal Academy of Arts and Sciences in a professorial robe. There, he encounters a portrait of Christian Huygens, the son of his good friend Constantin, and prophetically (or anachronistically) recognizes the successful scientific career of the young man. Then he recalls the death of the young scientist's mother. These moments are my (Bergsonian) ways of showing how we merge personal memories of childhood with what we notice about others and what we strive to achieve. Descartes's father was not proud of him the way Huygens was of his brilliant son. And he, too, had lost his mother, here invoked by a painting of the *Allegory of Teaching* by Ferdinand Bol (anachronistically, from 1663). Disgusted with the futility of ambition, he tosses the robe on a chair and leaves the grand room. Everything I just wrote about what went through Descartes' mind is nothing other than my interpretation of the actor's play in the setting.

Home again, a young collaborator (Reinier Schouten) is practicing the violin. Chanut comes to visit and whispers something in his ear, to which we are not privy. Upset, Descartes shouts out that Beeckman has betrayed him. The historical issue is that the mathematician appears to have spoken about the music treatise to others. Scholars agree that the philosopher's angry reaction is excessive; preparing for the issue of psychoanalysis, I tend to call it hysterical. The violinist attempts to take the fury over in his music. Chanut suggests René should see a 'soul doctor'; the theoretical fiction kicks in again. 'If it doesn't help, it will at least teach him something about the body-soul relationship; instruct him about the 'passions of the soul', says Chanut – anachronistically citing the subject and title of his last and, for me, most important book.[22]

So, to figure how Descartes came to become the inventor of psychoanalysis, instead of making him talk about it, I stage him as going into analysis. To the 'soul doctor' he reveals his childhood traumas – but to avoid implausible self-declarations, we only hear it from the doctor, not from Descartes himself. The attempt to get professional help with his anger fits come to naught when the doctor picks up on a metaphor Descartes' father had used to malign his son: he was ashamed to have produced a son who 'let himself be bound between two layers of leather'. A historical anecdote, updated for what it would mean today, not then. The analyst (Henk Hillenaar) asks if the metaphor might have other connotations. The allusion disturbs the patient, who runs off in fury. End of story.

The scene is meant to hint at Descartes' possible interest in men, to inform viewers of this childhood trauma of repeated abandonment, and at the idea that his conception of the subject made psychoanalysis possible, at his childhood loneliness and at his present troubles with others. My academic claim is that his view of subjectivity – especially as articulated in *The Passions of the Soul* and in the correspondence with Elisabeth, as well as the (imagined) interaction with Kristina – will become the foundation of psychoanalysis. In these two scenes, *anger* is the mode of thinking; because he is 'beside himself' and directing his emotions to the people who challenge his mastery, he closes off his thought process. The relationship between the two scenes of anger fits is based on a sense of futurality. Not only does this excitable man have a great impact on the world in his inauguration of modern thought but also his own life is filled with hints to the future, including future difficulties anchored in his complex personality.[23]

Meanwhile, Queen Kristina (played by Marja Skaffari), impressed by his work that she has seriously studied, writes to him with her magnified metaphysical questions. One of these questions, concerning the nature of love, compels the philosopher to invoke a childhood memory to explain – when his first, 'scientific' explanation, doesn't satisfy the Queen. This exchange hints at the indispensable role these two women – Kristina and Elisabeth – had, in the footsteps of René's sister Jeanne, in nourishing the philosopher's thinking process. Chanut – now in his capacity as Kristina's ambassador – tries to persuade his friend to make the trip to Sweden. He, too, is subject to conflicting allegiances and loyalties. Knowing what happens next, the scene

FIGURE 9.3 *Descartes' anger. Photo: Margreet Vermeulen.*

is ambivalent. We see Descartes' wavering determination be influenced by flattery. The dream of grandeur wins over prudence. Ambition, often important for the insecure, is also a double-edged sword. In the end, we see a frail man, bent over, walking on the beach, insinuating his inevitable upcoming voyage north. Still walking, but beyond mastery.

Although this scene occurs in the film as well as in the installation piece, the effect is quite different. In a single-space installation, this ambivalent decision will run simultaneously with the encounter with Spinoza in Scene 1. Both are talking scenes, and the visitor, immersed in a cacophony, must choose what to listen to, how to listen, and when to change direction. This embodies the social buzz; the impact of the viewer as interlocutor. The image struggles with the sound. There, full of plans, Descartes is now going to his demise; suddenly the spring has left his step and the bent-over figure, filmed from a distance, looks old, as if already near dying. Chronology is made redundant. The installation of these two scenes together helps us understand yet another aspect of how thinking works. It makes tangible that a person is not just a one-moment subject, but carries along a life-long baggage of memories.[24]

From impatience as lifestyle to mis-encounters

The next two scenes bring the second main character in, and begin with an image of stretched-out time. In the third scene, Kristina – without Descartes,

FIGURE 9.4 *Kristina's insecurity. Photo: Przemo Wojciechowski.*

but with the philosopher constantly on her mind – is the character, and impatience as an element of thought is the subject of representation. The mood is irritation about the power of another over the self. She is impatiently waiting for Descartes's arrival. Meanwhile, she is failing in her personal relationships, as well as in her studying, and in managing the state and her estate. The beautiful palace where she lives becomes a prison. Time is stretching endlessly, something she cannot tolerate. Sadness and anger alternate. This scene concerns feeling time in confinement, and the resulting futility of beauty, riches and power. The end is a withholding of certainty in a moment where dream and expectation, fiction and reality, converge in music. No event can occur. The scene also reflects an essential feature of film – its basis in time. What is time like when nothing happens? This question, and the viewer's participation in the experiment, introduces the idea of heterochrony.[25]

What Kristina is 'really' doing during the long wait for Descartes' arrival doesn't matter. The scene presents us with the moods that come with the impatience enacted. The eternally mourning Queen Mother hovers over a daughter with whom she has no contact whatsoever. Two unhappy women, together but alone. Nothing can occur. Kristina runs, plays with her dog, and explores her palatial home like a tourist seeing it for the first time. She looks into mirrors and questions herself, and her physical beauty. Thinking, it seems, is foreclosed when time is the enemy. She does try to think – in fact, she does barely anything else. Reading bits and pieces in a number of books, she feels she is drowning in them. A Shakespeare poem she stumbles upon seems to summarize her plight: if she doesn't marry and procreate, everything she has will die with her. The entrance of her lady-in-waiting and friend Bella (Anna Podkościelna-Cyz) cheers her up for a while; but, shy of entering into another phase of the friendship, she blames the other, and the sweet moment is over. She roams around the palace.[26]

This roaming is the expression of her insecurity about who she is, and what she can do with her life. It is her mode of thinking; her variant of Descartes' walks. Coming upon a small sculpture of the famous French philosopher, she covers it with gauze, as if unwilling to show him – if and when he arrives – that she cares. Going through her house is a way of saying that she owns it all, while also expressing her estrangement from the worldly goods that – after Descartes' death – will no longer interest her.[27]

But then, she has a dream – of potential beauty. This is yet another form of thinking I am interested in – with psychoanalysis as my companion. Here, an artwork by Jane Harris, *Potential Beauty* (2004), visualizes her dream. This is a dancing dress, without a body inside it. But the dress acts; it bows, greets, displays itself and dances. This artwork explores the fine line between thought and cognition. It turns out beauty doesn't leave Kristina entirely indifferent. Her apparent disinterest is as defensive as Descartes' excessive anger. On some unconscious level, she would like to be more beautiful than she considers herself to be, or so it seems. But the sculpture in front of her on the mantelpiece, alternating her view with her own mirror image, is a bust of Medusa – stylized, yes; but still ... .[28]

A somewhat mysteriously talking valet (Wladislaw Chojecki) tries to reassure Kristina, to calm her impatience. His primary function is to make her speak out her disquiet; to express her arrogance while also showing the insecurity that generates it. In a fit of fury – comparable to Descartes' screaming about Beeckman's betrayal – she breaks the dishes in her kitchen. But when she orders a servant (Milja Korpela, who doubles as hair- and make-up artist) to clean up, in a fit of economic thinking, she tells her not to throw away the pieces. Finally, Descartes' arrival is announced. Nervously, she dresses up in a regal outfit – crown and all – looking outdated and a trifle carnivalesque, and sits down while Lulli's music resounds through an empty hallway, then filled with dreamy-looking women in baroque costumes who play the music. This music (by the Polish string quartet Con Affetto) coincides in a single-space exhibition with the man walking on the beach, and with the first meeting with Spinoza. Together, these three endings compress decades into a full, ambivalent moment, stretched out to last as long as the visitor wishes to stay. Thought and time stand opposed as the enemies they seem to be. It is up to the viewers to bring their own thinking to how they will look at and listen to this, and for how long.

FIGURE 9.5 *Kristina with sculpture of Descartes. Photo: Przemo Wojciechowski.*

The fourth scene begins with the arrival, and the encounter that doesn't go so well. The mood: awkwardness. In this scene the attempt is to show – again, rather than tell – how these two great minds of the seventeenth century did not manage to really meet. Both had based their interest on something different than what they get. Descartes had hoped for the magnificent recognition of his greatness by royalty; Kristina for a pliant servant, a great man at her beck and call. The scene is best characterized by the word 'painful'. But as we will see, in painfulness thinking also happens.

Upon entering her room, his nervousness is matched by hers. The failure of the long-awaited encounter is imaged through montage. The two figures, sitting in the same room, alternate, but do not meet in the same frame. This precludes the sociality needed for thinking. He begins to express an excessive but disingenuous gratitude, speaking to Kristina in the third person ('*votre majesté*') so that a personal conversation becomes impossible; then he shows off his philosophical personality somewhat pompously. Matching him in his attempt to impress, she shows of her mastery of the French language, criticizing its structural properties. What can you say when your new acquaintance tells you that your native language sucks? His reaction is clumsiness. When she

FIGURE 9.6 *Awkward conversation. Photo: Przemo Wojciechowski.*

then tells him to meet the next morning – and every day afterwards – at 5 AM, the man who has the habit of staying in bed, sleeping, then working until noon, stays behind in shock while the Queen rushes to welcome her cousin, who visits to attend an imminent concert. With a casual hand gesture, Kristina, who does not bother to introduce her guest to her cousin (Agnieszka Kalinowska), sends him to an adjacent waiting room. So far, no thinking is possible yet. There, the exhausted philosopher has a vision of the world, turning with its many problems. This is a fragment of the shadow play *Transgressions* by the artist Nalini Malani (2009).

After the concert, the two go separate ways. Descartes falls ill while Kristina makes plans for a ballet to celebrate the 'Peace of Westfalen'. She is angry when her valet tells her about Descartes' illness. His death during her planning is yet another imaging of temporal discrepancy, and the impossibility of chronology. A sense of social schizophrenia emerges. The endings of the different scenes add to this a sonic schizophrenia. Kristina, so far unable to show affection to Descartes, falls apart when she learns he has died. Self-centred, she considers herself a victim. But, thinking, she turns her sadness into a philosophical question: she sees the limit of her power of self-disposal. This, combined with her ambition, will ultimately enable her to change her ways, including her selfishness.

After-effects and pre-figurations

The mood in the last scene is a mix of sadness bordering on melancholia, and brave attempts to learn, after the fact, from the wisdom of the friend she has lost. The ending is one of the rare moments in the project that something really happens. This, too, is a futural moment. Kristina is devastated. For her, Descartes' death is an assault on her personal autonomy. Her loss of self-power also affects her body when we see her sink to the floor. Trying to pick up her life, she does the inevitable: continue her routine. Some of these images are presentations of small routine acts; some are symbolic expressions of self-loss, as when she disappears in a hollow tree. This disappearance is an example of visual thought, close to metaphor but embodied. Doing something that makes no sense is also an incipient thought: an experiential attempt at feeling loss as loss of self.

This makes it possible for another form of thinking to emerge. When sitting dejected in her large and beautiful, but empty, private room, Kristina has a vision: the spectre of Descartes visits her. Now she is able to say what she couldn't muster the openness to say during his lifetime: that she misses their discussions. Those discussions that constitute most fundamentally what thought in process can be. But Descartes contradicts her by saying that discussing is just what they are doing, *now*. Thus he points at yet another form thought can take: imaginary dialogue. In the same move, he foregrounds the importance of the present. He encourages her to continue with her work, and to practice the passion of generosity, the most important one according to him. Kristina understands the message: Descartes' friend, Princess Elisabeth of Bohemia, needs help, and she may be able to extend a helping hand to the other woman. After the spectre has disappeared, she picks herself up, and all the changes that will occur soon in her life are set in motion. The spectre, or vision, or dream, appears to have a kind of agency that is able to performatively set in motion a stagnating thought process.[29]

After the apparition, Kristina moves to Rome. Entering the city, she is tempted by the Church. Regardless of her actual conversion to Catholicism, my point was something else. The image shows the temptation itself as a form of thinking, dialogic and forever incomplete. There is not really an outcome. She ends up in her palatial dwelling, the Palazzo Corsini. There she faces antique imperial busts, as if matching her own status that she has given up to that of those prestigious predecessors. Seeing her surrounded by ancient art and old-master paintings, one feels the futility of the worldly riches that she cannot quite let go. A biographer shows up, who asks her a question about her interest in science and philosophy. While she answers by reminiscing about the foundation of a university in Uppsala when she was thirteen years old, another visitor is announced: the very Princess Elisabeth of Bohemia (Johanna ter Steege) she thought she should help, if she was to obey Descartes' spectre's injunction to be generous.[30]

The final scene stages Elisabeth's appeal to Kristina on behalf of her daughter Charlotte (Fleur Bongertman). This was the opportunity to recall the important moment when Descartes himself was in need of help. Whereas the scene is entirely fictional, the ideas it expresses, the faltering reasoning and the sympathetic thinking, Elisabeth's uncertainty about the meaning of some of Descartes' recommendations, and her insistence on gender difference, come from the correspondence between Descartes and Elisabeth as suggestively interpreted by Yaëlle Sibony-Malpertu. In the conversation between the two women, Elisabeth phrases some of her doubts about Descartes' universalizing claims.[31]

Kristina, trying hard to think with Elisabeth, but clearly not aware of the intricate discussions between her and Descartes, ends up recommending that she consult the 'soul doctor' in Amsterdam that Descartes had been seeing. This is a key word. Descartes, in the correspondence, actually called himself Elisabeth's 'doctor'. When, full of renewed hope, Elisabeth and Charlotte depart, the latter unexpectedly and inappropriately kisses the former Queen, who stays behind in confusion. What is the meaning of social behaviour? Is an inappropriate kiss a thought image, too? I think so. It marks the moment the traumatized, psychotic young woman re-enters the social domain. The prospect of healing beckons her. As psychoanalyst Françoise Davoine phrases it: she retrieves the capability to repair the broken social bond.[32]

The constructions of thought-in-process that constitute the body of this series of videos lack an explanation. Only hints, allusions and small details can make the audience think about what it is that brought Descartes and Kristina

FIGURE 9.7 *Kristina's vision. Photo: Przemo Wojciechowski.*

to genius and worldwide fame, through the activity of thinking. Obviously, answering that question can easily become callous – thoughtless satisfaction of immodest curiosity. There is the historical evidence, of course. For my project, this was both indispensable for the construction of a narrative layer, a character presentation, and a meaningful link between the lives and the modes of thinking, as well as the resulting thoughts. But it was especially crucial to begin my own thinking about how to audio-visualize thought: my thinking in film. These are the elements I have gleaned from the sources, and that became the incipient thoughts about this project. This is not a factual biography but my interpretation of why bringing these two figures together makes sense to understand the shape of thought. So, let me end on a biographical note, instead of beginning with it.[33]

Both Kristina and Descartes had a rather tough beginning in life. Kristina became a queen at age five, after her father's death on the battlefield. She had been close to him. She was alone, with a mother in desolate mourning for the rest of her life, who didn't care much for the daughter who should have been a son. René lost his mother at age one, and barely saw his father, who was too busy pursuing his career elsewhere. When his father re-married, he took his older son and daughter with him, leaving René behind. These childhood situations of different forms of abandonment, and subsequent orphan-like loneliness, predict adult turmoil. And so it happened.

FIGURE 9.8 *Elisabeth visits Kristina. Photo: Thijs Vissia.*

Both grew up to be brilliant, obstinate, easily angry, suspicious and capricious; ambitious and impatient with resistance. In common parlance, we'd call them paranoid, and otherwise neurotic. The Queen was barely of age when she organized her coronation and started to think about her abdication, practically at the same time, while also pondering a change of religion that she carried out shortly after. After Descartes' death, she left Sweden for a restless life of travel, ending up in Rome as the Catholic, as Descartes had been all along. Both loved music. The emphatically anachronistic choice of musical works I have staged in the project hints at experimental attempts that they both tried: Descartes in his theorizing music and Kristina in commissioning musical works, even if that didn't come to very much.[34]

Once he started showing his writings to others, the philosopher was constantly under ecclesiastic surveillance – or thought he was (Freud: being paranoid doesn't mean people aren't out to get you). He moved around, mainly in the United Provinces (now the Netherlands), refusing to leave forwarding addresses, and was considered a great man. But because glory is never enough for the fundamentally insecure, he managed to fall out with quite some friends he initially adored. This master of rationalism did his thinking often in the turmoil of extreme emotions. He was a good enough Catholic, yet dangerously close to heresy. He led the life of what the French called an *honnête homme*: someone of good breeding and education, whose talents and skills could not be captured by isolated disciplines. From biology to philosophy, astrology and medicine, Descartes also shone as an expert in what we would now call 'mental illness', when he comforted his friend Elisabeth who was suffering from a bout of it. Where did that skill come from? My guess is: it takes one to know one. This is why I credit him with the 'invention' of psychoanalysis – his conception of the subject making its later explicit invention possible.

I imagine both figures suffered from the symptoms of what we now call neurosis, specifically an *abandonment complex* – a tendency to reject affective bonds while constantly seeking them. Out of fear to be abandoned, they prefer to be the first to do the abandoning. This is what underpinned their passionate attachments to, then rejections, of others. Always craving, but feigning indifference out of fear that parental abandonment would repeat itself. And since these things tend to be reciprocal, they were seen as alternatingly attractive and repulsive. It also explains why the queen insisted so strongly on the meeting, but then didn't do much to take intellectual advantage of Descartes' presence. In the end, it also explains their brilliance, and the suffering it took to achieve it.[35]

Both Kristina and René declined to marry, choosing to spend time with people of their own gender than doing 'the proper thing'. Hints of homosexual practice circulated about both. René, who had an acquaintance burned at the stake for precisely this, had an additional reason for fear. Kristina was notoriously fond of a woman at court called Ebba; she called her Bella. This was not a reason to turn them into homosexuals, as Mika Kaurismäki did with Kristina in his film *The Girl King* (2015), made practically simultaneously with my project. His film turns entirely on Kristina's lesbianism, without giving the figure of the queen much character.

Paradoxically, this emphasis becomes disturbing instead of emancipating. I preferred to bring the hints of it in, without making it more than a hesitating sexual orientation. René surrounded himself with caring male friends that he adored, then broke up with, and depended strongly on his young valets. In my version, these are very affectionate relationships. One of them plays the violin as a comfort to Descartes when he is depressed, dejected and feels betrayed. In short, these two major figures of the seventeenth century had much in common, but this didn't help their friendship. Nevertheless, what they had in common made them ideally suitable to think in film what thinking can be when it happens, in the social buzz, performatively and across time. The qualifier 'post-Cartesian' can really be banned, lest we keep our blinders on about what these processual aspects of thinking entail. I prefer to enlist Descartes, as Spinoza's interlocutor, to theorize the place of affect and sociality in that activity we tend to consider hyper-individualistic: thinking.

Notes

1 I have developed the concept 'social buzz' and its impact on visual art in my book, *Of What One Cannot Speak: Doris Salcedo's Political Art* (Chicago, IL: University of Chicago Press, 2010).

2 To get a sense of the intellectual profile of the institute, see *ASCA Brief: Intellectual Traditions in Movement*, eds Mieke Bal, Thomas Elsaesser, Burcht Pranger, Beate Roessler, Hent de Vries, and Willem Weststeijn (Amsterdam: ASCA Press, 1998), and for my own view, *The Practice of Cultural Analysis: Exposing Interdisciplinary Interpretation*, ed. Mieke Bal (Stanford, CA: Stanford University Press, 1999).

3 The collective Cinema Suitcase began in 2002, and consisted of Mieke Bal, Zen Marie, Thomas Sykora, Gary Ward, Michelle Williams Gamaker. The collective is now reduced to two, Michelle Williams Gamaker and myself. Both ASCA and Cinema Suitcase are tokens of the importance of collaboration – the 'social buzz' included.

4 For an overview of my video work, see 'From Documentary to Fiction and Back', in [...] (*Ellipses*), Johannesburg, SA, nr. 1, 2016 (no page numbers) http://www.ellipses.org.za/project/from-documentary-to-fiction-and-back (with Michelle Williams Gamaker) (accessed 01 January 2017).

5 The result of rethinking Flaubert in this context is a feature film and video installation that have been widely exhibited; see the film http://www.miekebal.org/artworks/films/madame-b, and the installations http://www.miekebal.org/artworks/installations/madame-b/madame-b-installation-pieces (accessed 01 January 2017). On 'emotional capitalism', see Eva Illouz, *Cold Intimacies: The Making of Emotional Capitalism* (Cambridge, UK: Polity Press, 2007); and *Why Love Hurts* (Cambridge, UK: Polity Press, 2012). On the Freudian 'invention' of hysteria and women's desire, see Shoshana Felman, *What Does a Woman Want? Reading and Sexual Difference* (Baltimore, MD: The Johns Hopkins University Press, 1993); and Barbara Johnson, *The Feminist Difference: Literature, Psychoanalysis and Gender* (Cambridge, MA: Harvard University Press, 1998). The project to integrate a concern for beauty with a political thrust affiliates our work with Jill Bennett's book *Practical Aesthetics: Event, Affect and Art After 9/11* (London: I. B. Tauris, 2012). What Flaubert foresaw and predicted is and is now a deeply disturbing reality has been analysed in persuasive detail in Saskia Sassen, *Expulsions: Brutality and Complexity in the Global Economy* (Cambridge: MA: Harvard University Press, 2014).

6 I borrow the phrase 'thinking in film' from the artist Eija-Liisa Ahtila. She discusses it in an interview with Chrissie Iles: 'Thinking in Film: Eija-Liisa Ahtila in Conversation with Chrissie Iles.' *Parkett* 68 (2003), pp. 58–64. To my regret, it was only after finishing this article that I found the book by Kyoo Lee, *Reading Descartes Otherwise: Blind, Mad, Dreamy, and Bad* (New York: Fordham University Press, 2013), which is wholly consistent with the view of Descartes presented here, and even more radical. This author, too, considers Descartes' thinking 'cinematic'.

7 Mieke Bal, *Reasonable Doubt,* Festival of Film and Philosophy (Museum of Contemporary Art Kraków (MOCAK), Poland, 2016). These events were organized, and the exhibition curated, by Roma Sendyka. Needless to say how deeply grateful I am for her commitment and activity to make this happen. See http://www.miekebal.org/artworks/exhibitions/reasonable-doubt (accessed 01 January 2017) for this event.

8 For a more extensive reflection on 'thinking in film', see my book on the subject, Mieke Bal, *Thinking in Film: The Politics of Video Installation According to Eija-Liisa Ahtila* (London: Bloomsbury, 2013).

9 On the specific effects of video installation as a medium, see, in addition to the previous reference, Kate Modloch, *Screens: Viewing Media Installation Art* (Minneapolis, MN: University of Minnesota Press, 2010); and Mathilde Roman, *On Stage: The Theatrical Dimension of Video Image* (London: Intellect, 2016). The installation pieces can also be used to turn the film into a serial, with the five segments as a way of thinking about each at leisure, and starting the next day with the next piece.

10 An excellent study on the differences between video installation and film is Janna Houwen, *Comparing Film and Video: Intermediality and Medium Specificity in Moving Images* (London: Bloomsbury, 2017). On the encounter and the interaction between the two, see Jean-François De Raymond, *La reine et le philosophe. Descartes et Cristine de Suède* (Paris: Lettres Modernes, 1993). This short book contains letters Kristina wrote to Descartes, which demonstrate her philosophical questioning convincingly.

11 My primary sources for Descartes, in addition to the French volume in the Pléiade edition, are the autobiographical treatise *Discourse on Method and Meditations*, trans. Laurence J. Lafleur (New York: The Liberal Arts Press, 1960 [1637]); and *The Passions of the Soul*, trans. Stephen H. Voss. (Indianapolis and Cambridge: Hackett Publishing Company, 1989 [1649]).

12 Of course, I am not alone, or first, to consider this. I, too, am subject to the social buzz, which includes the thoughts of other intellectuals. My intuitive conviction that Descartes' thinking process – rather than his published thoughts only – laid the basis for psychoanalysis was confirmed when, thanks to Françoise Davoine, I got to read, belatedly, Yaelle Sibony-Malpertu's study *Une liaison philosophique. Du thérapeutique entre Descartes et la princesse Élisabeth de Bohême* (Paris: Stock, 2012). The last scene of my film, and the fifth installation piece are entirely based on that inspiring book. But also Michel Henry, *Généalogie de la psychanalyse* (Paris: P.U.F., 2015 [1985]) begins with a chapter on Descartes. The theoretical thrust of the childhood scene of Descartes is based on this chapter. On psychoanalysis as an emphatically *social* science, see the work of Fançoise Davoine, especially her book *Mother Folly: A Tale,* trans. Judith G. Miller (Stanford, CA: Stanford University Press, 2014), and the film and installation project we made on its basis, *A Long History of Madness* http://www.miekebal.org/artworks/films/a-long-history-of-madness (accessed 01 January 2017). The possibility to include the episode with Elisabeth – in a 'theoretical fiction' I designed after Sibony-Malpertu's book – was due to the generous help by and hospitality of Harald Hendrix, director of the Royal Dutch Institute Rome. Thanks to him, I received permission from the Italian Ministry of Culture to film in the palace where Kristina lived, and in the room where she died. I also thank Marlene Dumas for persuading the brilliant actress Johanna ter Steege to play Elisabeth.

13 See the exhibition catalogue by Gary Schwartz and Machiel Keestra, *Emotions: Pain and Pleasure in Seventeenth-Century Dutch Painting* (Rotterdam: nai010 publishers, and Haarlem: Frans Hals Museum, 2014).

14 The importance of music for Descartes, and doubtlessly the deeper source of his thinking in and about the unity of mind and body, is well known. His very first writing concerned music. I am grateful to Gary and Loekie Schwartz for allowing us to film the botany scene in their beautiful garden.

15 The most informative biography of Descartes – and for me the best resource because it integrates historical facts with an analysis of the philosophical ideas – is Desmond Clarke, *Descartes: A Biography* (Cambridge, UK: Cambridge University Press, 2006). The biography by Stephen Gaukroger, *Descartes: An Intellectual Biography* (Oxford: Clarendon press, 1995), is a useful complement, going deeper into the development of the ideas, but less into the life that makes up 'Descartes' as a thinking being.

16 Spinoza appears as the earnest young man he must have been at the time that Descartes was trying to link up with lens makers. As the ultimate evidence of the social buzz, Spinoza was able to turn Descartes' thoughts into an affect-based form of thinking that was possible, although barely, twenty-five years later. Bringing these two thinkers together is my way of performing anachronism as an element of thought. Spinoza's theory of affect as inherent in ethics is presently current in cultural philosophy and analysis. See the illuminating and very accessible study by Moira Gatens and Genevieve Lloyd, *Collective Imaginings: Spinoza, Past and Present* (London and New York: Routledge, 1999). They bring Spinoza's ideas to bear on post-colonial theory, among other subjects.

17 Henri Bergson, *Matter and Memory*, trans. N. M. Paul and W. S. Palmer (New York: Zone Books, 1991 [1896]), p. 168.

18 Ibid., pp. 218–19.

19 I have also benefitted from two other books by Bergson, *Time and Free Will: An Essay on the Immediate Data of Consciousness*, trans. F. L. Pogson (New York: Harper and Row, 1960 [1889]), especially for the concept of extensity; and *Creative Evolution*, trans. A. Mitchell. (Lanham, MD: University Press of America, 1983 [1907]), for the political potential of art.

20 On affect in the Deleuzian sense, and its importance for art and aesthetics, see Jill Bennett, *Empathic Vision: Affect, Trauma and Contemporary Art* (Stanford, CA: Stanford University Press, 2005) – especially the Introduction; and Ernst van Alphen, 'Affective Operations of Art and Literature', *RES: Journal of Anthropology and Aesthetics* 53/54 (Spring/Autumn 2008), pp. 20–30.

21 In addition to the excellent and very accessible work mentioned in note 16, two further studies have been indispensable for my understanding of Spinoza in relation to Descartes: Genevieve Lloyd, *Providence Lost* (Cambridge, MA: Harvard University Press, 2008); and Steven Nadler, *A Book Forged in Hell: Spinoza's Scandalous Treatise and the Birth of the Secular Age* (Princeton, NJ: Princeton University Press, 2011), that shows the incipient secularism already present in Descartes' thought. This supports my initial interpretation of the residual dualism. The concept 'theoretical object' was proposed by Hubert Damisch in an interview with Yve-Alain Bois, in Yve-Alain Bois et al, 'A Conversation with Hubert Damisch.' *October* 85 (Summer 1998), pp. 3–17.

22 Chanut's intervention is entirely fictional, an attempt to lay the basis for Descartes' inclination to develop an interest in mental illness. On Descartes' treatise on music, see H. Floris Cohen, *Quantifying Music: The Science of Music at the First Stage of Scientific Revolution* (Berlin: Springer, 1984), pp. 161–77; 188–97; and Jacomien Prins and H. Floris Cohen, 'Knowing Heaven and Earth Through Music', in *Cambridge History of Sixteenth-Century Music*, eds Richard Wistreich and Iain Fenlon (Cambridge, UK: Cambridge University Press, (orthcoming). I am grateful to professor Cohen for his explanations of a domain I have little understanding of. See also D. P. Walker, 'Joan Albert Ban and Mersenne's Musical Competition of 1640', *Music & Letters* 57, 3 (1976), pp. 233–55 for the anecdotal history of the occasion for the treatise.

23 In addition to the beginning chapter of Michel Henry's book *Généalogie de la psychanalyse*, a number of interpretations of Descartes' concept of the subject that, like a patchwork, move into that direction is the collection edited by Kim Sang Ong-Van-Cung, *Descartes et la question du sujet* (Paris: P.U.F., 1999).

24 Memory is crucial in thinking, and particularly so in the practice of psychoanalysis. See *Acts of Memory: Cultural Recall in the Present*, eds.

Mieke Bal, Jonathan Crewe, and Leo Spitzer (Hanover, NH: University Press of New England, 1999).

25 Heterochrony was an important concept in the exhibition by Mieke Bal and Miguel Á. Hernández-Navarro, *2MOVE: Migratory Aesthetics,* of 2007-08. See *2MOVE: Video, Art, Migration* (Murcia, Spain: Cendeac, 2008).

26 Since I don't read Swedish – and Kristina's writings are sparse anyway – I had to rely for this scene and the following on secondary literature. See especially the well-documented book by Veronica Buckley, *Christina Queen of Sweden: The Restless Life of a European Eccentric* (New York: Harper, 2005). I have also benefitted from an imaginative, 'first-person' novel by Françoise D'eaubonne, *Moi, Kristine reine de Suède* (Paris: Encre, 1979).

Although time as I discuss it here is alien to Descartes' thinking, there is an instance of thinking about time in his work. See Loet Leydesdorff, 'Uncertainty and the Communication of Time', *Systems Research* 11, 4 (1994), pp. 31–51.

27 This interaction with the sculpture has become a logo for the project, in a photograph by Przemo Wojciechowski, who was the set photographer in the scenes that were shot in Kristina's palace and garden. The photograph has been published (with a short essay) in 'Photography After Cinema' 8-9 in *Photoworks: Photography, Art, Visual Culture. Issue 22: Women,* eds. Mariama Attah and Ben Burbridge (Brighton, GB: Photoworks, 2015).

28 On the fine but decisive line between consciousness and cognition, see N. Katherine Hayles, *Unthought: The Power of the Cognitive Nonconscious* (Chicago, IL: The University of Chicago Press, forthcoming).

29 On spectral agency in the context of another kind of disempowered subjects, the subalterns such as servants or refugees, see the important study by Esther Peeren, *The Spectral Metaphor: Living Ghosts and the Agency of Invisibility* (London: Palgrave, 2014).

30 Ironically, after abdicating her throne, in Rome the historical Kristina became especially known for her performances in the milieus of papacy and royalty. For an excellent close analysis of one such performance, see Camilla Kandare, 'CorpoReality: Queen Chistina of Sweden and the Embodiment of Sovereignty', in *Performativity and Performance in Baroque Rome,* eds Peter Gillgren and Mårten Snickare (Franham, UK: Ashgate, 2012), pp. 47–64.

31 The gender aspect in the discussions between the two thinkers deserves another article – perhaps even another film. Suffice it to say that the crux of the disagreement between them is embodiment, something that – against the clichés – was very important for the philosopher. But then, Elisabeth replied, gender difference makes the universalism invalid. In addition to Sidony-Malpertu's book, Genevieve Lloyd, 'The Philosopher and the Princess', in Lloyd, *Providence Lost,* pp. 160–91.

32 This moment is an allusion to the earlier work I made with Michelle Williams Gamaker, *A Long History of Madness,* http://www.miekebal.org/artworks/films/a-long-history-of-madness (2011), based on a book by – and in collaboration with – Françoise Davoine. See note 12. This book is a 'theoretical fiction' based on actual analytical sessions. Davoine plays herself in the film, and was present on set to give advice.

33 With this phrasing 'shape of thought' I allude to Thomas McEvilley, *The Shape of Ancient Thought: Comparative Studies in Greek and Indian Phlosophies* (New York: Allworth Communications, 2002).

34 As it happened, in fact the musicians chose their pieces themselves. This is one of the aspects of my film-making – also reflected in the actors' contributions – through which I aim to make the collaborative nature of film-making as 'thinking in film' the projects' principal aspect.

35 On the abandonment complex and the way it can be acted out in fiction, see Han Verhoeff, *"Adolphe" et Constant. Une étude psychocritique* (Paris: Klincksieck, 1976).

References

Ahtila, E-L. and C. Iles, 'Thinking in Film: Eija-Liisa Ahtila in Conversation with Chrissie Iles.' *Parkett* 68 (2003), pp. 58–64.

Attah, M. and B. Burbidge (eds), *Photoworks: Photography, Art, Visual Culture. Issue 22: Women*, Brighton, GB: Photoworks, 2015.

Bal, M (ed.), *The Practice of Cultural Analysis: Exposing Interdisciplinary Interpretation*, Stanford, CA: Stanford University Press, 1999.

Bal, M., *Of What One Cannot Speak: Doris Salcedo's Political Art*, Chicago, IL: University of Chicago Press, 2010.

Bal, M., *Thinking in Film: The Politics of Video Installation According to Eija-Liisa Ahtila*, London: Bloomsbury, 2013.

Bal, M., *Reasonable Doubt*, Krakow: Museum of History of Photography, 2016, http://www.miekebal.org/artworks/exhibitions/reasonable-doubt/ (accessed 01 January 2017).

Bal, M., Crewe, J. and L. Spitzer (eds), *Acts of Memory: Cultural Recall in the Present*, Hanover, NH: University Press of New England, 1999.

Bal, M., Elsaesser, T., Pranger, B., Roessler, B., de Vries, H. and W. Weststeijn (eds), *ASCA Brief: Intellectual Traditions in Movement*, Amsterdam: ASCA Press, 1998.

Bal, M. and M. Á. Hernández-Navarro, *2MOVE: Migratory Aesthetics, of 2007–8, at 2MOVE: Video, Art, Migration*, Murcia, Spain: Cendeac, 2008.

Bal, M. and M. Williams Gamaker, *A Long History of Madness*, 2011, http://www.miekebal.org/artworks/films/a-long-history-of-madness (accessed 01 January 2017).

Bal, M. and M. Williams Gamaker, *Madame B*, 2013, http://www.miekebal.org/artworks/films/madame-b (accessed 01 January 2017).

Bal, M. and M. Williams Gamaker, 'From Documentary to Fiction and Back', in [...] (*Ellipses*), Johannesburg, SA, nr. 1, 2016 (no page numbers), http://www.ellipses.org.za/project/from-documentary-to-fiction-and-back (accessed 01 January 2017).

Bennett, J., *Empathic Vision: Affect, Trauma and Contemporary Art*, Stanford, CA: Stanford University Press, 2005.
Bennett, J., *Practical Aesthetics: Event, Affect and Art After 9/11*, London: I. B. Tauris, 2012.
Bergson, H., *Matter and Memory*, trans. N. M. Paul and W. S. Palmer, New York: Zone Books, 1991 [1896].
Bergson, H., *Time and Free Will: An Essay on the Immediate Data of Consciousness*, trans. F. L. Pogson, New York: Harper and Row, 1960 [1889].
Bergson, H., *Creative Evolution*, trans. A. Mitchell. Lanham, MD: University Press of America, 1983 [1907].
Bois, Y. A. et al., 'A Conversation with Hubert Damisch.' October 85 (Summer 1998), pp. 3–17.
Buckley, V., *Christina Queen of Sweden: The Restless Life of a European Eccentric*, New York: Harper, 2005.
Cohen, H. F., *Quantifying Music: The Science of Music at the First Stage of Scientific Revolution*, Berlin: Springer, 1984.
Clarke, D., *Descartes: A Biography*, Cambridge, UK: Cambridge University Press, 2006.
D'eaubonne, F., *Moi, Kristine reine de Suède*, Paris: Encre, 1979.
Davoine F., *Mother Folly: A Tale*, trans. J. G. Miller, Stanford, CA: Stanford University Press, 2014.
De Raymond, J-F., *La reine et le philosophe. Descartes et Cristine de Suède*, Paris: Lettres Modernes, 1993.
Descartes, R., *Discourse on Method and Meditations*, trans. L. J. Lafleur, New York: The Liberal Arts Press, 1960 [1637].
Descartes, R., *The Passions of the Soul*, trans. S. H. Voss, Indianapolis / Cambridge: Hackett Publishing Company, 1989 [1649].
Felman, S., *What Does a Woman Want? Reading and Sexual Difference*, Baltimore, MD: The Johns Hopkins University Press, 1993.
Gatens, M. and G. Lloyd, *Collective Imaginings: Spinoza, Past and Present*, London and New York: Routledge, 1999.
Gaukroger, S., *Descartes: An Intellectual Biography*, Oxford: Clarendon press, 1995.
Hayles, N. Ka., *Unthought: The Power of the Cognitive Nonconscious*, Chicago, IL: The University of Chicago Press (forthcoming).
Henry, M., *Généalogie de la psychanalyse*, Paris: P.U.F., 2015 [1985].
Houwen, J., *Comparing Film and Video: Intermediality and Medium Specificity in Moving Images*, London: Bloomsbury, 2017.
Illouz, E., *Cold Intimacies: The Making of Emotional Capitalism*, Cambridge, UK: Polity Press, 2007.
Illouz, E., *Why Love Hurts*, Cambridge, UK: Polity Press, 2012.
Johnson, B., *The Feminist Difference: Literature, Psychoanalysis and Gender*, Cambridge, MA: Harvard University Press, 1998.
Kandare, C., 'CorpoReality: Queen Christina of Sweden and the Embodiment of Sovereignty', in P. Gillgren and M. Snickare (eds), *Performativity and Performance in Baroque Rome*, Franham, UK: Ashgate, 2012, pp. 47–64.
Lee, K., *Reading Descartes Otherwise: Blind, Mad, Dreamy, and Bad*, New York: Fordham University Press 2013.

Leydesdorff, L., 'Uncertainty and the Communication of Time', *Systems Research* 11, 4 (1994), pp. 31–51.

Lloyd, G., *Providence Lost* (Cambridge, MA: Harvard University Press, 2008).

McEvilley, T., *The Shape of Ancient Thought: Comparative Studies in Greek and Indian Philosophies*, New York: Allworth Communications, 2002.

Modloch, K., *Screens: Viewing Media Installation Art*, Minneapolis, MN: University of Minnesota Press, 2010.

Nadler, S., *A Book Forged in Hell: Spinoza's Scandalous Treatise and the Birth of the Secular Age*, Princeton, NJ: Princeton University Press, 2011.

Peeren, E., *The Spectral Metaphor: Living Ghosts and the Agency of Invisibility*, London: Palgrave, 2014.

Prins, J. and H. Floris Cohen, 'Knowing Heaven and Earth Through Music', in Richard Wistreich and Iain Fenlon (eds), *Cambridge History of Sixteenth-Century Music*, Cambridge, UK: Cambridge University Press (forthcoming).

Roman, M., *On Stage: The Theatrical Dimension of Video Image*, London: Intellect, 2016.

Sang Ong-Van-Cung, K., *Descartes et la question du sujet*, Paris: P.U.F., 1999.

Sassen, S., *Expulsions: Brutality and Complexity in the Global Economy*, Cambridge: MA: Harvard University Press, 2014.

Schwartz, S. and M. Keestra, *Emotions: Pain and Pleasure in Seventeenth-Century Dutch Painting*, Rotterdam: nai010 publishers, and Haarlem: Frans Hals Museum, 2014.

Sibony-Malpertu, Y., *Une liaison philosophique. Du thérapeutique entre Descartes et la princesse Élisabeth de Bohême*, Paris: Stock, 2012.

van Alphen, E., 'Affective Operations of Art and Literature', *RES: Journal of Anthropology and Aesthetics* 53/54 (Spring/Autumn 2008), pp. 20–30.

Verhoeff, H., *"Adolphe" et Constant. Une étude psychocritique*, Paris: Klincksieck, 1976.

Walker, D. P., 'Joan Albert Ban and Mersenne's Musical Competition of 1640', *Music & Letters* 57, 3 (1976), pp. 233–55.

Williams Gamaker, M., *A Long History of Madness*, 2011, http://www.miekebal.org/artworks/films/a-long-history-of-madness (accessed 01 January 2017).

10

Thinking through the cello

Tim Ingold

Opening declaration

'I have nothing to say and I am saying it'. So began the composer John Cage, in his *Lecture on Nothing*, presented in New York in 1949.[1] Behind the play on words, Cage was being deeply serious. In this essay I want to explore what he was getting at, and to draw out its implications for the way we think, not just about the world we inhabit but about thought itself. In the spirit of Cage, I shall conduct my inquiry by way of an instrument. That instrument is a violoncello. In an ideal world, I would be present in person with my cello as you read this, so that you could both hear me speak and listen as I play. Instead, I will have to ask you to imagine my voice and my performance. I realize that this is a big ask, but it is critically important that you attempt it, since unlike Cage, I do have something to say, and it is to show why a thinking that opens up to hopes and dreams – that is, to life – must be one that is attentive to things, that brings them into presence so that we, in turn, can be present to them. For only in the presence of things can we feel them, and only through feeling them can we respond. My inquiry, in short, is into the conditions of what Cage called 'response ability', though for reasons I shall explain further, I prefer the term 'correspondence'. I want to establish the possibility of a form of scholarship that sets out neither to understand the world around us nor to interpret what goes on there, but rather to correspond with its constituents.

Imagine, then, that I sit down to play. Let us suppose that I play the opening bars of the prelude to the third suite for unaccompanied cello by Johann Sebastian Bach. If you are familiar with the piece, or if you are a cellist yourself, you will know that these bars launch the suite with such pomp and certitude as if you were throwing open the ceremonial doors to a great banqueting hall, after which the guests start streaming in. Later, they will perform a series of courtly dances, making up the following movements of the suite. The first bars of the prelude are tantamount to a declaration: let the festivities begin! Yet, in playing them, I have nothing to declare. No coded information is smuggled in with the notes. It is not as though I wrap some contraband into the sound which you unpack upon receipt, like the contents of a parcel. Nothing is sent or received. The bars stand only for themselves. Their force – to adopt a technical term from the philosophy of language – is *illocutionary*: it resides in the performance itself and in what it achieves, not in some semantic content to which it refers.[2] To play is to create an auditory ambience in which anyone within earshot can participate. And to listen is to harness one's own awareness to this ambience, to join with it and respond to it. In this, your entire body becomes an extended ear, alive to the sonorities of the environment. When I play those first bars of the prelude, I throw open the doors to the suite; as you listen, your ear-body sweeps through them into the gilded rooms that continue to unfold as the performance proceeds.

And this, precisely, was Cage's point. He wanted us to acknowledge that to listen is to be in the presence of sound, to lay ourselves open to it and attend, not to extract some meaning from the sound that has first been encoded into it and for which it serves as a vector of transmission. His aim, as he put it, was to 'set about discovering means to let sounds be themselves rather than vehicles for man-made theories or expressions of human sentiments'.[3] To achieve this, he explains, the first step is to cease thinking of sound, in the first place, as music, and of hearing as what we do, specifically, when listening to music. For no sooner do we declare that what we hear is music than we impute to it an intention by which it is distinguished from the unintended sounds of nature, whether of the wind or rain, or a waterfall, or thunder, or even the nervous excitation or heartbeat of one's own body. If there were no sound not deemed to be musical, then these 'natural' sounds would be expunged from conscious awareness. We would be deaf to all sound that does not disclose a motivation and that leaves no expression in its wake. That is why we are inclined to speak of the 'silence of nature', despite all the noise it makes! Straining to discern the music from its background, we close our ears not only to the terrestrial and subterranean echoes of earthly existence but also to the celestial sonorities of wind and weather.

In effect, this is to split music from life. 'When we separate music from life', said Cage, 'what we get is art (a compendium of masterpieces)'.[4] The cello suites of Bach are commonly considered to be masterpieces. But that is because the arbiters of high culture have decreed that they be apprehended not as sound but as formal compositions rendered in sound, much as the portraits hanging on the walls of the banqueting hall are rendered in paint.

But colour is everywhere, not just in paintings. So too, sound is everywhere, not just in music. We do not only see, as art historians sometimes seem to think, when looking at paintings; nor do we only hear when listening to music. A sound does not project itself as the expression of a thought, nor does it depend on other sounds for its elucidation. It is *there*, becoming itself, in all its urgency and singularity, unimpeded and energetically broadcast, 'occupied', as Cage put it, 'with the performance of its characteristics'.[5] To attend to sound *as* sound (or likewise, to attend to colour *as* colour) is to feel these characteristics – of duration, pitch, amplitude and timber – and to respond to them. Once we allow sounds to become themselves, once we attend to them as such – and not to anything that might be being conveyed by their means – we cannot remain unfeeling in their presence. The *feeling* of sound: that is what Cage meant by 'response ability'.[6] This feeling invests both my playing and your listening with a quality of attention.

The move, in Cage's thinking, from intention to attention is critical. For if intention separates subject from object, mind from nature and art from life, attention restores the player or listener to that which is real and present in the immediacy of lived experience. Etymologically, the word 'attention' comes from the Latin *ad-tendere*, meaning 'to stretch towards', and it well describes what happens when I begin to play the cello.[7] Perhaps I intend to practice or perform. I take the instrument from its case, apply rosin to my bow, adjust the endpin, take my seat and tune up. But once under way, it seems that I and my playing are one and the same. I *become* my playing, and my playing plays me. I am there, not in front, but in the midst of it, animated by its gesture and rhythm. I feel the pressure of the bow against the strings and the vibrato in the left hand as I stretch the sounds from the resonant chamber of the instrument, as if they were viscous or elastic filaments. Listening, you stretch your ears to join with them, as indeed I do myself, ever responsive to their perceived tonality. The thread of sound and the thread of feeling twist around one another, as each – in its ongoing movement – answers to the other, much as a stream, swollen by rain, answers to the earth through which it runs while at the same time continually reshaping it.[8] Like stream and earth, sound and feeling co-respond. That is what I mean by *correspondence*.[9] And if I prefer the term to Cage's 'response ability', it is for no other reason than the emphasis on the mutuality of the response, of going along together, conveyed by the prefix, *co-*.

What, then, is silence? In a world of life, according to Cage, absolute silence would simply be impossible. Silence could never be anything other than a quality of ambient sound, reliably if unpredictably present to those with ears to hear – ears not so preoccupied with their owners' intentions as to be inattentive to the world. 'Where these ears are in connection with a mind that has nothing to do', as Cage put it, 'that mind is free to enter into the act of listening, hearing each sound as it is, not just as a phenomenon more or less approximating a preconception'.[10] You were listening long before I began to play. You heard my chair-legs squeak on the floor as I took my seat; you heard me tune up; you heard the rustling crisp-packet of your neighbour and the cough from the back row. And now, you hear sound pouring from my cello. What's the difference? That there is a difference is not in doubt, since with my playing, I command your attention. 'Listen to me', I demand, 'and do not be distracted by coughs and crisp packets'. I would not go so far as Cage, however, in attributing the difference to the existence in my mind of a preconception, which the sound from my instrument is purported to deliver to your receptive ears. As I play those opening bars of Bach's third suite, I am declaring but have nothing to declare. I am opening the doors to the banqueting hall, but not providing an inventory of its contents. However certain the declaration, it does not give voice to a preconception. It has no propositional content. 'I have nothing to say', to repeat Cage's own declaration, 'and I am saying it'. The paradox is that if silence lies in having nothing to say, how come that it can be so overwhelmingly sonorous? Conversely, does saying something really make any sound at all?

The sound of feeling

'Whereof one cannot speak', concluded Ludwig Wittgenstein in the *Tractatus Logico-Philosophicus*, 'thereof one must be silent'.[11] Taken literally, this austere pronouncement would consign to silence all that we conventionally call music, along with every other occurrence of ambient sound. Nothing could surface from the ocean of silence save that which can be set out, linguistically or mathematically, in the form of logically connected propositions. This might seem an extreme position; however, it is not so very far from one that still commands widespread acceptance. This is to argue that whatever cannot be explicated belongs to the domain of the *tacit*. We owe the distinction between tacit and explicit domains of knowledge to the philosopher Michael Polanyi.[12] Of course, Polanyi's purpose was not to denigrate what he called 'the tacit dimension', but rather to highlight its contribution to thought. Knowledge, he insisted, is not confined to explicit representations. It rather rests upon habits and sensibilities of perception and action that develop through practice and experience, but which adhere so closely to the person of the practitioner that they remain out of reach of explication or analysis. The craftsman, it is supposed, is unable to explain, in propositional terms, how he works with the material to achieve his results. As a cellist, I cannot explain what happens when I sit down to play. What can be explained, Polanyi argued, is but the tip of an iceberg compared with this vast reservoir of knowledge that lies beneath the surface, but without which nothing could be practicably accomplished.

But why should Polanyi have used the word 'tacit' to refer to the submarine dimension? And what might he have meant by it? The word itself is tantalisingly ambiguous: derived from the Latin *tacere*, 'to be silent', it is commonly used to refer to that which remains *verbally* unstated. But there are plenty of ways of making one's presence felt, sonorously and audibly, without the use of words, as for example when I play my cello or hum a tune. And there are plenty of ways of using words that do not amount to statements with propositional or representational content, as in drama and storytelling, poetry and song. In an extended commentary on the tacit/explicit distinction, the philosopher of science Harry Collins makes it very clear that for Polanyi, the opposite of 'tacit' is not precisely 'explicit,' but rather 'explicable'.[13] The tacit, in other words, does not refer to things that could be made explicit but happen not to be – perhaps for reasons of discretion or security – but rather to things that *cannot* be made explicit. Now for Polanyi, there are two necessary steps to explication: these are *specification* and *articulation*.[14] To specify is to pin things down to fixed conceptual or referential coordinates; to articulate is to join these coordinates up to form an integrated assembly, rather like joining points on a graph. What cannot be specified and articulated cannot be explicated – though it can of course be known. This knowledge – unspecifiable, inarticulate and non-explicable – inhabits the domain of the tacit.

Granted, however, that there are ways of using words that are non-propositional, is it not also the case that there are ways of explicating propositions that are non-verbal, as for example in mathematics and symbolic logic? Could not music also be one of these ways? Did not Bach, for example, *specify* that I should open the third suite for unaccompanied cello by playing a middle C? And are this and the following notes, making up those first two bars of the prelude, not *articulated* to form an elegantly structured phrase? Might it not be argued, then, that a musical structure is indeed explicated in performance? Never mind that the music is composed of notes and phrases rather than letters and words, is the principle not the same in both cases? The notation of Bach, according to the visionary landscape architect Lawrence Halprin, 'is as precise and controlling as he could make it, what was left for the performer was a matter of technique and interpretation'.[15] Reaching out over the centuries, Bach leaves us with no alternative but to follow his specifications to the letter. The performer, for Halprin, is a mere technician; his task to execute in every detail an immaculately conceived design. In principle, a machine – less fallible and untroubled by affect – could do a better job! Now there are of course many ways in which this view can be faulted. It is historically inaccurate, in that Bach was writing long before the idea of the composer as the independent and sole author of complete musical works had even emerged.[16] And as anyone who has tried playing Bach's music knows all too well, so much is left unspecified in the notation that the same piece, in alternative hands, can sound altogether different. But that is not what presently concerns me.

My point is rather that it is simply impossible for a living being to play without feeling – without the awareness we have of our own movement, and of its correspondences, otherwise known as *kinaesthesia*.[17] With the cello as any other musical instrument, playing and feeling, and movement and attention, are two sides of the same coin.[18] Where there is life there is feeling and, as Cage taught, where there is feeling there is sound. The note printed on paper has no feeling, and is therefore soundless. But as soon as I begin to play, the note erupts into sound, into life. To feel is not to pin things down, but to join *with* them in their growth and movement. Thus what is notated on the score as a point becomes, in my playing, a sustained and vibrant line. To play even a single tone, such as middle C, is no simple matter. It is rather like drawing a straight line freehand. To achieve this one's body must be finely balanced and tensed throughout, with an acute awareness of its immediate environs, while the elbow of the right arm, holding the pencil, describes a trajectory at once outward and backward as the angle of the joint varies from obtuse to acute and the wrist adjusts to compensate.[19] Bowing involves similarly controlled movements of the right arm, elbow and wrist, to ensure that the position where the bow remains in contact with the string, between bridge and fingerboard, remains more or less constant. In short, the singular tone arises from a complex choreography of highly attentive, mutually attuned movements, of arm, wrist and bow. Feeling lies in this kinaesthetic attunement.

The ancient Greeks called it harmony (from *harmos*, meaning 'joint'), a word that originally had no musical reference at all. It could refer to the joining of beams and masonry, in the building of houses, temples or ships, but also to the joining of limbs in the body.[20] From the root syllable **ar*, common to both the noun *harmos* and the verb *ararisko* (to join), are derived a host of other words including the 'arms' of the body, the 'arts' of the builder and of course 'article' and 'articulate'. In modern usage, however, despite sharing the same root meaning of the join, 'harmony' and 'articulation' have parted company. Whereas harmony, now commonly applied to musical contexts, retains the sense of the joining *with* or correspondence of sympathetic movements, articulation has come to mean the connection of rigid and discrete parts. Such is the articulation of the bones of the skeleton, which, in anatomical reconstruction, appear joined *up* rather than *with*. Divorced from life, the bones feature as the elements of an assembly. So too, with standard notational conventions, musical notes are joined up on the stave, connected by ligatures. This distinction between joining *up* and joining *with*, or between articulation and correspondence, is critical. One is an exterior connection, a coupling of parts each of which is already formed to its own specifications. But in the other, every movement participates from the inside in the generation of every other, while at the same time distinguishing itself. I call this latter process *interstitial differentiation*.[21]

Compare, for example, cutting timber with a saw and splitting it with an axe. The cut is transverse: it divides the timber into separate pieces, which can then only be re-joined side-to-side or end-to-end. That is exterior articulation. But the split is longitudinal: it follows the grain of the wood, laid down when it was part of a living tree. The axe joins *with* the timber, while differentiating it from within. That is interstitial differentiation. It is no accident that the word 'skill', by which the allegedly tacit knowledge of the craftsman is commonly known, carries this precise connotation of splitting from the inside. The word has its roots in Old Norse *skilja*, 'to divide, separate, distinguish or decide', and is an etymological affine of 'shell', a casing opened up by splitting or cleaving along the grain. Skill, then, means finding the grain of things and bending them to an ever-evolving purpose.[22] So to return to the cello, as I move from note to note in the musical score, am I assembling the notes as I would a piece of timber already sawn into logs? Is my performance an articulation? Certainly not! A sustained tone, as we have seen, is a movement in itself. To transition from tone to tone is then to effect a movement in the movement. Dance philosopher Erin Manning calls it an *inflection* of movement: it is really 'movement-moving'.[23] Through inflection, every tone – itself a line of movement – emerges with its potential directionality, differentiating itself from what came before. Musical form thus arises not from the connection of points but from the inflection of lines. To play a phrase such as in the first two bars of the Bach suite is not to link predetermined tones into a chain but to split them from the inside through a series of inflections. It is an exercise not in specification and articulation but in interstitial differentiation.

The silence of the score

This exercise of differentiation is anything but 'tacit', if by that is implied silence or stillness. On the contrary, it is alive with movement, and vitally sonorous. Specification and articulation might be keys to logical explication, but they lock the door to feeling. And without feeling, there can be no sound. This brings us, however, to a surprising result. It is that nothing more effectively silences the world than representing it in explicit, propositional terms. Pinned down and joined up as on the printed score, reduced to mere notes, sounds are rendered lifeless and inert. They have no room to move or breathe. Indeed, *it is the explicit that is tacit*, not the reservoir of skill or know-how for which Polanyi reserved the term. The latter, on the contrary, is turbulent and sometimes noisy. It swirls around in between the points that explicit knowledge joins up, like waters flowing around and between the islands of an archipelago.[24] We have been persistently misled, I think, by the analogy of the iceberg, with the picture it presents of explicit knowledge at the tip and the mass of inexplicable know-how below. Far from having come to rest, frozen solid in submarine psycho-corporeal depths, know-how is restless, fluid and dynamic. Above all, it is not embodied, in the sense of having been deposited in an inert and stable substrate, housed in the lower levels of some imaginary column of consciousness, but fundamentally *animate* – immanent in the sensuousness of a body that is mobile, alive and open to the world. Such a body, far from retreating into silence, dwells in sound.

With this result in mind, we can proceed to reformulate Wittgenstein's famous injunction from the *Tractatus*. To speak, for Wittgenstein, meant the same as to explicate. And explication, as we have found, stops up feeling, and condemns us to silence. But if sound is what we want, or what we mean to hear, then we should cease our attempts at explication, remove or brush aside the stoppages that drive feeling underground, and allow things into sentient presence. *Whereof one cannot speak, thereof let it resound*! Consider again the difference between the melodic line that I stretch out from my cello and the sequence of connected notes printed as black dots on the stave. The line weaves its way through the field of ambient sound in rather the same way as a path through the variegated undergrowth of a forest or the grasses of a meadow. Made by walking and traced along the ground, the path marks a line of differentiation. It emerges from the interstices of the ground in the very course of walking it. But while the path-line thus differentiates itself from the ground, the reverse does not hold. As philosopher Gilles Deleuze puts it in his reflections on difference and repetition, the line distinguishes itself from the ground 'without the ground distinguishing itself from the line'.[25] The difference is unilateral. So too the melodic line, while it distinguishes itself from ambient sound, never parts from it. The line is rather woven into the texture of its ambience.

With the notes of the score, however, it is as if the line of sound were detached from the matrix of its generation and divided into measured segments. Each segment is then stopped up into a point, and each point staked out upon a flatly homogeneous surface. Every note is a stoppage, reconnected to other notes in sequence by means of ligatures which bear no more relation to the surface than does the surveyor's rope, tied between stakes, to the ground. Where the path differentiates itself from the ground without ever parting from it, the rope stands high and dry above the ground across which it is stretched. The path is the trace of a movement, the rope a connection of stoppages. As with the stakes and the rope, the notes of the score and their connecting ligatures are indifferent to the surface on which they are printed, as indeed is the paper to the notation. The paper and the notation correspond, respectively, to two aspects of indifference that Deleuze calls, respectively, 'white nothingness' and 'black nothingness'.[26] In the case of the score, the surface is a sheet of white paper, while the notation is printed in back. The score is literally black-on-white. On the score, difference is bilateral: as the notes and ligatures distinguish themselves from the paper surface, so the paper is distinguished from the notation printed upon it. Like an exploded diagram, the score specifies the elements of a completed work and shows how they articulate. Moreover, it is silent. Its silence is the empty, exoskeletal silence of a world already broken up and dismembered, all energy spent, eviscerated of any traces of affect.

There is however another kind of silence, which is just the opposite. It is the silence of a world so compressed, so concentrated and so tightly knotted, that nothing can move.[27] This is not the silence of an already exploded world, but of a world on the verge of exploding. It is the silence of the predator, all eyes and ears, waiting to pounce, or of ice before break-up or of the eye of the storm. Let us return to the score of the third prelude and to the very first note. It is middle C, and is marked by a solid black dot, crossed through by a ledger line one up from the five lines of the stave. Remember that in Bach's time, composition and performance were not clearly demarcated as they are today. One could almost think of the work of composition itself as a calligraphic performance, carried on not with instrument and sound but with pen and ink. We can imagine Johann Sebastian (or just as probably, his wife and copyist Anna Magdalena), pen in hand, hard at work on the score of the third suite. Think of how much mental energy is concentrated in the gesture by which he digs his pen (or she hers) into the manuscript to inscribe that first middle C. Think of the attention and expectancy that go into that black dot! Is the silence of the score, then, so empty after all? Perhaps it is so, in the mechanically printed reproduction, filed away in a drawer or on a shelf. But what of the handwritten original?

In his essay *Point and Line to Plane*, the great pioneer of modern abstract painting, Wassily Kandinsky, considered the dot of musical notation as one exemplar of the elemental point.[28] Like any other element, Kandinsky argued, the point can be experienced either outwardly or inwardly. Outwardly, the point or dot is simply doing its job within the conventions of a notational system, just like a well-functioning tool in a tool-box. In a verbal text, the full stop or *punctus* indicates the end of a sentence. A dot on the stave-score indicates a note. And so long as we remain on this outward level of the 'practical-useful', to which we are accustomed by force of habit, we remain indifferent to the stop or dot as a figure in its own right. Context is everything. But suppose instead that we wrench the element from its usual habitat and enlarge its mass. As we do so, Kandinsky writes, 'as we gradually tear the point out of its restricted sphere of customary influence, its inner attributes … come out of the depths of its being and radiate their energy. … In short, the dead point becomes a living thing'. Freed from the practical-useful, the point begins a new 'inner-purposeful' life as an *independent being*. To apprehend the point inwardly is to feel its explosive potential.[29] With this, the dot that marks middle C on the score appears no longer empty, but full to bursting. It is like a seed on the point of germination.

Were Bach and his wife, then, methodical gardeners, planting their seeds in orderly rows such that they will burst forth in an ever-growing tangle of vegetation? Digging the pen into the manuscript, as the gardener would press seeds into the earth, they would have sown their notes not in a void of silence but in the field of ambient sound, whence – in performance – they would take root and grow. Thus, far from inheriting from Bach a comprehensive set of specifications for the execution of an already completed work, as Halprin would have it, we find ourselves tending the garden that he and Anna Magdalena planted together – a garden that will continue to grow for as long as their music is performed. Playing the music of Bach, I draw the threads of sound from the dark, resonant cavity of my instrument, much as green shoots rise from their black, earthen depths. In performance, the inner tension compacted in the dot of the score is transferred to the outward tension of the string. At the moment when I apply the bow and the string begins to vibrate, the potential energy of the dot is released, and it becomes a line. Neither will seeds grow, however, nor will written notes erupt into sound, if filed away in a drawer or on the shelf. To come to life they must be restored to the open air. I am reminded of the words of one of the great contemporary exponents of experimental music, Cornelius Cardew: 'a musical score is a logical construct inserted into the mess of potential sounds that permeate this planet and its atmosphere'.[30]

The fission/fusion reaction

What, then, *is* sound? Is it a mechanical vibration in the medium, issuing from a source and destined to fall, among other constituents of the environment, on sensitive ears? Or is it a sensation confined within the mind of the hearer, beyond the reach of this vibration? Is the study of sound, its production and reception, a subject for physics or psychology? Or could it be both? These are perplexing questions, epitomized in the well-known conundrum of whether the tree falling in a storm makes a sound if there is no one around to hear it.

On the physical account, it does: ears do nothing for the existence of sound; all they do is establish its relevance or meaning for the hearer. On the psychic account, it does not: there can be sound, in this account, only on the hither side of hearing. Were we to ask what light is, we would face much the same dilemma. Is light an energetic impulse radiating from a source of emission that may happen to stimulate the receptors of creatures equipped with eyes? If that were so, then light would have no more need of eyes to exist than, in the parallel case, sound has need of ears. So why should we give the name 'optics' to the physics of light? And how can we account for the experience we have of inhabiting an illuminated world, when incident radiation penetrates no further than the back of the retina? Should we conclude, to the contrary, that light is not an energetic impulse at all but a purely mental sensation? Perhaps I may be permitted a brief detour into the question of light, since it could give some clues as to how to proceed with the question of sound. My argument, in a nutshell, will be that light is neither physical nor psychic but *atmospheric*, and that so, too, is sound.

Imagine what happens when we look up at the sky. What do we see? Skylight can hardly be an *object* of perception. A balloon floating in the sky might conceivably be regarded as such an object, but not the sky itself. To contemplate the blue of the sky, as phenomenologist Maurice Merleau-Ponty remarks, is not to be set over against it as acosmic subject to cosmic object, nor is it to grasp it cognitively by assimilating the raw material of sensory experience to some abstract idea of blueness. The sky is not an object of the physical universe, nor is it a concept in the mind of the observer. To see the sky is precisely to experience its luminosity *from within*. 'I am the sky itself', continues Merleau-Ponty, 'my consciousness is saturated with this limitless blue'.[31] To be sure, there could be no experience of skylight without the diffusion of solar radiation by atmospheric air, and without the excitation of photoreceptors in the retina. But the luminosity of the sky is reducible to neither. As the experience of inhabiting an illuminated world, it is not so much a scattering of radiant energy as an *affectation of being*. This experience, moreover, is entirely real. We can no more dismiss it as an illusion than we can write off the history of painting as a phantasmagoria born of the overstimulation of excessively susceptible minds, or deny the reality of blindness for the visually impaired. Light is real for the sighted, precisely because it is none other than the continual birth of visual awareness as it opens up to the cosmos. And in this opening, the visual field – that is, the sky in its entirety – is merged with the field of attention.[32]

I use the term 'atmosphere' to denote this blending of the cosmic and the affective. It is a term that already has well-established meanings, on the one hand, in the science of meteorology, and on the other, in the philosophy of aesthetics. These meanings are opposed, but complementary.

Where meteorology gives us an aerial domain evacuated of all traces of affect, aesthetics gives us a system of affects among subjects and objects that appear otherwise to exist in a vacuum.[33] In thinking of skylight as a phenomenon of atmosphere, I aim to bring the two meanings together, thus restoring an affective dimension to aerial life. All life, after all, is lived under the sun, and to inhabit the atmosphere is to see with its light. But might it be to hear as well? Like Merleau-Ponty, musicologist Victor Zuckerkandl also imagines himself looking up at the sky. What he sees, he reports, is not a 'thing out there' but 'boundless space, in which I lose myself'. But if Merleau-Ponty describes the experience as one of pure luminosity, for Zuckerkandl it is one of pure sonority![34] Could we not then say of sound – precisely as we have said of light – that it is the birth of awareness, now auditory rather than visual, as it opens to the cosmos? No more than light is sound reducible to its conditions, which in this case include mechanical vibrations in the medium, emitted from a source, and the receptors of the ears and their associated neural connectivities. Like light, sound is a phenomenon of atmosphere.

In order to elaborate on this idea, let me take the comparison with the phenomenology of vision a little further. In his essay 'Eye and Mind', Merleau-Ponty describes vision, rather cryptically, as 'the means given me for being absent from myself'.[35] He was referring to the uncanny capacity that vision confers on us to be at home in our bodies and to vault the heavens at one and the same time. It seems that vision divides us from ourselves only for us to discover, at the termination of this division, that we are back where we belong, and that the luminosity of the sky is none other than the light in our own eyes. When, for example, you open your eyes to the firmament, you do not find yourself looking out from holes in your head as through the windows of a house. On the contrary, it is as though the enclosing walls had vanished, allowing you, like an agile spirit, to span the cosmos. Where your head was, there's the world! Your awareness has exploded, leaving you stranded and at large in the open. What has detonated this explosion? For Merleau-Ponty, it is none other than the spark of vision – a spark that is ignited whenever sensing meets the sensible, or wherever our attention is let loose upon the world.[36] The fusion of the two poles of vision – the one corporeal, the other celestial – blows us apart such that at one and the same time, we remain where we stand, emplaced where our bodies are, and roam heaven and earth as our attention wanders the furthest reaches of the visual field. Light, for Merleau-Ponty, is the outcome of this fission/fusion reaction. Like a spark, it does not connect a source of emission with a recipient but bursts forth in the atmospheric in-between, in directions orthogonal to the line of their connection.

Now if that is true for light, could the same argument work for sound? I think it could. There are indeed corporeal and celestial poles of hearing which, when they collide, generate the experience of sound. And that very sound, born of the fusion of the affective and the cosmic, where what is heard turns out to be our own hearing, also divides us such that – much as in a dream – we are simultaneously at home in our bodies and at large in the cosmos.[37] That this is so for sound as it is for light can be confirmed by means of a simple, two-stage experiment. If you conduct the first stage, then I'll conduct the second. For the first, go outside and cast your eyes heavenwards. Then bring your index finger to your forehead and tap it gently. Feel the hard, bony surface. Yes, you are definitely still there, and have not melted into the ether! But on second thoughts you are not so sure, for you are perplexed to find that in the visual field your finger strikes no surface but rather looms as a ghostly, intruding presence that casts its shadow in the void. How, you wonder, can you be here, in place and at home in your body, and at the same time inhabit an atmospheric world that returns the body to you as a spectre? Now, for the second stage, let me repeat the experiment with my cello. I bring my finger down on the fingerboard and feel the hard, resistant surface. Yes: I am here, and here is my cello. Yet again, on second thoughts, the finger is but a phantom presence that touches nothing but has inveigled itself into the midst of the field of audition. How can the finger show up simultaneously in two such different ways, at once corporeal, in the haptic space of performance, and as a phantom, in the atmospheric space of explosion?[38]

Taking flight

This double-take accounts for the curious combination, in playing an instrument like the cello, of sedentism and flight. For I can be seated on a chair, right here, and yet be possessed of the means, as Merleau-Ponty would put it, to be 'absent from myself'. Sitting with the instrument between my knees and its endpin piercing the floor, I have become the equivalent of a centaur, with human arms and head, a trunk of wood and strings, and an endpin for a leg. Body and instrument are tightly conjoined into an anatomical unity. Yet in the moment I begin to play, something else happens. The instrument itself seems to explode into its constituent materials – of wood, varnish, metallic strings, bow hair, rosin and resonant air. Nor is it only the instrument that explodes. I do too! I am no longer a body with mouth, hands, arms and ears; rather my entire body, in its movements and sensibilities, *becomes* mouth, hand, arm or ear. I am mouth-body-becoming (breathing), hand-body-becoming (fingering), arm-body-becoming (bowing) and ear-body-becoming (listening). I often dream about my cello, and a persistent theme is that the instrument has literally fallen apart, along with what I experience as the disintegration of my own corporeality. The cello is in pieces and so am I. I used to be disturbed by these dreams. But I now realize that they re-enact the very conditions of performance. For only by breaking apart the therianthropic unity of body and cello can it be put together again, not organically or anatomically, but quite differently, *as a bundle of affects*. Where body and cello had been joined *up*, as a totality of parts, wood, varnish, metal, hair, rosin and air join *with* mouth, hands, arms and ears in the generation of atmospheric sound.

It is in the correspondence of affects – in their feeling for one another – that sedentism gives way to flight. Sound takes off, and I take leave of myself. The violinist and composer Malcolm Goldstein vividly evokes this correspondence in a poem entitled *The Gesture of Sounding*:

> Gesture of breath and contact
> in motion, touch
> of wind and finger upon
> wood, hair, skin and metal,
> gut, ivory and felt
> bodies/objects transformed in their sounding,
> as mouth releases, impressing,
> the air within
> outwards,
> and fingers and wrist articulate
> from root of spine (and deeper)
> the totality of who
> we are, that moment resonating
> both inward impulse and outward
> realization being
> one.[39]

Not only does sound take flight in the correspondence of affects, however. So, also, does thinking. It has become common, even conventional, to observe that pianists 'think with their fingers', and violinists and cellists likewise – though not with just their fingers but, as Goldstein suggests, with wrists, lungs and trunk, indeed the whole body. This observation lends support to the idea that thinking is not an exclusively inside-the-head operation, confined only to the brain, but is facilitated by the 'wideware' of a mind that extends across brain, body and instrument. One of the leading exponents of this principle of the extended mind is the philosopher of cognition, Andy Clark.[40] By way of analogy, Clark asks us to consider the prodigious talents of a fish, the bluefin tuna. Why, Clark asks, can the tuna swim so fast? The answer is that it couples its own bodily energies to the fluid dynamics of the water through which it swims, setting up eddies and vortices through the swishing of its tail and fins which themselves exert a propulsive momentum beyond any muscular force of which the fish alone is capable. We might be forgiven for thinking of the tuna fish as a swimming machine. However the real machine, Clark suggests, is not the tuna on its own. It is 'the fish in its *proper context*: the fish plus the surrounding structures and vortices that it actively creates and then maximally exploits'.[41] Thus, strictly speaking, it is not the fish alone that swims, but the fish-in-the-water.

Now Clark would have us compare the way the fish takes to the water to the way a mathematician may take up pencil and notepad in order to perform a calculation, or to the way a navigator takes up ruler and compass to plot a course. If the totality 'fish-plus-eddies-plus-vortices' comprises a mechanism for swimming, then the totality 'mathematician-plus-pencil-plus-notepad' or 'navigator-plus-ruler-plus-compass' comprises a mechanism for computation. The cognitive machine, in the human case, is extended in just the way that the swimming machine is for the fish. Except that it is not! Indeed, we can draw the parallel between the swimming of the fish and the thinking of the human to demonstrate, precisely to the contrary, why thinking cannot be understood as the operation of a cognitive mechanism, even if that mechanism be extended to articulate the brain with both the body and its extra-somatic instruments. For swimming is no more a motor effect for the fish than is thinking a computational effect for the human. Eddies and vortices cannot be connected up like the wheels, cranks and pistons of an engine, in such a way as to deliver propulsion. They are energetic movements in themselves, as indeed is the fish. To borrow an expression from another philosopher, Stanley Cavell, the fish-in-the-water – like every other living being in its proper medium – is a 'whirl'.[42] The whirl is not an object that moves but the emergent form of a movement. Likewise the fish is not a body that swims but the gyre of swim-body-becoming; not an articulation of organs, but a bundle of kinaesthetically attuned movements. Or, in short, *its coherence is not articulatory but harmonic.*

Returning now to Goldstein's poem, we can see that exactly the same applies to the violinist (in his case) or to the cellist (in mine). I play like a fish; I fly as the fish swims, precisely because flying – like swimming – is not the output of a mechanism but a correspondence of affects. How can a player armed only with a cello make such an immense and variable sound? Not because the player's brain, body and instrument together make up a 'playing machine'! It is not as though I take up my cello and bow, as I might a notepad and pencil, or ruler and compass, in order to achieve results that I could not accomplish unaided. As Goldstein intimates, I am not chained anatomically to the instrument. Rather, my breath, touch, manual gesture and spinal posture join in unison with wood, hair and metal in a correspondence of sensory awareness and vibrant materials – the one stretching or attentive, the other stretched or tensed – wherein consciousness, in the words of Deleuze and his collaborator Félix Guattari, is 'thought of the matter-flow' and material 'the correlate of this consciousness'.[43] In this correspondence, sound takes flight, even as I remain seated. And so, of course, does thinking. Thought cannot fly; only thinking can. There is movement in thinking because connections unravel, leaving loose ends in search of company to correspond or join *with*. Correspondence, not articulation, is the guarantor that thinking can carry on.

Explicit knowledge, as we have seen, calls for specification and articulation. Thought, it is often said, should be 'joined up'. But if all thought were thus finally connected, nothing could move. It is a mistake, I think, to conflate thinking with conceptualization, if by that is meant the accommodation of experience to a pre-existing framework. Thinking, surely, lies not in this but in the *excess* of experience over conceptualization – an excess we commonly associate with imagination. This is the realm of hopes and dreams in which overflowing experience, edging into form, has yet to surrender to partition and categorization.[44] Thinking unsettles thought. It reaches out beyond what is already explicable towards that which is not yet present or even conceivable, an improvisation that forsakes the security of the fragile centre that we may have drawn around ourselves for an uncertain and unknown future. Far from fixing us to a position or standpoint it drags us out of it. Thinking is in this sense a de-positioning, a practice of exposure.[45] It is tenuous, hesitant and fraught with risk. But only when we take that risk can thinking fly. 'One launches forth, hazards an improvisation', write Deleuze and Guattari. 'But to improvise is to join with the World, or to meld with it. One ventures from home on the thread of a tune'. Every line of flight, they say, has its loops, knots, speeds, movements and gestures, but above all, its sonorities: 'there is always sonority in Ariadne's thread'.[46]

Have you ever wondered why we should think that thinking is silent? This would never have occurred to our medieval predecessors, who would describe the practice of meditation by the same term, *rumination*, which was routinely used for cattle chewing the cud.[47] In their understanding, thinking goes in and out just as breathing does, 'both inward impulse and outward realization being one' – to recall the closing words of Goldstein's verse. Or as Merleau-Ponty insists in the same vein, 'there really is inspiration and expiration of being'.[48] He meant this quite literally. For when we breathe, it is not just the body that takes air in, and lets it out, as though the mind could be left to float in the ether of the imagination. We breathe with our entire being, indissolubly body and soul. Thinking is the breath of the soul, and its sound is a murmur, an undercurrent on the verge of forming itself into articulable words. But the modern science of cognition – in separating thinking from doing, intellection from performance – has silenced thought by attributing it to the mind of an interior subject, alone inside its head, at one with itself but closed off against the cosmos. And by the same token, it has reduced performance to inherently thoughtless, physical or mechanical execution. In this essay I have argued, to the contrary, that thinking-in-doing, while it opens to the cosmos, simultaneously separates the thinking subject from itself. Like light and sound, thinking is kindled by a fission/fusion reaction, born of the collision of the affective and the cosmic. My thinking through the cello, in a word, is not cognitive but atmospheric.

Acknowledgement

The research and writing of this essay were assisted by the European Research Council Advanced Grant, *Knowing From the Inside: Anthropology, Art, Architecture and Design* (323677-KFI, 2013-18). I am very grateful to the Council for its support.

Notes

1 John Cage, *Silence: Lectures and Writings by John Cage*, 50th Anniversary Edition (Middletown, CT: Wesleyan University Press, 2011), p. 109.

2 On the illocutionary force of linguistic utterances, see John Langshaw Austin, *How to Do Things With Words*, 2nd Edition (Cambridge, MA: Harvard University Press, 1975).

3 Cage, *Silence*, p. 10.

4 Ibid., p. 44.

5 Ibid., p. 14.

6 Ibid., p. 10.

7 On the meaning of attention, see George Home-Cook, *Theatre and Aural Attention: Stretching Ourselves* (New York: Palgrave Macmillan, 2015), p. 2.

8 The inspiration for this analogy comes from the writings of violinist Malcolm Goldstein, to which I return in the closing section of this essay.

> I follow the line,
> am molded by it, yielding, as I mold it
> like a brook after rain pours through
> dirt, rocks, trees and grass, finding
> new subtle twists and turns as things move,
> are moved in the flow.

Malcolm Goldstein, *Sounding the Full Circle: Concerning Music Improvisation and Other Related Matters* (1988), p. 4. http://www.frogpeak.org/unbound/goldstein/goldstein_fullcircle. pdf?lbisphpreq=1 (accessed

19 November 2016). This, and subsequent quotations from *Sounding the Full Circle*, are reprinted here with the kind permission of the author.

9 Tim Ingold, 'On Human Correspondence', *Journal of the Royal Anthropological Institute* (N.S.) 23 (2017), pp. 1–19.

10 Cage, *Silence*, p. 23.

11 Ludwig Wittgenstein, *Tractatus Logico-Philosophicus* (London: Routledge & Kegan Paul, 1922), §6.54.

12 Michael Polanyi, *The Tacit Dimension* (London: Routledge & Kegan Paul, 1966).

13 Harry Collins, *Tacit and Explicit Knowledge* (Chicago, IL: University of Chicago Press, 2010), p. 4.

14 Michael Polanyi, *Personal Knowledge: Towards a Post-critical Philosophy* (London: Routledge & Kegan Paul, 1958), p. 88.

15 Lawrence Halprin, *The RSVP Cycles: Creative Processes in the Human Environment* (New York: George Braziller, 1969), p. 12.

16 On the late eighteenth-century origins of the idea of the musical work as a complete composition, see Lydia Goehr, *The Imaginary Museum of Musical Works: An Essay in the Philosophy of Music* (Oxford: Clarendon Press, 1992), p. 203.

17 On kinaesthesia, see Maxine Sheets-Johnstone, 'The Imaginative Consciousness of Movement: Linear Quality, Kinaesthesia, Language and Life', in *Redrawing Anthropology: Materials, Movements, Lines*, ed. Tim Ingold (Farnham: Ashgate, 2011), pp. 115–28.

18 As I have argued elsewhere, 'to play is itself to feel, so that in playing, I put feeling *into* the music'. Tim Ingold, *The Perception of the Environment: Essays on Livelihood, Dwelling and Skill* (London: Routledge, 2000), p. 413.

19 I am indebted to the artist Jaime Refoyo for instructing me in how to draw a straight line freehand. After returning to my cello, I was struck by the parallel with bowing technique. See Jaume Guilera and Jaime Refoyo, *GEOCOCO: Geography of Corporal Consciousness* (unpublished ms).

20 On the etymology of 'harmony', see Petar Hr. Ilievski, 'The Origin and Semantic Development of the Term *Harmony*', *Illinois Classical Studies* 18 (1993), pp. 19–29.

21 Tim Ingold, *The Life of Lines* (Abingdon: Routledge, 2015), pp. 23–5.

22 See Tim Ingold, *Being Alive: Essays on Movement, Knowledge and Description* (Abingdon: Routledge, 2011), p. 211.

23 Erin Manning, *The Minor Gesture* (Durham, NC: Duke University Press, 2016), pp. 117–18.

24 On this analogy, see Tim Ingold, *Making: Anthropology, Archaeology, Art and Architecture* (Abingdon: Routledge, 2013), p. 111.

25 Gilles Deleuze, *Difference and Repetition*, trans. Paul Patton (New York: Columbia University Press, 1994), p. 29.

26 Ibid., p. 28.

27 Ingold, *The Life of Lines*, p. 111.

28 Wassily Kandinsky, *Point and Line to Plane*, trans. Howard Dearstyne and Hilla Rebay, ed. Hilla Rebay, from *Punkt und Linie zu Fläche* (1926), first published in 1947 by the Solomon R. Guggenheim Foundation for the Museum of Non-Objective Painting, New York City (Mineola, NY: Dover Publications, 1979), pp. 43–5.

29 Ibid., pp. 25–8.

30 Cornelius Cardew, 'Treatise Handboook', in *Cornelius Cardew: A Reader,* ed. Eddie Prévost (Harlow, Essex: Copula, 1971), pp. 95–134, see p. 108.

31 Maurice Merleau-Ponty, *Phenomenology of Perception*, trans. C. Smith (London: Routledge & Kegan Paul, 1962), p. 214.

32 Ingold, *The Life of Lines*, pp. 96–7.

33 Ibid., pp. 73–8.

34 Victor Zuckerkandl, *Sound and Symbol: Music and the External World*, trans. Willard R. Trask (Princeton, NJ: Princeton University Press, 1956), p. 344. I have compared the arguments of Merleau-Ponty and Zuckerkandl at greater length elsewhere (Ingold, *The Perception of the Environment*, pp. 266–9).

35 Maurice Merleau-Ponty, 'Eye and Mind', trans. Carleton Dallery, in *The Primacy of Perception, and Other Essays on Phenomenological Psychology, the Philosophy of Art, History and Politics* (Evanston, IL: Northwestern University Press, 1964), pp. 159–90. See pp. 186–7; also Ingold, *The Perception of the Environment*, pp. 263–4.

36 Merleau-Ponty, 'Eye and Mind', pp. 163–4.

37 Ingold, *The Life of Lines*, pp. 107–8.

38 Ibid., pp. 99, 109.

39 Goldstein, Sounding the Full Circle, p. 49.

40 Andy Clark, *Mindware: An Introduction to the Philosophy of Cognitive Science* (Oxford: Oxford University Press, 2001).

41 Andy Clark, 'Where Brain, Body and World Collide', *Daedalus: Journal of the American Academy of Arts and Sciences* 127 (1998), pp. 257–80. For the tuna fish analogy, see p. 272. The emphases are original.

42 Cavell speaks of 'the whirl of organism'. See Stanley Cavell, *Must We Mean What We Say? A Book of Essays* (Cambridge, UK: Cambridge University Press, 1969), p. 52.

43 Gilles Deleuze and Félix Guattari, *A Thousand Plateaus: Capitalism and Schizophrenia*, trans. Brian Massumi (London: Continuum, 2004), p. 454.

44 I borrow the phrase 'edging into form' from Erin Manning, by which she foregrounds 'the heterogeneity of a welling experience before it succumbs to the categorization of its parts'. See Manning, *The Minor Gesture*, p. 112.

45 The literal meaning of 'exposure' is being 'out of position'. On this, see Jan Masschelein, 'The idea of critical e-ducational research – e-ducating the gaze and inviting to go walking', in *The Possibility/Impossibility of a New Critical Language of Education,* ed. Ilan Gur-Ze'ev (Rotterdam: Sense Publishers, 2010), pp. 275–91. See p. 278.

46 Deleuze and Guattari, A Thousand Plateaus, pp. 343–4.

47 Tim Ingold, *Lines: A Brief History* (Abingdon: Routledge, 2007), p. 17.

48 Merleau-Ponty, 'Eye and Mind', p. 167.

References

Austin, J. L., *How to Do Things With Words* (2nd Edition), Cambridge, MA: Harvard University Press, 1975.

Cage, J., *Silence: Lectures and Writings by John Cage* (50th Anniversary Edition), Middletown, CT: Wesleyan University Press, 2011.

Cardew, C., 'Treatise Handboook', in E. Prévost (ed.), *Cornelius Cardew: A Reader*, Harlow, Essex: Copula, 1971, pp. 95–134.

Cavell, S., *Must We Mean What We Say? A Book of Essays*, Cambridge, UK: Cambridge University Press, 1969.

Clark, A., 'Where Brain, Body and World Collide', *Daedalus: Journal of the American Academy of Arts and Sciences* 127 (1998), pp. 257–80.

Clark, A., *Mindware: An Introduction to the Philosophy of Cognitive Science*, Oxford: Oxford University Press, 2001.

Collins, H., *Tacit and Explicit Knowledge*, Chicago, IL: University of Chicago Press, 2010.

Deleuze, G., *Difference and Repetition*, trans. P. Patton, New York: Columbia University Press, 1994.

Deleuze, G. and F. Guattari, *A Thousand Plateaus: Capitalism and Schizophrenia*, trans. B. Massumi, London: Continuum, 2004.

Goehr, L., *The Imaginary Museum of Musical Works: An Essay in the Philosophy of Music*, Oxford: Clarendon Press, 1992.

Goldstein, M., *Sounding the Full Circle: Concerning Music Improvisation and Other Related Matters*, 1988. http://www.frogpeak.org/unbound/goldstein/goldstein_fullcircle.pdf?lbisphpreq=1 (accessed 19 November 2016).

Guilera, J. and J. Refoyo (n.d.), *GEOCOCO: Geography of Corporal Consciousness*. Unpublished ms.

Halprin, L., *The RSVP Cycles: Creative Processes in the Human Environment*. New York: George Braziller, 1969.

Home-Cook, G., *Theatre and Aural Attention: Stretching Ourselves*, New York: Palgrave Macmillan, 2015.

Ilievski, P. H., 'The Origin and Semantic Development of the Term *Harmony*', *Illinois Classical Studies* 18 (1993), pp. 19–29.

Ingold, T., *The Perception of the Environment: Essays on Livelihood, Dwelling and Skill*, London: Routledge, 2000.

Ingold, T., *Lines: A Brief History*, Abingdon: Routledge, 2007.

Ingold, T., *Being Alive: Essays on Movement, Knowledge and Description*, Abingdon: Routledge, 2011.

Ingold, T., *Making: Anthropology, Archaeology, Art and Architecture*, Abingdon: Routledge, 2013.

Ingold, T., *The Life of Lines*, Abingdon: Routledge, 2015.

Ingold, T., 'On Human Correspondence', *Journal of the Royal Anthropological Institute (N.S.)* 23 (2017), pp. 1–19.

Kandinsky, W., *Point and Line to Plane*, translated from *Punkt und Linie zu Fläche* (1926) trans. H. Dearstyne and H. Rebay, ed. H. Rebay. Mineola, NY: Dover Publications, 1979.

Manning, E., *The Minor Gesture*. Durham, NC: Duke University Press, 2016.

Masschelein, J., 'The Idea of Critical E-ducational Research – E-ducating the Gaze and Inviting to Go Walking', in I. Gur-Ze'ev (ed.), *The Possibility/Impossibility of a New Critical Language of Education*, Rotterdam: Sense Publishers, 2010, pp. 275–91.

Merleau-Ponty, M., *Phenomenology of Perception*, trans. C. Smith, London: Routledge & Kegan Paul, 1962.

Merleau-Ponty, M., 'Eye and Mind', trans. C. Dallery, in *The Primacy of Perception, and Other Essays on Phenomenological Psychology, the Philosophy of Art, History and Politics*, Evanston, IL: Northwestern University Press, 1964, pp. 159–90.

Polanyi, M., *Personal Knowledge: Towards a Post-critical Philosophy*, London: Routledge & Kegan Paul, 1958.

Polanyi, M., *The Tacit Dimension*, London: Routledge & Kegan Paul, 1966.

Sheets-Johnstone, M., 'The Imaginative Consciousness of Movement: Linear Quality, Kinaesthesia, Language and Life', in T. Ingold (ed.), *Redrawing Anthropology: Materials, Movements, Lines*, Farnham: Ashgate, 2011, pp. 115–28.

Wittgenstein, L., *Tractatus Logico-Philosophicus*, London: Routledge & Kegan Paul 1922.

Zuckerkandl, V., *Sound and Symbol: Music and the External World*, trans. W. R. Trask, Princeton, NJ: Princeton University Press, 1956.

11

Aesthetic intelligence

Jill Bennett (JB) and Lynn Froggett (LF)

In this chapter, Jill Bennett and Lynn Froggett discuss the impact of arts-led health interventions in terms of a practice of intersubjective thinking. Reflecting on their collaborative work, in turn drawing on Bennett's concept of practical aesthetics[1] and Froggett's psychosocial methodology,[2] they consider the importance of aesthetic intelligence as a mode of thinking in the world.

JB: We have recently worked on a number of arts projects relating to mental health and memory loss. In such areas, art has long been a method of registering subjective experience – of expressing thought, emotion and experience that is beyond words. But I'm interested in the concept of an aesthetic mode of thinking; that is, an aesthetic practice grounded in the activation of thinking as opposed to the expression of thought. This is not an abstract proposition; I would like to think about how such a mode of thinking has an impact on mental health. As yet, this notion is relatively unexplored concept in the field of arts and health.

LF: The nature of aesthetic sensibility, and how it is brought to bear on everyday life, is poorly understood. It has not been regarded as a subject worthy of much empirical research, except perhaps in the fields of design and marketing where the understanding of 'tastes' has commercial applications.

However, there is an aesthetic intelligence at work in most people's lives (and in communities of practice), which has profound implications for the ways in which they negotiate the world in which they live. As described by Christopher Bollas, we apprehend this aesthetic intelligence at work when we register in ourselves the imprint of a person's distinctively embodied way of being.[3] However, it is rare that we consciously identify, characterize or interpret it. Much less do we ask how aesthetic intelligence is implicated in the ways in which we conduct our lives, look after our health, relate to others – or how it might inform our understanding of 'a good society'.

If the arts are at all transformative it must be through the activation of aesthetic intelligence and sensibility, without which other social or health effects are unlikely to occur.

Yet it seems to me this is the area where the operation of the aesthetic is the least well accounted for. Authors like Nato Thompson, Claire Bishop, Grant Kester and Shannon Jackson have sought to develop critical and political perspectives on socially engaged art practice.[4] Artists like Shona Illingworth and Mark Storor have engaged with an aesthetics of human interaction in specific areas of experience, as well in art science collaborations.[5] However, the area remains undertheorized. It seems to me that this is because of the absence of a perspective on how the aesthetic faculty develops and is expressed intersubjectively.

Professionals who work intensively with arts-based approaches to health tacitly adopt a view of the self that comes close to Bollas' 'aesthetic intelligence' that imprints its unconscious sense of form on the world with which it interacts. According to Bollas, when we attune ourselves to the specific quality of the other's experience, we register their idiom as a distinctive, psychic texture within ourselves.[6]

JB: I am interested in what art practice does in this transactive mode – or when it engenders a particular form of engagement and reflection. Arts-health as a practice or field is poorly served by art theory and sits uneasily with aesthetics. Because it prioritizes health impacts, arts-health is often dismissed as instrumental – as if a focus on transformative effects negates the experimental or expressive purpose of art.

To me, the potential for these effects is what is interesting about arts-health. Arts-health takes seriously the idea of putting art to work – which is a very unartworldy thing to do. The art world still retains this bourgeois sense that art must simply exude influence rather than being put to use – and there is reluctance to posit a theory of change or real-world impact among some of the writers you mention, such as Bishop. This is not just at a theoretical level; it is absolutely entrenched in mainstream exhibition practice, which otherwise adopts progressive positions. For example, the director of a recent Sydney Biennale, Stephanie Rosenthal, gave an interview during that biennale in which she said 'it's definitely important to talk about politics in art, but you're cheating yourself if you think you're going to change the world'.[7] Art, she claimed, couldn't be compared to real human rights work. Now, that may be de facto true of much gallery work that doesn't aspire to effect change, but it is not philosophically true. To make such a claim simply forecloses on a whole area of radical practice.

There is a real resistance when it comes to articulating what art does for us and how we use it. Less so with literature and music, which we are more likely to consume in our private worlds – and so use in quite functional ways to stave off insomnia and depression, for example. As David Foster Wallace said, 'fiction, poetry, music' are the arts through which the loneliness of mental illness may be 'stared down, transfigured, treated'. Visual art is more difficult to access in this way.

This tacit use of art takes for granted the principle of access; it requires an institutional familiarity and confidence to be moved or transfigured by art. What is great about arts-health as a concept is that it does not offer a product but proposes that a process of aesthetic engagement may be beneficial. However, such a process needs to be brokered. This raises questions about how we can deploy or activate aesthetic intelligence – perhaps through using an aesthetic stimulus, such as an artwork or a process of making.

We need to conceptualize exactly what goes on in an arts-health engagement. You mention Bollas' notion of aesthetic intelligence, attuning to the quality of another's experience; this is one part of the transaction. I would want to add the possibility of developing curiosity about one's own mental state, or about processes and experiences. Isn't this part of what happens in arts-health work, or even in an engagement with art?

LF: Attunement to the other's idiom occurs by means of imaginative identifications that express themselves in bodily states (in psychoanalytic terms, we might say that it involves a somatic counter-transference aroused by the quality of their presence). In lay terms, it is commonly referred to as 'chemistry' (positive or negative). However, idiom can be unconsciously imprinted or transmitted by what we create, or the distinctive way in which we do things. Artists leave the imprint of their creative intelligence on their work as a kind of existential signature.

However, in everyday life we cannot do other than express idiom – perhaps less strongly than artists do – through how we arrange our gardens, homes and offices, or in the snapshots we take, the meals we cook, the music we listen to and so on. As we move through a world of people and things, we select and combine them according to an implicit personal 'theory of form', often without even recognizing we are doing so. It affects how we eat, move, interact and how we pattern our daily activities. And of course if we engage in making things that involve any kind of craft, alone or in interaction with others, we are impelled to express this personal aesthetic intelligence. Art, from this perspective, is only a special instance of creative living as you have also argued in *Practical Aesthetics*.[8]

JB: Yes, I would want to argue for an aesthetic continuum – and have espoused the notion of *aistheisis* as a form of sensory-affective perception that is embodied and activated in art practice, but in many other places too.

LF: I should clarify that aesthetic in relation to the self's idiom has nothing to do with a post-modern assemblage of personal identity as a consciously chosen aesthetic construct expressed in consumer behaviour or lifestyle choice, as described by Zygmunt Bauman (among others), and deployed to great effect in marketing.[9] It is an intrinsic aspect of a subjectivity, and it is also thoroughly social in that it begins to develop in the earliest phases of life and then continues to be elaborated through our intersubjective exchanges.

JB: I think it is essential to locate aesthesis in this way, given the more general association of aesthetics with either cultivated taste or product. The limitation of post-modern aesthetic theory lies in simply extending the domain of aesthetics from high culture to popular culture, which are two sides of the same coin. You cannot move from there to asking, 'What is the role of art in transforming mental health?', or 'How does aesthetics contribute to human rights?' To approach the question of what arts-health does, we can't start with a redundant ineffectual concept of art; we need to locate aesthetic capacity, aesthetic intelligence or aesthetic interactions within the wider field of operations.

Also, I would say, that the aesthetic cannot be seen as an interloper – a kind of luxury pursuit that is secondary to the real life-saving work. The rationale for an arts-health intervention is that it delivers something beneficial that is in some way better than available alternatives. It is not 'alternative medicine' – even if it has a beneficial effect on mental health – because medicine does not minister in the same way to critical, social and affective faculties (for example).

LF: Yes. In fact, in health, the increasing strength of the arts has not only been as a complement or alternative to the bio-medical model. In the UK and in Europe I would link the growth of the arts in areas like health, youth justice, and to a lesser extent in welfare to the rise and rise of 'new public management' and the consumerization of public services, which has also been a powerful vector for an intensified technical-rationalism. This process, which gathered pace in the 1990s, has transformed the ways in which human services are delivered, and with it – in the eyes of many practitioners – the scope for attentiveness, compassion and creativity.

Critical voices and a utopian impulse are more likely to find expression through the socially engaged arts than in many other sectors. Sometimes this is explicitly anti-capitalist, but often it results in locally embedded forms of civic action, demands to humanize services, reject commodification and create liveable communities and spaces of creative illusion in which it is possible to imagine a future that is different.

Another strand of activity within the arts, less obviously 'activist' but nevertheless concerned to embed itself in fields of social practice, addresses human vulnerability, ill health, exclusion, inequality and other forms of disadvantage. Here, the arts-health movement has endeavoured to preserve a responsiveness to embodied subjectivity, and resist the evacuation of relationship from practice in the face of the seemingly unstoppable march of technical-rationalism.

JB: So you are suggesting that aesthetic intelligence is embedded in this responsiveness to embodied subjectivity. This implies a compassionate practice and, as you suggest, a critical practice, but we are also wanting to link this to the production of thinking in a self-reflexive mode.

LF: The work we are doing together in relation to professional and public understanding of dementia and dementia care would be an example. I think we are trying to understand better how to create the conditions in which people in various stages of dementia can engage and communicate their responses to complex artworks which themselves deal with questions of memory loss, and the problems in living that arise from this. We are exploring whether and how an aesthetic intelligence can still be expressed when memory and cognitive function is impaired.

JB: Yes, in that scenario, we have developed a technique to work with the aesthetic intelligence that participants bring to the encounter – but also to specifically enable a mutually supported critical engagement, building on the participants' capacity for attunement. In other words, we have worked with the idea that participants can come to learn about, talk about and understand themselves (and the mental and neurological processes they experience) via sensory affective or aesthetic connections.

Rancière's formulation of 'aesthetics of the sensible'[10] has to some extent recast aesthetics as a descriptor of social embedded interactions. Yet there is no empirical project underpinning Rancièrian aesthetics.

LF: Raymond Williams' concept of structure of feeling is perhaps more useful, or rather it's a mediating concept – between the trans-historical level that Rancière is talking about, and the way in which the sensible is experienced in everyday life through the everyday articulation of aesthetic sensibility.[11]

JB: We could point to artists whose work has pursued something similar in the context of finding oneself institutionalized or 'medicalized'. Jo Spence, after being diagnosed with breast cancer and subsequently leukaemia, described her illness as a 'peculiar disjuncture in my knowledge of the physical world [which] caused such total crisis in my thinking and activity'.[12] For Spence, the struggle for becoming well was a struggle for a 'subject language'. I have also recently written about the experience of memory loss (in relation to Shona

Illingworth's project *Lesions in the Landscape*), referencing Evan Thompson's (neuro)philosophical formulation of the 'body-body problem', the problem of relating one's subjectively lived body to the living body that one is.[13] The aesthetic as art practice here becomes a technique, grounded in an inchoate 'aesthetic intelligence'.

Rather than assuming that the key to arts-health lies in the practical transmission of art-making skills to a patient (or in some kind of predefined art therapeutic programme), we can dwell on the activation/exercise of aesthetic intelligence (which implies participation, but not necessary 'making' on the part of the patient/participant). The drive/aptitude for this comes from the 'patient' rather than artist.

LF: There is a level of interaction that is not easily identifiable in terms of what we can see in the interrelationship between person and phenomenon, and this is why we need an element of depth psychology, because aesthetic sensibility is also implicated in what we 'take in' or introject from the world and what we project into it. Or, to put it differently, aesthetic sensibility is implicated in transfers of affect in which we are constantly unwittingly engaged. These things are not easily observable, but they can be deciphered and interpreted with the right kind of data. I think we have to be open to the fact that there are things going on in the intersubjective encounter that are not transparent to either party, and that is why a psychoanalytically sensitized cultural perspective is also valuable.

JB: What's important and what's distinctive about your methods is this development of an empirical programme that supports intersubjective engagement – and thinking collaboratively – and that also extends analysis of the institutional level. Maybe we could talk a bit more about how you analyse the material.

LF: What I try to do is achieve the right kind mix between a closeness to experience and interpretive distance, and between sensitivity to the intertwined dimensions of subjective feeling and perception, and the institutional/sociocultural domain which mediates the operations of the aesthetic in both everyday life and high art.

This implies that we can't rely on methods in which the focus of analysis is either purely the individual or purely the institutional/cultural. We have to be able to observe how they are mutually constitutive of one another. Take the 'visual matrix' as an example.[14] We are using this method because it is designed to enable people to 'enact' rather than 'speak' their experience of an artwork in a shared setting – the matrix – where the ideas offered are imagistic and associative, rather than discursive, evaluative and explanatory, as would be the case in a focus group. The emphasis is on participants expressing responses to an aesthetic stimulus in the present moment, and because they also associate to one another's associations, the matrix is a shared 'creation' where flows and clusters of imagery from all its participants are interwoven. So, although what people present is rooted in subjective experience, this experience becomes intersubjectively communicable by virtue of the shared cultural content of the imagery, which falls into patterns that reflect collectively held institutional or societal ideas and preoccupations.

You may remember the visual matrix we did with artists and scientists, that we nicknamed 'stonewall'. It literally began with images of stone walls borrowed from the film the participants had just watched together. Through their contributions, we understood how individuals were affected in the moment by the stony, abandoned signs of human habitation in the harsh landscape of the film. As it turned out, 'stonewall' also metaphorically framed what people were doing – their struggle to listen to one another in the face of the disciplinary divide.

This I think does reflect 'a structure of feeling' in what Snow called 'two-culture' societies where the arts and sciences are traditionally quite separate areas of activity.[15] In the setting of the matrix, we could observe mutual diffidence and incomprehension between artists and scientists being played out in the affectively laden, aesthetically textured microinteractions and figurative conversational turns of the participants. To get to this kind of analysis, we need an interpretive process that begins 'close up' to the experience of the intersubjective exchange, and progressively 'pans out' for a richer contextual understanding.

JB: Yes, an 'experience-near' approach that combines a means of analysing the institutional structures and frameworks that shape behaviours. I think this is particularly important if we understand the aesthetic and the affective as always already within or rubbing up against those political and institutional frameworks rather than extracting the aesthetic moment from the grip of politics.

LF: That's right, aesthetic experience is threaded right through the intra-, inter- and trans-subjective, if you like, and into the sociocultural and the institutional domain.

JB: I think it's also important when we start talking about a psychoanalytic framework to note that your work and analysis is very much focused at the level of group interaction – and on the emergence of a kind of collective expression.

LF: It is, but I would qualify that by saying that what is critical is the point of articulation between that which is individually and biographically produced and the group interaction. What people offer as individuals in the matrix, for example, is certainly grounded in subjective and biographical experience. But it is offered into a shared space – and I use the word 'shared' rather than 'collective' because this isn't really a group phenomenon. People speak their personal associations – based on imagery that arises in their mind's eye – into a shared space where it becomes intelligible in a shared cultural domain. This shared space is therefore 'in-between' the subjective and the cultural, and that I think is where aesthetic experience arises – at that point of intersection. This is in line with both Rancière and Williams – the aesthetic is a point of mediation. It's where subjectively felt experience takes on a cultural form, through the symbolic repertoires that are available to give it expression.

JB: Yes, so here we can think about arts-health projects as aesthetic interventions, in this sense that they are providing a means to elaborate or to extend what you call the available symbolic repertoires. You have also worked with the UK-based artist Mark Storor on a project that addresses a human condition of extreme sensitivity.

LF: I did this study with my colleague Julian Manley. *Barometer of My Heart*, which first showed in London in 2015, is about male impotence – though it starts with the bio-medical problem of erectile dysfunction. The painstaking research and development process involved a collaboration with Leighton Seal, consultant endocrinologist at St George's Hospital, where Mark, with the permission of patients, was able to attend consultations. The material he gathered was woven together with small stories and observed enactments of suffering – from encounters with taxi drivers, war veterans, rugby players and men from other walks of life where maleness is both evoked and called into question. The many threads were then reinterpreted by Storor through a trusted group of actors. In their hands, as well as an agonizing bio-mechanical 'malfunction', impotence became a trope for the social anxieties of masculinity; a health indicator of body and mind, an existential crisis for those who suffer it, a challenge for intimate partnerships, a universal metaphor for human vulnerability and an insistent demand for compassion and recognition. Audiences were walked through a series of scenes, linked by a distinctive aesthetic that the company evolved through their work together. The show was performed in an NHS Health Centre building, where the audience became witnesses to the emotional devastation of this experience, while they were confronted with the personal and cultural significance of impotence, and an intimation of acts of care that offered hope.[16]

JB: What is at stake in this kind of work, and what does the subject matter of erectile dysfunction gain from its articulation through aesthetic intelligence – and through art, in particular, as opposed to another kind of medical or therapeutic modality?

LF: From a medical perspective, Seal expressed the hope that it opened up for public discussion an otherwise 'unspeakable' topic, and a public awareness of some of its possible health indications (erectile dysfunction as an early indicator of heart disease, for example). It did this easily, but through the visual matrix we could also see that it did much more. We were able to gain evidence of deep affective engagement among the audiences, and an ability to express – through chains of association – the cultural, symbolic significance of impotence in personal biographies, and in areas of life that ranged from parenting to education, the workplace, politics, healthcare and cultural media. In the responses of selected groups, we could see what was gendered and beyond gender, and the same could be said of sexual orientation. What Storor and his actors provided through their combined aesthetic intelligence and the distinctive idiom of the show were a multitude of 'forms for feeling', so that the often inexpressible individual anxieties aroused by the subject matter could be shaped into imagery and thought and shared with others.

JB: The visual matrix essentially creates a third space to examine 'forms of feeling' in action, so that a radically new understanding can emerge in dialogue in an expressive language that is adequate to the emergent experience.

LF: In this sense, artworks like *Barometer of My Heart* function as an aesthetic third between personal experience and the cultural realm. The distinctive aesthetic of the art activates the aesthetic idiom of the individual through the sensory symbolic registers it deploys (imagistic, acoustic, performative), which are culturally intelligible – the resulting trans-subjective experience is intersubjectively communicable.

JB: The interpretive protocols you use are multi-layered. I notice that when you look at the data – let's say the transcript of an interview or the visual matrix – you tend to work through a series of lenses. You start by simply asking what is said or presented (what is the content or affect?). Then, you move to the performative – how it was said or presented – before you contextualize and approach an explanation. So, where do we see the aesthetic emerging – in the middle performative modality? Or is it embedded throughout, and thus inseparable?

LF: I do see it as emerging there, but we mustn't forget that it is grounded in subjective experience as well. I mean, to talk about it emerging at the point of institutional structures without retaining that sort of groundedness in embodied experience – which also means individual bodies and brains – would lose the imaginative 'fuel' that comes from the participants themselves, and from all their life resources. But these things become available for contemplation in a setting that is carefully devised to bring the individual subject into interaction with others, in a culturally shared space.

JB: Yes, embodied subjective experience is registered in this shared space of the visual matrix in quite a unique and free-flowing way. That seems to me to be what makes this a really political project. Rancière talks about the inscription of a certain regime of the sensible or subjective experience.[17] But how is the first-person experience reported in sensory affective terms – and understood as such? In the visual matrix, we have a method of investigating how individuals – bodies and brains – situate and express themselves, and work through these cultural and performative modalities.

LF: And are themselves then inscribed by them.

JB: Yes, the visual matrix can become a way of registering and analysing, and of positioning oneself in relation to the more rigid inscriptions or medicalizations of conditions that people have experienced. We have found this using the visual matrix method with people who have experienced repeated hospitalisation, for example.

This allows us to look at what the aesthetic does, how it operates in the everyday – and how then Art with a capital 'A' becomes a vehicle, whether you're a producer or a kind of consumer.

LF: … which brings us back to Bollas. I do think that this is why a theory of how aesthetic sensibilities are generated in the first place is useful –it's why a certain kind of psychoanalytic perspective is useful, and more specifically why Christopher Bollas's work is helpful. Bollas sets himself the task of understanding the distinctiveness of personal idiom, as he calls it. He is referring to a kind of existential signature that each of us bears as we move through the world. It accounts for the nature of our presence, the imprint we leave on others when we encounter them as well as the way in which we live our lives according to an implied personal theory of form. This, in turn, accounts for how we perform a myriad of interactions in the everyday – and also, of course, is something that we register to a degree in action within a crafted setting like the visual matrix.

Now, when he talks of personal idiom, he is not referring to an essential biological characteristic of the individual; idiom is always already social and located in the earliest experiences of care, which are the earliest experiences of human interaction. The infant responds to the distinctive way in which his or her body is tended or cared for – the stroking, soothing, cooing actions of the primary caretaker, usually the mother. And from those earliest experiences of interaction, the infant gains a sense of embodied form. Bollas describes this as the earliest experience of being transformed in the presence of – literally in the hands of – another, which then becomes elaborated with development. It is important to stress that the modalities of cleansing, caring, cuddling and so on are culturally shaped and socially transmitted.

JB: So, the very way that they're formed (and offered or withheld) proceeds from the social institutions that transmit culture?

LF: Yes, but unconsciously, through the mother's own theory of form – her idiomatic expression of her own aesthetic sensibility, which impresses itself on everyday tasks. So, in my view, this already is a psychosocial way of viewing the development of the aesthetic, even though Bollas doesn't use that term. It does what we were just talking about. It threads through from the intra- and intersubjective, and the cultural/ institutional dimensions of the experience.

Bollas is useful as an account of how a very early development of aesthetic sensibility is a crucial way in which we mediate our relationship to the world – and it therefore cannot be separated off from other areas of experience, in the way in which art historical discourse has attempted. Of course, it will then transfer into cultural production and consumption, but at the same time it also transfers into ways of living. This can be more or less creative, or destructive.

There is a wealth of clinical wisdom on how to create the conditions for the patient to find his or her way to a manifestation of idiom. In the tradition of Bion, much of it has to do with negative capability – or the 'evenly hovering attention' – that allows the analyst to attune to the patient, and thus use him or herself as an instrument of knowing.[18] The non-intrusiveness of the analytic stance is paramount. It is much more difficult to create these conditions in other welfare settings, and the routinization and regulation of practice ensures that the situation will get no easier.

For example, social workers who trained in the 1970s were taught of the therapeutic value of the one-to-one encounter, and the necessity to provide a space apart – where the relationship became the prime medium of intervention and could be psychodynamically understood. It is not just the psychodynamic model, but the intersubjective space itself that has collapsed under current practice conditions.[19]

It is about working creatively within the intersubjective space – this is still a marginal concern within health services, and even more so in the welfare sector. There are plenty of qualitative case studies of the intersubjective benefits of arts-based approaches, but they encounter the problem of replicability, which is why empirical studies that lead to theoretical development are so important. On the basis of work that I have done over a number of years, I would make a strong claim that while art-making requires and reproduces particular conditions essential to creating 'thirdness', communicative relationships can be generated in a range of creative activities, and there is plenty of energy and enthusiasm for it.

Ironically, the hybridity and interdisciplinary radicality of this work cuts it adrift from mainstream arts, which have not recognized its emergent politics of subjectivity.

JB: The arts-health movement has aimed to get beyond excessively instrumental forms of practice – led by outcome measurement and targets that are often imposed for political reasons. The irony is that the use of arts in health care has itself been criticized for instrumentalizing the arts.

LF: The questions of institutionalization and medicalization are a good example of the difficulties. There has been some research here, especially in the area of mental health. For example, art therapy, like other health professions, is obliged to establish to establish a stronger evidence base to defend its position and distinctive contribution. There is strong pressure here to submit to the hierarchy of evidence where the randomized controlled trial (RCT) is at the apex of gold standard research. However, RCTs are extremely problematic in this area, and even if they can demonstrate effectiveness, they lack explanatory power. They are even less suitable for the more informal (and often time and funding limited) art projects in psychiatric wards and community settings, where innovative work is going on.

JB: An important question at stake with medicalization is how an aesthetic intelligence is overwhelmed or surrendered in the face of powerful scientific and institutional pressures, and how an arts practice may be able to re-activate it, rather offering another form of intervention with definitive but reductionist outcomes. But the deeper, potentially enduring impacts of this will be hard to capture by traditional measures.

LF: To give an example, I undertook an evaluation of a dance programme in a secure psychiatric ward a few years ago, which not only visibly enlarged a range of expressive movement previously impaired by psychoactive medication, but was acclaimed by participants in insightful and metaphorically dense narratives of experience. I was startled to find that according to standard measures (an adapted version of the Herth Hope index),[20] their hope for the future had declined, despite the fact that an aesthetic intelligence had indeed been activated in the 'in-between' space between the hospital and the prospect of 'ordinary life' that dance provided. This expressed itself through a newly embodied sense of psychosocial integration, or its fragility, in the face of gathering realism in relation to the challenges of life beyond the ward. This is a complex outcome to do with changes in what you call the 'body-body problem' – the problem of relating one's subjectively lived body to the living body that one is, in the world one inhabits. Confronting the dissonance may not occasion immediate optimism, but working through the problem in a medium that affords an opportunity to re-align relationships to body, self, other and world can offer a far-reaching hope for change. The problem was that I could not persuade the consultant psychiatrist that realistic ambivalence was a significant gain. As he saw it, in the short term 'there were no robust positives' with which to defend the continuation of the programme.

Arts-based practice is nearly always 'relational' practice, and aesthetic intelligence cannot be understood outside of the human relationships through which it develops, and which it animates and sustains in turn. This kind of intuition is at work in many of the arts-health initiatives in both clinical and community settings, and can be seen as complementary to mainstream health practices, or as a rather inchoate push back against advancing medicalization.

JB: So in summary, we are proposing arts-health as the particular case that illustrates some pervasive issues?

Firstly, the instrumentalization of the arts, especially in cultural policy – an issue that people in both arts-health and the arts sector are very much aware of; and secondly, the lack of an empirical research programme informed by a theorization of practical aesthetics or aesthetics in everyday life, along with adequate methods to explore it. Our collaboration is beginning to address this.

LF: Exactly. All of this is exacerbated by the institutional split between the arts establishment and the uses of the arts in other sectors such as health, criminal justice, environment and so forth.

JB: Yes. We are suggesting that we need to be able to talk about and theorize the practical 'uses' of art in these sectors, without instrumentalizing the aesthetic. Instead, we want to build on the concept of aesthetic intelligence, and to find ways to realise and reflect on the thinking that it engenders.

Notes

1 Jill Bennett, *Practical Aesthetics: Events, affect and art after 9/11*, Radical Aesthetics Radical Art Series (London: I. B. Tauris & Co, 2012).

2 This method was developed with Alastair Roy and Julian Manley at the University of Central Lancashire, UK. See: Lynn Froggett, Julian Manley and Alastair Roy, 'The visual matrix method: imagery and affect in a group-based research setting', *Forum Qualitative Sozialforschung / Forum: Qualitative Social Research* 16:3 (2015), http://www.qualitative-research.net/index.php/fqs/article/view/2308/3849 (accessed 1 May 2017).

3 See Christopher Bollas, *Being a Character: Psychoanalysis and Self Experience* (New York: Hill and Wang, 1992); Idem., *The Shadow of the Object: Psychoanalysis of the Unthought Known* (London: Free Association Books, 1987), pp. 1–29 on 'The Transformational Object'.

4 See, for instance, Nato Thompson, *Living as Form: Socially Engaged Art from 1991-2011* (Cambridge, MA: MIT Press, 2012); Claire Bishop, *Artificial Hells: Participatory Art and the Politics of Spectatorship* (London; NY: Routledge, 2012); Grant Kester, *The One and the Many: Contemporary Collaborative Art in a Global Context* (Durham: Duke University Press, 2011); Shannon Jackson, *Social Works: Performing Art, Supporting Publics* (London: Routledge, 2011).

5 See Mark Storor, *The Barometer of My Heart* (Liverpool: FACT, 2015); Shona Illingworth, *Lesions in the Landscape* (Liverpool: FACT, 2015).

6 Bollas, *Being a Character*, pp. 33–46.

7 Curator Stephanie Rosenthal quoted in an interview with journalist Miriam Cosic, 'Sydney through fresh eyes: artistic director Stephanie Rosenthal on the city's Biennale', *The Guardian*, 11 March.

8 Bennett, *Practical Aesthetics*.

9 See, for instance, Zygmunt Bauman, *Consuming life* (Cambridge: Polity, 2007); Idem., *Globalization: The Human Consequences* (New York: Columbia University Press, 1998).

10 Jacques Rancière, *The Politics of Aesthetics: The Distribution of the Sensible* (London; New York: Continuum, 2004).

11 See Chapter 9, 'Structures of Feeling' in Raymond Williams' *Marxism and Literature* (Oxford; New York: Oxford University Press, 1977), pp. 128–35.

12 Jo Spence, *Work: Part I and Part II* (London: Jo Spence Memorial Archive, 2012).

13 Jill Bennett and Shona Illingworth, *Lesions in the Landscape: A Project by Shona Illingworth* (Liverpool: FACT, 2015); Illingworth, *Lesions in the Landscape*; See Evan Thompson and Robert Hanna, 'The mind-body-body problem', *Theoria et Historia Scientiarum: International Journal for Interdisciplinary Studies* 7:1 (2003), pp. 23–42.

14 Froggett et al., 'The visual matrix method'.

15 C. P. Snow, *The Two Cultures and the Scientific Revolution, Rede Lecture* (New York: Cambridge University Press, 1959).

16 Mark Storor, *The Barometer of My Heart*.

17 Rancière, *The Politics of Aesthetics*.

18 W. R. Bion, *Attention and Interpretation; a Scientific Approach to Insight in Psycho-analysis and Groups* (New York: Basic Books, 1970).

19 Here, I am quoting directly from my chapter, 'Artistic output as intersubjective third', in S. Clarke and P. Hoggett (eds), *Object Relations and Social Relations: The Implications of the Relational Turn in Psychoanalysis* (London: Karnac, 2008), p. 107.

20 Kaye Herth, 'Abbreviated instrument to measure hope: development and psychometric evaluation', *Journal of Advanced Nursing* 17 (1992), pp. 1251–9.

References

Bauman, Z., *Consuming Life*, Cambridge: Polity, 2007.

Bauman, Z., *Globalization: The Human Consequences*, NY: Columbia University Press, 1998.

Bennett, J., *Practical Aesthetics: Events, affect and art after 9/11, Radical Aesthetics Radical Art Series*, London: I. B. Tauris & Co, 2012.

Bennett, J. and S. Illingworth, *Lesions in the Landscape: A Project by Shona Illingworth*, Liverpool: FACT, 2015.

Bion, W. R., *Attention and Interpretation; A Scientific Approach to Insight in Psycho-analysis and Groups*. New York: Basic Books, 1970.

Bishop, C., *Artificial Hells: Participatory Art and the Politics of Spectatorship*, London; NY: Routledge, 2012.

Bollas, C., *Being a Character: Psychoanalysis and Self Experience*, New York: Hill and Wang, 1992.

Bollas, C., *The Shadow of the Object: Psychoanalysis of the Unthought Known*, London: Free Association Books, 1987.

Cosic, M., 'Sydney through fresh eyes: artistic director Stephanie Rosenthal on the city's Biennale', *The Guardian*, 11 March 2016 https://www.theguardian.com/culture/2016/mar/11/your-city-through-fresh-eyes-artistic-director-stephanie-rosenthal-on-the-sydney-biennale (accessed 28 April 2017).

Froggett, L., 'Artistic output as intersubjective third', in S. Clarke and P. Hoggett (eds), *Object Relations and Social Relations: The Implications of the Relational Turn in Psychoanalysis*, London: Karnac, 2008, pp. 87–111.

Froggett, L., Manley, J. and A. Roy, 'The visual matrix method: imagery and affect in a group-based research setting', *Forum Qualitative Sozialforschung/Forum: Qualitative Social Research* 16:3 (2015) http://www.qualitative-research.net/index.php/fqs/article/view/2308/3849 (accessed 1 May 2017).

Herth, K. 'Abbreviated instrument to measure hope: development and psychometric evaluation', *Journal of Advanced Nursing* 17 (1992), pp. 1251–9.

Illingworth, S., *Lesions in the Landscape*, Liverpool: FACT, 2015.

Jackson, S., *Social Works: Performing Art, Supporting Publics*, London; NY: Routledge, 2011.

Kester, G., *The One and the Many: Contemporary Collaborative Art in a Global Context*, Durham: Duke University Press, 2011.

Rancière, J., *The Politics of Aesthetics: The Distribution of the Sensible*, London; New York: Continuum, 2004.

Snow, C. P., *The Two Cultures and the Scientific Revolution, Rede Lecture*, New York: Cambridge University Press, 1959.

Spence, J., *Work: Part I and Part II*, London: Jo Spence Memorial Archive, 2012.

Storor, M., *The Barometer of My Heart*, Liverpool: FACT, 2015.

Thompson, E. and R. Hanna, 'The mind-body-body problem', *Theoria et Historia Scientiarum: International Journal for Interdisciplinary Studies* 7:1 (2003).

Thompson, N., *Living as Form: Socially Engaged Art from 1991–2011*, Cambridge, MA: MIT Press, 2012.

Williams, R., *Marxism and Literature*, Oxford; New York: Oxford University Press, 1977.

PART SIX

Spectrums of experience

12

Reading Leslie Marmon Silko's *Ceremony* with autist Jamie Burke, or remembering the sensorimotor future

Ralph James Savarese

I

I am in the midst of writing a book about discussing classic American novels with autistic readers. To conduct such discussions, my collaborators and I use Skype. They hail from places like Portland, Oregon; Austin, Texas; and Syracuse, New York – I live in Iowa City, Iowa. Those who cannot speak type their comments on the sidebar; those who can speak converse as anyone might, and I record what they say. We read slowly, a few chapters at a time, and meet once a week online. I ask my collaborators to prepare notes for the chapters and to respond to what they have read with their own writing. The project is ethnographical, a form of qualitative research, but it takes pains to acknowledge, in a scientific way, the very different brains that autistics have. The project is also 'neurocosmopolitan', a term that I have coined to denote both a posture of cognitive hospitality and a space of fluid neuro-interaction.

When we think about 'thinking in the world', we must include neurodiverse brains. We must think, that is, about different kinds of thinking in the world, different kinds of embodied cognition. To me neurodiversity is not just a liberal platitude; it is a working neurological proposition. As opposed to the vast majority of autism experts, I interpret that proposition generously, wondering not only whether there might be a different way of performing higher-order cognitive tasks such as reading and discussing literature but also whether an autistic neurology might in fact be better suited, in some respects, to literature's especially embodied form of language. Recent neuroscientific research has shown the degree to which poems and novels strive to simulate experience, not just to denote it in an abstract way. That simulation depends as much on activating more primitive sensing regions in the back of the brain as it does on activating the vaunted frontal lobes. As experts have begun to focus on the role of the sensory in autism, the idea of literary autistics seems much less preposterous than it once did.[1]

In this essay, I relate my discussions of the novel *Ceremony* with autist Jamie Burke. Authored by the Native American writer Leslie Marmon Silko and published in 1977, *Ceremony* tells the story of Tayo, a Second World War veteran of mixed Laguna-Pueblo and white ancestry who returns from combat in the Philippines with a severe case of battle fatigue, or what we now call post-traumatic stress disorder. After convalescing for a period at a Veterans Affairs hospital, Tayo travels to the impoverished Laguna reservation in New Mexico where his aunt and grandmother reside, still haunted by the death of his cousin Rocky during the infamous Bataan Death March of 1942. He had promised to look after Rocky, whose head a Japanese soldier had sadistically cracked in two. Western medicine fails to help Tayo, who like many Native Americans was encouraged to leave the old customs behind in favour of the material promises of assimilation. In his case, he joined the army.

The novel tracks Tayo's agonizing descent into alcoholism and destructive behaviour as he fleetingly recalls, through his grandmother and the New Mexico landscape itself, a long-forgotten way of relating to the world. Eventually, the ministrations of the mixed-race medicine man Betonie and a phantom woman (or spirit figure) bring about Tayo's recovery. That recovery coincides with the return of rain to the drought-plagued reservation. During combat in the Philippines, Tayo cursed the jungle's unending deluge; the curse, he comes to realize, worked too well. At the end of the book, he completes a ceremony that restores 'harmony with [his] natural surroundings and … with [his people]',[2] as Silko remarked in an interview. What makes the novel so relevant to the theme of 'thinking in the world' is (a) its insistence on the value of traditional Native American thought to Western ways of thinking and (b) its experimentation with literary form to convey the feeling of this sort of thought dynamically.

But first, a few words about Jamie Burke. Diagnosed with classical or 'severe' autism, Burke was included as a very young child in a regular classroom and taught to type on a keyboard using that much-maligned technique called facilitated communication. Eventually, he learned how to type independently, and at the age of thirteen began to speak what he pecked out, two fingers at a time, like an oilfield pumpjack or 'thirsty bird', as that contraption is sometimes called. An innovative occupational therapist used a range of movement therapies, including rhythmic drumming and a metronome, to mechanically coax a voice from Burke's fingertips.

At first, he could only speak while typing; then he could only read aloud something that he himself had typed, the memory of having produced the words with his fingers somehow guiding his mouth. Now he can read aloud another person's text and even speak without first typing what he wants to say. When he is nervous, however, he still prefers to prime his voice motorically, as he did when the two of us were interviewed on Iowa Public Radio as part of a show about the neurodiversity movement. It was the first live radio interview with a formerly non-speaking autist. At the beginning, the show's host explained to the audience that it would be hearing the sound of a keyboard before Burke spoke. And then, together we all talked about a different way of looking at autism.

I had been friends with Burke for a decade before we began our collaborative discussions, and I knew that, having recently graduated from Syracuse University, he missed what he called 'structured learning'. I also knew of his fascination with Native American culture. I remembered hearing a talk by him at an inclusion conference and being moved by the spirit of acceptance that he had found in this analogously oppressed and dehumanized group:

> I have noticed that in the study of the Native Americans, there seems to be a calling for … demonstrating the life-worth of all communities of people, whether they are the Nations of the Haudenosaunee, Iroquois, or Mohawk, or communities of people who … struggle with communication, motor dysfunction, or sensory regulation. [Everyone] deserves to be valued just for being the humans they are.

At the end of his talk, Burke argued for greater inclusion of classical autistics in higher education, delighting in the respect that his Native American professors had shown him as a learner. (He is only the seventh or eighth American with classical or 'severe' autism to earn a degree.)

> My joy on this journey wants to include so many others who should have the opportunity to be at a college or university, where worlds of odd literature and explanations of staying safe in sex and dating, and soulful revelations of an Ojibwa professor regarding the truth of the destruction of the Native Americans, are boldly open to all.

By asking Burke to participate in my project, I wanted to explore literary identification across not only neurological but also ethnic divides. I chose *Ceremony* because it staged a collision of Western and Native notions of health, and I was eager to see whether the latter had at all shaped his commitment to neurodiversity. I was especially eager to talk about his emergence into speech in the context of the novel's recuperation of ceremonial movement. But I had other, broader questions, too. Could a long-standing aversion to medicine in the field of disability studies be modulated by a Native notion of healing? Disability studies, after all, similarly foregrounds the relationship of the patient to her community, speaking of the 'social construction of disability'. What would a ceremony for autism look like?, I wondered. Or, more to the point, how might an autist design a ceremony that could heal our *collective* woes – from ecological destruction to the denigration of people who are different?

I knew going into our discussions that autistic readers tend to wonderfully scramble typical patterns of readerly identification. When I had discussed *Moby Dick* with Tito Mukhopadhyay, I was astonished by how much he identified with the book's other mammals – he especially loved Ishmael's descriptions of the very different ways that whales hear and see, linking these descriptions to his own neurodiverse sensing. When I had discussed *Adventures of Huckleberry Finn* with my son DJ, I was astonished as much by his ferocious identification with the runaway slave Jim as with the lonesome river itself. Its melancholy intelligence seemed akin, he said, to that of a non-speaking autist – both remain unrecognized. And when I had discussed *Do Androids Dream of Electric Sheep?* with Dora Raymaker, I was astonished by her love for the non-human replicants, especially the animal ones.

Jamie, in contrast, was more conventional. He naturally identified with a Native American protagonist and immediately empathized with his debilitating fear. (I say 'conventional' because a novel encourages the reader to get behind its hero, even as, in the case of *Ceremony*, it may tamper with the conceit of a strictly individual or human one.) 'I have journeyed in my own system of terror to a dimension of peace', Burke said in one of our Skype conversations. That terror was the recognition of 'being abnormal in the social world' and possessing a sensory system so differently integrated and intense as to produce constant anxiety. 'Fundamental to know others suffer and greatly emerge', he commented about Tayo. About native peoples generally, he said, 'I love their strength to develop the hope of living in liberation after being devastated in life.' The connection to the novel's protagonist was strengthened by his father's service in Vietnam. 'My father', he explained, 'effected love as a natural discourse to leave the memories behind.' In the novel, of course, Tayo also finds love and in the process begins to heal.

Burke's understanding of traumatic recovery strikes me as profoundly astute: it involves, in his words, 'not vitally destroying the emotion of fear but moving through the connection it brings to life'. When we discussed the difference between the white man's medical response to trauma and the Native American's ceremonial response, we lingered over the medicine man

Betonie's remark: 'In that hospital they don't bury the dead, they keep them in rooms and talk to them.'[3] In Burke's analysis, 'white people deem pills as returning to health, but Native Americans believe that the soul of the past within the physical must be healed first. The body will follow.' 'When the mind and the soul are in illness, the physical', he clarified, 'can be recuperated but not whole. It is as a living death.' The ceremonial response to trauma, which is at once communal and somatic, seeks to heal the failure of relation – to render even the end of life a kind of living dance.

Accordingly, to identify with Tayo was to identify with other entities as well. The land, or 'place that always was', if not a character per se, is certainly a presence, even a conscious being, in *Ceremony*, and Burke shared both the author's non-linear sense of time and her ecological politics. Just as Laguna-Pueblo territories have been contaminated by nuclear waste in the novel, so Haudenosaunee territories have been contaminated by commercial industry in Burke's hometown of Syracuse. (Lake Onadaga was, at one point, America's most polluted body of water.) The novel, to put it simply, doesn't have a setting: the Laguna people don't live *on* the land; rather, they live *in* and *through* it. Because Silko refuses all manner of dichotomies and instead insists on something like dynamic simultaneity, Burke's identification with Tayo wasn't finally a conventional gesture at all. Rather, by identifying with him, he was identifying with the Native dream of wholeness in which the alienated individual falls away and a place and a people, along with its vital history, stand proud.

While *Ceremony* obviously presents a story, it dramatizes space, not time, the customary engine of narrative. In fact, it does away with the latter altogether, or at least its unidirectional version, because for Native Americans, it has come to signify inexorable ruin. At one point in the novel, as Tayo searches for some cattle that white ranchers have stolen, he muses, 'The ride into the mountain had branched into all directions of time. … Rocky and I are walking across the ridge in moonlight. … This night is a single night; and there has never been any other.'[4] By treating time as space, Tayo begins to escape the iron logic of loss. He experiences the fullness of the past through something like radical stereopsis, or depth perception. The image of Rocky gestures at unseen dimensions, including the 'four worlds below', where the spirits of the dead reside, and the space of mythological figures such as Corn Mother and Thought-Woman.

When I inquired as to why Silko interrupts the story with Native legends and poems, Burke replied, 'Through the poems, memories and ceremonies are slowly returned to Tayo's mind. They are the voices of the past seeking connection to the present. They exist outside of the novel and must somehow be brought in.' 'Tayo', he remarked in a startling figure, 'is listening with more than ears.' And Burke, it seemed to me, was reading with more than eyes. He was using his considerable visuospatial prowess to illuminate the novel's spiritual geography. Betonie's counsel that 'the becoming must be cared for closely'[5] thus applies as much to the protagonist as to the reader who is asked to piece together the novel's own spatial 'becoming'.

A Native American professor at Syracuse had once described Burke's writing as 'dreamy'. There was indeed something to this description, but the *Brigadoon* quality often seemed more diagrammatic than pictorial – more math, you might say, than mist. Imagine a kind of divine geometry, with all manner of shapes floating in the air: the cathedral of life rendered as a set of three-dimensional (3-D) plans. An aficionado of complex symmetry, Burke attempted to translate his spatial perceptions, which are governed largely by the right cerebral hemisphere, into language, which is governed largely by the left, with all of the syntactical and usage challenges that this entailed. For example, he called the business of talking about how a book intersects with our lives 'dimensional truth'. Laguna chants were 'harmonies of elevation'. Human voices 'carry visual form'. Ceremonies 'can structure visual connection with the grounding of the past'. When he liked something I said, he would respond with 'highly structural'. There was no greater complement he could give than to appreciate an entity's essential organization.

In *The Autistic Brain*, Temple Grandin provides a clue as to what may be going on. Whereas in her groundbreaking work *Thinking in Pictures* she simply conceived of neurotypicals as verbal thinkers and autistic thinkers as visual ones, in this book she ruffles the binary in order to account for autistics who are verbal thinkers and autistics who are visual thinkers but in ways very different from herself. 'What I called a *picture thinker*', she reports, '[the new research] called an *object visualizer*, and what I called a *pattern thinker*, [it] called a *spatial visualizer*.'[6] Grandin excelled at the former but was surprisingly poor at the latter. Spatial visualizers can manipulate objects in their heads, moving them at will in a kind of organic calculus, as though they were determining the volume of a solid of revolution without equations. Grandin can see these objects in astonishing detail, but to map them she must move around the object herself, as though she were holding a video camera.

Neuroimaging has shown that there are two visual pathways in the brain: the ventral, which handles the appearance of objects, and the dorsal, which handles the position and relation of objects in space. As Grandin notes, 'People obviously use both pathways, relying more on one or the other depending on the task.'[7] But in autism, a particular path may be dominant, exceedingly so. In the 1920s, a German psychologist noticed that hallucinations – from drugs, migraines, flickering lights and other causes – took one or more geometric forms: tunnels, spirals, lattices or cobwebs. In the 1980s, a mathematician at Cal Tech hypothesized that 'because hallucinations moved independently of the eye, the source of the images was not on the retina but in the visual cortex itself'.[8] In other words, the hallucinations were a reflection of the fractal geometry that undergirds functional sight, a geometry that turns out to be ubiquitous in nature. When you hallucinate, you see seeing. It's quite possible that in autism, where bottom-up processing is the norm, spatial visualizers behave a bit like a computer, a natural one, synthesizing and manipulating visual information to discover the living essence of objects in space. They see an object, at least initially, the way that a dorsally driven visual cortex, and not the eye in service to the frontal lobes, would 'see' it.

In this way, Burke increasingly believed that the novel welcomes an autistic neurology – in particular, the talents of a spatial visualizer. 'How would Silko understand autism?' I asked, intrigued by the prospect that Burke's affinity for Native American culture was as much a matter of cognitive style as it was analogous marginalization and oppression. Although he certainly experienced the equivalent of 'the Native American world of challenges', something about his own sensing lined up with what he had encountered in his studies of Native American culture at Syracuse and in his reading of *Ceremony* with me. Pointing to the mute boy Shush who lives with Betonie and who is said to have been raised by bears – think of him as a Native twist on the feral child – Burke said that Silko would reject the prevailing stereotype of autistics as 'deeply tuned out'. She would view the condition not only as a potential shamanic gift, he maintained, but also as a mark of profound connection with nature. 'Perhaps Shush is autistic', he speculated, 'in that he sees beyond the purely physical.' To see 'beyond the physical' is to see less an entity itself than its position in a larger, spatial ecology.

In a conceit that reflected Silko's desire to preserve the endangered values and traditions of an oral culture in a print medium, Burke presented autism as a kind of literacy instructor. 'Autism plays ideas as a mother in the reading of books', he said, 'meaning that the mother, or earth, formulates connection in the strong sense of the Indian language.' I remember being perplexed by this statement but also having a sense of what he meant. Autism, according to Burke, is at once a mother instructing her children to read and Mother Nature herself, a source of interpretable, life-sustaining lessons. Literacy in this understanding becomes a way of being in the world as much as a phonological, orthographical, semantic, syntactical and morphological technique. The book of life, as reflected in the language of the Laguna people, emerges from the land broadly – and indeed deeply – construed. Like Silko, Burke refused to accept a strict dichotomy between reading and living or between thinking and seeing.

II

I have gestured at the cognitive aspect of my argument, but let me provide some more context. For the last decade, researchers have proposed that autistics possess a 'non-verbal, visually oriented processing style'[9] – what Temple Grandin famously called 'thinking in pictures'.[10] Whereas autistics rely more heavily on posterior sensory regions of the brain to think, neurotypicals rely more heavily on their frontal lobes; autistics also rely more heavily on the right cerebral hemisphere. Autistic brains appear to evince what scientists call long-distance underconnectivity and local overconnectivity. In other words, there seems to be less communication among discrete brain regions but tremendous communication within a particular region. When Grandin was tested using high definition fibre tracking (HDFT), her visual track was shown to be 400 per cent of a control subject's; in contrast, the 'say what you see' connection, which links vision with language, was 1 per cent of a control subject's.[11] She attributes her ability to draw complex, 3-D cattle-processing designs to the enhanced visual, and reduced linguistic, skills of autism.

Though neurotypicals almost never view their own neurology as in any way disabling, Grandin shows how it might be. Because they rely so much on their frontal lobes, neurotypicals, she believes, are 'abstractified in their sensory perceptions as well as their thoughts'.[12] Autistics 'don't see their ideas of things', she stresses. 'They see the actual things themselves.'[13] Grandin illustrates the difference between the two groups by pointing to what their brains look like in a scanner when performing an Embedded Figure Task. In that protocol, subjects must find a figure hidden within a complicated picture – autistics tend to find the figure much more quickly than neurotypicals. Using a remarkable poetic analogy, Grandin compares the visual centre of autistic brains during the test to 'a little bright cabin out in the snowy wilderness'.[14] 'Everything else is shut off, but [it] is turned on really bright',[15] she says. Neurotypical brains, by contrast, remind her of a lamp store: 'There's so much stuff turned on that the visual stuff gets obscured.'[16]

For some autistics, this sort of visual acuity manifests itself as a blizzard of detail. Initially, they see bits and pieces of things, micro-facets. They struggle to generate what scientists term 'central coherence'. Autist Tito Mukhopadhyay calls this phenomenon 'hyperfocusing'.[17] 'Hyperfocusing makes the world seem shattered', he explains in his most recent book – before offering an important qualification: 'I would say the world *is* shattered. Underlooking makes it seem whole.'[18] It is easy to understand how 'underlooking' would constitute an advantage in most contexts, but it does come at a cost. Our capacity for generalization depends on abstraction, which is to say, 'the act of considering something as a general quality or characteristic, apart from concrete realities'.[19] We let our categories – our homogenized, frontal lobe sense of the world – do much of our seeing, hearing, smelling and touching for us. As a result, particularity gets lost.

Even in language, the autistic predilection for the visual shows up. In a study from 2006, researchers compared how autistics and neurotypicals process high- and low-imagery sentences. For example, 'The number 8, rotated 90 degrees, looks like a pair of eyeglasses.'[20] For neurotypicals, a wealth of neuroimaging data has confirmed 'a greater involvement of sensory … areas in concrete word processing … and a more focal activation of … "language" areas for function words as well as abstract nouns'.[21] To comprehend the aforementioned high-imagery sentence, you must activate not only your traditional language centres but also your parietal lobes, which integrate sensory information and facilitate spatial awareness, and your occipital lobes, which enable both sight and the production of visual mental imagery. In the high-imagery setting, autistic and neurotypical brains looked most alike to the fMRI scanner, though the former activated sensory regions more than the latter.

In the low-imagery setting, however, where 'sentences … did not refer to spatial objects or relations'[22] – for instance, 'Addition, subtraction, and multiplication are all math skills' – autistics continued to rely on mental imagery.[23] They continued to read, that is, in 3D mode, though the sentences themselves did not present visuospatial images. Neurotypicals, in contrast, activated only their traditional language centres. Although scientists found no difference in the error rate or response time of the two groups, they interpreted autistic processing as inefficient. It never occurred to them that there might be different ways of skinning a higher order cognitive cat, or that diminished sensory thinking in neurotypicals could ever be a problem.

It is important to remember that autistic brains are as varied and as plastic as neurotypical ones. To be clear, I am talking about strong neurological predispositions – not immutable biology. In contrast to the persistent notion of autism as 'an intelligence scarcely touched by tradition or culture … strangely pure',[24] as Hans Asperger put it so many years ago, I have proposed the concept of neurocosmopolitanism, a kind of fluid and evolving exchange among different neurotypes. As I explain elsewhere,

> If cosmopolitanism is the idea of a trans-national community, the feeling of being respectfully at home everywhere in the world, then neurocosmopolitanism is the idea of a trans-neurocommunity, the feeling of being respectfully at home with all manner of neurologies. By 'neurocosmopolitan' I mean not just an openness to neurological difference but, rather, a denaturalization, even a dethronement, of privileged neurotypicality. In *Postcolonial Melancholia*, Paul Gilroy advocates 'methodic[ally] cultivati[ng] … a degree of estrangement from one's own culture and history' so as to forestall unfavorable judgments about the other. Traveling to autism, we must do the same. By 'neurocosmopolitan', I mean as well the effect on autistics of the journeying I mentioned – what might be termed neurohybridity or mobility.[25]

Burke's metaphorical understanding of autism as a maternal force of connection reflects precisely the mapping of acquired knowledge about Native American culture unto a neurology that, while clearly still autistic, long ago began to change as a result of acculturation. That Burke feels at home in Native American thought – 'I simply love the idea of the earth as valuable essence of life' – or that he has assimilated this group's history of oppression – 'I experience the Native American world of challenges' – makes plain the cosmopolitan inheritance. From the time he was a boy, he enjoyed reading about the different nations, and over the years, he memorized all manner of Native American creation stories, including a delightful one called 'The First Strawberry' that he recited to me over Skype.

Of course the evolving cosmopolitan inheritance depended on evolving neurological adjustments. Just as Grandin learned to express her visuospatial intelligence linguistically, so too did Burke, though he acknowledges that the translation from the visual to the verbal continues to be frustrating. Unlike Grandin, however, who claims not to 'get' literature, Burke loves it. 'Literature is very vital to my knowledge', he explained. Again and again in our conversations, he would tell me, 'Dearly pleased to talk', and at one point he asked, 'How do kids search in their hearts when they cannot read these books? So lovely accessing thoughts about the true understanding we critically create.'

When Burke reported that he 'really enjoys the strong visual emotions that Silko extends to readers' or references her 'words of visual courage', he could be said to confirm what cognitive scholars already know: that literature's concrete diction elicits mental imagery in the minds of readers. As Alan Richardson argues, leaning on the work of Elaine Scarry, 'Readers produce mental imagery "under the instruction" of the writer.'[26] But when Burke says, 'I enhance the process of interpreting the patterns of language in order to demonstrate the progress of movement in the visual' or 'I work in the beauty of the production of image evolving in my world of interpretation', he points to something conspicuously autistic: the kind of videographic imagination that Grandin and others have talked about.[27] 'My creation of visual mind is something I am passionate about', he emphasized. Here, literature becomes more like 3-D film. And it may be, as I have come to believe, that in Silko – and in Native American culture generally – Burke has discovered a kind of cognitive hospitality.

As previously noted, one consequence of significant local connectivity and a reliance on posterior sensory regions to think is what scientists term 'weak central coherence': a preference for details over categories and the concrete over the abstract. Before thinking 'tree', for example, Burke takes in 'the molecular structure of the good freedom of the natural world'. 'Details are my friends', he explains. Like a Derridean of the visual, he celebrates each tree's irreducible particularity, noting, 'The wood of the forest of trees perhaps engages the brain to connect with the work of differences.' The category 'tree' and the even bigger category 'forest' emerge slowly. 'I believe it's seeing the tree in the process of creation', he remarked. To quote Betonie again, 'The becoming must be cared for closely.' With this kind of seeing, the world doesn't exist in advance as something to be used or mastered.

In a very different context, Ian Watt writes of 'delayed decoding'.[28] Such decoding, it turns out, facilitates extraordinary pattern detection in autism. In fact, the ability to think beneath the category is crucial for seeing how ostensibly discrete things might connect or how ostensibly linked things might connect differently. Over the course of our discussions, Burke revealed his considerable ability to 'sequence the pattern'; 'the pattern is what I see in the first look', he said. 'I like following it. Truly I am summoning the answers and revealing what the information connects.' That sounds a lot like motif tracing. Once more, I took note of how he had translated a non-conceptual autistic propensity into a conceptual neurotypical one – or, phrased more elegantly, in literature he had located a meeting point for the two processing styles. 'Books are patterning on thoughts', he said confidently.

Ceremony, of course, makes great use of patterns – and not just in the way that a skilled author does. Rather, the ritual that restores Tayo to health literally requires improved pattern detection. Tayo is said to be 'involved with other things [than words]: memories and shifting sounds heard in the night, diamond patterns, black on white; the energy of the designs spiralled deep, then protruded suddenly into three-dimensional summits, their depth and height dizzy and shifting with the eye'.[29] The woman with whom he makes love wears a blanket. Tayo 'did not miss the designs woven across the blanket in four colours: patterns of storm clouds in white and grey; black lightning scattered through brown wind'.[30] When I asked Burke about this passage, he replied, 'The pattern is of the universe and through her he will receive the heavens of the brain.' To be certain that I hadn't missed the import of this insight (or his miraculous phrasing), he added, 'I mean that this pattern will open the thought to remembering what Betonie has spoken of and seen as vision.'

In my copy of *Ceremony*, an actual picture of 'the pattern of stars the old man drew on the ground that night' appears.[31] 'Why would a novel, which is an art form made of words, include a drawing of a constellation right in the middle of it?' I asked. 'It is important to reveal the vital process of emotion, especially when those stars will passionately interpret a pattern of return. To me the drawing looked simply as a thought of pure energy', he replied. How interesting: Burke seems to put his finger on Silko's need at this moment in the novel for something like an autistic, which is to say visuospatial, intelligence. The patterning of words alone, she hints, is inadequate; the writer's tiny graphic signifiers can't quite depict the volumetric depth or annulated shape of prophecy.

Neurobiological accounts of trauma, interestingly enough, suggest an analogous over-reliance on the brain's posterior sensory regions and right-hemispheric limbic structures. What matters to such an intelligence and what seems more likely to initiate healing in trauma is not language alienated from the body – the so-called talking cure – or language alienated from the environment, but embodied, communal activities such as yoga and dance that holistically incorporate language. Traumatic images become healing ones, Silko suggests in a Native American context, through ceremonial movement. But new patterns are paramount. They bring new thoughts, new possibilities. A multiracial author thus insists on a multimedia form. The future depends, as Betonie understood, on adapting the old ways, including the transformation of oral storytelling into printed narrative. Burke called this sort of 'changing with the present' 'intelligent continuation', and the phrase can be applied as much to Tayo's 'journeying into the place of memory' as to his own journeying into the place of typing and speech.

III

For as long as I had known Burke, I had marvelled at his ability to type independently, which is rare in classical autism, and to speak aloud what he had typed, which is even rarer. He had distinguished himself in these (and other) respects, but how exactly had he done so?

Over the last ten years, the scientific literature has confirmed what autistics, parents and clinicians have suspected for some time: 'ASD is associated with significant and widespread alterations in motor performance',[32] as a 2010 meta-analysis concluded. The study went so far as to propose that motor differences constitute a 'core element' of autism and that 'interventions aimed at improving … motor coordination (i.e. gait and balance, arm functions and movement planning)'[33] should be developed.

This perspective on autism emerged when the stranglehold of mechanistic thinking about the brain began to relax. Scientists abandoned modular notions of brain functioning – this controls that, etc. – in favour of complex networks that connect otherwise distinct regions in intricately patterned ways. Even the oldest, most primitive, 'reptilian' regions, such as the basal ganglia and cerebellum, which had been thought to contribute narrowly to motor function, were implicated in higher-order thought. (Put crudely, the basal ganglia enable voluntary motor actions whereas the cerebellum regulates coordination and timing.) In fact, Gerald Edelman coined the phrase 'basal syntax'[34] to emphasize the fundamental relationship between movement and language.

Speaking, to be sure, is one of the most complicated motoric things that humans do – speaking as the act of making discernible sounds but also the act of stringing such sounds together in a fluently sequential way. Language, argued Marcel Kinsbourne, is an 'elaboration, extension and abstraction of sensorimotor function'.[35] It evolved from 'utterances that were coincident with and driven by the same rhythm as the movement in question'.[36] Or as Iain McGilchrist put it more recently, 'The deep structure of syntax is founded on the fixed sequences of limb movement in running creatures.'[37] These researchers point to the fully integrated and embodied nature of human cognition: it is neither modular in its operation nor cut off from the flesh. Indeed, the brain depends on a body – a very active body – to think.

Listen to the editors of a groundbreaking book on movement differences in autism. I quote them at length because they effectively depict what typical maturation accomplishes and, in turn, help us to see the hidden challenges that autistics, especially classical autistics, face:

> When the sensations from our ever changing physical motions emerge as a stable percept that we can reliably predict, we begin to anticipate the sensory consequences of our impending actions with remarkable certainty. ... We begin to understand cause and effect in the physical world that we interact with, a world that includes others in social motion as well. The understanding of our own actions through their sensations helps us scaffold social cognition by establishing first the sense of self as an anchor, and then the sense of others and their relative motions. ... It is through the sensations of our own movements and through those of the movements of others as we sense them kinesthetically and visually that we learn to mentally navigate actions, to acquire a sense of agency and autonomy, and to eventually imagine, in a disembodied way, what it would be like to perform a physical action without actually having to do it.[38]

If we remember the pithy formulation of systems scientists Esther Thelen and Linda Smith – that 'to move is to perceive, and to perceive is to move'[39] – then we can begin to fathom the crucial importance of this dynamic feedback loop.

Analyzing the movements of typical toddlers, Elizabeth Torres discovered that three-year-olds 'do not yet have statistical predictability of temporal features of their limb movements'.[40] It's not only that they lack the control and motor fluency of four-year-olds, but also that their movements are still conspicuously random: there's too much noise, and too little signal, as they respond with their bodies to a moving and endlessly variable world. Even when they attempt to produce the same movement, the movement is different – that's the point. The organism must be able to adapt spontaneously to the demands of the present, which in all of its swirling specificity only vaguely resembles the moment just before it. These toddlers haven't yet assimilated what Torres and the philosopher Maria Brincker call 'sensorimotor priors':[41] a sturdy, 'probabilistic expectation about the variability itself'.[42] In this key respect, classical autistics operate motorically like typical three-year-olds.

Brincker views '"sensorimotor priors" ... as a kind of predictable probabilistic body, an abstract body that we can "bring into" counterfactual scenarios and thus use to navigate and make decisions in spaces we do not stand in current embodied relations to'.[43] In contrast, classical autistics must 'rely on their "here & now" body and world sensation'.[44] They are, we might say, beautifully stuck in the present, unable to leverage the past to create a motorically feasible, if much more homogenous, future. They are living quite literally *in the moment* – again and again and again. I am unaware of anyone who has proposed a link between 'weak central coherence' – the business of sensing so much detail as to make forming conceptual generalizations difficult – and a lack of 'sensorimotor priors'. In both cases, as probabilistic expectation offers little guidance, perception and movement stall: autistics remain immured in mesmerizing intensity, not propelled by the customary procedures of temporal abstraction.

For this reason, researcher Pat Amos argues that autism should be considered a temporospatial processing disorder (TSPD) akin to Parkinson's syndrome or certain traumatic brain injuries. She writes,

> It is often observed that the sense of time appears to work differently for many people with autism. That would not be surprising, given the increasing evidence that autism involves challenges to neural connectivity and different ways of assembling experiences. What has to be connected in order to accurately sense time is something even more complicated than, for example, connecting speech sounds with facial movements. Time is not a mode or channel of sensory experience, but an amodal property that unites the perceptions of different senses. We sense time through comparisons of our experiences, bootstrapping from events of known duration to establish expectations about other events; repeated events in the world and familiar rhythms of the body come to stand for intervals of time, with which new events can be compared.[45]

Amos concludes, 'If these embodied experiences are unreliable for people on the autism spectrum, it might make sense that the comparison process also would prove challenging, resulting in a panicked feeling of being adrift in a sea of time.'[46]

Enter the drum and metronome. We have known for some time that audible rhythm activates a person's motor systems, but there is also 'evidence of rapid motor synchronization to an external rhythmic cue in persons with and without neurological disability'.[47] As anyone who has ever attended a dance or tapped their fingers to a song knows, a particular beat can physiologically commandeer our bodies, prompting us to move in concert with it. Scientists call this phenomenon 'entrainment', and it has far-reaching implications for rehabilitative interventions. Research has demonstrated that auditory rhythmic cueing offers a 'temporal template for [the] organization of motor output'.[48] It affects both 'the timing of movement and the total movement pattern'[49] by 'add[ing] stability in motor control immediately (within two or three stimuli) rather than through a gradual learning process'.[50] By 'influence[ing] motor anticipation ... the [listener's] response pattern gradually becom[es] automatized'.[51]

Such cueing can compensate for damage to the basal ganglia or cerebellum, and for the problem of underconnectivity, and it can perhaps even encourage cortical plasticity. After all, the cerebellum has been shown to aid 'in computing the temporal parameters of incoming sensory stimuli and outgoing movements as well as in novel, temporally precise motor movements'.[52] It is the organic 'comparator' of which Amos speaks. It 'predicts the timing of an upcoming movement, utilizes sensory feedback from the current movement, compares ongoing performance to an internal model, and then adapts responses such as force and/or trajectory'.[53] Like a kind of motorized auditory wheelchair, rhythmic cueing can move the struggling autist along. It can do much of the work of 'sensorimotor priors'.

Neurological drumming and a metronome helped Jamie to type independently, to tie his shoes, and eventually to speak. 'So many things were hard for me to learn', he reported. About that second milestone, which he had achieved at the age of fifteen, he said, 'My brain moved into hiding the reason for not being able to do it. ... Like saying letters, mostly there was no pattern to follow in my brain for tying my shoelaces. After much practice ... it seemed a pattern moved into my brain, giving directions to my hands. I think my music therapy gave help with this.' (In a published interview with me, another autist, Tito Mukhopadhyay, all but says that William Blake, the eighteenth-century British poet, taught him how to tie his shoes.[54] The rhythmic cueing of iambic tetrameter worked like a drum or metronome.[55] Wrapping the beat, in his words, around his fingers, he managed to coax them to execute the necessary movements.) By 'pattern', Burke means something like a path or continuum, a kind of impetus that helps to string a series of motor actions together. His body needed the conviction of a moving sidewalk at the airport or a bowling ball that's kept out of the gutter by bumpers – momentum and direction driving intentionality forward and instilling confidence. According to researchers, 'Building an anticipatory means of motor control in autism might ... facilitate the development of internal models for motor planning.'[56] This seems to be what happened with Burke.

When he appeared on the aforementioned radio show about the neurodiversity movement, the host began by asking him why he needed to type his answers before speaking them. As he hunted and pecked in the background, I tried to establish a context for his answer, explaining the problem of poor sensory integration in autism and noting the way that Burke's communication device joined the visual and the auditory in real time. 'It's seeing and hearing together',[57] he had once said to some education professors. When he typed, the word would dutifully emerge on the screen and then just as dutifully be voiced by the mechanical synthesizer. Both print font and voice remained stable.

Whereas typical children move from speech to literacy by connecting the sounds they produce with ease to the graphic marks on a page, Jamie moved in the opposite direction by connecting the graphic marks on his Litewriter to the sounds coming out of the synthesizer. The Litewriter served as prompt and model; the metronome, as external motor planning device. With his eyes, in effect, being asked to move his tongue, and his ears, in effect, being asked to move his limbs, he jerry rigged a voice. Aggressive auditory-visual and auditory-motor coupling overwhelmed the considerable obstacles to speech. What was most intriguing to me (and what obviously couldn't be explored on the radio) was that motor memory in one domain (typing) could facilitate motor performance in another (speech). On a basic level, that made sense: movement has to be translatable from one form to another – in this case, from arm and hand movements to tongue and voice-box movements. But how could the *memory* of the former aide the performance of the latter?

A recent study revealed that listening to unfamiliar music activates the listener's motor systems.[58] Even more interesting, the interstices between songs on a *familiar* CD do the same.[59] The researchers hypothesized that motor areas support sequential mastery and, in the process, provide a memory boost. This is why we all know which song is coming next on our favourite CD. Think of it as silent rhythmic cueing. It is as if our motor systems create an essential continuum by constantly anticipating – we might even say, by constantly remembering – the future. They listen, in Jamie's phrase, 'with more than ears'. They listen when technically there is nothing to listen to and, in so doing, provide 'intelligent continuation'. Perhaps Jamie's tongue and voice box moved with more than arms. Perhaps, in perfect stillness, they remembered how to talk.

Exercise guru Carol Welch once commented, 'Movement is a medicine for creating change in a person's physical, emotional, and mental states.' It is also a way of uniting people. A study from just a few months ago pointed to yet another benefit of auditory rhythmic cueing. It confirmed that, 'having listened to a rhythmic beat, individuals' movements become more aligned to the frequency of that beat'[60] and, even more important, that 'when alignment to the rhythmic stimulus occurs in two interacting individuals, manifesting as increased motor coupling, their interpersonal attitudes toward one another become more positive'.[61] Here, we have the very basis of Native American community: the social bonding through ritual that neurologically knits people together.

In this context, prophecy is less an actual prediction than a holistic sense of how the body moves in the world. 'There were transitions that had to be made in order to become whole again',[62] Betonie explains. We might think of these transitions as akin to the gaps or interstices in a familiar CD: remembered sound in a rhythmic void. Call what is required to navigate them *spiritual priors*. By 'spiritual priors' I mean, to bend the words of Maria Brincker, something like a predictable, probabilistic spirit, a spirit that can be brought into counterfactual scenarios, and thus be used to make decisions in spaces that we do not stand in current spiritual relation to. A spirit, in short, that might be able to navigate the brutal hegemony of Western values.

And yet, the 'here and now' spirit of world sensation must not be renounced. Tayo needs a sense of time that is at once productively linear *and* spatial. In touch with the spirit world, the latter rejects the so-called ruin of Native history; discovering the living essence of the past in space, it sees, in Burke's language, 'dimensional truth', 'harmonies of elevation'. The former insists on pushing pragmatically forward; it knows that the past must adapt if it is to be useful. The future will not be worth living, however, if it cannot be remembered motorically.

A line from one of the poem-like chants that interrupt the novel proclaims, 'I am walking back to belonging',[63] and Tayo himself is described as 'want[ing] to walk until he recognized himself again'.[64] At the end of the novel, as he moves ceremonially through the landscape with the woman who has drawn him out of traumatic remembrance, we are told, 'Every step formed another word.'[65] Movement is language, a fully embodied and embedded narrative of healing. There is simply no point in talking about Native recovery apart from the body or place of belonging. 'The ear for the story and the eye for the patterns were theirs',[66] the novel declares. 'The feeling was theirs: we came out of the land and we are hers.'[67]

As we read *Ceremony* together, Burke saw in Tayo's story his own story of coming to life through speech. 'The ability to speak with voice curiously created many new patterns of access', he noted. 'Before I had voice, I couldn't write because the letters were wavy.' 'The shapes', he continued, 'were wading in waves. I could absolutely see the language, but when my voice moved forward, it formulated the form differently.' 'Now', he reported, 'I am simply reading text when I see the words.' Learning to speak also changed how Burke retrieved language, and it gave his own language feeling. 'When I lived in silence there wasn't emotion', he said, adding, 'Keyboards carry no energy' and 'Typing cannot return the emotion.' Burke is alluding, of course, to 'emotional prosody', that crucial quality of the spoken word. Summing up his neuroplastic, sensorimotor journey and calling out experts who presume not only mental, but also social, incompetence in autism, he asserted, 'I vitally correct the movement of much truth in the challenge of speaking.'

The account of autism in the *Diagnostic and Statistical Manual of Mental Disorders* cannot make sense of Burke's journey because it begins and ends in the narrowest sense of pathology. Like the doctors in Tayo's hospital, it talks *at* autism in a modular way. Rendering him and other autistics lamentably static, it cannot conceive of what movement therapies might do; this account, you might say, is lamentably static. It will not move, and in refusing to move, it cannot perceive autistic potential and, indeed, autistic strengths. Like Tayo, Burke had to walk – or, rather, to type and drum – his way back to belonging. And I, his friend and teacher, had to believe in different ways of thinking in the world and of reading literature.

It is more than a bit ironic that Western neuroscience has begun to embrace a notion of the integrated and holistic body that is similar to ancient Native notions – without, of course, the spiritual dimension, which Burke relishes. The current concepts of embodied, embedded and extended cognition depict human beings in a world of tangible affordances – one might even say, of undeclared assistive technologies. Disability reveals the arrogant fiction of the self-reliant individual by emphasizing the complex accommodative ecologies that make life possible for all of us.[68] In this way, an idea of medicine as facilitating relationship, not correcting lamentable physiological flaws, is completely compatible with the concept of neurodiversity. Understanding his own progress as a mover in physical, mental and spiritual terms, Burke maintained, 'We are just people on the transition, Ralph.' 'Harmony for me', he said, 'is all structural realities and great worlds connecting with people and dimensions to create peace and calm and engagement of hearts and minds, which then move in the dear success of lovely life.'

Notes

1 See Ralph James Savarese, 'What Some Autistics Can Teach Us about Poetry: A Neurocosmopolitan Approach', in *The Oxford Handbook of Cognitive Literary Studies,* ed. Lisa Zunshine (Oxford: Oxford University Press, 2015), pp. 393–414.

2 Thomas Irmer, 'An Interview with Leslie Marmon Silko', *The Write Stuff,* 1995. http://www.altx.com/interviews/silko.html [accessed 31 December 2016].

3 Leslie Marmon Silko, *Ceremony* (New York: Penguin, 2007), p. 114.

4 Ibid., p. 179.

5 Ibid., p. 120.

6 Temple Grandin and Richard Panek, *The Autistic Brain: Thinking Across the Spectrum* (Boston: Houghton Mifflin, 2013), p. 155.

7 Ibid., p. 156.

8 Ibid., p. 153.

9 Hideya Koshino, P. Carpenter, N. Minshew, V. L. Cherkassky, T. A. Keller, and M. Just, 'Functional Connectivity in an fMRI Working Memory Task in High-functioning Autism', *NeuroImage* 24 (2005), pp. 818–19.

10 Temple Grandin, *Thinking in Pictures* (New York: Vintage, 1996).

11 Grandin and Panek, *The Autistic Brain*, pp. 44–5.

12 Temple Grandin and Catherine Johnson, *Animals in Translation: Using the Mysteries of Autism To Decode Animal Behavior* (New York: Mariner Books, 2006), p. 30.

13 Ibid.

14 Quoted in Verlyn Klinkenborg, 'What Do Animals Think?' *Discover Magazine* (May 2005). http://discovermagazine.com/2005/may/what-do-animals-think [accessed 15 October 2015].

15 Ibid.

16 Ibid.

17 Tito Rajarshi Mukhopadhyay, *Plankton Dreams: What I Learned in Special Ed* (London: Open Humanities Press, 2015), p. 37.

18 Ibid.

19 Infoplease. http://dictionary.infoplease.com/abstraction [accessed 15 October 2015].

20 Rajesh Kana, T. A. Keller, V. L. Cherkassky, N. Minshew, and M. Just, 'Sentence Comprehension in Autism: Thinking in Pictures with Decreased Functional Connectivity', *Brain* 129 (2006), p. 2484.

21 Frida Martensson, M. Roll, P. Apt, and M. Horne, 'Modeling the Meaning of Words: Neural Correlates of Abstract and Concrete Noun Processing', *ACTA Neurobiologiae Experimentalis* 71 (2011), p. 456.

22 Kana et al., 'Sentence Comprehension in Autism', p. 2887.

23 Ibid., p. 2990.

24 Quoted in Ralph James Savarese, 'Organic Hesitancy: On Speechlessness in *Billy Budd*', in *Secret Sharers: Melville, Conrad, and Narratives of the Real*, eds Paweł Jędrzejko and Milton M. Reigelman (Zabrze: MStudio, 2011), p. 307.

25 Ralph James Savarese and Lisa Zunshine, 'The Critic as Neurocosmopolite: What Cognitive Approaches to Literature Can Learn from Disability Studies', *Narrative* 22:1 (2015), p. 20.

26 Alan Richardson, 'Imagination: Literary and Cognitive Intersections', in *The Oxford Handbook of Cognitive Literary Studies*, ed. Lisa Zunshine (Oxford: Oxford University Press, 2015), p. 227.

27 Temple Grandin's *Thinking in Pictures* begins like this: 'I think in pictures. Words are like a second language to me. I translate both spoken and written words into full-color movies, complete with sound, which run like a VCR tape in my head. When somebody speaks to me, his words are instantly translated into pictures. Language-based thinkers often find this phenomenon difficult to understand, but in my job as an equipment designer for the livestock industry, visual thinking is a tremendous advantage.' p. 19.

28 Quoted in Melba Cuddy-Keane, 'Narration, Navigation, and Non-conscious Thought: Neuroscientific and Literary Approaches to the Thinking Body', *University of Toronto Quarterly* 79:2 (2010), p. 690.

29 Silko, *Ceremony*, p. 212.

30 Ibid., p. 165.

31 Ibid., p. 166.

32 Quoted in Ralph James Savarese, 'Moving the Field: The Sensorimotor Perspective on Autism', *Frontiers in Integrative Neuroscience* 7:6 (2013). http://journal.frontiersin.org/article/10.3389/fnint.2013.00006/full [accessed 01 February 2017].

33 Ibid.

34 Gerald Edelman, *Second Nature: Brain Science and Human Nature* (New Haven: Yale University Press, 2007), p. 61.

35 Quoted in Iain McGilchrist, *The Master and His Emissary: The Divided Brain and the Making of the Western World* (New Haven: Yale University Press, 2012), p. 11.

36 Ibid.

37 Ibid., p. 119.

38 Elizabeth Torres and Anne Donnellan, 'Introduction', in *Autism: The Movement Perspective*, eds Elizabeth Torres and Anne Donnellan (eBook: Frontiers in Integrative Neuroscience, 2015), p. 2. http://journal.frontiersin.org/researchtopic/801/autism-the-movement-perspective [accessed 15 October 2015].

39 Quoted in Pat Amos, 'Rhythm and Timing in Autism', in *Autism: The Movement Perspective*, eds Elizabeth Torres and Anne Donnellan (eBook: Frontiers in Integrative Neuroscience, 2015), p. 141. http://journal.frontiersin.org/researchtopic/801/autism-the-movement-perspective [accessed 15 October 2015].

40 Quoted in Maria Brincker, 'Navigating Beyond "Here & Now" Affordances – on Sensorimotor Maturation and "False Belief" Performance', *Frontiers in Psychology* 5 (2014). http://www.ncbi.nlm.nih.gov/pmc/articles/PMC4266020 [accessed 01 February 2017].

41 Maria Brincker and Elizabeth Torres, 'Noise from the Periphery of Autism', in *Autism: The Movement Perspective*, eds Elizabeth Torres and Anne Donnellan (eBook: Frontiers in Integrative Neuroscience, 2015), 175. http://journal.frontiersin.org/researchtopic/801/autism-the-movement-perspective [accessed 15 October 2015].

42 Ibid.

43 Brincker, 'Navigating Beyond'.

44 Ibid.

45 Amos, 'Rhythm and Timing in Autism'.

46 Ibid.

47 Michael W. Hardy and A. Blythe Lagasse, 'Rhythm, Movement and Autism: Using Rhythmic Rehabilitation Research as a Model for Autism', in *Autism: The Movement Perspective*, eds Elizabeth Torres and Anne Donnellan (eBook: Frontiers in Integrative Neuroscience, 2015), p. 90. http://journal.frontiersin.org/researchtopic/801/autism-the-movement-perspective [accessed 15 October 2015].

48 Ibid., p. 90.

49 Ibid., p. 93.

50 Ibid., p. 90.

51 Ibid., p. 93.

52 Ibid., p. 90.

53 Ibid., p. 92.

54 Ralph James Savarese, 'More Than a Thing to Ignore: An Interview with Tito Mukhopadhyay', *Disability Studies Quarterly* 30:1 (2010). http://dsq-sds.org/article/view/1056/1235 [accessed 15 October 2015].

55 Research has confirmed that metrical poetry specifically activates the listener's motor systems. See Andre Aleman and Mascha van't Wout, 'Subvocalization in Auditory-verbal Imagery: Just a Form of Motor Imagery?' *Cognitive Process* 5 (2004), pp. 228–31.

56 Hardy and Lagasse, 'Rhythm, Movement and Autism', p. 93.

57 Alicia Broderick and Kristi Kasa-Hendrickson, '"Say Just One Word at First": The Emergence of Reliable Speech in a Student Labeled with Autism', *Journal of the Association for Persons with Severe Handicaps* 26:1 (2001), p. 21.

58 Josef Rauschecker, B. Green, J. Salmi, I. Jaakselainen, and M. Sams, 'Differentially Recruited Brain Areas for Familiar and Unfamiliar Segments of a Progressively Presented Musical Sequence', *Presentation, Neuroscience 2012 Conference* (New Orleans, LA).

59 Ibid.

60 Martin Lang, D. J. Shaw, P. Reddish, S. Wallot, P. Mitkidis, and D. Xygalatas, 'Lost in the Rhythm: Effects of Rhythm on Subsequent Interpersonal Coordination', *Cognitive Science*, doi: 10.1111/cogs.12302 (2015), p. 11.

61 Ibid.

62 Silko, *Ceremony*, p. 57.

63 Ibid., p. 133.

64 Ibid., p. 143.

65 Ibid., p. 218.

66 Ibid., p. 236.

67 Ibid.

68 Ralph James Savarese, 'Cognition', in *Keywords for Disability Studies*, eds Rachel Adams, Benjamin Reiss and David Serlin (New York: New York University Press, 2015), pp. 40–2.

References

Aleman, A., and M. van't Wout, 'Subvocalization in Auditory-verbal Imagery: Just a Form of Motor Imagery? *Cognitive Process* 5 (2004), pp. 228–31.

Amos, P., 'Rhythm and Timing in Autism', in E. Torres and A. Donnellan (eds), *Autism: The Movement Perspective*, eBook: Frontiers in Integrative Neuroscience, 2015. http://journal.frontiersin.org/researchtopic/801/autism-the-movement-perspective [accessed 15 October 2015].

Brincker, M., 'Navigating Beyond "Here & Now" Affordances – on Sensorimotor Maturation and "False Belief" Performance', *Frontiers in Psychology* 5 (2014). http://www.ncbi.nlm.nih.gov/pmc/articles/PMC4266020 [accessed 15 October 2016].

Brincker, M. and E. Torres, 'Noise from the Periphery of Autism', in E. Torres and A. Donnellan (eds), *Autism: The Movement Perspective*, eBook: Frontiers in Integrative Neuroscience, 2015. http://journal.frontiersin.org/researchtopic/801/autism-the-movement-perspective [accessed 15 October 2015].

Broderick, A. and K. Kasa-Hendrickson, 'Say Just One Word at First': The Emergence of Reliable Speech in a Student Labeled with Autism', *Journal of the Association for Persons with Severe Handicaps* 26:1 (2001), p. 21.

Cuddy-Keane, M., 'Narration, Navigation, and Non-conscious Thought: Neuroscientific and Literary Approaches to the Thinking Body', *University of Toronto Quarterly* 79:2 (2010), pp. 680–701.

Dick, P., *Do Androids Dream of Electric Sheep?* New York: Del Rey Books, 1996.

Edelman, G., *Second Nature: Brain Science and Human Nature*, New Haven: Yale University Press, 2007.

Gilroy, P., *Postcolonial Melancholia*, New York: Columbia University Press, 2006.

Grandin, T., *Thinking in Pictures*, New York: Vintage, 1996.

Grandin, T. and C. Johnson, *Animals in Translation: Using the Mysteries of Autism to Decode Animal Behavior*, New York: Mariner, 2006.

Grandin, T. and R. Panek, *The Autistic Brain*, New York: Mariner Books, 2014.

Hardy, M. W. and A. B. Lagasse, 'Rhythm, Movement and Autism: Using Rhythmic Rehabilitation Research as a Model for Autism', in E. Torres and A. Donnellan (eds), *Autism: The Movement Perspective*, eBook: Frontiers in Integrative Neuroscience, 2015. http://journal.frontiersin.org/researchtopic/801/autism-the-movement-perspective [accessed 15 October 2015].

Infoplease. http://dictionary.infoplease.com/abstraction [accessed 15 October 2015].

Irmer, T., 'An Interview with Leslie Marmon Silko', *The Write Stuff*, 1995. http://www.altx.com/interviews/silko.html [accessed 01 February 2017].

Kana, R. K., Keller, T. A., Cherkassky, V. L., Just, M. and N. Minshew, 'Sentence Comprehension in Autism: Thinking in Pictures with Decreased Functional Connectivity', *Brain* 129 (2006), pp. 2484–93.

Kieffer B., 'Autism as Neurodiversity', *River to River*, Iowa Public Radio, 2012. http://news.iowapublicradio.org/post/autism-diversity [accessed 15 October 2015].

Klinkenborg, V., 'What Do Animals Think?' *Discover Magazine*, May 2005. http://discovermagazine.com/2005/may/what-do-animals-think [accessed 15 October 2015].

Koshino, H., Carpenter, P. A., Minshew, N. J., Cherkassky, V. L., Keller, T. A. and M. A. Just, 'Functional Connectivity in an fMRI Working Memory Task in High-Functioning Autism', *NeuroImage* 24 (2005) pp. 810–21.

Lang, M. et al., 'Lost in the Rhythm: Effects of Rhythm on Subsequent Interpersonal Coordination', *Cognitive Science* 40:7 (2015), doi: 10.1111/cogs.12302.

McGilchrist, I., *The Master and His Emissary: The Divided Brain and the Making of the Western World*, New Haven: Yale University Press, 2012.

Melville, H., *Moby Dick*, New York: Longman, 2006.

Mukhopadhyay, T., *Plankton Dreams: What I Learned in Special Ed*, London: Open Humanities Press, 2015.

Rauschecker, J. et al., 'Differentially Recruited Brain Areas for Familiar and Unfamiliar Segments of a Progressively Presented Musical Sequence', *Presentation, Neuroscience 2012 Conference*, 2012.

Richardson, A., 'Imagination: Literary and Cognitive Intersections', in L. Zunshine (ed.), *The Oxford Handbook of Cognitive Literary Studies*, Oxford: Oxford University Press, 2015 pp. 225–45.

Sacks, O., *An Anthropologist On Mars: Seven Paradoxical Tales*, New York: Vintage, 1996.

Savarese, R. J., 'More Than a Thing to Ignore: An Interview with Tito Mukhopadhyay', *Disability Studies Quarterly* 30:1 (2010). http://dsq-sds.org/article/view/1056/1235 [accessed 15 October 2015].

Savarese, R. J., 'Organic Hesitancy: On Speechlessness in *Billy Budd*', in Paweł Jędrzejko and Milton M. Reigelman (eds), *Secret Sharers: Melville, Conrad, and Narratives of the Real*, Zabrze: MStudio, 2011.

Savarese, R. J., 'Moving the Field: The Sensorimotor Perspective on Autism', *Frontiers in Integrative Neuroscience* 7:6 (2013). http://journal.frontiersin.org/article/10.3389/fnint.2013.00006/full [accessed 15 October 2015].

Savarese, R. J., 'What Some Autistics Can Teach Us about Poetry: A Neurocosmopolitan Approach', in L. Zunshine (ed.), *The Oxford Handbook of Cognitive Literary Studies*, Oxford: Oxford University Press, 2015.

Savarese, R. J. and Zunshine, L., 'The Critic as Neurocosmopolite: What Cognitive Approaches to Literature Can Learn from Disability Studies', *Narrative* 22:1 (2015).

Silko, L. M., *Ceremony*, New York: Penguin, 2007.

Torres, E. and A. Donnellan, *Autism: The Movement Perspective*, eBook: Frontiers in Integrative Neuroscience, 2015. http://journal.frontiersin.org/researchtopic/801/autism-the-movement-perspective [accessed 15 October 2015].

13

The philosophical role of illness

Havi Carel

For what is it to be ill? Is it that you are near the severance of the soul and the body?

– EPICTETUS, *DISCOURSES*.[1]

Introduction

This paper examines the philosophical role of serious, chronic or life-threatening illness.[2] Illness has been a theme in the history of philosophy, in particular in relation to its moral, existential and spiritual value. For example, Epictetus, Seneca, Marcus Aurelius, Boethius and Descartes write about illness and its contribution to the modes and themes of philosophizing, as well as the relationship between health and virtue, and health's contribution to the good life.[3] We find Descartes commenting in his *Discourse on Method*: 'For even the mind depends so much on the temperament and disposition of the bodily organs that if it is possible to find some means of making men in general wiser and more skilful than they have been up till now, I believe we must look for it in medicine'.[4] He sees health as 'the chief good and the foundation of all other goods in this life'.[5] Perhaps most famously, Montaigne, following Socrates, claims that the whole point of philosophy is to prepare us for illness and ultimately death.

Philosophical reflection on illness in the Western tradition has tended to be shaped by Stoic, Epicurean and, later, Christian philosophies, each of which emphasize the importance of achieving a reflective coping with illness, seen as an essential feature of the world. Why this reflective attitude to illness is essential differs, though, by tradition. The Stoics seem to argue that everything that exists, including ostensibly bad things like illness, are all essential components of the rational order of the cosmos, so the properly philosophical response is to recognize this and reflectively accept illness. We find Epictetus saying: 'A man who has a fever may say: If I philosophize any longer, may I be hanged: wherever I go, I must take care of the poor body, that a fever may not come. But what is philosophizing? Is it not a preparation against events which may happen?'[6]

But for later Christian thinkers, such as Boethius, illness is a mark of our corrupt, imperfect state, and hence not an original feature of God's design. Boethius characterizes wickedness of the soul as akin to bodily sickness; while the former deserves hatred, the latter should be treated with pity.[7] So the properly philosophical response is to use illness in a doubly edifying way: first, as a reminder of the frailty and corruption of our mortal status, and second, as a source of moral and spiritual improvement.[8]

This is now largely a lost theme in philosophy because of the gradual erosion of philosophy's phronetic role.[9] I propose that this theme should be reawakened, and that more work needs to be done to examine and describe the philosophical role of illness. This paper outlines some of the ways in which illness is philosophically relevant, as part of the attempt to ignite this reawakening.[10]

I suggest that illness is relevant to philosophy because it uncovers aspects of embodied existence and experience in ways that reveal additional dimensions of human life. It does this by broadening the spectrum of embodied experience into the pathological domain, and in the process shedding light on normal experience, revealing its ordinary and therefore overlooked structure. Illness broadens the range of bodily as well as mental experience (e.g. delusions, dementia). Moreover, illness is (at present) an integral part of biological life, and thus must be taken into account when considering human life as a whole. Discussions of the good life, human relationships and ethics would be incomplete if they did not take into account the full spectrum of human life and experience, spanning sickness and health, childhood, adulthood and old age. In addition, illness is an opportunity for reflection because of its distancing effect, which illuminates taken-for-granted values and expectations by destroying the assumptions that underpin them (e.g. assumptions about longevity, capability and autonomy). I suggest that these characteristics warrant illness a philosophical role.

However, illness is a unique form of philosophizing. While the execution of most philosophical procedures such as casting doubt or questioning is volitional and theoretical, illness is uninvited and threatening. Illness throws the ill person into a state of anxiety and uncertainty. As such, it can be viewed as a radical, violent philosophical motivation that can profoundly alter our outlook. I argue that the radical nature of illness should be utilized to sharpen and expand philosophical discussion.

I conclude by examining the ways in which illness may impact upon the practice of philosophy. I argue that illness can be integral to philosophical method in a number of ways: in shaping and influencing philosophical methods and concerns, modifying one's sense of philosophical salience and conception of philosophy, and increasing the urgency and appeal of particular philosophical topics.

The structure of the paper is as follows. The first section outlines the centrality of the body for human experience, and discusses how illness changes embodiment, meaning and being in the world. The second section discusses illness as a form of *epoché* performed through objectification and uncanniness. The last section discusses illness as a motivation to philosophize and outlines how illness may change our modes and styles of philosophizing.

Illness modifies embodiment, meaning and being in the world

Three aspects of existence are significantly modified by illness: embodiment, meaning and being in the world. Embodiment is the fundamental characteristic of human existence.[11] Cognition and behaviour cannot be accounted for without considering the perceptual and motor apparatus that facilitates our dealing with the world.[12] The body is the condition of possibility for perception and interaction with spatial objects, and our means for having a world. As Gallagher and Zahavi write: 'the body is considered a constitutive or transcendental principle, precisely because it is involved in the very possibility of experience'.[13] Every worldly experience is mediated and made possible by embodiment.[14] Or as Merleau-Ponty put it, the body is 'that which causes [things] to begin to exist as things under our hands and eyes'.[15]

Counter to a purely naturalistic understanding, the body is not merely a thing among things. Embodiment determines spatial relations and temporal experiences, while also participating in these relations as a secondary form. The body is 'the centre around which and in relation to which space unfolds itself'.[16] According to Husserl, motility and tactile experience are fundamental not just for perception, but for any organized subjective experience.[17] In this sense, the body is the foundation of human experience. As Taylor Carman writes, the body 'plays a constitutive role in experience precisely by grounding, making possible, and yet remaining peripheral in the horizons of our conceptual awareness'.[18] Or to use Merleau-Ponty's famous formulation, the body is 'our general medium for having a world'.[19]

The form of my embodiment serves as part of the background of my experience.[20] This structure defines, for example, the coordinate system of my visual field and my proprioception. Different sensory fields are bound together to create a unified stream of meaningful experiences, united by a body with an established repertoire of habits, activities and style.[21] In Husserl's terms, the constitution of my body is essential to the constitution of objects appearing to me, and indeed to the constitution of space and time.[22]

Given how central the body is, a change to a bodily function entails a change to one's way of being in the world. Such a change will also affect the meaning of experience. For example, the experience of dancing will be radically altered by respiratory disease, both on the level of bodily feeling, which turns from a pleasurable experience to one of exertion, and on the level of meaning, when it changes from an experience of 'I can' to an 'I cannot'.[23] The types of changes affected by illness may range enormously, from changes to sensory experience, meaning, and to cognitive and emotional experience. If we think about symptoms as disparate as loss of mobility, loss of memory and incontinence, we can see that such changes are radical and they remove the ill person from the realm of familiar, predictable and well-understood experience. This displacement from the familiar destabilizes the structure of experience and reveals new aspects of our being, such as our ability to adapt, mourning and dependency. The bodily foundations of autonomous adulthood are often removed, revealing the tentative and temporary nature of these foundations. Illness can disclose finitude, dis-ability, and alienation from one's body as extreme modes of being.

The philosophical illumination offered by the study of illness has been recently explored by Matthew Ratcliffe, who studied the experience of time in depression.[24] Ratcliffe argues that there is strong evidence that the experience of time is affected in a number of ways in depression. He offers a phenomenological analysis of this experience, using Thomas Fuchs's application of Husserl's notion of retention and protention to the experience of time in depression. On this account, time both slows down and accelerates in depression. This alteration to the normal experience of time can be explained by the effects of depression. On Ratcliffe's account, depression removes meaning, obliterates the desire to carry out projects and stops the attribution of value to different projects in the depressed person's world.[25] Ratcliffe claims that the breakdown in such cases is not merely in the *contents* of experience, but in the *structure* of experience itself.

Because illness can affect many body parts and functions, it can delineate different aspects of embodiment by serving as a limit case.[26] The loss in illness may be of overall functionality, but also of flexibility and variability.

With a narrowed spectrum of activity, one's motility, assessment of duration, and notions such as 'difficult' and 'far', are modified. The restriction is not only a conscious understanding but underlies the kind of action one's body spontaneously performs. Here is a description of such pre-reflective modification:

> Every time I tried – and failed – to do something that was too strenuous my body stoically registered the failure and thereafter avoided that action. The change was subtle, because this happened by stealth [...] I stopped feeling all the things I could not do. They were quietly removed from my bodily repertoire in a way so subtle I hardly noticed it.[27]

Illness may lead to a collapse of meaning, or what Heidegger calls anxiety (*Angst*).[28] In anxiety, one's overall sense of purposeful activity is lost, leaving the person experiencing anxiety unable to act. Action is grounded in meaning: I pull a shirt over my head in order to get dressed. I get dressed in order to go to work. I go to work in order to earn a living, and so on. Ultimately, this nested set of goal-directed activities comes to an end, and human existence is ungrounded. A realization of the groundlessness of human existence leads to anxiety (*Angst*). In anxiety, purposefulness disappears, and the meaning of entities is lost. They turn from being ready-to-hand (*Zuhanden*) entities we use (t-shirt, shoes and reading lamp) to being present-at-hand (*Vorhanden*) entities which confront us with their lack of usefulness, and hence their lack of meaning. In anxiety, intelligibility is lost because the practical coherence of entities has been lost with the sense of purposefulness.

Loss of meaning is often reported in cases of mental illness. Matthew Ratcliffe cites a schizophrenic patient who says:

> When, for example, I looked at a chair or a jug, I thought not of their use or function – a jug not as something to hold water and milk, a chair not as something to sit in – but as having lost their names, their functions and meanings.[29]

Illness can also give rise to another kind of loss of meaning, related to the loss of the ability to perceive things as useful tools, and experiencing the contingency and irretrievability of meaning. In somatic illness, a ready-to-hand entity like a staircase can turn from being a practical tool to being a present-at-hand entity, or even a conspicuous obstacle. S. K. Toombs, a philosopher suffering from multiple sclerosis, writes: 'the bookcase outside my bedroom was once intended by my body as a "repository for books"; then as "that which is to be grasped for support on the way to the bathroom," and is now intended as "an obstacle to get around with my wheelchair."'[30] Somatic illness may cause a sudden and often disturbing sense of the contingency of the meanings and uses we assign to things: 'The bookcase holds books. Of course it does! What else might it do? It might obstruct, impede, sadly remind ...' There is also a sense of the irretrievability of certain meanings: 'The bookcase will always be an obstacle and will only cease to be so once I cease to be so.' The sense of inhabiting a space of possibilities can be replaced by a sense of this space becoming delimited and static.

The changes brought about by illness are not localized to a specific object, but modify one's entire interaction with objects and the environment, that is, their being in the world. For a wheelchair user, it is not just this shop or that doorway that are inaccessible, but the environment as a whole becomes less inviting or even hostile. Illness can expose not only the limits of human existence but also the biases of an environment.[31]

Illness may be philosophically salient in one of two ways. It is, in some cases, a severe and sudden disruption of our life. In this situation the illness is something foreign, threatening and disruptive, which we seek to get rid of. A bout of 'flu or gastric infection are examples of this type of illness. This type of illness is philosophically useful because of its acute disruption of the everyday; it makes visible the taken-for-granted manner in which we structure our routine life. We take for granted that we can plan our day, perform a variety of activities and get from one place to another. These tacit assumptions are placed in abeyance in the case of a sudden illness. Feelings of missing out, being useless and feeling unwell expose the underlying sense of participation, purposefulness and potency that has been disturbed.[32]

But illness may also appear more subtly and tacitly. The symptoms may be minor and not quite noticeable until they reach a certain threshold, or until they are picked up in routine screening. In this case the illness is not an acute disruption of the everyday, but still alters the everyday capacities of the ill person, and thus may also give rise to philosophical reflection, albeit of a different sort. Shaun Gallagher describes this kind of illness as one that 'either sneaks up on us, or that we become so habituated to (perhaps because it won't go away) that it defines our form of life – it becomes us, or we become it'.[33] Whereas in acute illness the expectation that the illness will 'go away' is very much part of the experience of illness, this expectation disappears in chronic illness. Arthur Frank contrasts his heart attack, which he interpreted as 'an incident', with his cancer:

> After an incident like my heart attack I was able to bounce back. [...] That's accurate because in most cases we do not sink into an experience, we only hit the surface. I may have bounced back from a heart attack, but with cancer I was going to have to sink all the way through and discover a life on the other side.[34]

The second type of illness is not a disruption, but a 'complete form of existence', as Gallagher writes, following Merleau-Ponty.[35] In this case, the disturbance runs deeper and longer, and thus must be dealt with in a different way than a passing illness such as food poisoning. When illness becomes a complete form of life, concepts (such as 'worthwhile' or 'difficult') are modified, the expectations the ill person has of her life change, and her understanding of time and value needs to be readjusted. Chronic or progressive illness is a comprehensive realignment of meaning, values and ways of being that culminates in illness becoming one's complete form of existence. This process is a kind of distancing from one's previous form of existence, and as such it throws it open to philosophical examination.

Illness as *epoché*: objectification and uncanniness

Because illness removes the taken-for-granted nature of motility and bodily capability, it makes what is normally natural and unreflective become artificial and conscious.[36] In this section, I explain how this process gives rise to philosophical reflection. It is characterized by *objectification* and *uncanniness*, which I use in this section to demonstrate the role of illness as a mode of philosophizing.

Illness can be seen as a crisis of meaning in one's life. This crisis arises from a collapse of the ill person's life narrative,[37] but also a disruption of routines, habits, expectations and abilities. This disruption shakes one's everyday life, and provides a distance from it. This distance has been described by Arthur Frank as a 'dangerous opportunity':

> Critical illness offers the experience of being taken to the threshold of life, from which you can see where your life could end. From that vantage point you are both forced and allowed to think in new ways about the value of your life. Alive, but detached from everyday living, you can finally stop to consider why you live as you have.[38]

This brings to mind the ancient Greek conception of philosophy – introduced by Socrates and embraced by the Stoics, and later valourized by Montaigne – that to philosophize is to learn how to die.[39] Learning how to die in this context may mean more than accepting one's mortality. It furnishes this highly abstract demand with concrete content. Learning how to die means learning to be ill, confronting pain and disability, accepting diminishing abilities and dealing with mourning, envy and sadness. In the words of Epictetus: 'What is it to bear a fever well? Not to blame God or man; not to be afflicted at that which happens, to expect death well and nobly, to do what must be done'.[40]

Illness calls upon the ill person to explore her life, its meaning, priorities and values; this personal quest is well documented in sociology of medicine, medical anthropology, qualitative healthcare research and cancer psychology.[41] But illness can also be used as a distinctively *philosophical* tool to move beyond the idiosyncratic and personal to more general and abstract exploration of embodiment as a source of meaning, and the condition of possibility for the self. In particular, the anxiety, loss of meaning and de-familiarization described in the previous section give rise to a peculiar form of what Husserl termed the *epoché*, the bracketing of the natural attitude. The *epoché* asks us to dislodge ourselves from everyday habits and routines in order to reflect on them; this, I suggest, is what happens in illness, albeit in a raw and unformulated manner.[42] Illness is a particular form of *philosophical motivation*, characterized by violence, negativity and being forced upon the ill person. The *epoché* asks us to shift our focus from objects to acts of perception, but does not involve ceasing to perceive; it is not a sceptical procedure. It is not a removal from the world but a shift in a way of being in the world that enables philosophical reflection, without ceasing to take part in the world. Exercising the *epoché* involves stripping away of shared meaning, known uses and familiar connections between person and object. The object then becomes estranged and appears in novel ways. Thus the experience of illness, or anxiety, as a particular type of *epoché* can shed new light on taken-for-granted aspects of the world.

Illness suspends the natural attitude – the taken-for-granted, meaning-laden and metaphysically determined way of experiencing the world. Such suspension does not mean doing away with the natural attitude, as that is impossible, but maintaining the attitude while suspending the underlying metaphysical beliefs underpinning it. This is the neutralization of one's belief in the existence of the world or of an object, which Husserl called the *epoché*. This neutralization is employed in the shift from the natural to the critical attitude.[43]

We do not affect the *epoché* in order to 'deny, doubt, neglect, abandon, or exclude reality from our research, but simply to suspend or neutralize a certain dogmatic attitude toward reality [...]'.[44] Bracketing the natural attitude is a withdrawal from the ordinarily implicit commitment to the reality of the world.[45] Bracketing turns the world into a phenomenon of being, instead of something that is. As Husserl makes clear, this is not a sceptical or idealist position. Rather, this 'inhibiting' or 'putting out of play' of the natural attitude exposes 'my pure living [...] the universe of phenomena in the phenomenological sense'.[46] This suspension neither questions nor negates reality; rather, it allows under-theorized aspects of experience to become an object of enquiry, because it enables us to shift attention from the given object to the way in which it is given and its modes of appearance. As Husserl writes in *Ideas I*: 'the whole prediscovered world posited in the natural attitude [...] is now without validity for us; without being tested and without being contested, it shall be parenthesised'.[47] But importantly, the *epoché* 'leaves everything exactly as it is'.[48]

Zahavi characterizes the *epoché* as a philosophical entry gate.[49] I suggest that because of its de-familiarizing effect, illness is such an entry gate into philosophy. It is an invitation to investigate subjectivity under the conditions of illness, and thus to expand the conditions under which subjectivity is studied. As such, it can reveal novel facets of subjectivity that otherwise remain unnoticed. For example, Merleau-Ponty gives a philosophical analysis of the case of Schneider, a World War I soldier with brain injuries, studied by neurologists Adhemar Gelb and Kurt Goldstein in 1918.[50] Merleau-Ponty interprets Schneider's inability to perform abstract movements, initiate sexual relations or stray from a daily routine as the breakdown of his intentional arc:

> The life of consciousness – cognitive life, the life of desire or perceptual life – is subtended by an 'intentional arc' which projects round about us our past, our future, our human setting, our physical, ideological and moral situation. [...] It is this intentional arc which brings about the unity of the senses, of intelligence, of sensibility and motility. *And it is this which 'goes limp' in illness.*[51]

This breakdown of normal human existence provides a unique opportunity to uncover facets of normal existence that are not visible under normal conditions. Similarly, Shaun Gallagher discusses the case of Ian Waterman, who suffered from de-efferentation from the neck down.[52] Waterman was forced to use vision to locate his limbs and identify his posture. Gallagher uses this case to provide an in-depth account of normal proprioception.

In illness, the *epoché* is *forced upon* the ill person because of the modification to and limitation on her body imposed by illness. The ill person may have no interest in philosophy and no desire to undergo existential change. However, illness – an uninvited guest – forces itself upon the ill person, and compels her to modify and thus re-examine her bodily habits; existential expectations; experience of body, space and time; and way of being in the world.[53] Illness is a form of violent removal of the natural attitude, which enacts a philosophical procedure in a way that is far more brutal than usual philosophical reflection. Illness motivates ill people, and often those around them, to confront practical concerns, and this, in turn, gives rise to theoretical reflection on one's embodied situation. It is an uninvited type of reflection, but such coping with practical concerns reveals the normal conditions under which one previously operated in health. It replaces health, which is 'life lived in the silence of the organs', as the French surgeon Leriche wrote.[54] This allows these conditions to be explored, as their silent function is lost and they become the object of explicit attention. The natural attitude is not immune to theorizing or meta-reflection, under circumstances which disrupt it. Illness is one such circumstance.

Merleau-Ponty characterizes the *epoché* as an experience of 'wonder in the face of the world'.[55] This sense of wonder, interrogation and puzzlement characterizes some experiences of illness. For example, it drove Randy Pausch to write *The Last Lecture*, a series of talks about life and death, after being diagnosed with pancreatic cancer. 'Many people might expect the talk to be about dying. But it had to be about *living*', he writes.[56] Because of changes to the somatic or mental architecture of one's body (or mind), one's contact with, and experience of, the world can be radically modified in illness. One's sense of comfort and familiarity may be displaced by alienation and a sense of 'not being at home'.[57] Merleau-Ponty writes: '[Reflection] slackens the intentional threads which attach us to the world and thus brings them to our notice; it alone is consciousness of the world because it reveals that world as strange and paradoxical'.[58] I suggest that illness is such a slackening of the intentional threads, which reveals the world and embodiment as uncanny. In other words, illness problematizes the relationship to one's world, or one's being in the world, thus lending itself to, or even forcing, philosophical reflection.

The *epoché* also arises from the rift between the biological and lived body, which becomes observable in certain cases of illness. In health the two aspects of the body usually cohere, or respond in harmony to a normal range of experiences.[59] In illness the biological body comes to the fore, as it ceases to cooperate with the ill person's desires. For example, a diabetic's biological body will be unable to cope with a chocolate mousse, despite her lived body's craving for it. In addition to the rift, the biological body also becomes the source of pain, disability and failure. In this respect, it becomes the source of negative experiences and the focus of medical attention, which often further distance us from it.[60]

Lawrence Hass views illness as conflict between the biological body and life projects. While the individual person's 'personal life' is engaged in a project, the biological body obstructs it. For example, one's personal aim may be to become a parent. However, if the biological body is infertile, the result is a clash between the desire to have a child and the biological barrier. The impersonal operations of the biological body, over which we have little or no control, interfere with the intentional arc of the person, the meaningful connection between person and world which is aimed at a particular goal.[61] This sense, that one's body is an obstacle, a problem, something that is no longer well understood, may initiate a kind of *epoché*. The metaphysical status of the body is thrown into question, because it is no longer familiar and predictable. In other words, the body is subject to a process of objectification in illness, as well as becoming uncanny – two processes to which we now turn.[62]

Objectification – the natural process secondary to experiencing the lived body is experiencing the body as an object among objects. In illness this process takes on a new dimension, as so much of modern medicine and the sciences underlying it rely on viewing the body as a physical object.[63] This objectification takes place under the dual experience we have of our bodies. The body is experienced as both a lived, pre-reflective body (my first-person experience of and through it) and as an objectified, observed, spatial object (the third-person experience of it).[64] It is both a physical object made of matter, *and* the seat of consciousness.

The exploration of objects implies a simultaneous self-exploration and self-constitution; there is a reciprocal co-dependency between the processes. 'The world is given to us as bodily investigated, and the body is revealed to us in this exploration of the world.'[65] We are aware of perceptual objects because we are aware of our bodies and how the two interact. When we investigate objects, this is always accompanied by some kind of bodily self-awareness. In illness, objectification gives rise to a distance between oneself and one's body, which is now reified into an object of medical inquiry and treatment. Objectification breaks down the natural taken-for-granted attitude towards the body, the seamless unity between the body as object and the body as subject.

Merleau-Ponty claims that the body is the first object we perceive *as* an object, thematizing and learning to interpret and judge it according to cultural standards.[66] Prior to that event, I do not experience my body; rather, I experience *through* my body. As Zahavi writes: 'Originally my body is experienced as a unified field of activity and affectivity, as a volitional structure, a potentiality of mobility, as an "I do" and "I can".'[67] Illness impedes the natural sense of ability and activity, and enables us to explore the volitional structures of embodiment. Our natural orientation is one in which the body serves as the perceptual centre of our experience, with our attention directed away from it, rather than to it. The negative, unwanted focus on the body in illness reorients our attention back towards the body, but this time viewed as an object. Many of us have had the experience of seeing an x-ray of scan of our bodies, and having to relate our subjective feeling of our body to this objectifying image.

The duality of the body plays a complex role in health care provision. The health professional experiences the patient's body as an object, but is also aware of its subjectivity (so will apologize for having cold hands when touching a patient). The patient may feel objectified by the physician's gaze, but this objectification is only possible because she is first a subject.[68] The physician perceives an appearance of an experienced object: a swollen arm. The patient perceives a localized sensing: the sore arm. She may also be shown an x-ray of her arm, and will thus oscillate between the two experiences – the immediate pain localized in the arm, and the arm as an object that is gazed at and imaged. She can focus on the sensing (observing the swollen arm) or the sensed (the arm itself), and each will yield a differently thematized experience.[69] Health professionals often view the body as thematized and objectified, focusing on a particular organ or function in order to understand it as a medical object. But for the patient, the awareness of her body as an object is secondary to her subjective experience of receiving health care.

As Fredrik Svenaeus claims, modern medicine expands the objecthood of the body through imaging and conceptualization of organs, functions and molecular processes.[70] The medical emphasis on the objecthood of the body contributes to the rift between the body as lived and the biological body. This intense experience of the objecthood of the body in illness alienates the patient from her body. Jean-Dominique Bauby, who suffered a stroke that resulted in locked-in syndrome, writes:

> Reflected in the glass I saw the head of a man who seemed to have emerged from a vat of formaldehyde. His mouth was twisted, his nose damaged, his hair tousled, his gaze full of fear. One eye was sewn shut, the other goggled like that doomed eye of Cain. For a moment I stared at that dilated pupil before I realised it was only mine.[71]

As this passage shows, illness may force us to adopt a reifying and abstract view of our own body – this is often the shift that is required from patients when discussing their disease with health professionals. However, although most of us can adopt an abstract view of our body, we are not able to sustain it; that is existentially unbearable. We cannot actually view ourselves *objectively* in any sustained sense, and it is unrealistic to expect that of others. Health professionals need to be aware of this because of medicine's way of privileging third-person perspectives. Objectivity is seen as an ideal by many health professionals, but when subjected to philosophical analysis, it can be seen that merely relying on an objective stance is a naïve and non-practicable ideal that ought to be replaced with a more nuanced understanding of intersubjectivity.

A further objectification takes place in the clinic. When a patient awaits her blood test results, she is as ignorant about her cholesterol levels, for example, as an objective observer. When she asks the physician 'how bad is it?', that is because she is genuinely unable to access this information by examining her bodily sensations. In that sense, the patient's body is an object not only to the physician but also to the patient herself. Other experiences of objectification can be seen in the encounter with medical technology. Seeing one's tumour as a set of CT images, or aligning one's limbs for a bone density scan, can make the objecthood of the body prominent in one's experience. These objectifying experiences may lead to a sense of alienation from one's body, and to treating that body as an aberrant object over which one has little control. The ill body becomes despised, feared and alien.

However, this objectification is not complete. There is an oscillation between treating one's own body as an object of medicine and the subjective experience of apprehension, feeling cold or flinching from the physician's touch. Husserl's example of two hands touching each other makes this duality salient.[72] When the right hand is the active, touching one, it is at the same time being touched by the left hand. If we consciously decide to reverse the roles and concentrate on the left hand as touching, we still oscillate between both dimensions, the active touching one and the passive dimension of being touched. According to Husserl, this duality of experience is a unique feature of human existence. In order to touch, one has to be a thing among things, a physical object. As such an object, one has to be open to the possibility that one can be touched. However, in illness, the natural movement between the two dimensions is disrupted because the passive dimension becomes prominent. For example, internal examination gives rise to an experience of being touched from within (e.g. one's cervix or intestines), expanding the domain of passivity. The body as object takes precedence in the clinical context, and its foreignness is accentuated by the inaccessibility of some medical facts to the patient other than via a third-person report. In illness, one's body becomes an object in ways it would not otherwise have.

Uncanniness – In illness, the body becomes an obstacle and a threat, instead of my home, a familiar place I inhabit. A change to one's body is a change to one's sense of being at home in the world. The body ceases to be the 'null centre' of my orientation towards the world,[73] and instead becomes the source of negative experiences. The primitive sense of 'I can' becomes replaced by a conscious, artificial, mediated sense of 'I cannot', or 'I once was able to, but am no longer'.[74] The perspicuous nature of bodily orientation as being the foundation of all experience becomes occluded with attention.

Illness can suspend the familiar setting and feelings that underpin normal everyday actions, giving rise instead to an experience of 'being not at home'.[75] Uncanniness arises most forcefully from the disruption of this background, which happens as a result of changed embodiment. Our concepts, habits, routines, expectations and norms may be disrupted, or even destroyed by illness. Uncanniness arises from a new, negative focus on one's body, a sense of this body becoming an alien destructive force, or even the threat of annihilation that become salient in serious illness. This changes the ill person's relationship to her environment, as well as her concepts. Illness causes disruption of the lived body, which interrupts the relationship between one's body and the environment. Concepts like 'far', 'difficult' and 'heavy' change their meaning for the individual, who may experience a further sense of alienation because her new use of concepts moves away from the norm. In addition, such concepts acquire new *objects*, for example, routine activities such as carrying a laptop bag, or nipping upstairs to pick up one's wallet, become marked as *difficult* in illness. Many concepts change their meaning, as well as attaching to new objects, and so expanding in scope. The change is not merely linguistic; the ill person actually *experiences* the physical world as less welcoming, full of obstacles and difficult. Distances increase, everyday routines take up more time, activities have to be forsaken or redesigned, and so on. Toombs describes loss of mobility as 'anchoring one in the Here, engendering a heightened sense of distance between oneself and surrounding things'.[76] Illness modifies not only one's body, but one's sense of space.

Not only do the experience of space and the use of concepts change in illness but the experience of time may also change and contribute to the sense of alienation and uncanniness brought about by bodily changes, fear, pain and limitation. Sustained pain or a poor prognosis may completely transform one's experience of time.[77] Activities may take more time, and thus expand, or may become impossible, which may cause the ill person to experience herself as 'useless' or as more disabled than she is.[78] Insecurity and anxiety about future health and ability may make one focus on the present.[79] And memories of a healthy past become objects of regret, yearning or a sense of discontinuity.[80] The experience of time may also change in response to an uncertain prognosis. Priorities might change and it is an opportunity to question how one has lived and how one would like to live.[81] These changes are fundamental and may lead to seismic shifts in identity and selfhood[82] as well as triggering philosophical questions. How plastic is the experience of space and time? What determines 'normal' experience? Can there be continuity in identity and personhood given the radical change in one's experiences of these fundamental categories? The way in which such questions can arise by bodily modification in illness demonstrates that illness can trigger philosophical activity. We now turn to examine in what ways this triggering is philosophically salient.

Illness as invitation to philosophize

So far I have explained how illness can be philosophically illuminating, by disrupting everyday taken-for-granted assumptions about embodied existence, and thus performing a kind of *epoché*.[83] In this section, I look more closely at this process, and suggest that illness is a peculiar kind of motivation to philosophize.

Illness is unwanted; it is almost never welcome or easily accepted into one's life. It is also a radical event: it gives rise to a rethinking of values and meaning, given the changed life conditions. Illness changes our relationship to our bodies, our environment and our plans and judgement. In short, serious illness is a dramatic life event that affects all aspects of life. Because of these features, illness can *motivate* philosophical reflection. However, the claim I wish to make is not simply that illness motivates the person who falls ill to become more reflective, although this is certainly true, but rather that the features that motivate reflection in individuals who become ill make illness salient to the practice of philosophy.

Illness certainly invites or inspires reflection of a philosophical sort. But it can also brutally force this reflection on ill people – for example, the way a poor prognosis may force the ill person to consider death. It also forces the ill person to consider such issues not in the abstract – a luxury of the healthy and young – but in their most intrusive application to one's own life. Illness does not permit inauthentic reflection on death, for example, as an abstract, far away event that may befall one at some point in the future. Illness forces the ill person to face her own death in the most concrete possible way. From practical arrangements to choosing one's funeral song, writing a will or saying what is pressing, illness is a strict philosophical instructor forcing the ill person to confront death in its most concrete and immediate. This can be seen as a fuller, more existentially salient form of philosophizing. Indeed, for Heidegger, authentically facing death demands precisely this kind of first-person engagement with death.

Illness is also different to other motivations to philosophize. Whereas normally one chooses to perform a philosophical procedure, of say, questioning or criticizing an argument, illness motivates in a non-volitional manner. It is violent, unwanted, destructive and uncontrolled. In this sense, illness forces the ill person to reconsider their situation. We normally take the practice of philosophy to be a matter of choice, whereas illness is almost never something we *choose* to happen to us. We think of reflection as a pleasant experience of intellectual challenge; but the reflection prompted by illness is all-consuming, extreme and terrifying.

Nietzsche argued that physical illness affords insights into the body, life and indeed reality. He saw illness as instructive as well as edifying, claiming that careful philosophical attentiveness to experiences of illness is an important feature of an examined life. Nietzsche describes how his illness sharpened his perceptions and inspired his philosophical view:

> It was as if I discovered life anew, myself included; I tasted all the good things, even the small ones, as no other could easily taste them – I turned my will to health, to *life*, into my philosophy [...] the years when my vitality was at its lowest were when I *stopped* being a pessimist.[84]

Illness affects different aspects of philosophical reflection; it can call for more radical and personal methods, such as existentialism or nihilism. It affects the philosophical concerns of the ill person – issues such as death, the good life, the injustice of the natural lottery, and time can be central and pressing for ill people in a way they would not be otherwise. Because it forces the ill person to engage with their physical or mental decline and death, it triggers reflection on finitude, dis-ability, suffering, injustice and so on. Similarly, the urgency and salience of particular philosophical topics may change in light of illness.[85] The very activity of philosophizing may change and become more urgent and personal. Illness may also change the ill person's conception of philosophy (if she has one) as a vital practice aimed at a good life, rather than an abstract theoretical enquiry seeking truths, for example, as can be seen in ancient philosophical schools such as the Epicureans and the Stoics. Illness may also bring about the sense that philosophical enquiry ought to be integrated into, and so intrinsic to, one's life as a whole. A case in point is Alasdair MacIntyre,[86] who stresses the fact of our vulnerable, dependent, afflicted state as a precondition for a style of moral philosophizing attentive to the human condition.

An important caveat is that illness does not always or necessarily fulfil its role as inviting to philosophize. It is disorientating and overwhelming, and can – like other extreme hardships – destroy reflection instead of bringing it about. Illness is not philosophical reflection in itself, but can be – and often is – a *way into* reflection. Illness is a compulsive invitation to philosophize:

> The experience of illness and its sweeping effect on every aspect of life shocked me into thinking about these issues. I found that I had to reinvent my life. ... I learned to rethink my aspirations and plans. I relinquished the sense of control I previously had. ... My experiences pushed me to reflect on health and illness.[87]

'True philosophy', Merleau-Ponty wrote, 'consists in relearning to look at the world'.[88] Illness forces us to relearn not just to look at the world, but also to cope with it, to negotiate new limitations and to continue to live to the best of our ability within new constraints brought about by illness. The consequences of such coping with practical limitations can be existential and philosophical illumination. Perhaps illness is a kind of philosophical *method*, which illuminates normalcy through its pathological counterpart. However, Merleau-Ponty calls on us to make this claim carefully:

> It is impossible to deduce the normal from the pathological, deficiencies from the substitute functions, by a mere change of the sign. We must take substitutions as substitutions, as allusions to some fundamental function

that they are striving to make good, and the direct image of which they fail to furnish.[89]

Merleau-Ponty is acutely aware in this passage that the pathological is not merely 'a change of the sign'. Rather, pathological cases allude to some function they are 'striving to make good' and in this striving, end up creating a complete form of life. It is this completeness that requires further philosophical investigation, to unravel how what may seem pathological and deficient may give rise to phenomena such as adaptability[90] and edification.[91] Canguilhem defined disease as 'a new way of life for the organism', the creation of new norms that govern the relationship of the diseased organism to its environment.[92] The richness of the experience of illness and the understanding of health and illness as distinctly *normative* activity attest to the fact that illness both requires and merits further philosophical exploration.

Acknowledgements

This paper was first published as 'The Philosophical Role of Illness' *Metaphilosophy* 45(1): 20–40, 2014. We are grateful to Wiley Publishers for their permission to reprint it here. This paper was written during a period of research leave funded by the Leverhulme Trust and revised during a period of leave funded by the British Academy. I am grateful to both funders. I would like to thank Ian James Kidd for helpful comments and suggestions that greatly improved the paper. I also thank an anonymous reviewer for helpful comments.

Notes

1 Epictetus, *Discourses*, Book III, Chapter X. Taken from: http://classics.mit.edu/Epictetus/discourses.3.three.html (accessed 18.2.19).

2 In the remainder of the paper I will use the term 'illness' to denote serious, chronic or life-threatening illness, rather than common and transient illnesses, such as 'flu. However, less serious conditions can also be philosophically important, as they disclose more minor interruptions to the flow of experience. Sartre gives the example of a headache as disrupting reading; see Sartre, Jean-Paul, *Being and Nothingness* (London: Routledge, 2003 [1943]).

3 For example, see Epictetus, *A Selection from the Discourses of Epictetus with the Encheiridion*, trans. G. Long (Project Gutenberg, 2004), http://www.gutenberg.org/files/10661/10661-h/10661-h.htm [accessed 20 August 2013];

Seneca, *On the Shortness of Life* (London: Penguin Books, 2004); Aurelius, Marcus, *Meditations* (New York & London: Penguin Books, 1995); Boethius, *The Consolation of Philosophy*, trans. H. R. James (Project Gutenberg, 2004), Book IV http://www.gutenberg.org/files/14328/14328-h/14328-h.htm [accessed 20 August 2013]; and Descartes, R. *Descartes: Selected Philosophical Writings*, trans. D. Murdoch and R. Stoothoff, (Cambridge: Cambridge University Press, 1988.)

4 Descartes, *Descartes: Selected Philosophical Writings*, p. 47.

5 Ibid.

6 Epictetus, *A Selection from the Discourses*, 'In what manner we ought to bear sickness'.

7 Boethius, *The Consolation of Philosophy*, Book IV.

8 See Ian James Kidd, 'Can Illness Be Edifying?', *Inquiry* 55:5 (2012), pp. 496–520.

9 There is much discussion in the philosophy of medicine about the concept of illness (and disease), and its relationship with the concept of health. But this conceptual analysis does not touch on the existential or philosophical role illness may have. For a notable exception, see S.Kay Toombs, *The Meaning of Illness: A Phenomenological Account of the Different Perspectives of Physician and Patient* (Amsterdam: Kluwer, 1999). See also Martha Nussbaum, *The Therapy of Desire: Theory and Practice in Hellenistic Ethics* (Princeton, NJ: Princeton University Press, 1994).

10 See also Kidd, 'Can Illness Be Edifying?'

11 See Maurice Merleau-Ponty, *Phenomenology of Perception*, trans. C. Smith (New York & London: Routledge, 1962 [1945]); Andy Clark, *Being there* (Cambridge, MA: MIT Press, 1997); Andy Clark, *Supersizing the Mind* (Oxford: Oxford University Press, 2008); Michael Wheeler, *Reconstructing the Cognitive World* (Cambridge, MA: MIT Press, 2005).

12 Paco Calvo and Toni Gomila, *Handbook of Cognitive Science: An Embodied Approach* (Oxford: Elsevier, 2008), p. 7.

13 Shaun Gallagher and Dan Zahavi, *The Phenomenological Mind* (New York: Routledge, 2008), p. 135.

14 Dan Zahavi, *Husserl's Phenomenology* (Stanford, CA: Stanford University Press, 2003), p. 99.

15 Merleau-Ponty, *Phenomenology of Perception*, p. 146.

16 Zahavi, *Husserl's Phenomenology*, p. 99.

17 Edmund Husserl, *Thing and Space: Lectures of 1907* (Dordrecht: Kluwer, 1997 [1907]).

18 Taylor Carman, 'The Body in Husserl and Merleau-Ponty', *Philosophical Topics* 27:2 (1999), p. 208.

19 Merleau-Ponty, *Phenomenology of Perception*, p. 146.

20 David W. Smith, *Husserl* (London & New York: Routledge, 2007), p. 223.

21 On style, see Darian Meacham, 'What goes without Saying: Husserl's Notion of Style', *Research in Phenomenology* 43 (2013), pp. 3–26.

22 Husserl, *Thing and Space*, §73.

23 Cf. Havi Carel, 'Phenomenology as a Resource for Patients', *Journal of Medicine and Philosophy* 37:2 (2012), pp. 96–113.

24 Matthew Ratcliffe, 'Varieties of Temporal Experience in Depression', *Journal of Medicine and Philosophy* 37:2 (2012), pp. 114–38.

25 Ratcliffe, 'Varieties of Temporal Experience in Depression'.

26 See Havi Carel, 'Illness, Phenomenology, and Philosophical Method', *Theoretical Medicine and Bioethics* 34:4 (2013), pp. 345–57. Death would not be the ultimate limit case but crossing the limit.

27 Havi Carel, *Illness* (Stocksfield: Acumen, 2008), p. 34.

28 Martin Heidegger, *Being and Time* (Oxford: Basil Blackwell, 1962[1927]).

29 Matthew Ratcliffe, 'Phenomenology, Naturalism and the Sense of Reality', in *Phenomenology and Naturalism*, eds H. Carel and D. Meacham (Cambridge: Cambridge University Press, 2013).

30 S. Kay Toombs, 'The Lived Experience of Disability', *Human Studies* 18 (1995), p. 16.

31 This bias underlies academic research in fields such as disability studies, gender studies, queer studies, black studies, deaf studies and so on. Academic inquiry in these fields is, in part, motivated by identifying biases and discrimination.

32 The experience of ageing may also give rise to these sensations, but more gradually than sudden illness.

33 Shaun Gallagher, 'Illness as a Complete Form of Existence', unpublished presentation delivered at the Association for Medical Humanities Annual Conference (University of Durham, 2009).

34 Arthur Frank, *At the Will of the Body* (Boston: Mariner Books, 1991), p. 28.

35 Gallagher, 'Illness as a Complete Form of Existence'. Cf. Merleau-Ponty, *Phenomenology of Perception.*

36 Shaun Gallagher, *How the Body Shapes the Mind* (Oxford: Oxford University Press, 2005).

37 Simon J. Williams, *Medicine and the Body* (London: Sage Publications, 2003).

38 Frank, *At the Will of the Body*, p. 1.

39 Michel de Montaigne, 'To Philosophise is to Learn How to Die', in *The Essays: A Selection* (London: Penguin, 1993), pp. 17–36.

40 Epictetus, *Discourses*, 'In what manner we ought to bear sickness'.

41 See: James Brennan, 'Adjustment to Cancer - Coping or Personal Transition?', *Psychooncology* 10:1 (2001), pp. 1–18; Sally Thorne and Barbara Paterson, 'Shifting Images of Chronic Illness', *Journal of Nursing Scholarship* 30:2 (1998), pp. 173–8; Sally Thorne et al., 'Chronic Illness Experience: Insights from a Metastudy', *Qualitative Health Research* 12:4 (2002), pp. 437–52.

42 Distancing can also arise as a result of other life events, for example bereavement, divorce and trauma.

43 John Drummond, *Historical Dictionary of Husserl's Philosophy* (Lanham, MD: Scarecrow Press, 2007), pp. 67–8.

44 Zahavi, *Husserl's Phenomenology*, p. 45.

45 Matthew Ratcliffe, *Feelings of Being: Phenomenology, Psychiatry and the Sense of Reality* (Oxford: Oxford University Press, 2008), p. 4.

46 Edmund Husserl, *Cartesian Meditations* (Dordrecht: Kluwer, 1999 [1931]), p. 20).

47 Edmund Husserl, *Ideas Pertaining to a Pure Phenomenology and to a Phenomenological Philosophy: First Book* (The Hague: Martinus Nijhoff, 1982 [1913]), p. §32, 62).

48 Arthur D. Smith, *Husserl and the Cartesian Meditations* (London & New York: Routledge, 2003), p. 23.

49 Zahavi, *Husserl's Phenomenology*, p. 46.

50 Merleau-Ponty, *Phenomenology of Perception*, p. 103ff.

51 Ibid., p. 136, my emphasis.

52 Gallagher, *How the Body Shapes the Mind*.

53 Carel, 'Phenomenology as a Resource for Patients'.

54 René Leriche, cited in Georges Canguilhem, *The Normal and the Pathological* (New York: Zone Books, 1991), p. 91.

55 Merleau-Ponty, *Phenomenology of Perception*, p xiii.

56 Randy Pausch, *The Last Lecture* (London: Hodder & Stoughton, 2008), p. 9.

57 Fredrik Svenaeus, 'Das Unheimliche – Towards a Phenomenology of Illness', *Medicine, Health Care and Philosophy* 3 (2000), pp. 3–16.

58 Ibid.

59 But see Havi Carel, 'Conspicuous, Obtrusive, Obstinate: A Phenomenology of the Ill Body', in *Medicine and Society, New Continental Perspectives*, ed. D. Meacham (Dordrecht: Springer, 2015).

60 Carel, *Illness*.

61 Lawrence Hass, *Merleau-Ponty's Philosophy* (Bloomington: Indiana University Press, 2008), p. 87.

62 Young, healthy embodiment is typically oblivious to the possibility that the body might be experienced in this way. The confidence in one's physical and cognitive capacities can occlude a sense that these capacities might change (even with natural ageing) and that this change will increasingly come to radically impact one's identity. This can be seen as a failure of moral imagination, compassion, humility, or even a misunderstanding or denial of the biological expiration that delimits human life.

63 This is a good thing. Modern medicine has made huge progress because of this objective view of the body.

64 Merleau-Ponty, *Phenomenology of Perception*; Sartre, *Being and Nothingness*.

65 Zahavi, *Husserl's Phenomenology*, p. 105.

66 Merleau-Ponty, *Phenomenology of Perception*.

67 Zahavi, *Husserl's Phenomenology*, p. 101.

68 Havi Carel and Jane Macnaughton, '"How do you Feel?": Oscillating Perspectives in the Clinic', *The Lancet* 379: 9834 (23 June 2012), pp. 2334–5.

69 The health professional may also alternate between the sensing (her experience of gazing at the x-ray or examining the arm) and the sensed (the arm or the x-ray), but this oscillation does not involve self-objectification.

70 Fredrik Svenaeus, 'Organ transplantation and personal identity: How does the loss and change of organs have effects on the self?' *Journal of Medicine and Philosophy* 37:2 (2012), pp. 139–58.

71 Jean-Dominique Bauby, 2007. *The Diving Bell and the Butterfly* (London: Harper Perennial, 2007), pp. 32–3.

72 Edmund Husserl, *Cartesian Meditations* (Dordrecht: Kluwer, 1999 [1931]).

73 Smith, *Husserl and the Cartesian Meditations*, p. 221.

74 Amy Kesserling, Amy, *The Experienced Body, when Taken-for-Grantedness Falters: A Phenomenological Study of Living with Breast Cancer*, PhD dissertation (UMI, 1990: unpublished).

75 Svenaeus, 'Das Unheimliche – Towards a Phenomenology of Illness', p. 9; Svenaeus, 'Organ Transplantation and Personal Identity'.

76 S. Kay Toombs, 'The Lived Experience of Disability', *Human Studies* 18 (1995), p. 11.

77 Ibid.

78 S. Kay Toombs, 'Illness and the Paradigm of Lived Body'. *Theoretical Medicine* 9 (1988), pp. 201–26.

79 Carel, *Illness*, Chapter 5.

80 Michael Bury, 'Chronic Illness as Biographical Disruption', *Sociology of Health and Illness* 4:2 (1982), pp. 167–82.

81 Elizabeth Lindsey, 'Health within Illness: Experiences of Chronically Ill/ Disabled People', *Journal of Advanced Nursing* 24 (1996), pp. 465–72; O. Lindqvist, et al., 'Reclaiming Wellness – Living with Bodily Problems as Narrated by Men with Advanced Prostate Cancer', *Cancer Nursing* 29:4 (2006), pp. 327–37.

82 Simon J. Williams, *Medicine and the Body* (London: Sage Publications, 2003).

83 This process may affect family members or carers who become distanced from shared practices and understandings by the limitations of illness.

84 Friedrich Nietzsche 'Why I am so Wise' In *Ecce Homo*, trans. Duncan Large (Oxford: Oxford University Press, 2009), p. 9.

85 For example, Seneca, *On the Shortness of Life*.

86 Alasdair MacIntyre, *Dependent Rational Animals* (London: Duckworth, 1999).

87 Carel, *Illness*, p. 7.

88 Merleau-Ponty, *Phenomenology of Perception*, p. xx.

89 Ibid., pp. 107–8.

90 Havi Carel, 'Can I be Ill and Happy?', *Philosophia* 35:2 (2007), pp. 95–110.

91 Kidd, 'Can Illness Be Edifying?'.

92 Canguilhem, *The Normal and the Pathological*, p. 84.

References

Aurelius, M., *Meditations*, New York & London: Penguin Books, 1995.
Bauby, J., *The Diving Bell and the Butterfly*, London: Harper Perennial, 2007.
Boethius, *The Consolation of Philosophy*. trans. H. R. James, Project Guttenberg, 2004. http://www.gutenberg.org/files/14328/14328-h/14328-h.htm [accessed 20 August 2013].
Brennan, J., 'Adjustment to Cancer – Coping or Personal Transition?' *Psychooncology* 10:1 (2001), pp. 1–18.
Bury, M., 'Chronic Illness as Biographical Disruption'. *Sociology of Health and Illness* 4:2 (1982), pp. 167–82.
Calvo, P. and T. Gomila, *Handbook of Cognitive Science: An Embodied Approach*, Oxford: Elsevier, 2008.
Canguilhem, G., *The Normal and the Pathological*, New York: Zone Books, 1991.
Carel, H., 'Can I be Ill and Happy?' *Philosophia* 35:2 (2007), pp. 95–110.
Carel, H., *Illness*, Stocksfield: Acumen, 2008.
Carel, H., 'Phenomenology and Its Application in Medicine'. *Theoretical Medicine and Bioethics* 32:1 (2010), pp. 33–46.
Carel, H., 'Phenomenology as a Resource for Patients'. *Journal of Medicine and Philosophy* 37:2 (2012), pp. 96–113. doi:10.1093/jmp/JHS008
Carel, H., 'Illness, Phenomenology, and Philosophical Method', *Theoretical Medicine and Bioethics* 34:4 (2013), pp. 345–57. doi:10.1007/s11017-013-9265-1
Carel, H., 'Conspicuous, Obtrusive, Obstinate: A Phenomenology of the Ill Body', in D. Meacham (ed.), *Medicine and Society, New Continental Perspectives*, Dordrecht: Springer, 2015.
Carel, H. and J. Macnaughton, '"How do you Feel?": Oscillating Perspectives in the CLINIC', *The Lancet* 379:9834 (23 June 2012), pp. 2334–5. doi:10.1016/S0140-6736(12)61007-1
Carman, T., 'The Body in Husserl and Merleau-Ponty', *Philosophical Topics* 27:2 (1999), pp. 205–26.
Clark, A., *Being There*, Cambridge, MA: MIT Press, 1997.
Clark, A., *Supersizing the Mind*, Oxford: Oxford University Press, 2008.
Drummond, J., *Historical Dictionary of Husserl's Philosophy*, Lanham, MD: Scarecrow Press, 2007.
Epictetus, *A Selection from the Discourses of Epictetus with the Encheiridion*, trans. G. Long, Project Guttenberg, 2004. http://www.gutenberg.org/files/10661/10661-h/10661-h.htm [accessed 20 August 2013].
Frank, A., *At the Will of the Body*, Boston: Mariner Books, 1991.
Gallagher, S., *How the Body Shapes the Mind*, Oxford: Oxford University Press, 2005.
Gallagher, S., 'Illness as a Complete Form of Existence', unpublished presentation delivered at the Association for Medical Humanities Annual Conference, University of Durham, 2009.
Gallagher, S. and D. Zahavi, *The Phenomenological Mind*, New York: Routledge, 2008.
Hass, L., *Merleau-Ponty's Philosophy*, Bloomington: Indiana University Press, 2008.
Heidegger, M., *Being and Time*, Oxford: Basil Blackwell, 1962 [1927].

Husserl, E., *Cartesian Meditations*, Dordrecht: Kluwer, 1999 [1931].
Husserl, E., *Ideas Pertaining to a Pure Phenomenology and to a Phenomenological Philosophy: First Book*, The Hague: Martinus Nijhoff, 1982 [1913].
Husserl, E., *Thing and Space: Lectures of 1907*, Dordrecht: Kluwer, 1997 [1907].
Kesserling, A., *The Experienced Body, when Taken-for-Grantedness Falters: A Phenomenological Study of Living with Breast Cancer*, unpublished PhD Dissertation available via UMI, 1990.
Kidd, I. J., 'Can Illness Be Edifying?' *Inquiry* 55:5 (2012), pp. 496–520.
Lindqvist, O., Widmark, A. and B. Rasmussen, 'Reclaiming Wellness – Living with Bodily Problems as Narrated by Men with Advanced Prostate Cancer', *Cancer Nursing* 29:4 (2006), pp. 327–37.
Lindsey, E., 'Health within Illness: Experiences of Chronically Ill/ Disabled People', *Journal of Advanced Nursing* 24 (1996), pp. 465–72.
MacIntyre, A., *Dependent Rational Animals*, London: Duckworth, 1999.
Meacham, D., 'What Goes Without Saying: Husserl's Notion of STYLE', *Research in Phenomenology* 43 (2013), pp. 3–26.
Merleau-Ponty, M., *Phenomenology of Perception*, trans. C. Smith, New York & London: Routledge, 1962 [1945].
Montaigne, M. de, 'To Philosophise is to Learn How to Die', in M. A. Screech (ed.), *The Essays: A Selection*, London: Penguin, 1993, pp.17–36.
Nietzsche, F., 'Why I am so Wise', In *Ecce Homo*, trans. Duncan Large, Oxford: Oxford University Press, 2009, pp. 7–18.
Nussbaum, M., *The Therapy of Desire: Theory and Practice in Hellenistic Ethics*, Princeton NJ: Princeton University Press, 1994.
Pausch, R., *The Last Lecture*, London: Hodder & Stoughton, 2008.
Ratcliffe, M., *Feelings of Being: Phenomenology, Psychiatry and the Sense of Reality*, Oxford: Oxford University Press, 2008.
Ratcliffe, M., 'Phenomenology as a Form of Empathy', *Inquiry* 55:5 (2012), pp. 473–95.
Ratcliffe, M., 'Varieties of Temporal Experience in Depression', *Journal of Medicine and Philosophy* 37:2 (2012), pp. 114–38.
Ratcliffe, M., 'Phenomenology, Naturalism and the Sense of Reality', in H. Carel and D. Meacham (eds), *Phenomenology and Naturalism*, Cambridge: Cambridge University Press, 2013, pp. 67–88.
Sartre, J.-P., *Being and Nothingness*, London: Routledge, 2003 [1943].
Seneca, *On the Shortness of Life*, London: Penguin Books, 2004.
Smith, A. D., *Husserl and the Cartesian Meditations*, London & New York: Routledge, 2003.
Smith, D. W., *Husserl*, London & New York: Routledge, 2007.
Svenaeus, F., 'Das Unheimliche – Towards a Phenomenology of Illness', *Medicine, Health Care and Philosophy* 3 (2000), pp. 3–16.
Svenaeus, F., 'Organ Transplantation and Personal Identity: How does the Loss and Change of Organs have Effects on the Self?' *Journal of Medicine and Philosophy* 37:2 (2012), pp. 139–58. doi: 10.1093/jmp/jhs011
Thorne, S. and B. Paterson, 'Shifting Images of Chronic Illness', *Journal of Nursing Scholarship* 30:2 (1998), pp. 173–8.

Thorne, S., Paterson, B., Acorn, S., Canam, C., Joachim, G. and C. Jillings, 'Chronic Illness Experience: Insights from a Metastudy', *Qualitative Health Research* 12:4 (2002), pp. 437–52.

Toombs, S. K., 'Illness and the Paradigm of Lived Body', *Theoretical Medicine* 9 (1988), pp. 201–26.

Toombs, S. K., 'The Temporality of Illness: Four Levels of Experience', *Theoretical Medicine* 11 (1990), pp. 227–41.

Toombs, S. K., 'The Lived Experience of Disability', *Human Studies* 18 (1995), pp. 9–23.

Toombs, S. K., *The Meaning of Illness: A Phenomenological Account of the Different Perspectives of Physician and Patient*, Amsterdam: Kluwer, 1999.

Wheeler, M., *Reconstructing the Cognitive World*, Cambridge, MA: MIT Press, 2005.

Williams, S. J., *Medicine and the Body*, London: Sage Publications, 2003.

Zahavi, D., *Husserl's Phenomenology*, Stanford CA: Stanford University Press, 2003.

PART SEVEN

Economies, ecologies, politics

14

Thinking love and politics in the world

Michael Hardt (MH) and Mary Zournazi (MZ)

In this chapter, Michael Hardt and Mary Zournazi consider what thinking in the world might mean in relationship to politics; what political practices, connections and relationships arise out of the world, and our understanding of it. This thinking involves our affective lives and labour; in other words, the systems of thinking and connection that can embed and expand social relations, as well as recognize the inherent exchange within the worlds in which we live. This resonates with idea of embodied and situated knowledges that are detailed in different chapters throughout this collection, but it also extends what thinking might mean through the political process itself, and as such, understanding the different social contexts and conditions for political thought.

Throughout this conversational essay, Hardt and Zournazi explore how *thinking with politics* might evolve, and how love as the co-substantiation of thought in the political sphere may enable different relations, negotiations and exchanges to evolve. They consider how this *thinking* might challenge the usual ways we understand the relationship between love and politics, and how this love includes a sense of our 'being in the world' and our thinking in place. And this thinking involves how we might live, feel and respond to each other in times of crisis and change.

Michael Hardt has written extensively on the issues of political love and democracy, and with his co-author Antonio Negri, he has helped to define and shape contemporary ideas and challenges to political thought. Co-author of such works as *Empire, Commonwealth* and *Multitude,*[1] his ideas on the political process help ground the materiality of thinking across different social and political contexts, and in particular his work with Negri on the idea of the multitude provides a rich framework for this conversation and *thinking with politics*. Multitude could be understood not as a unitary political subject or project, but a transformative project in which identities are not fixed, but are in the process of being created.

Mary Zournazi has written extensively on ideas of social hope, crisis and peace, and she has considered the affective and material implications through her scholarly as well as essay style documentaries. Ideas of love and hope are central to her *thinking through and with the world*, and how we make meaning in everyday encounters and political engagements.

They met several times over the course of a year in different locations and across different countries, and the following conversation is what their thinking together produced.

I Thinking

MZ: I'd like to start with what thinking in the world might mean, in the sense of thinking as a real active process in the world, and that it's the world itself – the materiality of the world – that creates our thought, rather than the other way around. So, one of the things that interests me is that relationship of *thinking with politics* and the material world.

MH: Can you say a little more about what thinking with politics means to you?

MZ: I'm trying to think how politics is often separated out from the way in which people think and live. So, how do we think in that sense of the organization of people from the ground up, how do we *think together with* tools and concepts? In other words, thinking as being part of the world itself, and our engagements with it.

MH: I would start with an obvious point, disrupting the traditional notion of the division between theory and practice – the agents of theory being intellectuals and the agents of practice being activists. And what interests me most, really, is the way that political theorizing is done collectively in movements: so that the production of knowledge and the intellectual work of politics is done in the political process itself. So, even just thinking about the location of where political thinking is done, the fact of it being done, not even just in conversation but actually collectively, that would be my first attempt at what I understand as 'thinking with politics'. Sometimes I say that all of my work together with Toni Negri is completely unoriginal, because of the ways we think with movements. The movements themselves are the ones who are the conceptual innovators, and in some ways we are registering the kind of intellectual work and the kind of theoretical work that is done in movements. I don't think that's completely true but I think it's a nice starting point.

MZ: So, yes it's about what is actually happening – and through people's ways of organizing themselves, somehow you're becoming part of the process of thinking and change. But, there's often a kind of dialectic produced in thought: there is the belief that it does have to be theory or practice, or this or that or the other. What is interesting – and thinking about your work – is the relationship between Deleuze and ideas of the multitude, and Marxist thinking. In a way these thinkers almost do not sit together, but somehow they also do, perhaps even more so with this idea of *thinking with politics*. Coming back to that relationship between registering movements, can you say a little bit more about what you mean by that?

MH: I think actually 'registering' is probably not the right word; maybe an introductory word but not quite right way of saying it. Maybe closer to it is 'thinking with movements', but it might be even better to say that there's a kind of relationship among the thinking we do in movements, the thinking we do in the library, and the thinking we do in academic contexts; that there are a variety of scenes of knowledge production or intellectual production – and even modes of it – and that it's probably best not to imagine a priority or a hierarchy among them, but to somehow facilitate their exchange, that's what I would say. I do a lot of my thinking in libraries or in cafes actually, for that matter.

And the originality of the thinking and the importance of the thinking that's done collectively in movements is often unrecognized. What's important, at least in the kind of the political theorizing that I'm interested in, is the relation to and with these other scenes of knowledge production, or scenes of thought.

MZ: Yes, that's what I'm interested in: that dialogue of production and how is that created; how does the dialogue in the library, or out on the street or wherever you're located, form relationships and systems of thinking that enable us? Thinking may not also be the right term, but thinking is often considered as purely a cognitive function or an individual notion of self. What I'm interested in is this: How do we understand the creation of thinking that can come out of the relations between different people and relationships *in* the world, and *with* the world?

MH: I think that's important, and also it's sometimes difficult to comprehend or register the collective innovations in thought, and not only how decisions are made – politically, collectively – but also how thought is advanced. It's much easier to register the one that you mentioned, of the individual thinking alone.

MZ: I am also thinking about the relationship to power, because power works so effectively in the world: it splits us and divides us when we think alone, but in the living world, things are connected. I think that's what I mean by something like ecological thought: that it is not a division between ecological movements and social movements but that there is a connection between thoughts. But power seems to fetishize – maybe fetishize isn't the right word – but it's successful because it harnesses the individual in particular ways, even though power doesn't necessarily work like that, it has a more productive force as we are well aware.

So, I guess the innovation of thinking about the multitude or thinking about the collective is how to articulate that, because at the moment, I think, there's quite a lot of repressive and punitive regimes that we're all experiencing – wherever we are, at whatever level – that subsume the productive force of power relationships. Maybe some examples would help here.

MH: Well, we'll get to examples later, I sense. As we were saying earlier, one path of response is trying to construct the exchanges among these different scenes of thought. I'm not one who would want to say that things done in the university or by academics have no value, but rather that their value should be worked politically, made use of. Finding ways of creating the kinds of dialogue or exchanges among those different scenes, like we mentioned before the streets and the library, or the streets and the university, seems at least one way to undermine the individualizing disciplines of power or the kinds of separation that we suffer under.

MZ: I'd say thinking in the world or thinking with politics is in the realm of affect, and it's the connection between all the different scenes of knowledge that you were talking about. Different spaces, the different places, involve a connection with people that is felt, is experienced, whether it be at a protest, or whatever it is. But at the same time, it's the recognition that we are also in relation to a world, a world that responds to how we act and think, and so on and so forth. So, that's a level of ecology as well.

MH: Of the thinking? And by that you're not explicitly thinking about the Earth, and only about our relation to the Earth?

MZ: I think the world can mean many different things, and we respond to the conditions of the world.

MH: That's another level of challenge in a way.

MZ: Yes, and if we open out this challenge to consider how economics, politics, and community involve the materiality of our experience – that we have to live in a world that is not a passive or limitless resource – then I think we cannot see the world in purely economic rationalist terms, or with political exclusiveness.

MH: That's absolutely right. We can address one face of this ecological challenge by broadening conventional conceptions of production (and reproduction) to include also the production of affects, the production of subjectivity, the production of forms of life. That's one strategy, at least, to extend beyond the traditional limits of economic and political rationalities.

MZ: Yes, and this does need a real shift in thought to consider how the living world becomes part of the conversation in thinking forms of life and politics.

II Love

MZ: I'd like to talk about love and joy, and this idea of thinking with politics – and I'm also thinking of love as a necessary prerequisite for thought, and the creation of social bonds.

MH: I have to start with two cautions about 'love' in politics. The two most common conceptions of love are, in fact, horrible in politics. The first one is of love being a process of merging into one. First of all, I find that disgusting in an intimate relationship anyway, but in politics it seems to me a recipe for fascism. And that's really almost indistinguishable from another notion, which is that you love those who are like you, and sometimes – or often – love of neighbours is interpreted in that way. So, love means either the love of those who are the same, or love as a process of becoming the same – it really amounts to the same thing. This can easily be recognized in white supremacy: the love of whiteness as white supremacy, something like that. And I think it is helpful to think of fascisms and various racisms, even populisms, as being based on that horrible notion of love. Not so much on hatred, I think the hatred is secondary, I think that what's primary for them is a kind of love, but a *horrible* love. So because of that, my first step in thinking about love politically is the necessity of its multiplicity. What it would mean to love in a political sense must mean to love difference, or to love becoming different, or that the plurality or multiplicity of it is necessarily central.

Love in this sense relates directly to joy, and here I revert to Spinoza's definitions: joy is the increase of my power to think and act, and love is joy with the recognition of an external cause.[2] So, what it means to love, then, is to recognize that my power to think and act are increasing, and to be able to identify another or an outside as the cause of it. In some ways, by loving that outside, it really becomes part of you. Here's my super simple example, and it's a very Spinozian example: when you find yourself with certain people – in fact most people, most groups you find yourself in – you are actually *less* able to think clearly. In all kinds of groups, you find yourself almost more confused or unable to express yourself, etc. But there are certain groups you find yourself in where your power to think is actually increased. That's a beautiful Spinozian notion of love: we, being together – either the two of us or a larger group – we recognize that we are able to think more powerfully. That we can more clearly express ourselves, more clearly understand our world – and that seems to me a really basic understanding of love and joy. I love the others in the sense that I recognize they are the cause of an intellectual joy in me. Something similar is also, of course, true in political movements; that the joy of movements is about an increase of our power when we're together: our power both to act and to think.

So, if you put those two things together – joy as the increase of our power collectively to think and act, and multiplicity, that the only love that is useful politically is one that is based on multiplicity and difference – if you put those two together, that is a good skeleton for starting to think of a political concept of love. Multiplicity and joy, I guess that's the summary of the two. So, anyway, that's my beginning, what's yours?

MZ: Yes, it's interesting because some of the secular notions that we've inherited around love come from a lot of Christian theology, and so on. And so one of the problems that have gone awry is how we understand that relationship, which might be a Christian ethics in a secular context, right? So, why I'm saying this is because I think of Simone Weil, and that she has quite a nice reworking of 'Love Thy Neighbour'[3] – that you love the stranger first, 'You love yourself as a stranger', not the stranger as yourself. So, there's something in that way of the outside, that thought is not you. I think it is what you're saying in the Spinozian idea of joy, and then the extension is the sense of love as the recognition of that potential. And I think this is what is the potential of Simone Weil, the idea of that stranger; it's something about the outside, it's something about that force or that energy or that feeling that is being generated between and among people, and so it's something that is being created. And I think social bonds are forged that way.

Of course the other thing that I think about, which is not necessarily adding anything, is Émile Durkheim's General or Collective Effervescence:[4] there's something in the joy of coming together that people feel, and respond to, and that can work for the good of humanity or its reverse, but it certainly offers some ways of understanding human bonds.

But coming back to the political question: we know the bad forms of love involve the ugly stuff where love is exclusionary, you exclude others to create bonds and loyalties to the leader, to the state, to the nation. This type of bond is harnessing capacities for both love and exclusion.

MH: That was a nice edition with the Simone Weil: we not only love each other as different, but also we love ourselves as different. That's a good first part. And then the second part really should be about equality; that we can only love each other as equals, I mean, because the reason I also started with those sorts of caveats is that love in the field of politics is dangerous, and there has to be some choices made. Not all love in politics is good; it can be the source of evil, if I can use that word.

MZ: Well, yes. It has been used very often in our cultures.

MH: And so it's therefore not just a matter of saying what love is in politics, it's also a matter of choosing what love should be, and what kinds of love in the field of politics should be struggled against.

For thinking that field of love and leadership, for a certain way of thinking or for certain audiences, Deleuze and Guattari provide not only a useful combat of familialism but also when they talk about love – and they do a number of times in *Anti-Oedipus* and *A Thousand Plateaus* – they emphasize the links among multiplicities. They come up with examples from Proust, for instance. In love, it's not like two individuals merge; it's more like – there's a composition that is created by partial objects, you know, aspects of me and you, 'It's the wolf in Charlus's voice that composes with the freckles on Albertine's face.' I might have the example a little off, but anyway, the multiplicity in love is always at the forefront for them.[5]

MZ: Yes, I think we need to move away from 'familial' models of love as the models for our existing social, as well as political, relationships, because equality might mean something different, and somehow the idea of composition can capture both the human and non-human elements. So I'm interested in how you are thinking about love and equality here.

MH: There's a lot to say about this, of course, but one could start, in the spirit of *Anti-Oedipus,* with a ban on the love of the leader as a mode of politics.[6] I'm thinking of Freud's claim that group formation in social and political terms is founded on love of leader – the Church and the army are his primary examples – and how love of leader for Freud is really a necessary and natural extension of the love of father.[7] One loves the leader in the place of the father. That's a familial mode of love cast in political terms that can have disastrous consequences. That is a first step towards addressing a mode of love founded on equality.

MZ: And I think we also need to consider different ways of understanding brotherhood as well. It might be more helpful to think of 'friendship' and those kinds of bonds that provide a mechanism for different ideas of equality, because a lot of violence has also been done in the name of brotherly love.

III Thinking life

MZ: I'm thinking about the relationship between democracy and leadership and how it fits into rethinking the relationship between politics and life.

MH: Yes, it definitely should. And that's something Toni and I have been struggling with a lot recently, because we're dissatisfied – I think everyone is – with the two common responses that are given to the so-called 'leaderless movements'. On the one hand there are those who say that everything is fine, that we're winning, that horizontal movements should continue on as-is. And the other side is saying: in order to be effective and long-lasting, you have to adopt traditional structures of leadership and hierarchy. Toni and I think neither of those is right. Those aren't our only choices. And so it then takes some doing to work out our alternatives. Partly it's a question about – what are the mechanisms for a way forward for the movements? And by forward, I'm referring both for the need for continuity or longevity, and the need to construct 'counter-powers' with the ability to contest the ruling powers. So, how to be effective in that sense?

And there would even be a third thing which goes one step further: it is not only a matter of effectively protesting the ruling power, but also the ability to organize an alternative social order. As you well know, I'm a great admirer of the successes of the cycles of social movements in the last ten years, but we also have to recognize their unfulfilled promises; the lack of continuity of counter-powers and the lack of ability to construct alternatives.

MZ: There are two things that are coming to mind: firstly I am thinking back to the Indignant Citizens Movement, at Syntagma Square (2010–12). I wasn't there, but from what I can gather and from things that I've read about it and so on, it sounds like it was such an amazing spontaneity of people coming together, and from all sorts of backgrounds – there wasn't any political party affiliation in that sense – people just came. But there were problems at different points – because Golden Dawn was also there, everybody was there against austerity, primarily. And then there was an eruption of violence between the police and some protestors, so what started out as a peaceful and joyful event changed.

But somehow the energy stayed. Even though when I first went to Greece in 2014 it felt quite tense – which was before Alexis Tsipras and SYRIZA had come to power – I could understand how civil wars could erupt because of Greece's history, and so on and so forth. And then when I went back again this year (2015) after Tsipras had got in, I think that with the current of the Indignant Citizens Movement and people's response to austerity, it helped to get him into power. And he has also been re-elected as prime minister, but from the world's point of view he's recapitulated his position by accepting the austerity measure put forward by the European institutions, and there's harsh criticisms, and so on. But there's still something that can't be taken away from people coming together and people's resistance.

So this is an interesting tension between a leader who promised a whole range of things – anti-austerity and the first radical Left government in Greece's history – and then this huge disappointment. And I guess it's this sort of relationship – the struggle that you're articulating. But I'm wondering how the energy continues; in some ways, without the anti-austerity movement, there would have been no possibility of any form of change. Even though it feels like it could be the end of the political Left, it's not because there's something happening on the ground, so I wonder: How do we creatively move ahead, even when it all seems to fall apart?

MH: Yes. One of the things you said that's interesting is that there's something that remains. I think one of the things that happens is that it's often times very hard for people to recognize the changes that are created by movements. Even movements that are defeated often turn out, in the long run, to have been successful in many respects. For example, I would put Occupy in the US in that category. The way that Bernie Sanders's presidential campaign took up so much from Occupy – its critiques of inequality, debt and so forth – was one symptom of its lasting effects. But the gains are sometimes subterranean, and oftentimes it's very difficult to recognize transformations that movements have brought about. Very often when I'm in conversation with someone who is, how shall I put it, dismissive of the importance of these movements, I would insist on that line.

But even while recognizing the important shifts they made, those three elements that I mentioned before still seem to be lacking. And those are the kinds of elements that lead some people to say, 'Therefore we need a traditional party' or, 'Therefore we need a traditional form of hierarchical or charismatic leadership.' And my response is double: one is that those traditional political forms will not succeed today in creating a counter-power and a lasting alternative – that's the first response. The second response is – and this is the more difficult one – that the movements must find a way to achieve what traditional forms of leadership used to accomplish. And so, that's the more challenging side, but that seems to me the direction that one has to go in this line of thinking. Rather than simply being satisfied with the ephemeral or periodic character of these social revolts, or reverting to assuming that a traditional party or traditional political forms will do it, I think we have to both demonstrate that a democratic mode is possible, and organize it so that it is lasting and effective. It would be interesting – and you know more about the Greek situation than I – to try to figure out to what extent a dynamic like this has already been developed. I know much more about Spain.

MZ: Maybe you could tell me more about that, because in some ways, at the moment, Spain is suffering similar kinds of issues really, in the Euro-zone (if not the whole of Europe, in some ways).

MH: I see the current situation of Podemos as representing, from the perspective of the movements, a kind of wager; a wager that the party will not claim to represent them, but rather will open a space for, and foster the activity and development of, the movements. Rather than essentially saying 'Podemos will take over, and therefore you might as well go home because we'll do it for you, we'll represent you', it's kind of the opposite: the idea that an electoral force could nourish and expand the power of the movements. Since we can talk Deleuze here, this is a point he makes in the *L'Abécédaire* when he gets to 'G' for Gauche, and he says something like, 'There is no such thing as a government of the Left, there is only possibly a government that opens a space for the Left.'[8] So, that's the kind of wager I feel that the activists involved with Podemos are taking; that it could be an electoral force that opens space for the movements, rather than a party that represents the movements. This is even more clear with the municipal governments in Barcelona and Madrid.

MZ: Yes, I think that was the initial space that Tsipras was operating within, even though SYRIZA is a hybrid political organization. But I think that what he was offering – in that sense of leadership – was the idea of *hope* (which I have written about in a different context).[9] But I'm interested in this hope now, because the whole spirit of this event was about arguing for the recognition of the humanitarian crisis that's happening in Greece. They have been arguing for a hope to bring back people's dignity – all this other kind of logic – which was trying to counter the economic logic, which was saying, 'You have to do this, we're not going to allow you to continue unless you do this.' And so they were trying to open up this other space, or at least some other series of questions, or possibilities. And I think that's still open, it's just that they're forced to take on measures that are hurting people from all classes and social groups.

So this idea of opening up space for the Left is perhaps a more useful way of thinking about it. At the same time, it is the relationship between thinking in the world, not as an abstraction – a theorization – but the real world of experience, and what is being acted on and spoken and heard. That's the kind of relationship I'm wanting to work with, in considering what thinking in the world might mean. In other words, how do we create the space and the ways to move forward with it, even when things are working in the opposite direction.

MH: And it does seem to me that Greece and Spain right now present excellent scenes of experimentation, scenes for trying to work this out. Better than others right now.

MZ: Yes. The problem, I think, is the balance of things. Things can slide very easily – and what I mean is that it can slide easily into violence, because everything is precarious, and there are systems of power and services being cut, and real things that are affecting people's day-to-day lives. So, how can we integrate that experience, that affective realm, into what we're talking about? That can make some sort of change, because the real issue is people are experiencing the pain of austerity. This is serious stuff for a country that already has a ragged history in terms of divisions. And so the violence I'm talking about is also a neo-fascism too: Golden Dawn, that xenophobic response, and we also have at the same time this influx of migrants coming from Syria which is its own kind of nightmare for Greece and Europe, who have yet to understand how to respond to it.

But there's something in that space of what you were saying of trying to imagine the democracy – trying to imagine the democracy of what the party might do, but not the party doing it, in a sense. What could something like this look like?

MH: The formula Toni and I are working with (which I'm not sure if I can make clear quickly) is about the inversion of strategy and tactics. Traditionally, strategy was the responsibility of leaders, and tactics was what the rank-and-file did. Tactics is partial and temporary, whereas strategy is long-seeing and long-term planning, across the entire social field. Our idea is that leadership is still necessary, but in a tactical way, leaders can be used and dispensed according to the occasion. But that's not actually the hard part, conceptually; the harder part conceptually is how the multitude, or some democratic form, is capable of strategy, is capable of long-term organization of society. And that's the kind of thing that we have been trying to think through – it reminded me of it when you said a minute ago, what is the possibility of democracy is not that the party would do it, but that the party would relate to it.

I was describing this to some Turkish friends who had been involved in the Gezi Park protest, and they thought this notion of tactical leadership was like playing with fire; any time you give these people power, they're going to take all of it, and the movements can't successfully control and disperse these structures of leadership when they are no longer necessary. And I understand that as a danger. But it seems more important to me to start with the other pole: How can we understand the capacity for democracy itself, because by democracy I do mean something quite different from elections?

MZ: How do we open out this question of democracy, then?

MH: Conceptually it's very simple: democracy is collective self-rule. So that concept doesn't seem too difficult to me – that we rule ourselves together. What's much more difficult, it seems to me, is to identify and confirm the capacities for democracy. It's a mistake to think that we all spontaneously or naturally have the ability to rule ourselves together. Not only to rule ourselves individually – which is a different kind of capacity – but to cooperate in such a way that we can govern. That requires verification. Consider, for instance, the caricature of anarchist thought — not what most anarchists think, but a caricature of anarchism — that assumes that once we remove all forms of social repression, all forms of repressive power, that then people will spontaneously, or naturally, through mutual aid, be able to rule themselves and each other.

I would put much more accent on the *learned character* of the capacity for democracy. That we're not born with it, but it's something that we learn it by doing. That would be the direction I would go, or the direction Toni and I are going in thinking about this question about leadership and democracy, or leadership and transformation.

MZ: Yes, as I was listening to you, it made me think about how the question of the learned element is also something to do with an ethical response as well, isn't it? It's a kind of learning what is the notion of right, in that sense. Not based on – we know that the notion of right, and even human rights, comes from a kind of history of declaring one's right to property – but the right that is separate to that: an ethics or a right that can determine relationships, or work with relationships; that can allow cooperation and community. And I think it's very hard to do, but not impossible. I think it's much harder to do at this point in time – not because there aren't movements happening all over the world, but rather the ways in which we understand 'right'. I don't really know how to articulate the force of power that does inhibit and restrict peoples' potential to activate this more ethical register, or this more ethical response to others.

MH: And so partly this response to others, related to your notion of being in the world, or rather I would give it a more active definition, like, *learning how to be in the world* –

MZ: Yes, something like that.

MH: I understand that. Being in the world now is partly about understanding how you do, and can, cooperate with others, live with others; I understand that as what you're referring to as the ethical component.

MZ: So, the thinking is not in that sense done from categorical imperatives about good and evil in that sense; rather, it's a system of relationships that start to forge those meanings that are between what we understand to be 'the good' – something like that, something along those lines.

MH: So, we got there by talking about the challenges faced by the current movements, and the ways in which the electoral parties do and don't address those challenges. Like I said before, I see it more – and I assume this is also true for at least a certain activist population in Greece – as a kind of wager. That's definitely the way I understand it for those I feel closest to in Spain; they recognize that the leadership group in Podemos can have, at times, a relatively closed mentality, a hegemonic direction, but that they also have the possibility of being even forced to interact and respond with the movements. I definitely appreciate and understand those who would say, in such a situation, 'Well, it's a risk, but it's worth the risk. Let's try.'

MZ: I think very particularly of Yanis Varoufakis, who was the Finance Minister for SYRIZA and the Greek government, and who disagreed with the austerity package, and has now formed other kinds of alliances, which is interesting: for example, DIEM25, whose aim is to democratize Europe. So, it's ways of trying to still work with this problem, which is the sort of fiction: What is Europe? It's meant to have come together to solve certain problems; the idea of Europe or the European Union, but it is not that at all. And I guess what he's doing is starting to articulate this idea of the common. It's very Marxist, in that sense of how to think the international (the global), but I think there is something that crosses over with your idea of the common, and what that might mean, for instance: Can we think economics and can we think humanitarian crisis together? I mean in real terms, and this is the *thinking the world* differently. How do we understand this awkward relation of punitive measures and human experience?

MH: That makes sense to me. I often start my reasoning about the common negatively with property: the common is not property, neither private property nor public property – meaning State property. And so, what are sometimes thought of as strategies of survival – in the situation of austerity – are completely conducted in terms of the common; not in terms of property, but in terms of sharing resources and making decisions collectively over them. That is one point where the common enters into these discussions about austerity. One of the interesting things about it, to me, is there are certain ways in which discussions about the common, or certain perspectives from which it sounds really far out, that seem completely unrealistic. But then, from other perspectives, it's quite clear that that's the way most people are conducting their lives already, in the terms of sharing and making decisions together, about the terms of living. 'Resources' doesn't quite capture the kinds of things I'm talking about.

MZ: But somehow 'resources' is not a bad word, I think, because we're always told about resources in the more economic sense of the word. But the resources you're talking about are coming more from the people, the spirit, the place, the context.

MH: Right. That's true, we use the term 'resources' in that way, too, don't we? We talk about 'one's own resources'; that's interesting. One's own powers and capacities as resources. In situations of social disaster, the possibilities for living in terms of the common become more clear and apparent.

And so, this notion of the common is not only a defensive manoeuvre; it also has to have an offensive meaning. In other words, it has to also re-appropriate and transform forms of property.

MZ: By re-appropriation, we might mean something different in this context – so that thinking resources and the common in new ways involves *thinking together with the world*, and this world includes our social, as well as physical, environments, or perhaps understanding how we can sustain and live in the world, and how this is part of a 'common' project in which we all share: which is the world itself.

IV The world

MZ: Let's come back to love and joy. The disposition towards joy changes the dynamic of how you might participate, or how you might work together with people, or how you might share things in a different way. But I think that people are often closed off to other possibilities of a more continuous relationship with each other, but also with the world itself. For example, how we consider our own relationships, how we consider relationships to institutions, our relationships to the economy, and then also that which is called the world, and how we all interrelate. There's something in joy that is also the opening out of love; love which fits into the propensity towards giving, but not necessarily receiving.

MH: Let me try a little detour and then come back to the love part; maybe you can help me think through this. This is my own narrative of my coming to political action or way of life. When I was in college in the US as a twenty-year-old, I felt very distant from political activities. It's partly that I felt that other students were just posing at being political, and not really being political. But it wasn't so much that. It was more that I felt there was a kind of moralism that dominated political activism. First of all, that we're expressing our solidarity for others suffering. We're not struggling on our own behalf, but rather we're making a sacrifice. Even more, expressing a solidarity with those suffering elsewhere. At the time – confronting apartheid in South Africa, US-backed wars in Central America – these kinds of things were of my generation of twenty-year-olds. I just felt I couldn't find my place in it.

When I made my way, then, to Central America, and found ways of participating with – or at least observing – their struggles, politics seemed to be a completely different thing. I discovered from them the joy of politics. It wasn't just that it always involved dancing, although it certainly did. There wasn't this cloud of moralism or of constant reference to other peoples' suffering. It was, rather, not even reference to suffering so much, but to the joy of struggling together. Suddenly, I could see a political life, where I couldn't previously. It was because of this, like I say – Does it make sense to use this phrase? – the joy of struggle. It seemed to be a joyful mode of life, rather than as a seasonal activity, or as a duty that one had, even responsibility to others. I did it because I loved it. That's what I wanted.

It seems to me important to do politics that way. First of all, not out of a duty for others, but to recognize one's own joy and desire in it, which has to do with the struggle itself. I'm stumbling a little bit here, because I don't want to just say the struggle is all that matters. The achievements and the goals are also important. I don't even want to subordinate the one to the other, but in some ways they feel indistinguishable to me. The joyfulness in the struggle, in part, is already an achievement.

MZ: Yes, in the coming together itself, in that way. Is that what you mean?

MH: Yes. In some ways, this is all a kind of antidote to the poisons of moralism, resignation, and depression. The joys of struggle continue through victories and defeat.

MZ: Yes, and it's what strangely survives, if anything. Otherwise, you wouldn't continue at all, if you really took stock of everything that's happening, in whatever context of violence or forms of oppression that have happened. Joy, in a way, is the antidote to hope as well, I think.

One of the things I noticed, and this is also a detour, but it links to what you're saying: when I was in Greece to make my film *Dogs of Democracy*,[10] there were two strikes within the space of ten days. The first one was a general strike. The second one was also a general strike. The first one I attended. It was a very peaceful, joyous kind of event. People with their music; it was a gathering, and almost festive in the way that these things can be. It was coming from people's hearts, what they felt: that they needed to be out in the street, they needed to be saying these things that they were unhappy with the cuts that were happening – to everything, really; the cut to pensions being a main issue.

During the last five to ten minutes of this march that moved up and down the square, there were some organized protestors who started to throw petrol bombs. That's when the violence erupted. Everything completely changed from something where people were united together in their difference – there were old people, young people, all sorts of different people – to a moment where it erupted into violence, which dissipated all of it. Joy, somehow, is essential to act against violence. I think that violence is what prohibits or stops the potential for things to move, at least in that kind of setting.

What people remember becomes a question, too: Do people remember the bits in which people came together joyously? Or do they remember the police, the bombs that were going off? In terms of a global media, this all that you see: the tear gas and the riot police. I filmed the event. What you saw wasn't just riot police. I filmed the riot police as well, but what was interesting was the riot police were walking side-by-side with the protesters, before any violence erupted. There was a lot of anger towards the riot police. There's something in that too, the spiralling of violence within it at all. That's just an observation.

Maybe it's coming back to what you're saying also about the moralism that people have around the participation in events. From a point of view of those who want to save 'others' – and then those who don't want to participate at all, and see the coverage, and respond to the violence and say: 'We'll see. See what happens when you let them out on the street.' They're both clashing kinds of moralisms.

MH: The violence question is complicated.

MZ: Yes, I know.

MH: It creates a homogeneity of experience.

MZ: Yes. It doesn't give value to this other ... it becomes this only one thing. It becomes violent. I mean, it becomes this demonstration of violence. And it reduces the experience to just that, as if that is all that people are feeling, and working with. People are angry. The hate is interesting, because there's more serious levels of hate – other than the sense that you hate your ice-cream or you hate this or that thing. When it's more serious, that is not hate to me, it's a kind of indifference towards others – you really don't care – whereas hate, I think, has got an element of care, and it still has some connection. Even though it doesn't play out that way, there's still some relation to whatever it is. If you're indifferent, then there's nothing.

MH: The opposite might be sadness for me. It might be that sadness and indifference are closely related.

MZ: Maybe. Why sadness?

MH: Because it's a decrease of what we can do together. It's related in some ways to depression. I don't mean that as a psychological designation but a lack of possibilities, a lack of potential; I guess that's what I'm thinking of.

MZ: Sadness seems to me to be a softer version. Sadness feels like it could lead to the possibility of joy, whereas I don't think indifference can.

MH: I see what you mean.

MZ: I think it's not even on the same plane.

MH: Let's stick with indifference then. Let's try something about love, too, that might connect us. I think love only makes sense as a progressive political concept when it's a multiplicity; in some ways, an open multiplicity, an unbounded number. It's helpful, I think, to start with one, two – but it's not even three. Then the question becomes: How does one negotiate? What kind of lasting bonds that empower us are constructed among the many of us?

I think, to come back to your description of the general strike, one could even think of the day as enacting something like that. Of course it wouldn't just be the day, because I think it's important for love to be a lasting bond. I don't mean lasting forever, but I mean ...

MZ: So, it's potential to be something that's ongoing is what you're saying?

MH: Yes. There's an open-endedness to love. It never makes sense to say, 'Here's a love but it'll be gone tomorrow.' Or, 'Here's a love but it'll be gone next Thursday.'

MZ: Yes.

MH: There always has to be ...

MZ: Well, it has an infinite sense to it.

MH: Yes, indefinite at least. Love is not infinite, but it never comes with a fixed endpoint.

MZ: Yes. I mean that really is the problem; we don't understand this infinite relation or notion of love ...

MH: Yes, that's exactly it. So one challenge, then, about this political notion of love, is the negotiation of relationships among multiplicities. The second is the indefinite temporal nature – looking to a future – and then the third I think has to be its transformative nature. Because in love, one always becomes different. What it means to love is to allow yourself to become different.

MZ: Yes, love which is not romantic, it's something else. It's the confusion I think between desire and love in that sense. There's a difference.

MH: Say a little bit more about that.

MZ: Well, we usually think of love as an outcome of desire. The joy that is connected to love is not about a lack of desire or something you've lost.

MH: Fulfilling a lack.

MZ: Yes, I know that's not what you're saying, but that's the usual kind of way of associating desire and love together. Whereas joy gives you a whole different register: on the one hand, temporality, and on the other hand, a sense of how things can continue in a different way. Even though when you feel joy, it's not something you can capture. Together you feel it more exuberantly. It's not even feeling good, actually. It's not even that. I think it's a different lived experience; it's a different conceptual model. I think about temporality, difference and the multiplicity. I know exactly what you're talking about with multiplicity, but I'm thinking what is the *real* in the multiplicity?

MH: What do you mean?

MZ: I'm thinking about this materiality of the world. If things are not coming from our desire towards things, but somehow a gathering from outside of ourselves, how do we live that real, in a sense? Of course it's multiple, and it is a multiplicity, but I'm wondering if you can give an example.

MH: This isn't really an example – I find it useful to think about this in terms of composition, like a musical composition. I'm responding to your point about lack. You're saying it's not a matter of fulfilling a lack but rather involves composing a number of different elements that together form something different. It's holding that composition together, or the bond that's created by such a composition. That bond is one thing we have to explain in love. The other is the transformative character of it. I think the third is this open temporality. Love is ...

MZ: Yes, that bond is important, and it's that which creates something else ...

MH: Well, one doesn't want to get lost in scripture, but this notion about love being stronger than death is about our love being the strongest bond. It's what can hold us together.

MZ: That's what I was seeing at the strike: the bond that was bringing people together in a way, with all of the different feelings people were having, and then the rupture was the violent part – which did nothing to help the bonds of resistance, if you want to call it that. I guess it closed things down, rather than opened things out, which is what the openness of love can do. I think the Scriptures can be very helpful in some respects, or virtues that they can open out for us; it's just they have to be rethought, but the understanding of love is a central element.

MH: Maybe we should link this to what we were saying before, regarding a form of love that is based on indifference. I think that's the horribly destructive kind of love. The kinds of bonds that are created through that indifferent relationship, we should say it as a kind of love, but a destructive kind. In some ways, what I'm struggling with often in this, is how to make distinctions among forms of love, some of which I want to valourize and some I want to ...

MZ: But I think that indifference is useful, because it starts to think through the fact that it is a creation of something, it just doesn't move us along in a particularly helpful way.

MH: It can trap us in a horrible way.

MZ: Yes, well the trap is the danger.

MH: Could we link this notion of love in multiplicity – or an 'anti-indifferent love', let's call it that – with the notion I was fumbling with earlier, about joy and struggle? I would like the two to be the same thing – that open temporality of it; also the openness to a kind of multiplicity, rather than being fixed. And, what I was complaining about – a moralism – was a flattening of political issues onto an almost symbolic screen.

MZ: I think what is helpful with thinking indifference in that way is to recognize, or be able to engage with, that which you don't like. Because one of the problems with moralism is that you're always right. I mean, you're always doing the right thing, the right cause; you're helping those who are suffering. Whereas if you're recognizing your own involvement in a certain sort of indifference, whatever that might be, and that your own commitment to moralism can produce indifference to the reality of what people are living or feeling or needing.

MH: We're developing a polemic against a love based on indifference or a bond based on indifference. Indifference in the way we've been using it is somewhat odd but I think helpful.

V Encounters

MH: I was never in Syntagma, but I was in many of the other squares. One of the things that seemed magical about these squares was the kind of open space of encounter. People were really together, and together in a way that was different.

MZ: Yes, I think the extended encounter is interesting, because it's something that happens only between people when they encounter each other.

MH: Right – the space for that being possible. I mean, that's what I thought was so distinctive about the movement of squares: that suddenly there seemed like a social space that hadn't existed previously, in which people could encounter each other.

MZ: Yes, it's still continuing – even with what's been happening in Greece – I think it's still continuing for people, even if we call it sadness for a moment. People are still connecting somehow, and I guess it's those bits of connection that I find get missed in the way we document and talk about them.

MH: In some ways, at least, a full notion of encounter requires breaking up indifference, or rather, indifference obstructs having actual encounters.

MZ: And it's the encounters in some way that can make the difference, and it can keep things moving along.

MH: This sequence – encounter, joy, love – makes sense to me, each building on the last; or, what were you going to say? A different order?

MZ: I was going to say it's love, encounter, joy; but then I think it is encounter because it is that materiality of experience that then creates the relation.

MH: I'm thinking that encounter can at least be thought of as a temporary period – a short time period – whereas love is open in its temporality.

MZ: Yes, that's why I was thinking the love was open in its temporality, and therefore the encounter is part of the temporality.

MH: I see. It makes sense.

MZ: Now I'm thinking you need the action for it to exist. In other words, the relational proximity or distance that's part of the encounter.

And I don't think it has to be necessarily a real encounter. You don't have to live an experience, but it is something to do with being able imagine the suffering, and it moves beyond empathy or sympathy – it is about a certain understanding and grace. What I mean by grace here is as a force that only comes through the movement of love, rather than in that moralism way of: I'm going to do good for myself, by going out there and saving people, whatever it is you're going to save. The encounter is something altogether different, in quality and response. How you live it, how you express it, how you work with it, particularly now, I think, because we have to extend this thinking with the Syrian crisis – it's unprecedented in terms of population movement in Europe.

Of course, the recent Paris attacks is another example of the ways in which we formulate these things and understand them, and in this formulation it will lead us into worse situations, or into trying to work out something that is helpful. Not just us sitting here and talking about it and thinking this is what we want, when it's something that's real and being activated.

MH: That's the in the world part.

MZ: That's the in the world part, yes.

MH: That's the theme for the whole series of things, right?

MZ: Yes, I'm not entirely sure what it all means in the end, but it is a starting point to think politics in the world, not just about it.

Post script

We finished our conversation a day after the US presidential elections. It occurred to me that the 'horrible' love that we were looking at has never been more dangerous, not just in the US, but across the world.

This 'horrible' love is a love nonetheless that must be understood. Love as exchange in whatever form it takes is one of the most powerful forces of *thinking* that exists in the world. And in the real world of experience, we must understand how this thinking takes hold, but is often ignored in the political process itself by the closing down of discussion on either side of politics. So that the call to 'thinking with politics' must involve how we can understand what makes people live and feel disenfranchised, but also what are the elements of dialogue and respect that might allow the space for a different kind of love.

Since the election, many anti-Trump protests have been cast as love versus hate. On the one hand, this misrecognizes the desires coming from the majority of the Trump electorate – even, or especially, those driven by feelings of white racial belonging. By recognizing these feelings as being motivated by love does not endorse them; on the contrary, as we discussed in this chapter, the point is to understand and counter this destructive mode of love. By simply posing the alternative to Trump as a movement based on love is good, but insufficient without making more precise the mode of love necessary and as we suggested, it is not as love versus hate but as a contest between two modes of love that must be understood. And it might be that this requires a form of grace – the exchange that acknowledges the affective and social experiences of people, rather than those based on identity politics – and in this way it may offer more productive encounters between a range of communities and experiences to help us rethink and refresh love and politics in the world.

Notes

1 See Michael Hardt and Antonio Negri, *Empire* (Cambridge, MA: Harvard University Press, 2000); Michael Hardt and Antonio Negri, *Multitude* (New York: Penguin Books, 2004); Michael Hardt and Antonio Negri, *Commonwealth* (Cambridge, MA: Harvard University Press, 2009).

2 Baruch Spinoza, *Ethics* (London: Dent, 1989).

3 Simone Weil, *First and Last Notebooks,* trans. Richard Rees (London: Oxford University Press, 1970), p. 284.

4 For a description of the concept of General or Collective Effervescence, see Émile Durkheim, *Elementary Forms of Religious Life*, trans. Karen E. Fields (New York: Free Press, 1995).

5 See Gilles Deleuze and Félix Guattari, *A Thousand Plateaus: Capitalism and Schizophrenia,* trans. Brian Massumi (Minneapolis: University of Minnesota Press, 2005); Gilles Deleuze and Félix Guattari, *Anti-Oedipus: Capitalism and Schizophrenia,* trans. Brian Massumi (Minneapolis: University of Minnesota Press, 2008).

6 Deleuze and Guattari, *Anti-Oedipus.*

7 Sigmund Freud, *Group Psychology and the Analysis of the Ego,* trans. James Strachey (London: The International Psychoanalytic Press, 1922).

8 *L'Abecedaire de Gilles Deleuze, avec Claire Parnet*, dir. Pierre-André Boutang (Paris: DVD Editions Montparnasse, (1996) 2004).

9 Mary Zournazi, *Hope – New Philosophies for Change* (New York: Routledge, 2003).

10 See Mary Zournazi (Director), *Dogs of Democracy* (Canberra: Ronin Films, 2016). http://www.roninfilms.com.au/feature/13955/dogs-of-democracy.html

References

Deleuze, G. and F. Guattari, *A Thousand Plateaus: Capitalism and Schizophrenia,* trans. B. Massumi, Minneapolis: University of Minnesota Press, 2005.

Deleuze, G. and F. Guattari, *Anti-Oedipus: Capitalism and Schizophrenia,* trans. B. Massumi, Minneapolis: University of Minnesota Press, 2008.

Deleuze, G. and C. Parnet, *L'Abecedaire de Gilles Deleuze avec Claire Parnet,* dir. P.-A. Boutang, Paris: DVD Editions Montparnasse, (1996) 2004.

Durkheim, E., *Elementary Forms of Religious Life*, trans. Karen E. Fields, New York: Free Press, 1995.

Freud, S. *Group Psychology and the Analysis of the Ego*, trans. James Strachey, London: The International Psychoanalytic Press, 1922.

Hardt, M. and A. Negri, Empire, Cambridge, MA: Harvard University Press, 2000.

Hardt, M. and A. Negri, *Multitude*, New York: Penguin Books, 2004.

Hardt, M. and A. Negri, *Commonwealth*, Cambridge: Harvard University Press, 2009.

Spinoza, B., *Ethics*, London: Dent, 1989.

Weil, S., *First and Last Notebooks*, London: Oxford University Press, 1970.

Zournazi, M., *Hope – New philosophies for Change*, New York: Routledge, 2003.

Zournazi, M. *Dogs of Democracy*, dir. M. Zournazi, Canberra: Ronin films, 2016, http://www.roninfilms.com.au/feature/13955/dogs-of-democracy.html [accessed 01 January 2017].

15

Thinking with interdependence: From economy/environment to ecological livelihoods

Ethan Miller and J. K. Gibson-Graham

Introduction

The world calls us to respond to the rising inequality between those who struggle daily for sustenance and the tiny minority that is drowning in financial wealth; to the unprecedented global displacement of human beings from the lands they call home – more than 65 million people seeking refuge from violence and socio-ecological devastation; to communities of colour in settler colonial societies around the world, besieged by the white supremacist violence of policing, prison and enforced poverty; to the white working class despair, anger and resentment over the growing impossibility of dignified work and a stable future; and to the escalating dynamics of fear, blame, scapegoating and division that these converging processes bring forth.[1] Meanwhile, as human communities battle over the construction of new walls between and within them, an anthropogenic geological-scale expulsion of CO_2 continues daily to push the planet's climate system towards irrecoverable destabilization. In the USA and Australia, we watch appalled as the powerful coal lobby pushes for expanded fossil fuel mining and burning, while politicians in one country abandon environmental regulation and in the other blame the failure to cope with extreme heat on the unreliability of renewable energy.

One could be forgiven for concluding that humans today, especially those residing in our nooks of the minority 'developed' world, have decided to stop thinking for themselves, and certainly of others. In the 'post-fact' era, critical thought is not encouraged, and creative, empathetic thinking is deemed suspect. Yet never before have there been stronger calls to attend to the world and wake up from the anaesthesia-inducing flow of information about who we can be, what we can and should have, and which 'others' might be standing in the way of our self-fulfilment. These calls should form the conditions of possibility for thought, and should indeed *force* thought – not merely as the agential act of a rational, individual self, but as an emergent collective response with, as, against and for the world.

But cries such as these are falling on the deaf ears of just enough of the voting population of powerful nations around the world to be institutionally ignored. The ability to *think with* the challenges of climate change and the suffering of fellow humans, let alone other species facing extinction, is blocked. How might social theorists and action researchers work to open new pathways and help prompt a mass thinking event of the magnitude that will be needed to move on from 'the Enlightenment' to 'the Sustainment'?[2]

In this short essay we seek to both challenge and think beyond some key contributors to this shared blockage: contemporary articulations of 'the Economy' and 'the Environment.' For the moment, we capitalize the 'E's to denote their common articulation as singular, distinct, coherent and law-governed domains, though our aim is precisely to *de-capitalize* them (in both senses of the word, pun intended). As we describe in more detail below, the distinction between these two domains, and the particular ways in which they are each constituted in conventional contemporary discourse, severs us from transformative, ethically infused encounters with our constitutive interdependencies. By dividing our *oikos* (habitat) into two tension-ridden domains, and by articulating these domains in terms of a law-governed sphere of (capitalist) market activity ('the Economy') and a separate, law-governed non-human sphere of resources ('the Environment'), this pair of categories makes it exceedingly difficult to develop collective accounts of and interventions into *how we are actually sustained*, and *with whom/what we are actually interdependent*.

In today's world, complex negotiations of multi-species community and livelihood have been deflected into modes of non-thought such as 'jobs versus environment', or 'cost/benefit analysis' or 'necessary trade-offs.' These formulations appear to provoke serious collective consideration, yet in practice block the creative potentialities of thinking. They assume too much about what the world is made of, what is inevitable and what may yet be transformed. In Isabelle Stengers' terms, following Deleuze, this is 'stupidity' – not an ignorance that can be attributed to particular individuals, but rather a collective affect that is born when the contours of the world are ossified and frozen, and change is rendered impossible. 'Stupidity,' she notes, 'is active, it feeds on its effects, on the manner in which it dismembers a concrete situation, in which it destroys the capacity for thinking and imagining.'[3] This non-thought allows us to maintain diabolical illusions of hyper-separation, whereby *Homo economicus* makes a (paid) living free of dependency on 'handouts' from others, and humankind stands apart from obligations to planetary ecological processes. It is a recipe for the scapegoating of those in our midst who 'take from hard working people' or those at some distance who 'steal our jobs', and for denigrating those privileged hippies who 'want to protect some endangered plant or animal' or those who 'jump the queue' and, because of their difference, 'threaten our way of life'. As long as Economy and Environment continue to divide and obscure our relations of sustenance, many of us will remain in a fantasy land, believing that action against climate change, solidarity with refugees and undocumented migrant workers, or protecting groundwater from profit-thirsty fossil fuel development is 'not in our interests', while a tax cut for billionaires *is*! The necessity of challenging and transforming these kinds of dynamics cannot be understated at this juncture of history.

What is to be done? How can we think *with* the world, with the fullness of the interdependencies that make us? How can we act in the midst of this thinking? Such work of exposing interdependence and its ethical demands is, simultaneously, an *impossible* and a *necessary* task. It cannot be done, and yet it must be engaged. This is the condition, perhaps, of life itself – call it, with Simon Critchley, the 'infinite demand' or, with Jacques Derrida, a justice always 'to come';[4] call it ~~ecology~~, crossed out to mark its impossible necessity and necessary impossibility.[5] The challenge of rethinking economy and re-embedding economy within ecology is one that has been taken up by members of the Community Economies Collective,[6] an international group of action researchers who share an interest in exploring and supporting diverse practices of sustenance beyond the narrowly defined boundaries of capitalist economics. Inspired by various threads of Marxian, feminist, post-colonial and post-structural thought, and committed to embedding our work in the 'here-and-now' of particular places and communities, we have developed a range of thinking practices that help us, and those we work with on the ground, to open and expand pathways for thinking interdependence and negotiating the ethical dynamics that emerge in our myriad constitutive relations. After elaborating the problem of Economy and Environment, we will present one particular approach to this work and conclude with some speculations about using these thinking practices in place.

The economy and the environment, as we know them

It is, at this point, common sense – something called 'the Economy' is the system by which most humans in industrialized nations effectively make their livings. It is composed of the dynamic monetary transactions associated with myriad producers and consumers, and is ultimately animated towards necessary, endless growth by the twin drivers of capitalist profit and individual utility maximization. One cannot easily deny nor defy the Economy, as it is widely understood to punish those who go against its logics or demands, and it stands as a central site of intervention for governments, policymakers, and the owners and managers of its central institutions – capitalist firms. At the same time, something called 'the Environment' confronts us from beyond, from the *outside*: whether constituted as a collection of resources to be mined (carefully), a space for dumping and discharging the wastes of production, a set of services to be rendered 'sustainable' in their availability to human enjoyment and endless economic growth or a sovereign limit-setting force of Nature, the Environment stands as a distinct, non-human realm to be variously ignored, managed, obeyed or 'saved'.[7]

The Economy and the Environment constitute what we call a 'hegemonic assemblage' in contemporary life. Despite their contingent, historical production as core categories of industrial modernity, these terms appear in common understanding to name pervasive and inevitable contexts within which human action must unfold.[8] They are 'assemblages' (perhaps even two parts of one assemblage) in the sense that they are constituted discursively and materially; produced by various practices of measurement, representation, institution and discipline; and rendered semi-durable by their inculcation as habits of materiality (forms of landscape, tools, etc.) and subjectivity (imagination, desire, etc.).[9] What these assemblages produce (and are, in turn, produced by) is a *form of life*, an ontological formatting of a particular terrain in which certain kinds of problems and possibilities appear while others are rendered non-viable or pushed to the margins.[10]

What is it that appears? First, we are confronted with a seemingly-inevitable landscape of conflict and tension. The *oikos* is divided by these two articulations, and we find ourselves dependent on two spheres of life that are effectively at war. We are warned of what the Economy will do to us if we take a step towards, for example, curbing carbon emissions or allowing more people to settle in our communities and nations. Meanwhile 'the Environment' has either an infinite capacity to absorb pollution and recover from degradation or a delicate 'carrying capacity' that cannot possibly withstand an increased population footprint, especially (so the population discourse often tacitly implies) of certain *colours* of feet. For those who are threatened with job loss, with not being able to pay the rent or mortgage, or with the inability educate their children, 'the Economy' – that is, wage labour and debt – appears to be something in which they are obliged to participate at the threat of extinction, and 'the Environment' appears as something whose care merely detracts from these desperate priorities (if, in fact, it needs care at all, since the 'environmentalists' appear here as little more than a privileged special interest). This frustrating agency deficit married with a victim sensibility is easily whipped up into simplistic and misdirected antagonisms, while at the same time a coterie of experts are empowered to repeatedly reinforce this scene and pronounce the constraints within which we must live. Thinking – as a transformative practice of engaging a dynamic and possibility-filled world – is shut down.

The second set of consequences produced by the hegemonic articulation of Economy and Environment is the rendering-invisible of a whole host of constitutive relations that lie outside the sphere of either the capitalist market or purified Nature. On one side, the capitalist Economy appears as the singular site for the production of livelihood, while at the same time excluding or marginalizing vast swaths of human sustenance activity – all of the crucial labour and relationships that cannot be capitalized, monetized or, in many cases, even measured. On the other side, the Environment appears as external Nature, while rendering invisible all of the complex ways in which human and more-than-human worlds are constitutively interwoven and inseparable – made up of myriad interdependencies that continually transgress all divisions between nature and culture, wild and cultivated, urban and rural, and creation and production. Trapped between the twin poles of Economy and Environment, with both claiming the crown of the sovereign, the whole actual world of interdependent planetary sustenance is made exceedingly difficult to see, to engage and to collectively negotiate. This hegemonic articulation, to use another of Isabelle Stengers' terms, serves to *anaesthetize* us to the demands of our complex interdependencies, and to the ethical responsibilities and vulnerabilities they call forth. To build new pathways for action and possibility in this era of planetary ecosystem destabilization, the assemblage of Economy and Environment (as we know them) must be unmade.

Tipping the assemblage

How does one unmake an assemblage? We begin by recognizing that no assemblage is ever completed; hegemony is never total.[11] The assemblage is at once both a site of *instituting* worlds and a site in which worlds are always already *becoming-otherwise*. 'A territory', write Deleuze and Guattari, 'is always en route to an at least potential deterritorialization'.[12] As powerful as Economy and Environment may be to map the terrain of possibility in contemporary life, these articulations fail to capture everything, fail to cover all space with their measurements and modes of discipline, and are in fact shakier and less stable than their 'common sense' appearance might suggest.

It is precisely the task of amplifying this instability that J. K. Gibson-Graham has taken on in her critique of 'capitalocentric' models of economy and in the development of a notion of diverse economies.[13] The Diverse Economies framework, which is often introduced via the image of a floating iceberg (Figure 15.1), helps to identify and amplify the myriad practices and relations that continually 'escape' the hegemonic narrative of the Economy. These practices are shown below the waterline, submerged under those activities that are seen as part of the 'real' economy – working for a wage or salary in a job connected to business and transacting commoditized goods and services via the capitalist market.[14]

Parallel work is unfolding relative to the domain of the hegemonic Environment, as post-humanist ecological thought increasingly challenges hyper-separated notions of an external 'nature' and begins to map the complex interbecomings of a more-than-human ecological 'mesh'.[15] What emerges from this work – intimately connected with and expressive of transversal practices on the ground – is a profound sense of the world that lies 'beyond' the hegemonic assemblage, a 'world of becoming' in which we are *connected* in ways we barely imagined, *responsible* to and with each other in ways we can barely grasp, much less fully respond to, and *called* towards new possibilities for world-making that we have only just begun to glimpse.[16]

But amidst all of this, we are still gripped by the Economy and the Environment. Their power in shaping imagination and possibility is real. We must face the ways in which we *depend on* the very assemblage we seek to undo – embedded as we are in the workings of the Economy and invested as we must be in certain modes of engaging the Environment. 'If you blow apart the strata [the sedimented structure of assemblages] without taking precautions ... you will be killed, plunged into a black hole, or even dragged towards catastrophe'.[17] How, then, are we to respond? Deleuze and Guattari propose that we make radical, effective change not by simply ripping up the entire current order of things, not by 'wildly destratifying', but rather by 'gently tipping the assemblage':[18]

> This is how it should be done: Lodge yourself on a stratum, experiment with the opportunities it offers, find an advantageous place on it, find potential movements of deterritorialization, possible lines of flight, experience them, produce flow conjunctions here and there, try out continuums of intensities segment by segment, have a small plot of new land at all times.[19]

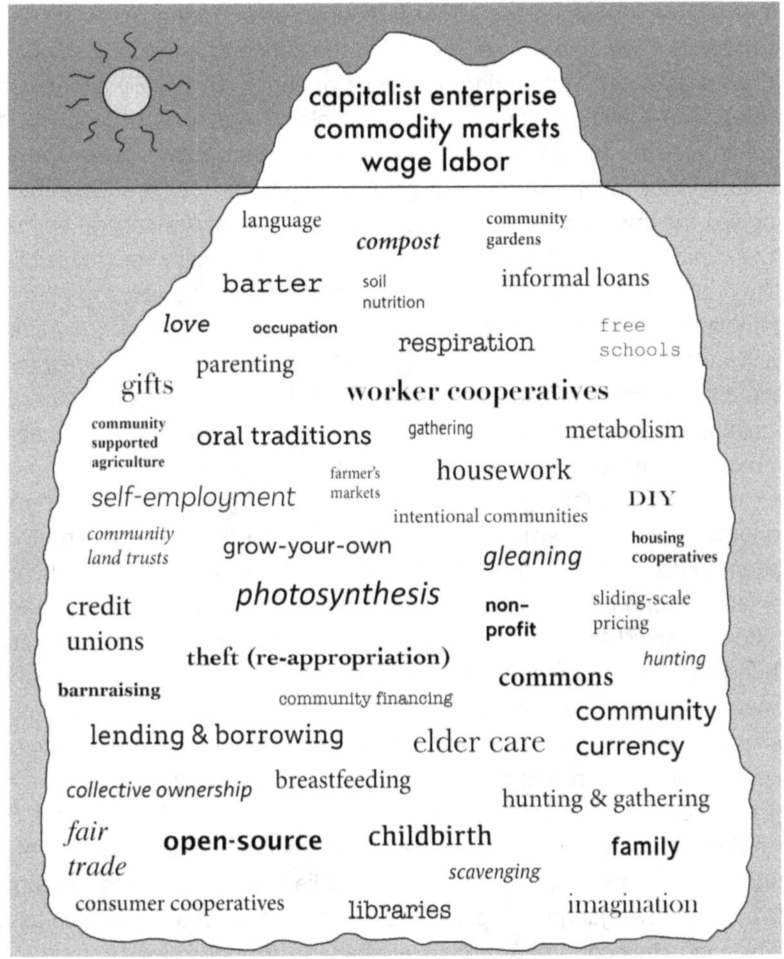

FIGURE 15.1 *The economy as an iceberg. Original image by Ken Byrne, modified text by Ethan Miller.*

To think the new and to make the new, we stand where we are, all the while rendering this place into something other than it has been – finding all of the ways that our current reality is already otherwise and already becoming more of this otherwise. We amplify these becomings (lines of flight) and experiment with their possibilities, all the while recognizing that some mode of ongoing stability is necessary for life to continue. Strategic displacement, in other words, demands *belonging* – both for the economically disenfranchised and for those for whom the hegemonic assemblage still seems to 'work'. Exposing ethical interdependence calls for some comfort that one's whole world (whoever one might be) won't come wholly unravelled in the process.

If revolution means ripping all of reality apart and building anew, we refuse revolution. But we also refuse 'reform' in the sense of a moderate tweaking that never asks earth-shattering questions or seeks to radically alter existing modes of life. Revolution and reform are political practices of stupidity: the first animated by the twin utopian refusals to either locate oneself in time and place (succumbing to the thought-stopping fantasy of the Perfect) or to recognize the complex implication of means and ends; the second animated by the cynical refusal to participate in the birth of radically new possibilities for life and livelihood. We seek, instead, to proceed by destabilizing dominant assemblages while anchoring ourselves to practices upon which we already rely. We want to develop tools to help emerging movements think/act in this space: the lived space of ethical negotiation of diverse livelihoods; the ongoing production of the *oikos* and its inhabitants; and the ongoing production of commons and uncommons amidst this interdependence.

Much of our past writing has focused on rethinking and reframing 'economy' from a hegemonic space of capitalist dominance to an always-indeterminate space of diverse relations, identifying existing practices of alternative economic subjectivity and ethical negotiation as sites for (potential) transformation.[20] More recently, and in multiple collaborations, we have sought to bring more-than-human human ecological relations 'in' to this expanded economic space of becoming.[21] The language of 'community economy' has been a central strategy for fostering counter-hegemonic assemblage-tipping, where 'community' refers not to locality or shared identity, but to the raw, ethical exposures of coexistence in our myriad relations of sustenance.[22] As we reflect now, however, on the dense, anaesthetizing articulations of the Economy and the Environment described earlier, we are called to experiment with a different language to express this broad project. What if we were to stop re-signifying 'the economic' – continually battling its hegemonic connotations – and instead mobilize a different, more transversal language for the articulation of transformative relation and movement beyond the Economy/Environment machine? Building on both the substance and spirit of past work, we seek to transpose now into a new key.

Thinking with interdependence: Ecological livelihoods

Instead of thinking along the lines of an Economy and an Environment, we propose to experiment with reconstituting the landscape of current action and possibility in terms of *ecological livelihoods.*[23] This term *livelihood* is commonly used to indicate, quite generally, the work of sustenance. It has been used in

English, via a variety of spellings (*lifelode, liflade, lyvelode, lyveliod, livelyhoode* and others) since at least the thirteenth century.[24] It is certainly not a wholly neutral term, but it also lacks the historical baggage and disciplinary power that comes with 'economy' or 'economics.' It evades categorization relative to the Economy/Environment pair. It is a term of *practice*, of experience, a simple articulation of complex lives lived and negotiated from the inside, *par le milieu*, rather than categorized from without.[25] Livelihood is what unfolds in the space of life's action, the middle-space in which the hegemonic division of Economy/Environment blurs and dissolves into the power-laden specificities of encounter and negotiation. Having not been wholly captured by a particular hegemonic metrology, it indicates a diversity of activity, a variety of skills and knowledges, a plethora of possible sites of action, and multiple configurations of ever-changing relations and processes that cannot be captured by a generality. Livelihood is, in this way, a minor (as opposed to a major) category: it resists unification under a singular standard of measure, image of action, or domain of life.[26] When invoked, it most often comes linked to particular contexts, stories and strategies: How do people make a living here, and there? We do it in *all kinds* of ways. Moreover, livelihood also has the nice resonance of *lively*, which beckons towards some kind of normative commitment to *joy* in the Deleuzian/Spinozan sense of enhancing a body's capacities through connection, and it also serves to remind us of the 'lively matter' in which we participate and from which we continually emerge.[27]

The language of 'livelihoods' as an intervention in the field of development is not, of course, a new proposition. It has been previously mobilized in a number of forms, from Karl Polanyi's *The Livelihood of Man* to the 'Sustainable Livelihoods Approach' in international development practice.[28] In all of these cases, this language is used to displace the hegemony of paid work and monetary exchange via capitalist markets: humans make livings, through all kinds of paid and unpaid, and reciprocated and unreciprocated activities, and in relation to all kinds of institutions, motivations and contexts. At the same time, however, these approaches all tend to merge the economic and the social without challenging an articulation of 'the environment' as a domain of resources. The *human* remains at the centre of action, and (often in the form of individuals and households) still navigates – even 'optimizes' – amidst a world of objects or resources. To develop a truly 'transversal' articulation that cuts across and through the hegemonic categories, and opens new ethical and political space, livelihoods must be articulated in a more radically *ecological* sense.[29]

By 'ecological,' we do not refer to a synonym for 'environmental,' nor to its common mobilization as a kind of scientific holism. Rather, we mean it as precisely that which escapes domestication or even signification, 'not the name of a totality but of the impossibility of any such totality'.[30] This is Timothy Morton's sense of ecology in *The Ecological Thought*, the mind-boggling interdependence that we can never master and never know, and that calls us towards an ethics we have only begun to explore.[31] Livelihoods would indicate, then, not the ways in which we – the 'autonomous' agents – make a living for ourselves in relation to some 'outside,' or in the midst of 'enabling resources' and 'constraints,' but rather the complex, reciprocally-negotiated composition of habitat (*oikos*) and that which inhabits (*us*, along with *others*). Livelihoods must refer to an 'ecopoiesis' – the active creation (*poiesis*) of *oikos*.

The point here, we must emphasize, is not to propose that thinking in terms of ecological livelihoods is more 'accurate' to what is 'really happening – in other words, that we are seeking to reveal a new truth with our approach. We are committed to an understanding that language can be performative, helping to bring into being that which it names.[32] To speak of ecological livelihoods is to propose an intervention: What kinds of relations, connections and possibilities might be opened by a language that refuses to distinguish an Economy and an Environment as the ultimate spheres in which we must live? What might it *do* to say, instead, that we make our livings in diverse ways, in complex power-laden relations of interdependence that cannot be reduced to or contained by the hegemonic articulations? This is an *experimental proposition*.[33] How, more specifically, can this proposition encourage thought? How might it, in the words of Sylvia Wynter, help us 'to think *outside* the terms in which we *are*? Think *about* the processes by which we institute ourselves as what we are, make these processes transparent to ourselves?'[34]

Making,receiving, providing: Three dimensions of livelihood

Livelihood can be understood or 'mapped' in terms of three dimensions: *making* a living, *receiving* a living made for us by others (human and non-human) and *providing* livings for others. 'I' am, 'we' are, continually emergent at the convergence of these three dimensions (Figure 15.2). *Making* a living is the dimension of livelihoods most often and overtly acknowledged. We weave together multiple life-making activities, including paid work as well as unpaid labouring in home, community, garden or 'country'; buying, giving, sharing, and swapping goods and services; working for others in private enterprises, for ourselves in a small business, or with others in a cooperatively owned and run enterprise, not-for-profit or social enterprise. In all these activities, humans or others exercise particular forms of perception, skill, knowledge and power. They engage in some degree and form of self-making or, to extend a term developed by Humberto Maturana and Francisco Varela, 'autopoiesis.'[35]

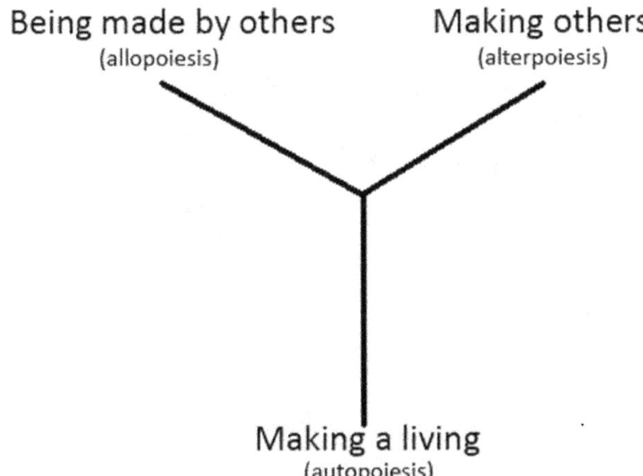

FIGURE 15.2 *Three dimensions of livelihood: receiving, making, providing. Image by Ethan Miller.*

This active work of doing, producing and procuring the means of subsistence is the classic site often associated with 'agency,' and it serves as a key form of social validation for many people raised in cultures that emphasize the virtues of individual effort (think, for example, of the status of the 'self-made man'). Indeed, in so many Western cultural articulations of the human, autopoiesis is seen as the very definition of the species – *Homo faber* and *Homo economicus* – and it should be no surprise that myriad crises of identity and self-worth emerge in post-industrial communities that are no longer able to access traditional forms of wage work. Autopoiesis is, in this sense, both how we are made and how some of us are *unmade,* and it can become a site of disastrous failure and shame. How difficult it is for so many to see that making a living is not, in fact, ultimately the work of individuals; it is, rather, the key site where a particular agency condenses, congeals or is momentarily *realized*, while its actual sources are 'distributed' throughout the whole triple assemblage of livelihood relations.[36] This is precisely why it is not enough to reduce livelihood to the work of *making*.

Prior to any making of a living, we *receive* livings made by others. This is the livelihood dimension that we can also call 'allopoiesis' (*allo,* from the outside). The over-emphasis on agency always risks re-inscribing an impossible normative demand towards a notion of autonomy that we need to confront and transform.[37] Our culture is ripe with praise for those who are represented as pulling oneself 'up by the bootstraps'. In a world where public policymakers classify citizens as lifters or leaners, it is not surprising to hear those who have the least proudly claiming, 'I don't need a handout from anyone'.[38] Yet we are all *utterly dependent* on beings and forces that exceed us. Consider, for example, those at a distance whose labour makes our lives possible, or the web of plants, animals, microbes and geological formations that feeds, clothes, warms and heals us. The hard-working American citizen who decries the 'theft' of jobs by 'illegal aliens' is eating an apple picked by immigrant hands as they call out their condemnations. The stockholders who gain from fossil fuel investments find, at the very same time, their habitats fundamentally transformed in terrifying and uncertain ways by atmospheric carbon accumulations. We all rely, fundamentally, on the labours of human and non-human others. We are all on the dole. Some of our constitutive others we know; most of them we will never know, and a whole host of ethical questions are opened up here, since *we do not even know with whom we are connected.*[39]

Finally, we *provide* livings for others. We might call this 'alterpoiesis' (*alter* as in other). Despite all the emphasis on 'self-making' in the hegemonic articulation, so much of what we do is about making livings *for* others – those we know, and those we will never know. In some cases, this takes the form of involuntary relations such as exploitation in capitalist firms that provides surplus for owners at our expense, playing host to (other kinds of) parasites or becoming compost when we die. In other cases, providing for and making others forms a core part of our intention: birthing the next generation, supporting our families, contributing to our communities, caring for our places or enacting solidarity with those who live beyond the immediate bounds of our daily connections. Does alterpoiesis become a site of resentment as we support those who we feel to be 'undeserving'? Does it become a site of hospitality and generosity? It is with us, and *from* us, regardless.

Let us bring this triad of relations together: 'we' emerge as a site of continually enacted agential articulation between the *habitats that we make for ourselves*, the *habitats that we receive* and the *habitats we participate in making for others*. 'I' and 'we' become relays in a complex ecological meshwork, and a politics of the negotiation of ecological livelihoods unfolds here. *Life is the negotiation of multiple, overlapping, co-constitutive habitats.*[40] In such a context, to 'make an honest living' would not entail severing or even reducing one's dependencies on others as is often suggested. Rather, it would entail taking active responsibility for interdependence, for one's constitutive reliance on both human and non-human others and the ethical questions this reliance entails, for the dynamics of self-making and for the many ways in which one participates (or not) in making others.

The framing of ecological livelihoods sketched out here seeks to open an explicit space to acknowledge the myriad interdependencies in which our sustenance is implicated, thus challenging the conventional frame in which each of these three dimensions is partially *obscured* by the enclosures and exclusions of the Economy and the Environment. So for example, what is called 'economic development' can be seen here, in its hegemonic form at least, as one particular way of articulating an alienated, restricted and deeply conflicted mode of livelihood at the intersection of making, receiving and providing. At the same time what is called 'the environment' can be seen as constituting an alienated, restricted and conflicted framing of habitat at the same triple intersection. In this articulation, making a living involves securing one of the 'jobs' generated by economic 'growth'. But for the past 200 years, growth has been fuelled by, and synonymous with, the plundering of fossil fuels and habitat degradation. It has taken quite some time for us to see that the living we receive is being severely compromised by our actions to make a living. It seems even harder for us to recognize that our ability to provide

Making a living

- ☐ What do we really need to survive well? How do we balance our own survival needs and well-being with the well-being of others and the planet?
- ☐ How do we secure the things we cannot produce ourselves? How do we conduct ethical encounters with human and non-human others in these transactions?
- ☐ What do we really need to consume? How do we consume sustainably and justly?

Having a living made for us

- ☐ What are the gifts we receive from others, from nature and from past generations that enable us to live well?
- ☐ How does a community maintain, replenish and grow this natural and cultural commons? What do we make and share with human and non-human others?
- ☐ How might we render our interdependencies more visible while also recognizing the impossibility of any complete accounting?
- ☐ What forms of responsibility can we construct towards the myriad others (beings, places, times) whose bodies and worlds are shaped by the 'makings' that we take and receive from them?
- ☐ How do we gain, as the well-known 'serenity prayer' has it, the wisdom to discern the difference between those dependencies that can be transformed and those to which we are truly at the mercy of?

Making livings for others

- ☐ To whom are we obliged to offer ourselves, our energies and our lives?
- ☐ What's left after our survival needs have been met? How do we distribute this surplus to enrich social and environmental health?
- ☐ How are our makings-of-others connected with our being-made, recirculating energies and matter in ways that maintain our habitats and those of others, and to what extend is this connection severed by various extractive mediations?
- ☐ What do we do with stored wealth? How do we invest this wealth so that future generations may live well?
- ☐ To what extent are these relations shaped by forms of coercion and violence, and to what extent can we transform such relations?

FIGURE 15.3 *Questions of livelihood. Image by Ethan Miller.*

safe livings for others, particularly future generations, is diminished in drastic ways. Today the life expectancy of Beijing citizens is declining by more than five years because of toxic air pollution – the result of coal-fuelled industrial growth, itself fuelled by the need for jobs growth and for cheap 'goods' around the world.[41] In China, to make a living (by having a job) is to be denied a living (in terms of air quality and longevity). In Australia, the immediacy of this feedback loop is attenuated: to make a living is to deny a living to our children. We might wonder, which is more stupid?

To challenge these categories and ask, instead, about *the relations themselves* is to radically foreground collective mutual dependence. It is to ask dangerous questions about who we are truly dependent upon, how we actually make our livings and to whom we might be obligated (Figure 15.3). And it is to crystallize more precisely the various sites of struggle that emerge around each of these questions when the grip of the Economy and the Environment are loosened – thus opening the question of what possibilities for new modes of collective life might emerge when livelihood and its negotiations are articulated in a more ecological and ethically-oriented frame. The concepts of commoning and uncommoning, to which we now turn, can help to make the ethicopolitical stakes and dynamics of this reframing even clearer.

The politics of commoning (and uncommoning)

The language of 'ecological livelihoods' is a tool for de-anaesthetizing, a strategy for thinking in and with the world that we are continually becoming. It is not a proposal for an alternative system, a vision for how 'we all' should or should not live, nor a vehicle for the elevation of a specific set of codified morals. It is about opening new space for emergence and 'learning to be affected', enabling 'a process whereby one becomes sensitized to (affected by) a world that in turn becomes more highly differentiated'.[42] But can effective transformative politics grow from a perspective that appears oriented only towards opening questions and proliferating sites of encounter? We see the practice of 'commoning' as the collective politicization of livelihood.[43] Commoning, or making common, refers to the myriad ways in which complex relations of livelihood are rendered into *explicit sites of ethical negotiation*. This may unfold as a momentary rupture or revolt against the ossification of hierarchical relations in a community, a nation state or a workplace, or it may be enacted (and renewed continuously) in forms of institution that seek to render livelihood relations and their stakes into sites for democratic deliberation. Commoning, in all forms, is the ongoing production of a shared space of mutual exposure to the ethical demands of interdependence.

The practice of commoning involves *identifying and supporting* practices and articulations that render our interdependencies explicit and open to collective negotiation and transformation, and *challenging* and *dismantling* all that seek to close these spaces down. Commoning constitutes shared and explicit 'matters of concern', where 'matter' should be taken in both senses of the word at once.[44] It is not that *all things shared* are commoned (we discuss this later), but that all shared matters are commoned to the extent that they appear as questions, concerns or sites of struggle and decision. Commoning is at the heart of all labours of thinking in and with the world.

Such labour unfolds, then, as the composition of an innumerable set of variable 'spheres' of concern and negotiation that articulate livelihood triads together in explicitly common habitat assemblages. Particular ecosystems, diseases, experiences of shared oppression, cultural traditions, mutual relations with distant others and the planetary climate system, all may be commoned by their rendering as sites of connection and negotiation. How will we live together? Commonings are the sites where *oikoi* (habitats) overlap, converge and become sites for asking this crucial and transformative question. When interdependencies between citizens and new immigrants become visible in a public struggle over working conditions and wages, or in a direct encounter at the farmer's market, in school, or at a community meeting, this is where commoning can emerge in the form of new shared action and commitment. When the climate crisis becomes a site for shared concern and a movement begins to emerge that renders this concern into a new convergence of energy and collective labour, this, too, is commoning.

As sites of connection and community, commonings are also often *boundary-drawing* sites, since they entail explicit relations between particular participants and not others, particular negotiated settlements and stalemates that must often be bounded in order to remain stable. Thus commoning cannot always be contrasted – as it often is – with enclosure.[45] While some enclosures disrupt and destroy commons (the privatization of water, for example), others actually *constitute* them. A community says: 'The water is ours, we share it. It cannot be privatized!' This is a boundary-drawing. The ethicopolitical question must, then, shift from its commonly-articulated form as 'commons versus enclosure' to *What enclosure, for whom, for what purpose and to what effect?* It matters a great deal which *side* of a given enclosure one ends up standing on.

For clarity's sake, then, we oppose processes of commoning with those of *uncommoning*. If commoning is a making explicit of the negotiations of the common, then uncommoning is an anaesthetization of the common, an ethical closure or a rendering-non-negotiable of habitat relations.[46] The commodity form, for example, as Marx showed us, renders our interdependence with the apple pickers into a site of uncommoning to the extent that the social relations of production – and thus our potentials for transformative connection – are obscured. Uncommoning in its various forms is not a *non*-common, since being-in-common itself cannot be undone as a shared condition of existence,[47] and nor does it always entail the destruction of commons. Uncommoning is, in a strange way, still an articulation of the common, and is even a production of commons (that is of shared matters of concern), but this production is *alienated* or estranged – dispossessed, in varying degrees, of the means of encounter, negotiation and response ability. The conventional capitalist factory is a space of the common, of a shared existence for those who work there, but until workers organize to challenge or rupture capitalist discipline, it remains an *uncommoned common* or a *common site of uncommoning*. Such dynamics can also be seen in the domains of climate and migration.

The earth's climate system has constituted a dynamic, shared field of experience for humans and other organisms since their evolutionary emergence. Over the 'long summer,' the earth's climate regime has provided a relative stability that supported the human species to make livings from agriculture and industry.[48] Yet the climate only became a site of commoning when certain humans became aware of their active role in undermining the livelihoods we receive from our climate system, and they began to experience climate as a site of ethical and political engagement.[49] When the global community of nations negotiated the Montreal Protocol and agreed to ban the production and continued use of CFCs, they made a stand for livelihoods – agreeing to change how livings were made, to provide improved livelihoods for future generations and to receive the livelihood protection that a repaired earth's ozone layer can give. As a result, this dangerous rupture in the chemical structure of our open access stratospheric commons has started to heal.[50] Substantive, large-scale action to halt global warming has not yet followed suit, and the commoning of the climate at a planetary scale remains only an urgent, but unfulfilled, possibility. Might attempts towards climate stabilization unfold as regimes of capital accumulation and national division are challenged by new modes of collective ecological action? Or might they take the form of large-scale privatizations that serve to reinforce relations of exploitation and inequality in the name of 'necessity'?[51]These are questions of commoning and uncommoning, and the stakes could not be higher.

The earth's land surface and the geographical distribution of its population is another shared field of experience. As our ultimate commons, the planet is a shared home – its land masses the ground upon which terrestrial livelihoods are built and its oceans the watery abode of marine life. It is also the stage upon which the most violent acts of habitat destruction have played out as colonial conquest, war, resource extraction, labour exploitation and capital accumulation. At the very same time, these and other processes have woven together a vast integrated network of production, trade and consumption upon which many humans now depend. We are co-implicated, in profoundly unequal ways, in a historically unprecedented web of planetary livelihood. At various historical junctures, the situation of 'displaced people' has become a shared matter of concern that has led to the commoning of habitats and the welcoming of strangers across the boundaries of nation state enclosures. This is not so today. We are anaesthetized to what we have received from so many 'strangers' – the livelihoods provided for us by those who care for our elderly, our sick, our children, or those who work in the more unpleasant and low-paid industry sectors. We wallow in the resentments and victimizations of uncommoning. The goods and services that sustain us appear as anonymous commodities rather than manifestations of transformable social relations. Not only are we disconnected from populations of people seeking peace and secure livelihood in the face of violence and habitat destruction but so many of us see them as 'parasites' or 'dangerous others'.

In each of the three livelihood dimensions of receiving, making and providing, the complexities of the world call us to open spaces for commoning, even while the hegemonic assemblages within which we exist continue to close down or deny such spaces. Let us re-imagine more-than-human planetary ecologies, not as the Environment (itself a form of uncommoning in its hegemonic form), but as myriad sites of explicit ethical engagement around our responsibilities to those who make us and to those to whom we, in turn, provide. The climate is not an externality to be variously ignored, preserved or 'internalized' into the Economy via marketization; it is a crucial dimension of livelihood itself, always already internal to the direct life sustenance of every organism on the planet. Can we attend to and cultivate our memberships in communities that actively make and share (and thus common) the conditions of life? Yes, we *already are*! What are movements for climate justice if not modes of commoning the collective means of life in ways that refuse exploitation and inequality? What is the work of building ethical food systems and 'sustainable agriculture' if not the commoning of our relations with plants, soil, bacteria, bees and human food-eaters? A collective refusal is emerging in the face of a capitalist economy posing 'trade-offs' between ecological toxification and the feeding the world, or between climate stability and 'necessary' economic growth. Instead, the work of commoning seeks to continually render the distinction between an 'Economy' and an 'Environment' *impossible*. There is only the complex negotiation of livelihood.

Let us challenge, too, the image of the autonomous, self-made man who 'works for a living.' This creature, beholden to the Economy and its jobs, desperate to deny its existential debt to the labour of others (human and non-human) and bound up with an impossible demand to singularly provide for 'the family', thrives on resentment. The Economy, combined with toxic masculinity, racism, nationalism and ever-increasing financial instability, enables a collective turning-away from interdependence and its demands and possibilities. We end up with a tragically ironic situation of *resenting* those who are 'dependent', pretending that we (alone) work for what we have (no, it is given to us all), all the while enabling the accumulators to steal the very means of life and livelihood from us – at local and planetary scales – on a daily basis!

To challenge such uncommoning, we must honestly trace the complexities of our livelihood relations, and cultivate practices of taking collective responsibility for them. How have past generations of immigrants and refugees worked hard to make the felicitous conditions under which we now live? What forms of responsibility do we have towards the myriad others (beings, places and times) whose bodies and worlds are shaped by the 'makings' that we take and receive from them? How might our way of making a living change if we took greater responsibility for supporting these livelihoods? Commoning our interdependence means generating new relations of connection, hospitality and solidarity with immigrants and refugees, and with devastated environments and broken infrastructure. It means struggling against forces that displace human and non-human communities against their wills, challenging stories and concepts that render our own forms of exploitation invisible or 'necessary', and transforming resentments into desires for transformation and practices of hope.

Conclusion

Our task is to think with, as, against and for the world: *with* the world because the world is the condition of possibility for thought; *as* the world because we are this world in-the-making; *against* the world as it has been articulated in uncommoned forms; and *for* the world as it is already emerging in-common, differently. In this essay, we have foregrounded the role of organizing concepts and their material institutions – articulations – in shaping the possibilities and trajectories of active thought. The Economy and the Environment are potent tools for organizing a particular configuration of planetary power that tend to obscure many ethical dimensions of our constitutive relations and reproduce a sense of inevitability – stupidity – in the face of ongoing ecological destruction, growing inequality and entrenched injustice.

To counteract these categories and their associated practices, we seek to think with all of those relations that are already exceeding them, rupturing their coherence 'from within', and opening towards new forms of collective life and solidarity. We propose to think and act in terms of 'ecological livelihoods' and the three dimensions of receiving, making and providing as an experimental engagement with 'tipping the assemblage'. It is our hope that such a language might help us (and others) to develop new sensitivities to the demands of the world, to the ethical calls that confront us and to the possibilities that are already emerging in our midst. This is not a call for pure invention of a new mode of life, for creation *ex nihilo*; it is, rather, about building on and from the 'other' modes of life that are already present in the cracks – and perhaps even at the heart – of hegemony. How are we sustained by others? How do we sustain ourselves? (Who is 'ourselves'?) How do we participate in sustaining others? And where are the moments, practices and institutions of commoning in our midst that are rendering these questions into sites of collective struggle and deliberation? We have given some examples; it is our collective task to identify, amplify and cultivate a thousand more.

One might accuse us of a certain conservatism here, or of seeking to overly-domesticate the wild potentiality of transformation with our insistence on the here-and-now. We plead guilty to the extent that we are already in love with aspects of this present world, bound to them and obligated to conserve. And we, too, are domestic. We are creatures of homes, and in many ways it is home – the *oikos* – that we seek to passionately defend. But some concepts domesticate by alienating, closing and stopping thought – answering questions too quickly, before they are even really asked. Our aspiration is to domesticate *just enough* to hold onto our commitments to an *oikos*, or to *oikoi*, while also keeping open the movement towards radically transformative possibility. The 'sweet spot' that we seek is somewhere between the sublime, ethereal terror of 'the ecological thought' that everything is connected, and the messy, everyday comfort of washing dishes, cooking for the family and going to the neighbourhood association meeting.[52] We want to help find, acknowledge and strengthen the places where thought is engaged in the radical challenges that our interdependencies call forth, where beings are collectively exposed to each other, becoming-in-common in ways that are bound to transform all those involved.

We do not propose here a coherent 'theory of change'. We are not suggesting that capitalism can be overthrown in a particular way via a particular strategy (though we are sure that capitalism *can* be overthrown!). We do not know if the amplification and connection of multiple, diverse forms of commoning will be 'enough'. But we refuse to be certain that they will *not* be enough. We seek to think, and to be forced to think, by new forms of relation that might emerge from our collective experimentation. We seek to find ways to make the interdependencies of our webs of receiving, making and providing more visible, and thus to open up new spaces for commoning across the boundaries and divisions that have so often been built between us. How else are we to imagine the overcoming of the separations between those who seek to build walls and those who strive to tear them down?

Perhaps we can render their construction less viable by relentlessly asking – with our concepts, in our conversations, and in myriad forms of action research and organizing – how we are already connected across these real and imagined walls. We can refuse to accept that there is something called the Economy and something called the Environment that we must choose between, or that 'our' Economy takes priority over 'theirs', and focus on the transversal relations of ecological livelihood rather than the divided spheres of the hegemonic articulation. We might then more effectively foster a world in which fewer and fewer are forced to choose between feeding their family and being hospitable to unknown others, or between a steady job and a viable planetary life-support system for future generations. To paraphrase Spinoza, we do not yet know what our commonings of ecological livelihood can do.

Notes

1 Data on global refugees is from Adrian Edwards, 'Global Forced Displacement Reaches Record High', United Nations High Commissioner for Refugees (UNHCR), http://www.unhcr.org/news/latest/2016/6/5763b65a4/global-forced-displacement-hits-record-high.html (accessed 20 February 2017).

2 Tony Fry, 'The Sustainment' (Tasmania: The Studio at the Edge of the World, n.d.) http://www.thestudioattheedgeoftheworld.com/the-sustainment.html (accessed 14 January 2017).The Sustainment' (Tasmania: The Studio at the Edge of the World, n.d.) <http://www.thestudioattheedgeoftheworld.com/the-sustainment.html (accessed 14 January 2017).

3 Isabelle Stengers, *In Catastrophic Times: Resisting the Coming Barbarism*, trans. A. Goffey. (Lunenburg: Open Humanities Press, 2015), p. 119.

4 Simon Critchley, *Infinitely Demanding: Ethics of Commitment, Politics of Resistance* (London: Verso, 2007); Jacques Derrida, 'Force of Law: The Mystical Foundation of Authority', in *Deconstruction and the Possibility of Justice,* eds D. Cornell, M. Rosenfeld and D. G. Carlson (New York: Routledge, 1992).

5 Jean-Francois Lyotard, 'Oikos', in *Political Writings*, trans. Bill Readings and Kevin Paul Geiman (Minneapolis, MN: University of Minnesota Press, 1993); Bruno Latour, 'To Modernise or Ecologize? That Is the Question', in *Remaking Reality: Nature at the Millenium*, ed. B. Braun and N. Castree, trans. C. Cussins (New York: Routledge, 1998).

6 www.communityeconomies.org

7 Phil Macnaghten and John Urry, *Contested Natures* (London: Sage, 1998); Joel Kovel, *The Enemy of Nature: The End of Capitalism or the End of the World?* (London: Zed Books, 2007); Mick Smith, *Against Ecological Sovereignty: Ethics, Biopolitics, and Saving the Natural World* (Minneapolis: University of Minnesota Press, 2011).

8 Michel Foucault, *Security, Territory, Population: Lectures at the Collège de France, 1977–78*, ed. Michel Senellart, trans. G. Burchell (New York: Palgrave Macmillan, 2007); Karl Polanyi, *The Great Transformation* (Boston: Beacon Press, 2001); Timothy Mitchell, 'Fixing the Economy', *Cultural Studies* 12:1 (1988), pp. 82–101; Timothy Luke, 'On Environmentality: Geo-Power and Eco-Knowledge in the Discourses of Contemporary Environmentalism', *Cultural Critique*, 31 (1995), pp. 57–81; Macnaghten and Urry, *Contested Natures*.

9 Gilles Deleuze and Félix Guattari, *A Thousand Plateaus: Capitalism and Schizophrenia*, trans. Brian Massumi (Minneapolis: University of Minnesota Press, 1987); Gilles Deleuze and Félix Guattari, *A Thousand Plateaus: Capitalism and Schizophrenia*, trans. Brian Massumi (Minneapolis: University Of Minnesota Press, 1987); Bruno Latour, *Reassembling the Social: An Introduction to Actor-Network-Theory* (New York, NY: Oxford University Press, 2005).

10 This notion of a 'form of life' can be traced to Ludwig Wittgenstein, *Philosophical Investigations*, trans. G. E. M. Anscombe (London: Basil Blackwell, 1958).

11 Ernesto Laclau and Chantal Mouffe, *Hegemony and Socialist Strategy: Towards a Radical Democratic Politics* (London: Verso, 2001).

12 Deleuze and Guattari, *A Thousand Plateaus*, p. 326.

13 J. K. Gibson-Graham, *A Postcapitalist Politics* (Minneapolis: University Of Minnesota Press, 2006); J. K. Gibson-Graham, *The End of Capitalism (As We Knew It): A Feminist Critique of Political Economy*, 2nd edn (Minneapolis: University of Minnesota Press, 2006); J. K. Gibson-Graham, 'Diverse Economies: Performative Practices for Other Worlds', *Progress in Human Geography* 32:5 (2008), pp. 1–20; Gerda Roelvink, Kevin St. Martin, and J. K. Gibson-Graham (eds), *Performing Diverse Economies* (Minneapolis: University of Minnesota Press, 2015).

14 The kinds of diverse economic activities represented in his iceberg image have been more systematically identified by members of the Community Economies Collective via two frameworks: a 'diverse economies grid', mapping alternative and non-capitalist forms of enterprise, labour, exchange, property and finance (see J. K. Gibson-Graham, Jenny Cameron, and Stephen Healy, *Take Back the Economy: An Ethical Guide for Transforming Our Communities* (Minneapolis: University of Minnesota Press, 2013); and a circular 'diverse economic moments' schema linking processes of creation, production, transaction, consumption, surplus allocation and governance (see Ethan Miller, 'Solidarity Economy: Key Issues and Questions', in *Solidarity Economy I: Building Alternatives for People and Planet*, eds E. Kawano, T. Masterson, and J. Teller-Ellsberg (Amherst, MA: Center for Popular Economics, 2010); Ethan Miller, 'Rethinking Economy for Regional Development: Ontology, Performativity and Enabling Concepts for Participatory Vision and Action', M.S. Thesis (Amherst, MA: University of Massachusetts Amherst, 2011)).

15 Timothy Morton, *The Ecological Thought* (Cambridge, MA: Harvard University Press, 2010); Val Plumwood, 'A Review of Deborah Bird Rose's *Reports from a Wild Country: Ethics of Decolonization*', *Australian*

Humanities Review, 42 (2007), pp. 1–4; Deborah Bird Rose, *Reports from a Wild Country: Ethics of Decolonisation* (Sydney: UNSW Press, 2004).

16 The phrase 'world of becoming' is from William Connolly, *A World of Becoming* (Durham, NC: Duke University Press, 2011).

17 Deleuze and Guattari, *A Thousand Plateaus*, p. 161.

18 Ibid., pp. 160–161.

19 Ibid.

20 J. K. Gibson-Graham, *A Postcapitalist Politics*; J. K Gibson-Graham, *The End of Capitalism (As We Knew It)*; Jenny Cameron and J. K. Gibson-Graham, 'Feminising the Economy: Metaphors, Strategies, Politics', *Gender, Place & Culture* 10:2 (2003), pp. 145–57; Ethan Miller, *Solidarity Economy*; Ethan Miller, 'Community Economy: Ontology, Ethics, and Politics for Radically Democratic Economic Organizing', *Rethinking Marxism* 25:4 (2013), pp. 518–33.

21 Gerda Roelvink and J. K. Gibson-Graham, 'A Postcapitalist Politics of Dwelling: Ecological Humanities and Community Economies in Conversation', *Australian Humanities Review* 46 (2009), pp. 145–58; J. K. Gibson-Graham and Gerda Roelvink, 'An Economic Ethics for the Anthropocene', *Antipode* 41 (2010), pp. 320–46; Ann Hill, 'Growing Community Food Economies in the Phillipines', PhD Dissertation (Canberra: Australian National University, 2014); J. K. Gibson-Graham, 'A Feminist Project of Belonging for the Anthropocene', *Gender, Place and Culture* 18:1 (2011), pp. 1–21.

22 See J. K. Gibson-Graham, *A Postcapitalist Politics*, and also Ethan Miller, 'Community Economy'.

23 See also J. K. Gibson-Graham, and Miller, 'Economy as Ecological Livelihood', in *Manifesto for Living in the Anthropocene*, eds K. Gibson, D. B. Rose, and R. Fincher (Brooklyn, NY: Punctum Books, 2015); and Ethan Miller, 'Economization and Beyond: (Re)composing Livelihoods in Maine, USA', *Environment and Planning A* 46:11 (2014), pp. 2735–51.

24 Oxford English Dictionary (2008).

25 We draw this phrase '*par le milieu*' from Deleuze and Guattari, via Isabelle Stengers, 'History Through the Middle: Between Macro and Mesopolitics, an Interview with Brian Massumi', *iNFLeXions* 3 (2009).

26 Deleuze and Guattari, *A Thousand Plateaus*, p. 105.

27 Gilles Deleuze, *Foucault*, trans. S. Hand (Minneapolis: University of Minnesota Press, 1988), p. 19; Jane Bennett, *Vibrant Matter: A Political Ecology of Things* (Durham, NC: Duke University Press, 2010).

28 Karl Polanyi, *The Livelihood of Man*, ed. H. W. Pearson (New York: Academic Press, 1977); Robert Chambers and Gordon Conway, 'Sustainable Rural Livelihoods: Practical Concepts for the 21st Century' 296. IDS Working Paper (Brighton, UK: Institute of Development Studies, 1991); Ian Scoones, 'Sustainable Rural Livelihoods: A Framework for Analysis' 72. IDS Working Paper (Brighton, UK: Institute for Development Studies, 1998); and Scoones, 'Livelihoods Perspectives and Rural Development', *Journal of Peasant Studies* 36:1 (2009), pp. 171–96.

29 The term 'transversal' comes from Félix Guattari (*The Guattari Reader*, ed. Gary Genosko [Oxford: Wiley-Blackwell, 1996]) and has been further developed by Nira Yuval-Davis, 'What Is' Transversal Politics?' *Soundings*, 12 (1999), pp. 88–93.

30 Bronislaw Szerszynski, 'Reading and Writing the Weather: Climate Technics and the Moment of Responsibility', *Theory, Culture & Society* 27:2–3 (2010), p. 14.

31 Morton, *The Ecological Thought*.

32 J. K. Gibson-Graham, 'Diverse Economies: Performative Practices for Other Worlds', *Progress in Human Geography* 32:5 (2008), pp. 1–20.

33 Bruno Latour, *Politics of Nature: How to Bring the Sciences into Democracy*, trans. Catherine Porter (Cambridge, MA: Harvard University Press, 2004).

34 David Scott, 'The Re-enchantment of Humanism: An Interview with Sylvia Wynter', *Small Axe*, 8 (2000), pp. 206–7.

35 Humberto Maturana and Francisco Varela, *Autopoiesis and Cognition: The Realization of the Living* (Holland: D. Reidel Publishing Company, 1980).

36 See Bennett, *Vibrant Matter* for a discussion of 'distributed agency'.

37 Sarah Whatmore, 'Dissecting the Autonomous Self: Hybrid Cartographies for a Relational Ethics', *Environment and Planning D* 15 (1997), pp. 37–54.

38 This classification of 'lifters' and 'leaners', referring to those who give and those who merely take, comes originally from a poem by Ella Wheeler Wilcox and has been taken up by numerous people in the world of social ministry, nonprofit organization and social work.

39 Latour, 'To Modernise or Ecologize? That Is the Question'.

40 We draw the term 'meshwork' from Morton, *The Ecological Thought*.

41 Benjamin Haas, 'Beijing Creates Anti-smog Police to Tackle Air Polluters', *The Guardian*, 2017 https://www.theguardian.com/world/2017/jan/09/beijing-creates-anti-smog-police-to-tackle-air-polluters (accessed 9 January 2017).

42 Gerda Roelvink, 'Learning to Be Affected by Earth Others', in *Manifesto for Living in the Anthropocene*, eds K. Gibson, D. B. Rose and R. Fincher (Brooklyn, NY: Punctum Books, 2015). See also Gibson-Graham and Roelvink, 'An Economic Ethics for the Anthropocene'; Bruno Latour, 'How to Talk about the Body? The Normative Dimension of Science Studies', *Body and Society* 10:2–3 (2004), p. 205.

43 The term 'commoning' is drawn initially from the work of Peter Linebaugh (*The Magna Carta Manifesto: Commons and Liberties for All* [Berkeley: University of California Press, 2008]) and Massimo de Angelis (*The Beginning of History: Value Struggles and Global Capital* [London: Pluto Press, 2007]), has been taken up by members of the Community Economies collective and many others in recent years as a key language for articulating the politics of explicit, collectively-negotiated interdependence.

44 Latour, *Reassembling the Social*, p. 114.

45 A similar point about avoiding the opposition of commons and enclosure is made by David Harvey (*Rebel Cities: From the Right to the City to the Urban Revolution* [London: Verso, 2012], p. 70).

46 We could speak, then, of particular *commoning enclosures* and of *uncommoning enclosures*.

47 Jean-Luc Nancy, *The Inoperative Community* (Minneapolis: University of Minnesota Press, 1991); Jean-Luc Nancy, *Being Singular Plural* (Stanford: Stanford University Press, 2000).

48 Dianne Dumanoski, *The End of the Long Summer: Why We Must Remake Our Civilization to Survive On a Volatile Earth* (New York: Crown Publishers, 2009).

49 Ibid.

50 J. K. Gibson-Graham, J. Jenny Cameron and Stephen Healy, 'Commoning as Poscapitalist Politics', in *Recovering the Commons*, eds A. Amin and P. Howell (London: Routledge, 2016). See also Susan Solomon, Diane J. Ivy, Doug Kinnison, Michael J. Mills, Ryan R. Neely and Anja Schmidt, 'Emergence of Healing in the Antarctic Ozone Layer', *Science* 353:6296 (2016), pp. 269–74.

51 We are thinking here of various market-driven pathways such as carbon credit trading, as well as capital intensive and power-centralizing visions for geoengineering.

52 Morton, *The Ecological Thought.*

References

Bennett, J., *Vibrant Matter: A Political Ecology of Things*, Durham, NC: Duke University Press, 2010.

Cameron, J. and J. K. Gibson-Graham, 'Feminising the Economy: Metaphors, Strategies, Politics', *Gender, Place & Culture* 10:2 (2003), pp. 145–57.

Chambers, R. and G. Conway, 'Sustainable Rural Livelihoods: Practical Concepts for the 21st Century', 296. IDS Working Paper, Brighton, UK: Institute of Development Studies, 1991.

Connolly, W. E., *A World of Becoming*, Durham, NC: Duke University Press, 2011.

Critchley, S., *Infinitely Demanding: Ethics of Commitment, Politics of Resistance*, London: Verso, 2007.

De Angelis, M., *The Beginning of History: Value Struggles and Global Capital*, London: Pluto Press, 2007.

De Landa, M., *A New Philosophy of Society: Assemblage Theory and Social Complexity*, London: Continuum, 2006.

Deleuze, G., *Foucault*, translated by Sean Hand, Minneapolis: University of Minnesota Press, 1988.

Deleuze, G. and F. Guattari, *A Thousand Plateaus: Capitalism and Schizophrenia*. Translated by Brian Massumi. Minneapolis: University of Minnesota Press, 1987.

Derrida, J., 'Force of Law: The Mystical Foundation of Authority', in D. Cornell, M. Rosenfeld, D. G. Carlson (eds), *Deconstruction and the Possibility of Justice*, New York: Routledge, 1992.

Dumanoski, D., *The End of the Long Summer: Why We Must Remake Our Civilization to Survive on a Volatile Earth*, New York: Crown Publishers, 2009.

Edwards, A., 'Global Forced Displacement Reaches Record High', United Nations High Commissioner for Refugees (UNHCR), 2016. http://www.unhcr.org/news/latest/2016/6/5763b65a4/global-forced-displacement-hits-record-high.html (accessed 20 February 2017).

Foucault, M., *Security, Territory, Population: Lectures at the Collège de France, 1977–78*, M. Senellart (ed.), G. Burchell (trans.), New York: Palgrave Macmillan, 2007.

Gibson-Graham, J. K., *A Postcapitalist Politics*, Minneapolis: University of Minnesota Press, 2006.

Gibson-Graham, J. K., *The End of Capitalism (As We Knew It): A Feminist Critique of Political Economy*. 2nd ed., Minneapolis: University of Minnesota Press, 2006.

Gibson-Graham, J. K., 'Diverse Economies: Performative Practices for Other Worlds', *Progress in Human Geography* 32:5 (2008), pp. 1–20.

Gibson-Graham, J. K., 'A Feminist Project of Belonging for the Anthropocene', *Gender, Place and Culture* 18:1 (2011), pp. 1–21.

Gibson-Graham, J. K., Cameron, J. and S. Healy, *Take Back the Economy: An Ethical Guide for Transforming Our Communities*, Minneapolis: University of Minnesota Press, 2013.

Gibson-Graham, J. K. and E. Miller, 'Economy as Ecological Livelihood', in K. Gibson, D. B. Rose, and R. Fincher (eds), *Manifesto for Living in the Anthropocene*, Brooklyn, NY: Punctum Books, 2015.

Gibson-Graham, J. K. and G. Roelvink, 'An Economic Ethics for the Anthropocene', *Antipode* 41 (2010), pp. 320–46.

Gibson-Graham, J. K., Cameron, J. and S. Healy, 'Commoning as Poscapitalist Politics', in A. Amin and P. Howell (eds), *Recovering the Commons*, London: Routledge, 2016.

Guattari, F., *The Guattari Reader*, G. Genosko (ed.), Oxford: Wiley-Blackwell, 1996.

Harvey, D., *Rebel Cities: From the Right to the City to the Urban Revolution*, London: Verso, 2012.

Hill, A., 'Growing Community Food Economies in the Phillipines', PhD Dissertation, Canberra: Australian National University, 2014.

Kovel, J., *The Enemy of Nature: The End of Capitalism or the End of the World?* London: Zed Books, 2007.

Laclau, E. and C. Mouffe, *Hegemony and Socialist Strategy: Towards a Radical Democratic Politics*, London: Verso, 2001.

Latour, B., 'To Modernise or Ecologize? That Is the Question', in B. Braun and N. Castree (eds), *Remaking Reality: Nature at the Millenium*, trans. C. Cussins, New York: Routledge, 1998.

Latour, B., 'How to Talk about the Body? The Normative Dimension of Science Studies', *Body and Society* 10:2–3 (2004), pp. 205–29.

Latour, B., *Politics of Nature: How to Bring the Sciences into Democracy*, trans. C. Porter, Cambridge, MA: Harvard University Press, 2004.

Latour, B., *Reassembling the Social: An Introduction to Actor-Network-Theory*, New York, NY: Oxford University Press, 2005.

Latour, B., 'A Plea for Earthly Sciences', in J. Burnett, S. Jeffers and T. Graham (eds), *New Social Connections: Sociology's Subjects and Objects*, London: Palgrave Macmillan, 2010.

Linebaugh, P., *The Magna Carta Manifesto: Commons and Liberties for All*, Berkeley: University of California Press, 2008.

Luke, T. W., 'On Environmentality: Geo-Power and Eco-Knowledge in the Discourses of Contemporary Environmentalism', *Cultural Critique*, 31 (1995), pp. 57–81.

Lyotard, J.-F., 'Oikos', in *Political Writings*, trans. B. Readings and K.P. Geiman, Minneapolis, MN: University of Minnesota Press, 1993, pp. 96–107.

Macnaghten, P. and J. Urry, *Contested Natures*, London: Sage, 1998.

Maturana, H. and F. Varela, *Autopoiesis and Cognition: The Realization of the Living*, Holland: D. Reidel Publishing Company, 1980.

Miller, E., 'Solidarity Economy: Key Issues and Questions', in E. Kawano, T. Masterson and J. Teller-Ellsberg (eds), *Solidarity Economy I: Building Alternatives for People and Planet*, Amherst, MA: Center for Popular Economics, 2010.

Miller, E., 'Rethinking Economy for Regional Development: Ontology, Performativity and Enabling Concepts for Participatory Vision and Action', M.S. Thesis, Amherst, MA: University of Massachusetts Amherst, 2011.

Miller, E., 'Community Economy: Ontology, Ethics, and Politics for Radically Democratic Economic Organizing', *Rethinking Marxism* 25:4 (2013), pp. 518–33.

Miller, E., ' Economization and Beyond: (Re)composing Livelihoods in Maine, USA', *Environment and Planning A* 46:11 (2014), pp. 2735–51.

Mitchell, T., 'Fixing the Economy', *Cultural Studies* 12:1 (1998), pp. 82–101.

Morton, T., *The Ecological Thought*, Cambridge, MA: Harvard University Press, 2010.

Plumwood, V., 'A Review of Deborah Bird Rose's *Reports from a Wild Country: Ethics of Decolonization*', *Australian Humanities Review* 42 (2007), pp. 1–4.

Polanyi, K., *The Livelihood of Man*, ed. H. W. Pearson, New York: Academic Press, 1977.

Polanyi, K., *The Great Transformation*, Boston: Beacon Press, 2001.

Roelvink, G., 'Learning to Be Affected by Earth Others', in K. Gibson, D. B. Rose and R. Fincher (ed.), *Manifesto for Living in the Anthropocene*, Brooklyn, NY: punctum books, 2015.

Roelvink, G. and J. K. Gibson-Graham, 'A Postcapitalist Politics of Dwelling: Ecological Humanities and Community Economies in Conversation', *Australian Humanities Review* 46 (2009), pp. 145–58.

Roelvink, G., K. St. Martin and J. K. Gibson-Graham (eds), *Performing Diverse Economies*, Minneapolis: University of Minnesota Press, 2015.

Rose, D. B., *Reports from a Wild Country: Ethics of Decolonization*, Sydney: UNSW Press, 2004.

Scoones, I., 'Sustainable Rural Livelihoods: A Framework for Analysis', 72. IDS Working Paper, Brighton, UK: Institute for Development Studies, 1998.

Scoones, I., 'Livelihoods Perspectives and Rural Development', *Journal of Peasant Studies* 36:1 (2009), pp. 171–96.

Scott, D., 'The Re-enchantment of Humanism: An Interview with Sylvia Wynter', *Small Axe*, 8 (2000), pp. 119–207.

Smith, M., *Against Ecological Sovereignty: Ethics, Biopolitics, and Saving the Natural World*, Minneapolis: University of Minnesota Press, 2011.

Solomon, S., Ivy, D. J., Kinnison, D., Mills, M. J., Neely, R. R. and A. Schmidt, 'Emergence of Healing in the Antarctic Ozone Layer', *Science* 353: 6296 (2016), pp. 269–74. doi:10.1126/science.aae0061.

Stengers, I., 'History Through the Middle: Between Macro and Mesopolitics, an Interview with Brian Massumi', *iNFLeXions* 3, 2009.

Stengers, I., *In Catastrophic Times: Resisting the Coming Barbarism*, trans. A. Goffey, Lunenburg: Open Humanities Press, 2015.

Szerszynski, B., 'Reading and Writing the Weather: Climate Technics and the Moment of Responsibility', *Theory, Culture & Society* 27:2–3 (2010), pp. 9–30.

Whatmore, S. J., 'Dissecting the Autonomous Self: Hybrid Cartographies for a Relational Ethics', *Environment and Planning D* 15 (1997), pp. 37–54.

Wittgenstein, L., *Philosophical Investigations*, trans. G. E. M. Anscombe, London: Basil Blackwell, 1958.

Yuval-Davis, N., 'What Is "Transversal Politics?"' *Soundings*, 12 (1999), pp. 88–93.

Index